Experience, Affect, and Behavior

Experience, Affect and Behavior

Psychoanalytic Explorations of
Dr. Adelaide McFadyen Johnson

Edited by DAVID B. ROBINSON, M.D.

With a foreword by
STANISLAUS SZUREK, M.D.

THE UNIVERSITY OF CHICAGO PRESS
Chicago and London

Library of Congress Catalog Card Number 69-19828

THE UNIVERSITY OF CHICAGO PRESS, CHICAGO 60637

The University of Chicago Press, Ltd., London W.C. 1

© 1969 by the University of Chicago
All rights reserved
Published 1969

Printed in the United States of America

To Louise, my wife,
and our
Peggy, Claire, Dana, Deborah, and Eleanor

—D. B. R.

ACKNOWLEDGMENTS

There has been no formal committee, grants or funding to promote the publication of this volume; however, I am grateful for the encouragement which came informally in response to my permission requests from the many co-authors who worked and wrote with Adelaide. Support has also come from the publishers of the books and journals contributed to by her. I am deeply indebted to their recognition of the fact that this volume is a tribute to an unusually fine person. During a time of difficult personal and professional demands on my energies and attention, my secretary, Mrs. Fran Rogers, has been invaluable in assisting with both the manuscript and all the minutiae involved in this project.

CONTENTS

Foreword by Stanislaus Szurek	xiii
Editor's Preface	xvii

Section I INTRODUCTION

1. Psychoanalytic Psychiatry (1947)	3
2. School Phobia (1941)	14
3. Collaborative Psychiatric Therapy of Parent-Child Problems (1942)	26

Section II PSYCHOSOMATIC PROBLEMS

4. Vertigo as the Primary Manifestation in Anxiety Neurosis (1940)	39
5. Brief Psychotherapy in Bronchial Asthma (1944)	45
6. Preliminary Report on a Psychosomatic Study of Rheumatoid Arthritis (1947)	55
7. A Case of Migraine (1946)	67
8. Recurrent Urinary Retention Due to Emotional Factors (1956)	98
9. Comments on Disposition of Amputated Body Parts (1952)	108

Section III ANTISOCIAL BEHAVIOR

10. Sanctions for Superego Lacunae of Adolescents (1949)	113
11. The Genesis of Antisocial Acting Out in Children and Adults (1952)	145

12. Parental Permissiveness and Fostering in Child Rearing and Their Relationship to Juvenile Delinquency (1955) — 155
13. Parental Influence in Unusual Sexual Behavior in Children (1956) — 168
14. The Sexual Deviant (Sexual Psychopath): Causes, Treatment, and Prevention (1957) — 181
15. Etiological Factors in First-Degree Murder (1958) — 205
16. Juvenile Delinquency (1959) — 207

Section IV COLLABORATIVE PSYCHIATRIC TREATMENT

17. Collaborative Psychotherapy: Team Setting (1953) — 245
18. Analysis of a Disturbed Adolescent Girl and Collaborative Psychiatric Treatment of the Mother (1944) — 282
19. Psychotherapy of a Mother and Daughter with a Problem of Separation Anxiety (1955) — 298

Section V PSYCHOANALYTIC THERAPY

20. Psychoanalytic Therapy (1953) — 313

Section VI THEORETICAL PAPERS

21. Some Etiological Aspects of Repression, Guilt and Hostility (1951) — 333
22. Factors in the Etiology of Fixations and Symptom Choice (1953) — 353
23. Observations on Ego Functions in Schizophrenia (1956) — 377
24. The Incest Barrier (1958) — 389

Section VII CHILD PSYCHIATRY

25. Some Applications of Psychoanalytic Insights to the Socialization of Children (1957) — 409

26. The Disturbed Child (1957)	430
27. The Adolescent and His Problems (1957)	459
28. Some Suggestions for Practice in Infant Adoptions (1954)	477
Bibliography of Writings by Adelaide Johnson	497
Index	503

FOREWORD BY STANISLAUS SZUREK

THIS volume is a most appropriate memorial to Adelaide McFadyen Johnson, a warmly remembered friend and deeply respected colleague of mine, by her student and later colleague, Dr. David B. Robinson. It is obvious from the selections and the concise editorial comments he has made that Dr. Robinson experienced similar feelings of admiration, respect, and warmth for her that her friends of earlier years experienced. Wisely he has let Adelaide Johnson speak largely for herself. His arrangement of her writings permits the reader to follow her development in her chosen field and at the same time to see almost at a glance the breadth and depth of her indefatigable explorations of the many aspects of this field which presented themselves to her amid the changing circumstances of her clinical work.

Thoroughly grounded in biological science and medicine, Adelaide Johnson came to psychiatry, child psychiatry, and psychoanalysis not only to make them thoroughly her own but also, as these writings testify, to make her significant contribution to their more dynamic and modern transformation. A very clear thinker in matters scientific, a worthy student of that giant, "Ajax" Carlson, our common tutor in biologic scientific principles, Adelaide Johnson was a careful practitioner of her art. She gathered observations and recorded them with such clarity and detail that any reader — but especially students in the field — might easily comprehend the clinical situations described and effortlessly follow the logic of her reasoning. By such qualities, all too rare in clinical psychiatric literature, her studies will continue her teaching among students who will not have had the advantage of encountering her vibrant voice and vivid personal delivery. Well might they emulate her approach, as reflected in these studies, for their own development as scientific clinicians and for the further growth of a humane and humanitarian knowledge of man.

Her studies were far-ranging, exploring a broad spectrum of psychopathological syndromes from a variety of childhood disorders, through "delinquent" behavior of adolescence and psychosomatic illnesses, to psychoses and murder. To most of these corners of the psychiatric universe she brought the brighter illumination of an idea, of a principle, which we came upon together in our days at the Institute for Juvenile Research in Chicago. And in each instance her enlightening studies helped much to make more comprehensible a particular kind of human trouble. In this respect her modesty about being a theoretician is indeed remarkable. Many an abstruse tenet of the physicalistic and "mechanistic" theory that we inherited from our intellectual ancestors has been transformed if not transcended by her studies — that is, by her observations and therapeutic work — if not always explicitly, then implicitly by her data. As in all valid theoretical advances, the old theory is subsumed in a wider and simpler generalization which includes and illuminates much older aspects of human knowledge and wisdom expressed in other forms. Thus the idea that experiences in the family affect deeply — at times for life — the feelings, impulses, decisions, and behavior of each of its individual members in unique yet predictable ways is not far from the biblical statement, "unto the third and fourth generation."

Memories of personal experiences with Adelaide are easily and vividly revived in rereading her writings. Such memories are of piece with those recorded in this volume by the editor and by her style of writing about people and hence inevitably about herself. I shall continue to treasure them as in the past; they contributed to one's expansion of the self. A warm hearted, energetic friend of great endowment, an intellectual companion of many years, and a collaborator without peer, Adelaide McFadyen Johnson will continue to live in her writings.

STANISLAUS A. SZUREK, M.D.

EDITOR'S PREFACE

I AM pleased to have been asked to compile and edit a book of Adelaide McFadyen Johnson's writings. Her pioneering work, her brilliance, originality, and warmth certainly deserve a memorial. Beyond this, her unique contributions to psychiatric thought merit publication in book form.

It was my privilege to know Adelaide Johnson from several different perspectives — as student, as analysand, as co-investigator, as friend, and then as colleague. I was well on my way to a career in internal medicine when I first attended one of her sparkling case conferences. She was an impressive figure, carefully groomed, tall, with jet black hair parted in the middle, an alert, strong face dominated by dark, intense eyes. With perspicacity, she sought out and found the crucial points and missing links in the data as it unfolded in a case presentation. She used her hands and cigarette holder both expressively and expansively. She smiled readily. Few would have guessed that this was a woman who had suffered much from tuberculosis and multiple surgery. She could not have children of her own but held open house for the neighborhood children regularly.

She had a high energy level — worked and lived to the hilt. She loved entertaining in her beautiful home, enjoyed Western ranches, ice hockey, and trips to far-off places away from the beaten track. She thoroughly enjoyed working with colleagues. There were many long, stimulating, and productive evenings spent talking, thinking, discussing, and writing in her living room or at the round table in her warm, spacious kitchen — of which she was especially proud.

Her premature death (age 55) came November 20, 1960, caused by constrictive pericarditis resulting from metastatic carcinoma.

Dr. Johnson's work on parental sanctions in the development of conscience defects (superego lacunae) has been accorded appropriately wide recognition. Her work on collaborative therapy is general knowledge in the field of child psychiatry and occupies a significant place in the therapeutic armamentarium of many child psychiatric clinics. The use of collaborative therapy as an investigative device is not as widely appreciated — especially in adult psychiatry.

Dr. Johnson's enquiring mind explored other areas with the same candor and perspicacity. As a scientist, she fearlessly questioned widely accepted basic premises — often to the consternation of those around her. Her early training with Dr. Anton J. Carlson, with whom she worked toward her Ph.D. in physiology at the University of Chicago, instilled in Dr. Johnson an appreciation for evidence and scientific rigor. She found the mental gymnastics of many psychoanalytic "theorists" of little usefulness, for she felt they were based on questionable premises without the support of solid evidence. Of course, this did not mean that Dr. Johnson was anti-psychoanalytic. She was a highly regarded training analyst with a deep sense of loyalty to the analytic movement. She did, however, regret the increasing institutionalization of the psychoanalytic movement with the attendant rigidification that comes to all social institutions over time.

In her work with child-parent problems, she became increasingly aware of the impact of the environment on the learning of behavior in the growing, developing child. She observed the determining influences of communication, kinesics, paralanguage, and double communications (in addition to identification) on the development of the child. She never denied inherent biologic, genetic factors as determinants of human behavior, but rather felt that these factors were all too often invoked as plausible "explanations" in the absence of accurate or complete data regarding early and continuing interpersonal life experiences. Locke's concept of the 'tabula rasa' appealed to Dr. Johnson. In many ways she incorporated Freudian psychoanalysis, learning theory, and Sullivanian psychiatry in her own conceptualizations. She admired the pragmatism of Meyer.

As a physiologist-turned-psychiatrist, Dr. Johnson developed an early interest in psychosomatic disorders. One of her earliest psychiatric papers, "Vertigo as the Primary Manifestation in Anxiety Neurosis," was written while at the Henry Phipps Psychiatric Clinic in Baltimore. Her interest in emotional alteration of somatic function and structure continued throughout her career. Her major work in this area occurred in Chicago, while working with Dr. Franz Alexander. Also while in Chicago, her consuming interest in child-parent relationships developed. This interest was enhanced by the development and expansion of collaborative techniques of psychotherapy from which new data and insights evolved. Her paper on "School Phobia" (with E. Falstein and S. Szurek), 1941, is perhaps a classic. From this work evolved her major interest in conscience development and the genesis of antisocial behavior. She later applied the basic principles of this work to attempts to understand other clinical syndromes and behavioral deviation. The papers on schizophrenia best exemplify this latter phase of her work.

With Alexander, she explored techniques of psychotherapy that might shorten the length and, therefore, expensive course of classical psychoanalysis. She was also interested in adapting and changing techniques to make possible the application of psychoanalytic theory (in the broadest sense) to the treatment of psychoses and psychosomatic disorders as well as to those disorders primarily characterized by "acting out." She felt that limit-setting with the latter group was often necessary for the working through of determinant conflicts. The limits were set only after the genetic material had evolved and after a reasonably strong positive transference had been established. In those many instances where the socially self-destructive acts were originally fostered unconsciously by the parents, Dr. Johnson observed that the patient transferred to the therapist and experienced in the therapist the parental "wish" for the same destructive solution. Just as the unambivalent parent obstructs self-destructive behavior in the child (despite the child's immediate anger of frustration), so the therapist actively intervenes through appropriately timed interpretation and subsequent prohibition of destructive behavior.

I have selected for this volume a representative sample of Dr. Johnson's work. The reader will then have at his fingertips all of the more important of Dr. Johnson's contributions to psychiatry and psychoanalysis. In addition, a complete list of her publications is to be found in the Appendix. I have purposely limited editorializing, interpretation, and explanation since, in my view, Dr. Johnson speaks well for herself.

SECTION I

Introduction

1

PSYCHOANALYTIC PSYCHIATRY

In 1947, on the occasion of celebrating its centennial year, Rockford College invited many leading scientists and educators including Adelaide McFadyen Johnson (class of '26) to speak at a conference on science. In her address, "Psychoanalytic Psychiatry," Dr. Johnson outlined her own "groping growth process" as she moved from a graduating bachelor of arts to her then current position as a staff member of the Chicago Institute for Psychoanalysis. She described her compelling interest in both understanding and modifying human suffering and behavior. She also alluded to her wish to avoid obtuse language (jargon). This concern contributed to her excellence as a teacher and made her writings comprehensible to non-psychiatrists and refreshing to psychiatrists.

Dr. Johnson's Rockford College address provides us with her own evaluation of psychoanalytic psychiatry and her role in the field as it was in 1947.

I LEFT Rockford College in 1926. In spite of the concept of the general public that a psychoanalyst is a rather eerie mixture of Oriental magician and glorified astrologer, I would like to try to convey to you that it is really not such a far cry from Rockford College graduation to becoming a member of the staff of the Chicago Institute for Psychoanalysis. Of course, I did not go immediately into psychoanalysis from Rockford College —

Reprinted with permission from *Proceedings, Conference on Science*, pp. 109–16. Rockford College, Rockford, Illinois, February 21–23, 1947.

between the two was a rather long intellectual and sometimes groping growth process. I received a Ph.D. in physiology and later an M.D., both from the University of Chicago. I spent the two extra years in physiology because I felt that the discipline acquired in basic scientific research under the great scientist, Dr. Anton J. Carlson, would be invaluable in later medical studies. Never for a moment have I regretted this extra time spent in study, since it gave me opportunity for association with that brilliant investigator and teacher.

In my medical school training I had *not one* course in psychiatry. During my internship at Billings Hospital, I was considering ophthalmology as a specialty, when I was told by several staff men that my talents were particularly attuned to psychiatry. I spent, therefore, an extra year at Billings Hospital studying the emotional aspects of internal medicine. Johns Hopkins Hospital, with the famous Adolph Meyer at the head of psychiatry, was recommended to me as the fountain-head of psychiatric knowledge and training in this country. I spent three years there with gifted colleagues and learned much about the field of psychiatry. I felt blocked and discouraged, however, that superficial reassurances and the best of sympathetic care were the only techniques of psychotherapy taught there. It seemed to me that there must be depths in the human mind that we did not reach, or know how to approach. I began to read more and more about psychoanalysis, the writings of Freud, and the discoveries of the new psychoanalytic institutes, especially the Chicago Institute under Franz Alexander.

At that time there was no psychoanalytically trained psychiatrist on the staff of Hopkins — in fact, psychoanalysis was frowned upon. I was shocked to realize that there may be intense resistance to new ideas even in great scientists. In addition to a doctor's own personal fears and defensiveness about looking into himself deeply, further resistance was created by the early writers of psychoanalysis. Their language of Greek derivatives instead of simple words exasperated readers. I once spoke of this to an older analyst who had known Freud and all the early analysts in Europe. I asked her why they wrote so abstrusely of what we can say so simply, and she replied, "You say it simply now because you understand now much more than they understood at first." This past year Johns Hopkins has changed the direction of their teaching in psychiatry to a more psychoanalytically oriented approach.

After my work at Johns Hopkins, I returned to Chicago and spent 5 years in training at the Institute for Psychoanalysis. At the same time I was doing psychiatric work at the Institute of Juvenile Research. Training in psychoanalysis, namely the learning of the methods of understanding and treating the unconscious conflicts at the basis of emotional illness, consists first of a personal analysis, then endless courses and seminars, and finally the supervised analyses of several patients.

I would like to explain the necessity of the personal analysis in any postgraduate training in psychotherapy. The analyst must have his own unconscious sensitive areas analyzed; or when his patient says something which deeply concerns the analyst's own conflicts, the physician may react with depression, or anger, or stupidity, and thus confuse his patient's analysis. Let me give a simple illustration. Recently a young psychiatrist came to me saying he could not risk further treatment of patients before he himself was analyzed. He told me that one of his patients mentioned a humiliating experience that had occurred in his childhood. The psychiatrist suddenly had an uncontrollable wish to laugh and then felt such a strong urge to weep that he could hardly finish the interview. The doctor had no conscious knowledge of the basis of this emotional reaction. Another example of this could occur when a patient tells his violent murderous fantasies to the therapist. If the analyst becomes frightened because unconsciously his own hates are aroused, he may be unable to listen objectively and casually, or to analyze with his patient the deep sources of the patient's hostility.

Of the 4,000 psychiatrists in the country to date, only about 300 have undergone psychoanalytic training. Since the war vast numbers of young psychiatrists are coming for training because they are more informed about psychoanalysis in medical schools and also because they saw in the armed forces that the analytically trained psychiatrists had more understanding of their patients, and as a result treated them far more skillfully.

Today there is a desperate need for specialists in emotional disorders, and a large part of the time of experienced therapists goes into the training of young psychiatrists. Training institutes are deluged with demands for training and for the personal analysis required of each candidate.

It would be unwise to allow research to lag behind because of the present need to emphasize training. The more we learn of the unknown conflicts at the basis of certain ailments, the more rapidly we can treat and alleviate these difficulties. At the Chicago Institute the time not given to training students is devoted to therapy and research. For the past 2 years nearly all of our research effort has been directed toward understanding what emotional conflicts, if any, give rise to arthritis, a widespread disease among the age group 20 to 30 years. I am not at liberty as yet to discuss our discoveries regarding the nature of the emotional conflict underlying this disease, but there is no question that a common causative factor exists. Asthma was the subject of an earlier research, and the results of this study have been published.

A major research issue at the Institute for 7 years was the

problem of how to decrease the time required to analyze a patient. After several years of working collectively on this problem, we finally developed some criteria for selecting patients who could be helped with fewer treatment hours than the standard method of psychoanalysis had required. We critically evaluated our own techniques of psychotherapy and found many new avenues of approach. Our findings were published in a book (1) this past year. This by no means implies that therapy can be shortened greatly for everyone; and it is wishful thinking to draw this conclusion on reading our book. We often get letters and phone calls asking if we can psychoanalyze Mr. X when he stops off for 2 or 3 hours between trains.

Emotional illness has existed for generations, but never have its genesis and treatment been so widely understood and popularly exposed as in the past 5 years through novels, movies and magazine articles. To be sure the movies still deal with the grossest and eeriest pathological situations. At least one person has to be murdered before the law or psychiatry overtakes the principal character. I often wish they would depict a capable but neurotic business man who never killed anyone, who goes to the psychoanalyst because he has frightful insomnia, and who is like 90% of the patients treated by analysts. The case reported recently in *Life Magazine* is an excellent example. People are beginning to realize that all of us have some deep conflicts which may cause emotional distress and impaired effectiveness in life. Such moderate disorders as migraine, asthma, anxieties and depression do not mean that a patient is insane, and people seek help from the psychiatrist with far less fear than formerly.

What do we mean when we say that an unconscious conflict may cause anxiety, depression, asthma, migraine, high blood pressure, undue sensitiveness, nightmares and scores of other symptoms? In simple terms the following takes place. In earliest childhood everyone has to learn to tolerate a certain degree of frustration. A little child may be terribly frustrated through the death of his parents, or by exaggerated hostility or coldness in his parents; he may be made to feel too guilty about his hostility toward the new baby in the family; he may have been punished too severely for misdemeanors or made too guilty about his dependent needs as a little child. A child who has suffered extreme frustration of his needs will be filled with hatred and fear toward those on whom he is dependent. He dares not display such hatred, but he may deny these feelings to himself, and they may become unconscious so that he does not have to be aware of their existence. Sooner or later such hatred may begin to work its way back into consciousness. For reasons too complex to explain here, the hostility often appears in disguised forms such as high blood pressure, anxious over-protectiveness of the younger brother or sister, fears of leaving the mother and going to school, etc.

In this connection I am reminded of a 10-year-old girl who for 6 years had become increasingly protective of animals — to the extent that her concern was fantastic. She was so busy caring for mice, dogs, snakes and birds and so worried about them that she had no energy for school or friends. In her analysis we finally unearthed the following facts. She remembered that at 4 years of age she had had a dream in which she was being chased by millions of baby animals that wanted to hurt her. I commented that it was peculiar that she who loved animals should dream of baby animals wishing to injure her. I suggested that possibly at that time she had been angry and wished to hurt some baby animal herself, since in her dream she felt they were all her enemies.

The next time I saw this child she said that after leaving me she remembered a "horrible thing." She recalled that when she was 4 years old her parents talked continually of wanting a baby. In school at this time the class had a pet rabbit which was loved by the group. Then a baby rabbit was brought into the play group.

All the children cared only for the baby rabbit and completely ignored the older one. The patient was so angry about this that she lay awake at night for weeks planning how to kill the baby rabbit. She finally took a paper sack to school, placed the baby animal in it and buried it alive in the sand pile. When this was discovered several days later, the teacher and parents called the child a murderer. In her analysis the little patient could see that she had feared and hated the possibility of a new baby at home, and after seeing the older rabbit ignored for the baby one, her hatred was acted out against the baby rabbit. She was so guilty about this that the next six years of her life became increasingly devoted to atoning for her early cruelty to an animal. As this conflict was worked out in analysis the fantastic need to care for and protect animals subsided.

A woman of 30 years of age came to treatment because she realized she could not love people as warmly as she knew others did and she suffered increasingly from violent headaches. She knew her mother had died when she was 2 years old. She maintained that this meant nothing to her, that she had always loved her stepmother. This patient was terrified at the thought of having a baby. In analysis over a long period, she finally was able to express the forgotten overwhelming loneliness and terror she had felt when her own mother died. This part of the analysis was an ordeal for her, but when the terror of the little girl's losing someone on whom she had been so dependent returned to consciousness, she was able to face it as an adult. The emotion then became dissipated instead of stored up. She had been afraid to love anyone ever since the death of her mother because of her fear of losing a loved person. Now she was no longer afraid to love other people and she could dare to love children and wish to have some of her own. After these feelings were expressed, she became a much happier woman and the headaches improved.

These are only two examples of the fears and hatreds that may be stored up within us. It is a well known fact that much of the hostility in race prejudice and in war springs from our own personal unconscious storehouse of hostility, and a certain personal relief from the tension of repressing such animosity comes when it is expressed in the socially accepted channels of war and race prejudice. Man's inner hostilities, usually not apparent to himself, can explode in the atomic destruction of other men or may be dissipated by being brought to light cautiously and slowly through analysis of the basic causes of his hatred.

One particular line of research that I have followed since my Institute for Juvenile Research days has been the understanding and treatment of children, especially of a certain adolescent group, who grow up with a poorly developed conscience. By this I mean children who engage in antisocial behavior such as stealing, truanting, fire-setting, cruelties or promiscuity. Volumes have been written stating that delinquency is a constitutional or hereditary defect. Then numbers of excellent case histories were published attempting to prove that when parents were cold and rejecting and a child did not develop any love for them, he could not develop feelings of guilt or conscience and thus would give in to any impulse that arose in him. Some of us became especially interested in further causes of delinquency. Coldness on the part of the parents could not be the whole story, for many rejecting parents have children who have strong consciences and who often seem to be over guilty about their misdemeanors. Also some warm, loving parents may have a child who has no guilt about stealing. What is the explanation?

Dr. Szurek and I, working collaboratively, one of us seeing the child and the other the parent or parents, became aware of certain rather unpleasant but undeniable facts. Sometimes consciously, but more often unconsciously, the parent, due to his own partial defects in conscience, was fostering the asocial behavior in the child. In other words in a non-delinquent, non-slum area, if a child is brought to treatment because of stealing, or fire-setting, or excessive truanting, lying or promiscuity, the etiology is no longer speculative if the significant parent's unconscious attitudes toward the delinquency are discovered. Unwittingly the parent soon exposes herself or himself as the initiator of such behavior in the child. How does the parent unconsciously give permission to the child to behave in such an asocial fashion? First the child identifies himself with a parent and adopts the parent's concept of right and wrong. The parent may upbraid Johnnie for lying, but if Johnnie hears his mother order the maid to tell the caller his mother is not at home, Johnnie has reason to vacilate. If he sees his father leave the grocery store smugly pleased that he was given too much change and did not reveal the mistake to the clerk, Johnnie will do likewise.

In a similar fashion, fantasies of the parents expressed to the child may arouse doubts in the child. For instance, 14-year-old Marion comes home and tells her mother that the neighbor girl Dorothy was caught stealing in school. Marion's mother might say, "If you ever do anything like that, I hope they will punish you." To make such a remark is to indicate doubt of her daughter's capacity to be honest, and Marion might spitefully take this as a permission. An anxious doubt of possible dishonesty in the child expressed by parents is highly destructive to the child's developing conscience. An adolescent girl, Ellen, who was in treatment with me came one day without an appointment, pale and obviously frightened. She told me the following story: She had just returned home from school and angrily told her mother that she hated her math teacher and was going to shoot him someday. Her mother had looked horrified and said, "Oh Ellen, don't bring any such tragedy on this family." Ellen said to me, "She actually thought I would murder someone! What is wrong with her?"

Fortunately earlier than this I had helped this mother to get into treatment with another analyst, for in my initial interview with the mother I had felt her fears about the child were actually fears about her own deeper impulses. Only such an approach will clarify the details of how any child or adolescent becomes a delinquent or criminal. If a parent has a thoroughly sound conscience, he will tell the little child what is right or wrong without anxiety or embarrassment.

We finally had to face the fact that treatment of the child was often impossible without concomitant treatment of the permissive parent. Sometimes we treat only the parent. The following case is an illustration of this method of treating the child through treatment of the significant parent. Anne, an intelligent 17-year-old girl was failing in school and was becoming increasingly disturbed emotionally. Since she refused to see a psychoanalyst, her mother came to see me. The mother was a very fine woman of high intelligence. Because of the circumstances of her own early life, she had mixed feelings of love and hostility toward her daughter. She could not be firm with her daughter for fear she would become too angry with the child. She had given in to Anne's demands that the mother write fraudulent excuses to the school whenever Anne cut classes. The girl knew this was dishonest and must have felt very uneasy that her mother was corruptible. I analyzed many different facets of the mother's feelings toward Anne, including the significance of this mutual corruption in regard to cutting classes. Finally the mother could be firm with Anne without being hostile; and as a consequence the young girl settled down rapidly, graduated from high school and has done well in college for three years. In many cases of this nature no treatment is possible; for in spite of our most tactful and subtle approach, parents may refuse to go for any treatment themselves.

In summary I should like to emphasize that as a psychoanalyst

I derive pleasure not only from teaching, treating patients, and doing research; but what is even more basic, I find it gratifying and stimulating, both intellectually and emotionally, to be able to understand why people behave as they do.

Why do some people eat to the point of obesity? Why do some brilliant children fail in school? Why does one child in a fine well-to-do family steal and the others in the family do not? Why do some people go into a deep depression when they are offered a promotion on a job? Why are some people utterly unable to make friends? Why does a woman think her little son is a joy but feels distant and critical toward her little daughter? Why do some people appear even-tempered and pleasant at every turn while their blood pressure is mounting to higher and more malignant heights? Why does a man marry and get divorced several times, resort to sedatives, continually change his job, and seek all kinds of doctors before he dares face his problems and come to an analyst to seek the deeper sources of his maladjustment? I do not maintain that we know all the answers to these questions, but we do understand much more than we formerly did about these once insoluble mysteries, and we are always seeking new solutions.

REFERENCE

1. Alexander, Franz; French, Thomas M.; *et al. Psychoanalytic Therapy.* New York: Ronald Press, 1946.

2

SCHOOL PHOBIA

With Eugene I. Falstein, M.D., S. A. Szurek, M.D., and Margaret Svendsen

The earliest paper on emotional disturbances in children derived from work at the Institute of Juvenile Research, Chicago. This paper, presented at the 1941 orthopsychiatry meeting, was based on therapy of children with "school phobia." Although it was only her third contribution to the psychiatric literature, it is recognized as a classic paper by many child psychiatrists.

FOR years psychiatrists have recognized that there is a type of emotional disturbance in children, associated with great anxiety, that leads to serious absence from school. This is a deep-seated psychoneurotic disorder fairly sharply differentiated from the more frequent and common delinquent variety of school truancy. The syndrome, often referred to as "school phobia," is recognizable by the intense terror associated with being at school. The child may be absent for periods of weeks or months or years, unless treatment is instituted. The children, on fleeing from school, usually go straight home to join the mother. Eventually they refuse to leave the house. When the child is superficially questioned, he cannot verbalize what he fears and the whole matter appears incomprehensible to parents and teachers. It seems to us that this syndrome is not a clean-cut entity, for one finds overlapping of the phobic tendencies with other neurotic patterns, such as those of an hysterical or obsessive nature.

Although this type of problem is seen fairly frequently in any child guidance clinic and can become very serious, there has been very little written about it. In 1932 Dr. Isra T. Broadwin (1) described this syndrome in his paper entitled, "A Contribution to the Study of Truancy." The title might suggest that it is only another article on delinquent truancy but it does attempt to describe the psychoneurotic elements in this disorder.

There are all degrees of school phobia ranging from those that are abortive and clear quickly, to those requiring intensive treatment. The severe school phobia that is left untreated may develop into a seriously crippling condition. This is well exemplified by a case of a woman of 31 who was analyzed by one of the writers, (E.I.F.). Her first acute anxiety began in the school room at 13 and soon developed into a severe school phobia which was untreated. This rapidly spread to include phobias of many varieties from which the secondary gains were so great that after 18 years they constituted an insurmountable barrier to any very successful analytic therapy.

Fairly intensive clinical experience with eight children treated at the Institute for Juvenile Research has resulted in a somewhat clearer insight into the dynamics of school phobia as well as its therapy. The group studied includes an equal number of male and female children. The age range at time of appearance of the phobia was from 6 to 14 years of age. The symptoms had existed from 10 days to 2 years, one 8 year old boy never having gone to school. There was no consistent determinant so far as ordinal position was concerned. Intelligence ranged from low average to extremely superior — the majority of the children being in the superior group. In the 8 cases studied the 4 boys were submissive and obedient to their mothers, whereas the girls were aggressively defiant. All of these children had a definite history pointing to the presence of considerable anxiety in their early years, such as night terrors that were striking, promotion anxieties, earlier short periods of phobia regarding school, severe temper tantrums, asthma and eczema. The children came from homes of varied economic levels.

The outstanding common factors in initiation of the school phobia which seem to be operating in all 8 cases are, first, *an acute anxiety in the child*, which condition may be caused by organic disease, or by some emotional conflict manifested in hysterical, hypochondriacal, or compulsive symptoms precipitated by arrival of a new sibling, promotion in school, etc. Second, and equally important, an *increase of anxiety in the mother* due to some simultaneously operating threat to her satisfactions, such as sudden economic deprivation, marital unhappiness, illness, etc. Third, there seems always to be a strikingly poorly resolved early dependency relationship of these children to their mothers. How these three cardinal factors become interrelated in the production of the school phobia will be seen most easily perhaps from study of a case summary and excerpts from others.

Summary of Case. Jack, age 9, the middle child in a family of three, developed school phobia eight months before coming to the Institute. After a mild organic illness associated with unnecessary trips to various medical clinics accompanied by his over-solicitous mother, with two or three months of absence from school the boy refused to return to school and developed hypochondriacal complaints, temper tantrums, fears of storms, etc. Soon a full-blown school phobia was very evident. Early in her clinic visits the boy's mother said, "It made me sick to see Jack so pale and anxious, angry and upset. Jack and I had such arguments about his going to school and I became so sick and upset that last spring his father decided it would be better for Jack not to go to school. Jack has always been so lovable — always worried about my illnesses — more than the other two children." The mother stated that people in her community said the boy was "working her" and she felt their view might be justified. Patient was described as "very cuddly, always needing more love than the others." The mother felt "he would have been better off had she devoted all of her time to him."

The child's maternal grandmother had been in bed for years with an hysterical disorder, and was growing increasingly demanding at this time of her younger daughter, the child's mother. The latter suffered from many somatic neurotically conditioned disorders that sent her to bed for days. She was a very dependent, hostile woman and while in a resentful mood, used her illness as a way to punish herself and her mother, to enslave her husband and this boy. Unconsciously she exploited the boy's guilt regarding his resentments toward her in order to bind him to herself. When treatment began at the Institute regularly once a week, she developed more severe disorders which at first were used as an excuse for not making the long trip. The family lived 250 miles from the clinic. She wrote, "I know I'm impeding Jack's progress by not coming in, for my husband can tell you nothing." Though the boy enjoyed his treatment hours from the start, his mother early used every excuse to keep him home. Finally criticism from the school and community operated to increase the mother's anxiety to the point where she came to the clinic regularly. Very quickly she developed a dependent transference to her psychiatrist (male) and subsequently seldom missed treatment hours. The boy was treated in a playroom by a woman psychiatrist. In this situation he lived through in play activity and verbally his conflicts with the family as brought out in relation to the therapist. Relationship interpretations were given to the child as seemed necessary to the resolution of his conflicts.

In the five months of regular weekly treatment hours the patient worked through a great deal of his ambivalence and rivalries toward both parents and siblings. Especially was he concerned early with rage and guilt against the mother because of her demands upon him for obedience and attention, and because of her resentment of any independent strivings. After he had been in treatment for some time he sent her a rather expensive present to cover both Mother's Day and her birthday. The mother complained bitterly to her therapist that Jack was "No longer her dear little Jack who had always given her two separate presents before." There were periods of fearfulness, especially when his mother would be very sick and, as these were worked through, patient brought out clearly at times his intense hateful wishes against her. As he asserted himself with the mother and turned more to outside interests, the mother interpreted this behavior as a real rejection. Often during treatment it was obvious that the boy felt very unhappy regarding his absence from school, recognized the crippling to himself and felt keenly the blow to his self-esteem when children became critical of him.

The mother discussed with her therapist her own unresolved dependence on her mother, her sister, and the therapist. She discussed also her bulimia when left alone, her longing for love, her feeling of inability to give it to her children, and her competition with Jack for attention, e.g., she often complained that her headaches were worse than his. Her "pride was cut to the quick by Jack's not going to school" and she saw his refusal to go as defiance of her. This led to discussion of her wish to dominate the boy as she was being dominated by her neurotic bed-ridden mother. Early in the treatment she vacillated in her wish to have Jack home, developed guilt as a result and tried to put the responsibility for forcing him to go to school on Jack's therapist. She also tried to prove that Jack's therapist was inadequate and exploited every opportunity to keep the boy near her. As she worked through her own frustrated, dependent needs with her therapist and felt indulged without criticism, she became much more giving with the children and husband and demanded less appreciation and nursing care. She became able to assert herself with her own mother, to sidestep the mother's attempts to make her guilty and to feel far better physically. After five or six months of treatment the boy returned to school and a year later a detailed letter stated that there was no more trouble with the boy and that the mother was feeling better than she had for years.

Dynamics. Consideration of the dynamics of this case with a few illustrative excerpts from the others seemed to point to the following impressions.

Jack suffered some acute anxiety associated with organic illness which created a tendency to regress to a greater dependency on the mother for the moment. This is the first crucial step in the cycle to follow. The mother had been recently more hostile and frustrated because of the increasing demands made by her neurotic mother. This is an equally important factor in the genesis of the disorder.

Study of the early life situations of these mothers always shows an inadequately resolved dependency relationship to their mothers with intense repressed resentments. One recalls that Jack's mother felt she could never give him enough love — that she should have been free to devote all her time to him as a little boy. This with many other similar comments suggests strongly the dependency relationship of Jack to his mother was never well resolved. What happens when Jack's mother, herself recently deprived and needing new satisfactions, begins to renew overindulgence to her child for the gratification it affords him and her? Though gratified to some extent because of the child's revived dependence on her, she feels aroused within her at the same time great resentment regarding granting to anyone that which she was not given. Thus Jack's mother reacted to his bid for renewed dependence with indulgence first and then with hostile envy. She clearly indicated her envy and resentment by competing with him in the sphere of illnesses, her headaches became worse, she felt that he should serve her refreshment in bed, etc. She felt guilty regarding her resentment, however, and sensing his rage at her none too subtle frustrations and begrudging, she began to vacillate in firmness in all situations. Furthermore, his rage aroused in her a recognition of a mirror image of her own reaction to her mother's dependent, infantile demands and begrudgings, and this in turn led to even further guilt and vacillation in firmness on her part. "When he looks so wild and angry and pale," said the mother, "I cannot stand it — it scares me and I give in. I can't make him go to school."

Occurring concomitantly is the ever-present conflict over the child's efforts at independence. The mother of one boy said, "I can't stand to see Bob such a sissy. I want him to stand his own ground like other boys," and a few minutes later commented, "I told him to go to bed at nine o'clock and at nine-thirty he walked into my bedroom fully dressed, hands in pockets and whistling — just defying me — a mother should be considered an authority."

In treatment Jack felt less dependent on his mother and gave her one gift to cover Mother's Day and a birthday which were one day apart. She was angry and complained bitterly. On the one hand, tired and resentful of the child's dependence she urges him to stand on his own feet, but on the other, when he tries this, she resents it as rejection and affront to her authority. In countless subtle ways these mothers create intense guilt in the children for their independent strivings.

What does the child do in these various situations? Sensing his mother's wish to have him dependent again, he at once exploits it. One girl utilized her asthma attacks with the anxiety they aroused in her mother to exploit indulgence to a great degree. One child early inveigled his mother into taking him to Florida to rest, "He looked so sick and pale." When the mother becomes angry regarding the degree to which she is asked to give, the child is furious and more demanding. The same rage appears when the child's attempts at independence are thwarted. All these reactions lead the child to wish to punish the mother in various ways, particularly through not going to school. Sooner or later all these mothers were humiliated and miserable with the criticism leveled at them regarding the child from the community and relatives. As one mother put it, "It is like a knife through my heart." Also the child punishes himself for his hostile rages in a typically self-destructive way by falling behind in school and crippling himself for life, if not treated. All of the children show fears and sensitiveness regarding this. Frequently they will stay indoors all day and be seen on the streets only after children are home from school. Furthermore, being home permits the child to reassure himself and check up to be sure his hostile destructive wishes against the parents, particularly the mother, do not ensue. One boy frequently said to his mother with real venom, "You're so old and haggard looking I doubt if you will live long and I want to be with you."

A fundamental step in this vicious circle is finally that of mutual restitution which involves loving, giving, over-solicitousness regarding one another's comforts with the need to be near each other. This constitutes the end and beginning of the circle and they begin again with mutual indulgence of dependence and of all that we now know follows this first step.

Very early in this chain of events there enters as a factor the school itself. When the teacher, as a more consistent disciplinarian, frustrates the child, she arouses his rage. Being less dependent on the teacher, who is a diluted form of the mother, the child's rage inhibited toward the mother can now find expression through displacement, and the teacher in her milieu becomes the phobic object. To avoid the teacher and school is now the defense against being placed in the situation in which the overwhelming anxiety is aroused. Often a child early complains that the teacher dislikes him.

It must be emphasized that in any clinic dealing with children we encounter countless histories of abortive school phobias and all gradations of transient anxieties with reference to going to school. These constitute the so-called "self-cures" which were possibly brought about by sufficient shift in the balance of life situations to offset anything more serious. A word should be said about the relation of this acute and deep anxiety which produces absence from school and the common form of truancy where the child often absents himself from school and dallies here and there about the neighborhood. He does not rush home as the phobic children do. In the cases of phobia where the child hurries home, the reaction seems to be part of a crystallized circle of mutually partially inhibited rages and need to make restitution where dependence and guilt of child is far greater with respect to the mother. In school phobias the mother is, in her vacillating moments, more affectionate, and therefore guilt is greater in the child, whereas in common truancy the child senses far less genuine love from the parent.

Treatment. Because of the vicious circle of guilt already indicated to be operating, it was believed that this circle best be broken into by a therapy which involved a collaborative dynamic approach to mother and child — treatment carried out by two therapists who co-incidentally attempted to relieve the guilt and tension in both patients. The aim in each was to foster a positive dependent transference in which each patient was permitted indulgence of his or her dependent needs and at the same time the expression of hostilities as lived out with the therapist. The particular conflicts which led to the acute anxiety in both at the onset of the disorder, as well as the basic neurotic dependence problem, had to be resolved. This led to ultimate release of tension and anxiety in both. Treatment of the mother led to a calmer and more secure firmness in her attitude toward the child. The child recognized in her a new firmness and this, plus his own treatment, led to a resolution of the previous conflict. It cannot be overemphasized that the mother needs and is given treatment as intensively as is the child, and by treatment we do not mean advice.

Six children were treated in a playroom where their conflicts, reflected in behavior toward the therapist, were dynamically understood and interpreted to them. One pre-adolescent and one adolescent child were treated in the usual interview situation as were the mothers in each case. Of the eight children, seven have returned to school and seem to be well along in their adjustment. One boy is still in treatment and only in the past three months was it seen that nothing fundamental could be accomplished unless his mother received regular treatment by another psychiatrist for her neurotic role.

Early in our studies the mothers were frequently treated by the social worker and the child by the psychiatrist, but it soon became clear that the most difficult problem had been given to the social worker, and to treat mother and child adequately in most instances two psychiatrists had to work collaboratively treating mother and child equally intensively. The duration of regular once a week treatment was from five months to over a year. In considering the factors operating in effective treatment one must recognize not only the depth to which the therapists are able to go with both patients, but also those community attitudes which are frequently vital to the mother and operative in bringing her to the clinic before she has developed any transference. Other factors are the relative secondary gains of child and mother from the existent phobia, for if at any time the balance of secondary gain moves too much to one or the other, such an imbalance becomes an asset in breaking into the vicious circle. The history of earlier neurotic episodes in mother and child, length of time the phobia has existed, and especially present life satisfactions of the mother, are important criteria of the prognosis. Treatment of the child alone might be all that is necessary if the child is older (pre-adolescent, and if he has not been ill too long). With younger children especially, a collaborative type of treatment seems to us more efficacious because such a child is more dependent upon the mother and the latter will not free the child without intensive treatment herself. Such collaborative treatment by two psychiatrists has been used by this clinic in treating a number of deeply crystallized intra-familial neurotic disorders, but this is a matter for elaboration in a subsequent paper.

Little has been said of the role of the father and treatment of him, but in several cases fathers have been seen many times. The impression has always been gained, however, that though he and his neurosis played into the mother's difficulties and led to greater disturbance and frustration in her, and thus indirectly to greater conflict in the child, still, treatment of the mother with clarification of her feelings about the father has seemed the more direct route to a resolution of the conflicts for the child. Fortunately, from a practical point of view, the mother is freer to come for treatment than would be the average father.

Discussion and Conclusion. Just how does this neurosis differentiate itself from other childhood neuroses? The syndrome of school phobia does not seem to us to be a qualitatively new and specific entity. It is a symptom developing under very definite circumstances. First, it appears to us that there is present a history of a poorly resolved dependency relationship between the child and its mother. With this background, two specific factors now enter in to initiate the phobia. There always occurs at the outset in the child some acute anxiety, produced either by organic disease or some external situation which arouses conflict, and manifested in hysterical or compulsive symptoms. Simultaneously the mother must be suffering from some new threat to her security — marital unhappiness, economic deprivation, or demands that she resents. Newly frustrated in her satisfactions, she has need now to exploit the child's acute anxiety and his wish for dependence. On the basis of an early poorly resolved dependency relationship, both readily regress to that earlier period of mutual satisfaction. Now the cycle begins which soon results in the school phobia if the child is of school age, with the teacher, in her milieu, made the phobic object.

REFERENCE

1. Broadwin, Isra T. "A contribution to the study of truancy." *Am. J. Orthopsychiatry* 2 (1932): 3.

3

COLLABORATIVE PSYCHIATRIC THERAPY OF PARENT-CHILD PROBLEMS

With Stanislaus Szurek, M.D., and Eugene Falstein, M.D.

> The technique of collaborative therapy by two psychiatrists was initially utilized at the Institute of Juvenile Research to treat an especially refractory instance of school phobia — one of the cases outlined in the preceding paper. The following paper, in which Dr. Johnson collaborated with Dr. Szurek (as senior author), defines the nature of such treatment, some of the requirements for effective application of the method, and emphasizes that it not only can facilitate therapy but also can provide a valuable research tool. From this development much of the material included in section III, Antisocial Behavior, evolved. In some of the examples presented in this paper, there are early reflections of several of the many questions Dr. Johnson pursued at length in later publications. For this reason the paper is presented in its entirety.

THIS paper describes a technique for psychiatric treatment and research in the behavior problems and psychoneurotic disorders of children in which concomitant therapeutic efforts are made by two psychiatrists, one of whom deals with the significant

Stanislaus Szurek, M.D., Adelaide Johnson, M.D., and Eugene Falstein, M.D., Collaborative psychiatric therapy of parent-child problems, *American Journal of Orthopsychiatry* 12(1942): 511–16. © American Orthopsychiatric Association, Inc. Reproduced by permission.

parent and the other directly with the child. Although the rationale of the approach has been indicated by Lowrey (1), and at times even explicitly stated in the literature by Almena Dawley (2), Greig (3), Anna Freud (4), Silberpfennig (5), and Rogers (6), people who are clearly aware of the importance of the parental neuroses in the treatment of children, it seems that the type of procedure which has been elaborated in this clinic might be of interest to record, not only because of its therapeutic value, but also because of its research possibilities.

There is an increasing awareness on the part of clinicians dealing with children that the behavior of a child is to be understood fundamentally only in the context of the intrafamilial interpersonal relations. Pathological relationships between mother and father and child play a great role in helping to maintain the distorted and unintegrated tendencies in the child.

It is unnecessary here to refer to the many years of excellent and successful collaborative work that has been done with the psychiatric social worker seeing the mother and the psychiatrist seeing the child in treatment disorders that are not too firmly crystallized. Such collaborations between psychiatrist and social worker will continue to constitute the predominant method of treatment in a child guidance clinic (7). This paper deals exclusively with those severely distorted child-parent relationships where the techniques of two psychiatrists well trained in dynamic psychiatry seem to be necessary for alleviation of the presenting problems.

Because it had been impossible to treat severe school phobias by treatment of the child alone,[1] in this clinic the mother, or the

[1] The one child reported in *School Phobia* (8) [reprinted above, p. 14], who had not returned to school was one whose mother had not been treated. Four months after the mother came into treatment he went back to school.

more significant parent, and the child were each treated by a psychiatrist concomitantly and, as it seemed, more successfully (8). Such collaborative therapy has been expanded in treating many behavior problems and other severe neuroses. Experience over a period of about three years with this technique has led the writers to the impression that: (1) many severe cases cannot be treated at all without the use of it; (2) it becomes a valuable tool in carrying research further in the study of interpersonal relations; and (3) many cases, where child or mother might be successfully treated alone, still seem to progress more rapidly when the two are treated concomitantly.

Probably the most fundamental requirement of such therapy is that the competitiveness of the psychiatrists involved in treatment shall be at a minimum. A psychiatrist treating the mother, for example, with unconscious rivalrous attitudes toward the other therapist, may quite unwittingly block the mother's expression of jealousy and hostility toward the child's therapist. Such complications can become manifold. A competitive therapist may unconsciously fail to give all of his available information to the other therapist for discreet use, or may ignore as superfluous what the other therapist could make available to him. Thorough training may reduce the problem, but a long training in dynamic psychiatry may not entirely resolve the sources of these competitions.

The writers do not draw too sharp a line between the neuroses and behavior problems, but there are certain quantitative distinguishing characteristics. The provocative or self-frustrating activities of the child with the behavior disorder seem to stem from the fact that there has been less warmth and support in the environment, and therefore less guilt about his greater tendency to direct seeking of gratification of impulses in an ungenerous and unsympathetic milieu (9).

In addition, there appears to be in these children as much wish to punish the hostile environment as to punish themselves, if not more. The self-punishing element has usually been more stressed in the literature. Because of these considerations it is difficult at times to know what is the more basic motive in the provocative behavior of such a child. Sometimes, the psychiatrist working alone with the child, sees only the child's guilt, anxiety and resentment, and not the provocation from the parent. Two psychiatrists in such a situation can observe better than one how mutually gratifying to all involved is the particular mode of interpersonal behavior, no matter how distorted or disguised the symptom or technique may be. It is as inaccurate to say that the mother alone fosters the behavior in the child, as to say that the child on his own stimulates certain responses in the mother. It is a mutual exchange, built of techniques slowly evolved between them. A few brief examples follow.

Elaine, IQ 150, a middle child with two brothers, in a very moralistic, respectable family, at age 12 suddenly began stealing and revealed to her mother that she had had intercourse many times with a high school boy. The mother was horrified and brought the child for treatment. It soon became obvious that this behavior was in defiance of and designed to injure the mother. The child only became guilty and depressed after she became aware of her mother's reactions. The mother, in treatment at the same time, gradually became aware of impulses and attitudes toward the child that were thoroughly hostile and designed to provoke situations where Elaine would be confronted with some impasse. She had no such feelings toward the sons, but was over-identified with the daughter who was named after her. Elaine was in treatment a brief time and was relieved of anxiety and depression, whereas the mother continued for a long period. No further difficulty arose with Elaine. The mother saw how she pushed the child into the father's lap, so to speak, and then reacted to the child with intense jealousy. She recalled episodes in her own early life of an attachment to her father about which she had great guilt and she was fearful of seeing the same reaction develop in Elaine. At the same time, however, by unconsciously fostering such an attitude in Elaine, she derived vicarious gratification of her own unintegrated infantile impulses.

Another mother, whose boy was extremely sadistic toward her, revealed with tears during her treatment that she had derived real gratification from his having twisted and hurt her arm. She wondered why she had permitted him to do it. Her own masochistic tendencies led her unconsciously to foster sadism in her son.

In this clinic, collaboration between psychiatrists in treating so-called behavior problems and neuroses has raised a number of significant hints about the matter of "choice of symptom." This term implies too much of conscious volition. The symptom itself is an on-going process expressing interplay of unconscious tendencies. How does a child, and later an adult, happen on a certain type of behavior such as stealing books or fire setting, or tearing the clothes, or promiscuity? How does a child evolve enuresis, vomiting, or a reading inhibition as one symptom of his neurotic disorder? In the following instance it was possible to see that one factor directing the child's expression of her tensions was the specific neurotic anxiety of the mother.

Doris, 13, suddenly set the family apartment on fire. The child had never destroyed with fire before, although she enjoyed bonfires very much. When the mother came into treatment, she revealed with considerable anxiety the deep hostility between her and Doris, an exact repetition of the rage existing between the mother and her sister after whom Doris was named. Three weeks before the fire setting the mother told her own therapist that she had gone to a fire several blocks away. While at the fire she thought, "My own apartment will be the next to burn and Doris will be the one to start the fire." The mother went home and told Doris and her father about it, saying children had set the fire, although of this she was not at all sure. On the day she heard that her apartment was on fire she knew instantly that Doris was responsible. Also, when she came into treatment she was horrified by the fact that ever since the fire she had had the firm conviction that Doris would be struck by an automobile. The violent feelings felt by this woman toward her own mother and sister were projected onto Doris and unconsciously the mother fostered the acting out of her own frightening, forbidden feelings which dealt with years of hostile death wishes against her family by burning. For a few days before Doris set the fire, the mother had been extremely hostile and provocative, as she later told her therapist.

Another example in a family studied in detail was David's mother who "had a horror of a stealing child." In handling David she was vacillating and uncertain when it came to advising him firmly of property rights. Further discussion with the mother gradually revealed her own early stealing tendencies, the conflict about which had not been resolved.

In another family James promptly became a party to an interesting reaction manifest in his mother during his and her treatment. The mother said in discussing her own problems that she "could not stand bedwetting in a child." A week later she returned and reported that for the first time in his life 13 year old James had wet the bed four nights in a row.

These symptoms or pathological techniques become complicated when several family members are involved. For example, in the case of Marion who was extremely provocative with her mother it was found that the father fostered much of the child's acting out because of the vicarious gratification he derived from seeing his wife injured.

The behavior of parent and child in relation to their two therapists is illustrated by a brief incident in the treatment of Robert and his mother. Robert had almost recovered from his school phobia when suddenly he became much worse and his mother called the boy's male therapist. He at once referred the mother to her own therapist, a woman, and in the following interviews it became quite clear that the mother's need to see the boy's male therapist was in part an expression of her own unresolved oedipal conflicts. It was obvious that she provoked Robert, making him much worse, and thus felt she now had sufficient excuse to talk to Robert's therapist herself. This was one of numerous efforts on her part not to work through her own difficulties with her therapist but to "seek advice" from the boy's therapist.

On the basis of 22 cases studied in detail and illustrated by these brief excerpts it seems clear that in some instances the parent unconsciously gives the child a cue. It may be an expression of a specific fear, as in the fire setting case, or an ambivalent anxious reaction to some behavior or symptom of the child. This combination of events has seemed to fix the form of the clinical picture through which the parent's own unintegrated and forbidden impulses are afforded vicarious gratification.

Although it is frequently easier to see the forbidden impulse vicariously fostered by the significant adult in the behavior problems, there are also strong hints of the presence of the same factors in the more disguised pathologic formations of the neuroses.

We have had occasion to study several sets of identical twins, which material will be reported in greater detail in a later communication. In these studies one could see the mother, and at times the father, splitting off their acceptable tendencies from the forbidden. They fostered the unacceptable trends in one twin and the acceptable in the other. One mother brought her normal boy for treatment and for a long period was protective and secretive about the really sick boy who represented for her gratification of certain tendencies in herself which she had great difficulty in facing and giving up.

Since its reactions are gratifying somehow to the parent, the child is not brought for treatment until the secondary gains or gratifications of the child exceed those of the mother or father, when the latter speaks of *complaints*. At that time, too, the excess is usually sufficient to cause anxiety in the parent to bring the child for treatment but not to accept treatment for himself. Getting the parent into treatment depends upon such factors as the skill of the therapist, and the anxiety of and gratification to the parent.

From the experience of this clinic impressions concerning treatment of behavior problems and neuroses differ somewhat. These impressions may be summarized as follows.

1. Almost no serious behavior problem regardless of the child's age can be treated unless the significant parent is in treatment.
2. Any serious neurotic adjustment between parent and child necessitates the treatment of both parent and child with the following possible exceptions: (a) an adolescent neurotic child, not too bound by the parent, can often be successfully treated without treatment of the parent, if the child is old enough to be able possibly to identify with the therapist toward a satisfactory emancipation; (b) treatment of the parent alone with a child under 4 or 5 may be satisfactory; (c) intensive treatment of the child of 5 or under, suffering from a neurosis of recent origin, may be sufficient occasionally. Levy (10) has reported the successful treatment of this type of conflict.

The logical outcome of such collaborative experiences is that it would seem better in treatment to avoid, on the whole, giving much in the way of advice. The educability of parents bringing children as disturbed as are seen in this clinic is rather limited. In other words, it is not suggested that a mother "show more restraint" or "give more love," for she would have done this if she could have, and she may regard the advice as criticism. It does little good to urge a parent to give a stealing child an allowance without understanding the parent's own deeper attitudes about giving and stealing. For instance, Mrs. A. clearly indicated as her treatment progressed that although she had given Ted an allowance according to earlier advice of a therapist, she deeply envied the boy and begrudged him his allowance. The boy sensed her attitude and stopped stealing only when her own conflicts over envies had been resolved.

Often out of anxiety or hostility, parents may become very demanding for concrete advice. The skillful therapist will see beyond this device and deal with the anxiety back of the demand. For the same reason it is not very helpful in training the young social worker or beginning psychiatrist to "advise" that they never give advice to demanding, hostile parents. In other words, the young therapist must deal with his own feelings in the situation and do the best he can. Even the experienced psychiatrist at times finds himself giving advice. He may tell parents he can do no more for their boy until they relax their pressure on the child for achievement, but the psychiatrist soon finds he has only shifted responsibility and has not done therapy. Parents, out of guilt, may try to lighten their pressure, but the child senses the artificiality and anxiety, and feels less assurance as to where he stands. Through some measure of reliving early unresolved conflicts with their permissive therapist the hostility beneath the anxiety in the parents is lessened with the gaining of some insight.

Workers interested in the socially delinquent child have had some hope that these collaborative psychiatric techniques would be effective in treatment. It is apparent that such children, in very little conflict with their social group, possess a defect in conscience with regard to the larger community. Such children cannot develop guilt and self-restraint in relationship to the larger community without much more warmth and firmness than can be offered in the weekly psychiatric interviews. At times these aims can be attained by the warm, consistently firm and basically friendly foster-parent with whom the child lives, or in the institution properly staffed for such treatment, such as Aichhorn's. As for getting the parents of the child in for collaborative treatment they usually are unavailable for the same reasons as apply to the child, i.e., they usually cannot be won by the brief psychiatric interview.

In conclusion, it would seem that a collaborative approach by two psychiatrists is frequently necessary and more rapidly effective in treatment of most behavior problems and the more severe neuroses. It is recognized that facilities for such studies are sometimes not available. But beyond the clinical advantages, and really of more fundamental importance, are the research opportunities made possible by this direct participant observation of the dynamic interplay between parent and child. Out of such observations have come rather clear impressions that the unconscious gratifications parents derive from their unintegrated tendencies, is a powerful stimulus in fostering certain behavior or determining a neurotic symptom in a child. It is apparent that for the complete study of the genetics of so-called "symptom choice" or pathologic formations in children, one must know the meaning of such manifestations to the parent. Such collaborative techniques make it possible to observe something of the genesis of behavior and, eventually, of character traits.

It seems this method permits direct empirical observations

bearing on these questions instead of depending upon speculations and reconstructions from studies of adult neurotics or from the study of the neurotic child alone. It affords a further avenue of inquiry before retreating to such concepts as "constitutional tendencies."

REFERENCES

1. Lowrey, Lawson G. Trends in therapy: evolution, status and trends. *Am. J. Orthopsychiatry* 9 (1939), no. 4.
2. Dawley, Almena. Trends in therapy: inter-related movement of parent and child in therapy with children. *Am. J. Orthopsychiatry* 9 (1939), no. 4.
3. Greig, Agnes Bruce. The problem of the parent in child analysis. *Psychiatry* 3 (1940): 539.
4. Freud, Anna. *Technic of child analysis.* New York: Nerv. & Ment. Dis. Pub. Co., 1928.
5. Silberpfennig, Judith. Mother types encountered in child guidance clinics. *Am. J. Orthopsychiatry.* 11 (1941), no. 3.
6. Rogers, Carl. *The clinical treatment of the problem child.* New York: Houghton Mifflin, 1939.
7. Szurek, S. A. Some problems of collaborative therapy. *AAPSW. News Letter* 9 (1940): 1.
8. Johnson, Adelaide; Falstein, E. I.; Szurek, S. A.; and Svendsen, Margaret. School phobia. *Am. J. Orthopsychiatry* 11 (1941), no. 4. Reprinted above, p. 14.
9. Szurek, S. A. Notes on the genesis of psychopathic personality trends. *Psychiatry,* 5 (1942): 1.
10. Levy, David. Release therapy. *Am. J. Orthopsychiatry* 9 (1939), no. 4.

SECTION II

Psychosomatic Problems

PSYCHOSOMATIC PROBLEMS

One of Dr. Johnson's earliest psychiatric papers was in the area of psychosomatic interests. This was "Vertigo as the Primary Manifestation in Anxiety Neurosis" which appeared in 1940. Although the body of the paper has been abbreviated for presentation in this section, the case report is given en toto as an example of her ability to present the meat of pertinent data and, simultaneously, to retain color and vitality in an abbreviated description of her patient.

This early interest in psychosomatic medicine was a natural extension of her early interest in physiology. Under the tutelage of Dr. A. J. Carlson, whom she admired greatly, Dr. Johnson worked in the physiology laboratories at the University of Chicago and in 1930 earned her Ph.D. in Physiology. Her three earliest publications were in the field of Physiology (1931–33) (see Bibliography, p. 497, first three articles).

During the years of close association with Dr. Franz Alexander at the Chicago Institute for Psychoanalysis, her psychosomatic interest continued to grow and resulted in publications on bronchial asthma, migraine, and rheumatoid arthritis (1944–47). Although this psychosomatic focus of interest was subsequently diluted by competing interests, it remained as a continuing and recurring theme as manifested by her coauthoring papers on eating problems (1955), facial disfigurement (1956), anorexia nervosa (1957), urinary retention (1956), and convulsive seizures (1957). In each of these instances, the "senior" author was a junior colleague whose study was, in large part, encouraged and stimulated and sensitively guided by Dr. Johnson. Unlike some self-aggrandizing academicians, she refrained from usurping the limelight.

4

VERTIGO AS THE PRIMARY MANIFESTATION IN ANXIETY NEUROSIS

A^N analysis of the case of a young woman in whom vertigo was the outstanding symptom of her neurosis, raises some pertinent questions about the interpretation, etiology, and management of vertigo. Cases in which vertigo is just one of several equally evident symptoms of neurosis or anxiety are commonly referred to the psychiatrist, and are discussed frequently in the psychiatric literature. Cases, however, in which severe vertigo is the one primary complaint, obscuring less obvious and often overlooked neurotic manifestations, are more frequently seen by the neurologist and neurosurgeon alone, without psychiatric consideration.

By what objective criteria may we with assurance differentiate an organic from a functional vertigo? What of the Barany tests? French (2) says that "an increased irritability of the semi-circular canals is . . . reported to be the usual finding in neuroses in which vertigo is a symptom. Barany states, indeed, that 'neurasthenia' increases in particular the duration of the horizontal nystagmus following rotation in the verticle plane." Brown (1) reports the Barany tests to be of "little help in differential diagnosis." Patroni (3) reports a case of a young man who for twelve months suffered from severe vertigo, with subjective whirling from left to right, nystagmus, and temporary deafness. The Barany varied from attack to attack in both ears. Because the

Abbreviated version of the original article which first appeared in *Illinois Medical Journal* 77 (1940): 86–89. Reprinted with permission.

patient "recovered" without treatment, Patroni concluded that vasomotor dysfunction was responsible. Unfortunately there is no history of the patient's personality, so that we cannot answer the question which is legitimately raised: Might not this case — presenting the classical pictures of true Meniere's syndrome — have been of functional origin?

It is frequently stated that "functional" vertigo may be distinguished from organic vertigo by the presence of whirling sensations in the organic variety. But in the case of depression which he was analyzing, French (2) described sensations of objects moving circularly about, and showed these sensations to be definitely a part of the functional disturbance. Whirling was also a prominent feature of the case to be reported here.

It has been suggested that vasomotor disturbances such as spasms might be responsible for disturbed vestibular sensitivity or whirling sensations. Such suggestions usually carry the implication that if this be true, the condition is of "organic" origin. But could not also a purely *"functional"* vascular spasm markedly affect the sensitivity of the vestibular receptors, modify the Barany tests, and produce whirling sensations? Indeed, might not such spasms, repeated frequently enough, produce actual structural changes in the vestibular (and even cochlear) organs?

REPORT OF CASE

A married woman of 34 years, the mother of two children, entered the Phipps Clinic of Johns Hopkins Hospital with this story of vertigo as the outstanding complaint: Ten and seven years ago the patient had had brief attacks of light-headedness without whirling, at a gathering of people. Six years before coming to the clinic she married, and a little later she became so dizzy at a theatre party that she had to leave. Since this time she

Vertigo in Anxiety Neurosis

has insisted on having aisle seats at the theatre, and has attended fewer and fewer social functions. Nine months before admission, during a serious and protracted illness of her husband, she had her first violent attack of vertigo, while she was shopping. She felt she was being rapidly whirled about. Reeling, she sat on the curbing, extremely nauseated. The severe whirling continued for five or six hours after she was carried home and put to bed. There was some diarrhea for a day.

As other equally severe attacks followed with increasing frequency, the patient developed a strong fear of leaving the house or being left alone without help. She entertained no guests for fear of an attack in their presence. Although her husband recovered from his illness three months before the patient entered the hospital, her attacks and agoraphobia continued.

At a large eastern clinic the patient was advised to go to Johns Hopkins Hospital for a nerve section. At the suggestion of a lay friend who knew some of the Phipps Clinic staff, the patient visited this clinic first. The psychiatrist who saw the patient could not be sure of the primary difficulty, but recognized evidence of emotional tension behind the story of severe vertigo. The patient was told that a period of observation would be desirable, to determine whether nerve section was indicated.

The consultant in otolaryngology stated that the caloric tests showed hypersensitivity bilaterally, and added, "if this is Meniere's syndrome, we cannot tell which side is involved." There was no history or objective evidence of deafness or tinnitus. Neurological examination was otherwise negative, and the neurosurgical consultant thought the case to be one of pseudo-Meniere's syndrome. The blood pressure was 125-70, and the serological examination was negative.

On the ward it soon became clear that underlying the major complaint was a great deal of anxiety. Obviously it was impossible at first to determine whether the anxiety was secondary to the attacks, or a primary cause of them. In either event it was felt important that the patient broaden her activities and associate with others. Interviews soon revealed the background and sources of the patient's more immediate anxieties.

The middle child in a well-to-do family of three girls, the patient was reared in a northern town. Her father was tyrannical with her mother and sisters, and interfered with the housekeeping to such an extent that finally the mother left all such matters to him. Consequently the daughters were taught nothing about housekeeping. The mother, socially ambitious, constantly criticized the girls in their choice of companions. The patient lived in constant fear of criticism, "boiling inside," but rarely rebelling openly. She felt that she seldom did as she pleased, although she had college and travel opportunities. She was a handsome, serious-minded girl, with little sense of humor. She was much disturbed by her lack of serious admirers.

On a trip to Europe seven years ago, she met and became engaged to a handsome, prominent and very wealthy southern bachelor of 35. Married to this man, she encountered in him much of what she had experienced in her father. In the husband's family, housekeeping was at a premium. The husband, as well as his sisters and mother, were masters of the art. The patient has always felt humiliated by her own muddled housekeeping, and was greatly upset by the slightest suggestion from her husband. The chief source of her immediate anxiety, however, was finally revealed with a great decrease in her tension and symptoms.

For the first two years of her marriage her husband was utterly devoid of all sexual interest in her, and he missed no opportunity to humiliate her, publicly or privately. He drank inordinately, causing still further chagrin. His behavior was entirely unexpected and without apparent cause. He refused to discuss his conduct with the patient. Suddenly at the end of two years he announced his desire for a child, which arrived in nine months. As this and another child grew older, the husband decreased his drinking "as an example to the children." Marital relations improved somewhat, but the patient's symptoms of dizziness increased, culminating in the attack described, during the illness of her husband nine months before her admission. With the patient's permission, the whole matter was discussed with the husband, who volunteered the following explanation of his behavior.

Three days before his marriage a friend had told him that he had no need to concern himself about contraceptives, because his fiancee had informed herself about such matters. This enraged the husband, who felt that "the first child should be allowed to come naturally." He set out to be deliberately cruel to his wife, and made it plain that she "might leave him whenever she wished." At our suggestion the patient and her husband discussed the entire matter, and thenceforth the patient showed a remarkably rapid loss of her vertigo.

This patient had developed the pattern of repressing anger and resentment toward her father, and she continued in this through the years of miserable existence with her husband. She seemed incapable of expressing her resentments, which she deeply repressed. Of significance is the fact that after her husband had informed her of the cause of his behavior, she still showed no anger at his prudish frigidity. Although it seemed clear that the patient had deeper anxieties to be relieved, she felt so well that she left the clinic after 2½ months of treatment. She remained comfortable for a month, and then she began to have symptoms of anxiety in the form of worries over trivialities about the house, fear of having been too extravagant or too niggardly, dread of the slightest criticism, increased shyness, and easy fatigubility. After four or five months she began to have mild attacks of dizziness, which have lately become more frequent but never so severe as her earlier attacks. Clearly the patient needs further analysis of the sources of her anxieties.

Since it is so difficult to differentiate organic from functional whirling sensations by objective tests or from the patient's description of his abnormal state, it is desirable that a careful psychiatric history be taken in all cases of this sort. It is unfair to the patient to conclude that neurotic elements in this case, such as fear of attacks, are necessarily consequences of the attacks, unless the history reveals no evidence of emotional instability or serious conflicts preceding the attacks, or unless there are correlated physical findings, or positive serology, or neurological changes in other systems than the eighth nerve complex.

Unquestionably a great many cases of Meniere's or pseudo-Meniere's syndrome are on a definitely organic basis primarily, bearing no relationship to the emotional condition of the patient. Yet it is important that the patient be given the benefit of a psychiatric examination if any doubt exists because the diagnosis of an organic basis for the Meniere's or pseudo-Meniere's syndrome carries with it (in some clinics) advice to the patient to submit to a serious operation.

Institute for Juvenile Research.

REFERENCES

1. Brown, Madeline R. *JAMA* 108 (1937): 1158.
2. French, T. M. *Internat. J. Psycho-Anal.* 10 (1929): 1.
3. Patroni, A. *Valsalva* 11 (1935): 661–66.

5

BRIEF PSYCHOTHERAPY IN BRONCHIAL ASTHMA

Thomas M. French, M.D.

> Although Thomas M. French was senior author of "Brief Psychotherapy in Bronchial Asthma," the bulk of this paper is based on a case treated by Dr. Johnson and upon a summary of the case prepared by her. (A second case has been deleted.) In addition to its elaboration of pertinent psychiatric information on bronchial asthma, this paper also provides us with an excellent example of Dr. Johnson's therapeutic skills as an analyst.

A STUDY of the psychogenic factors in bronchial asthma was made several years ago by the Chicago Institute for Psychoanalysis. Of the dynamic relationships uncovered by this research, one of the most significant was that between asthma attacks and confession. Throughout the lives of patients subject to psychogenic asthma attacks, there seems to run as a continuous undercurrent, more or less deeply repressed, a fear of estrangement from the mother. The cause of this fear is usually the patient's own forbidden impulses which he thinks will offend the mother. One device of which the asthmatic patient makes extensive use to protect himself against this danger of estrangement is confession

Reprinted with permission from *Proceedings, Second Brief Psychotherapy Council*, pp. 14–21. Chicago Institute for Psychoanalysis, January 1944.

of the disturbing impulse. If the mother or mother-substitute accepts the confession without being shocked, then all is well for a time. If, however, the patient is too uncertain of the mother's tolerance to dare make his confession, then an asthma attack is likely to be precipitated.

This dynamic relationship between confession and asthma attacks has obvious implications for psychotherapy. The psychotherapeutic situation offers first of all an opportunity for the patient to confess what is disturbing him. If the asthmatic patient can gain confidence to confess fully and freely the impulses that are at the moment responsible for his fear of estrangement from some mother-substitute, then we may expect relief from his asthma attacks until some new forbidden impulse arises to disturb him. This period of relief may be quite prolonged. When attacks occur again, the therapist's problem is to discover what is the new disturbing impulse and to encourage the patient again to find relief by confessing it.

This is an important principle in every psychotherapy. Many cases of psychogenic asthma, however, differ from other more complex psychotherapeutic problems in that the relatively uncomplicated cases of psychogenic asthma require little or no treatment other than that which aims to make the patient more and more secure in the confidence that nothing he may need to confess will be disturbing or offensive to the therapist.

The effect of such a therapy is at first merely symptomatic. By confessing what is disturbing him the patient gets relief for a time from his asthma attacks. Such symptomatic relief tends gradually to diminish deep underlying insecurity and dependence.

This theory suggests that we should be able to obtain satisfying therapeutic results with at least a considerable number of cases of bronchial asthma by means of briefer methods of psychotherapy. The objective in such therapy is to discover and help the patient to confess the particular matters that are disturbing him at the time of exacerbation of asthmatic attacks and then as soon as relief is obtained to diminish the frequency of treatments until other asthmatic attacks occur.

CASE REPORT

The patient was twenty-four years old and single. He had recently graduated from a medical school but felt himself quite unable to practice because of severe asthmatic attacks. Four years previously, skin tests had found him allergic to beef, pork and chicken.

He had a history of asthma since the age of fourteen. Before this age, he had weighed over 200 pounds but then went on a diet, reduced his weight to 155 and at that time began to develop asthmatic attacks. When he came for treatment, the patient was living with his father, a physician, his mother having died when he was three. Of this event he recalled only the mother's leaving home on a stretcher, fighting with the attendants and crying as they took her to the hospital where she died of pneumonia.

After the mother's death, the patient and his brother moved next door to live with their father's sister and her husband. They lived there until the patient was nine. At this time the father married again — a young woman nineteen years his junior. The patient states that they were married six months before anyone was told. He resented the new wife and mother very much and at first he fought with and was very mean to her, but as he came to know her he grew fond of her.

Four years before the patient came for treatment, the stepmother died of ulcer. At the time he began treatment, he was extremely frank about his intense dislike for his father which he attributed chiefly to the father's misuse of funds belonging to the patient's mother and stepmother. The patient also recalled that before the father's second marriage he had always sided with his aunt against his uncle, but rather early in the treatment he came to realize that the aunt was really a complaining, begrudging and resentful person.

The aunt was very fat and the patient had always told her that he wished to be fat like her. At the time of the treatment, however, he resented her obesity and looked upon her refusal to diet as part of her greediness and infantilism. His own impulse to be fat like her throws some light upon his own obesity in early adolescence before he began to diet. This attitude toward the aunt's obesity may probably be taken as an indication of a relationship which became plain later, that his obesity served the function of a defense against the conflict arising out of the attraction to his aunt and to his stepmother.

The patient was treated for a total of 45 interviews for the most part at weekly intervals. Almost immediately the analyst had opportunity to point out the patient's tendency to develop a relationship of great dependence upon her. In the second hour the patient told how for eight years he had warded off attacks of asthma by rising late in the morning, leisurely sitting on the toilet where he drank coffee for an hour or so. If anything interrupted or rushed him he was certain to get an attack. Later in the same interview, however, a topic came up which was related to his anxieties about sexual impulses. He said that the only kind of girl he liked was an older girl who would take full responsibility for any sexual relations entered into and would not nag him afterwards for attentions! Immediately after this statement he said, "I hope you will be critical of me and tell me just what to do so I don't do the wrong thing." The therapist said, "In other words you want me to be like the older girls who know what they are about, who see things clearly, who face the facts and re-

Brief Psychotherapy in Bronchial Asthma

lieve you of any responsibility for their acts." The patient laughed and said, "That's exactly what I want. You see I'm being dependent on you right away and I want you to be frank because I can't stand people to go round about things. I want to know where I stand with people."

The first asthma attack reported after the beginning of the treatment was attributed by the patient to the fact that he had to take his coffee rapidly and hurry around after he got up. He said he was watching himself to see whether he would have an attack and "sure enough he did." Later on in the same hour, however, he told of his extreme embarrassment with girls from the time he was six. Eventually he related this to the embarrassed uneasy feeling that he had when his uncle teased him about being snuggled by his obese aunt.

When the therapist asked how his aunt accepted his efforts to be more independent, he said she would not stand for it. Any attempt on his part to "talk up" met with a whipping. She thwarted any adventurousness on his part. She "stuffed him with food."

At this point the therapist told him it seemed that his asthma came when his dependence was threatened, whether in relation to women or when he was left alone on a job (as will be reported later). She pointed out that his asthma began at fourteen, after he had reduced his weight and was therefore more attractive in appearance, and she wondered whether the asthma had something to do with impulses in him that might threaten a pleasant relationship with a mother-person. After this interpretation the patient recalled that when he was nine he realized that his stepmother was very pretty and nineteen years younger than his father. She encouraged him to fondle her breast and rest his head on her bosom. She would draw him closer and closer until the father in a rage would order him off to bed. From the age of nine to fourteen when he was so obese, this seductive situation continued, associated on the patient's part with intense conscious sexual desire for the stepmother. He did not think of her as a mother and longed to get into bed with her but feared that she would tell his father. In these years there was extreme fear of his father and of dogs. At fourteen when he reduced drastically and felt more attractive physically, all the sexual play with his stepmother ceased and he had no further sexual feeling for her. It was at this time his asthma began to be disturbing.

Two months after treatment started, the patient took a job in a department store under his brother's supervision. An asthma attack occurred the first night when everyone went off and left him at midnight and he was alone at his work. To him this job signified an extension of the home with dependence on the brother although it did furnish an independent income. Attacks continued at night for some weeks when he was left alone.

The patient continued to feel elated about his treatment hours. He said nothing could make him leave them. The therapist at this point warned him about the possibility of later resistance. He protested, however, that he had told the therapist more than any other patient in so short a time. This the therapist interpreted as a wish to be the most cooperative of her patients and to confess all to her.

The patient failed to tell the therapist that he had had a mild asthmatic attack on the way to the office before the ninth hour, but he recalled this in the tenth hour. In discussing this attack the analyst finally elicited from him the following confession: "Well, last Wednesday before I came here when I felt the attack coming on, I thought of sexual feelings in connection with the red-head and the Jewish girl and my aunt and my stepmother and practically every woman I know, and nothing clicked." The therapist pointed out that it was significant he should have thought of sexuality in relation to practically every woman except herself.

This, however, he energetically denied. He emphasized instead his great dependence upon her.

At this point, three months after treatment began, the patient was very dependently attached to the therapist, was avoiding all girls and having almost no asthma. A month later he came in furious about having to meet his draft board. He was certain the men on the board would have no patience with the emotional basis for asthma. He felt all these men were as "dumb" as his father and he would die of asthma if he had to leave the therapist now. His asthma became worse. The analyst suggested that possibly he was angry at her for not intervening on his behalf with the draft board. In discussion of his intense anger, which soon appeared, he confessed that he had wished the therapist would "risk her reputation" in order to "save his life." The therapist's frustration of his dependence and her acceptance of his rage constituted one of the two major steps in his treatment. As a result the patient felt more independent.

It was after this hour that the patient for the first time was able to ask a "respectable girl" for intercourse, accept her refusal and ask for another date. Never before had he approached a girl who he thought might refuse him. He now began steadily dating an attractive girl.

Soon he mentioned that his girl had a former beau whom she sometimes thought about. He did not want to be a "second fiddle" and he asked what the therapist thought about the girl. The therapist suspected that by means of this question the patient hoped to find out something about her own sexual experiences and her attitude toward them. This suggestion apparently took him by surprise but he immediately recognized its validity. "By George," he said, "that's right. I wouldn't have thought of it." For several hours after this, the patient was preoccupied with the faithlessness of women as illustrated by stories of married women with whom he had had intercourse. To this the therapist commented, "I doubt if you have as much conflict about women who are unfaithful as about women who are faithful to their husbands." He felt this to be true but added that he was not so easily downed by a rival as formerly. He went on for two or three hours to say that he could not be in conflict with the therapist because she was too old for him. When a friendly opportunity arose the therapist wondered if it were that he feared he was too young for her. He was evasive; blocked and expressed amazement that he could not think of a thing to say for ten minutes. He said "only rarely" did he feel so uneasy talking to men or women as now. The therapist asked if it were necessary to bring the "men" in now and with great heat he said, "Why not?" He was breathing heavily. The therapist mentioned some possible concern in relation to her husband. The patient appeared startled but immediately became more relaxed and said he had wondered about him.

About this time the therapist went on vacation. The second hour after she returned may be regarded as the turning point in the treatment. On this day the patient came to the office breathing heavily, perspiring somewhat, and obviously having a rather severe asthma attack. He said that he had had to dismiss several of his patients from the office. He had had several attacks during the week, always at night, and had taken ephedrin. Several mornings he felt his breathing a little impaired but no real attacks developed. He wanted to explain all this on the basis of his having had to rush around in the morning, especially that morning.

The therapist listened to him for a few minutes. He said he had not been out with the girl that week and he thought that could not be a factor. He mentioned nothing about the therapist. She commented that she thought his feelings toward her had been relatively flat since she returned from her vacation and he said that this was true. She wondered if there were some feelings about her having gone away that were not just clear. He said that he was sure this was not so, that he could not even remember one thing they talked about before she went away. Thinking that he was probably very angry at her, the therapist merely said that she was thinking of the fact he had mentioned that when he found that the girl with whom he had been falling in love was still somewhat attached to a former beau, he had dropped her immediately. At this point the patient said, "Oh, yes, and probably that brings up your husband now. I was talking about your husband just before you went away and I felt he was too much of a rival in the picture. I felt that was one of the big factors inhibiting me in my feelings toward you."

At this point the asthma completely stopped. The patient breathed quietly, his face was no longer flushed and he began to laugh. He said, "I can't believe it. I have never had an attack stop so suddenly even with ephedrin." He said, "You mentioned that thing and I thought of your husband and what we were talking about before you went away and in thirty seconds the attack had stopped." The patient was amazed. He said that at last he was convinced the therapist was involved in his attacks and when he had the asthma attacks in the morning or at night it must be that there were some thoughts of her he was not conscious of.

Hours followed full of resentment toward the therapist with fears of humiliation, and speculations about her husband. He would like to marry her in order to have her take care of his attacks; there could be a sexual life also but he would not be in love with her. His bitterness and anger were mentioned briefly to him. At this time he wanted to call the therapist by her first name and to have her call him Dr. X. The feeling that the therapist would not be willing to concede him all his rightful prerogatives and respect as Dr. X. was pointed out and after this competition was worked through the patient and the therapist were both "Doctor."

After this he realized that he had begun to want to do things for women and to go out with them without any special interest in sexual intercourse. He finally came to tell the therapist that he could no longer be in love with her. There was much angry depreciation of her which she accepted without comment. After this he said he no longer felt the anxiety he used to feel when indicating to some girl he did not love her, whereas previously he had always feared this would throw the girl into a rage. From now on he felt a great sense of freedom, talked and acted with increased masculinity and independence, and was no longer hostile but friendly.

The patient has now been in the Army for almost two years. He came to see the therapist two weeks ago. He looked fine. He had one slight attack of asthma in a difficult situation a year and a half before. He is engaged and expects to marry soon.

It will be noted that the interpretations were directed primarily toward relieving the disturbance arising out of the frustrated dependence and out of the sexual wishes that the patient developed toward the therapist.

This case illustrates the great relief that the patient received from confessing disturbing impulses; in fact, the therapist's interpretations in the main served the purpose of anticipating and thereby facilitating the patient's confession.

6

PRELIMINARY REPORT ON A PSYCHOSOMATIC STUDY OF RHEUMATOID ARTHRITIS

With Louis B. Shapiro, M.D., and Franz Alexander, M.D.

THIS presentation will be restricted to the psychodynamic findings in a study of 33 cases of rheumatoid arthritis; 18 of these were seen in therapeutic sessions; 15 in anamnestic interviews. There were 4 male and 29 female patients. The psychodynamic formulations pertaining to women have accordingly a greater validity at this point.

The women patients show impressive similarities in nuclear conflict situations and in general personality structure. Although our findings on men are not sufficiently extensive to make generalizations at the present time, our impression is that in the male patients also, certain features are recurrent.

OVERT PERSONALITY FEATURES

A conspicuous characteristic of our women patients is a tendency toward bodily activity, manifesting itself in an inclination toward outdoor and competitive sports. In the period of latency and in adolescence they show decidedly tomboyish behavior. In contrast to this active tendency, they show in adult life a strong control of all emotional expression. Booth made similar observations on 45 cases. Halliday stressed this tendency to control and self-restriction.

In the majority of our female cases there is a striking need to be of service to other people. Although their dependence upon persons in the environment is obvious, it is subtly masked by service and activity, overtly masochistic in character. In respect to their children, the patients in our study are generally demanding and exacting. While they worry and do a great deal for their children, at the same time they dominate them. In a very small group, the masochism is not a character trend but appears to be restricted more to the concept of the feminine sexual role, against which they defend themselves in the manner of the hysterical woman.

The sexual behavior of all the female cases shows the common feature of an overt and easily recognizable rejection of the feminine role, the so-called masculine protest reaction. They assume certain masculine attitudes, compete with men, and cannot submit to them. The husbands are for the most part compliant, and more passive than their wives; several husbands even have physical defects. The husbands readily accept the part of serving their incapacitated wives.

PRECIPITATING EVENTS

On superficial inspection the precipitating factors of the disease seem to be without any common denominator. They cover a wide range of external and psychologically significant events; indeed they run the whole gamut of life situations; birth of a child, miscarriage, death in the family, change in occupation, sudden change in marital situation or sexual relationship, a great disappointment in some interpersonal relationship. It is, therefore, not astonishing that such an observant investigator as Halliday found little rhyme or reason in causative factors. If, however, we focus our attention on what these various events mean to the patients, we can reduce the precipitating causes to a few significant psychodynamic factors.

1. The disease process seems to have developed in these women patients when an *unconscious* rebellion and resentment against men increased, as for instance when a patient was abandoned by a man with whom she had felt safe, or when a previously compliant man became more assertive, or when a man in whom the patient had invested a great deal disappointed her.

2. The disease may also be precipitated by events which tend to increase hostility and guilt feelings, previously latent and adequately handled through the patient's self-sacrifice and service to others. The birth of a child with consequent reactivation of an old sibling rivalry may be the disturbing factor. Hostility and guilt may be mobilized because adequate opportunities for self-sacrificing service are thwarted, as in the event of a miscarriage or of the death of a hated dependent relative, or when circumstances force the patient into a situation where she must accept help beyond her ability to compensate with service.

3. Finally in a few cases the process appears to have begun when a masculine protest reaction was intensified in order to serve as a defense against fear of sexual attack. One woman developed an acute arthritis of the hips and knees when exposed to a sexual threat and a 16-year-old girl suffered an extreme stiffening of the back with arthritis after a sexual assault by the father.

IMMEDIATE UNCONSCIOUS BACKGROUND

The overt personality features in these women are defenses against their feminine and dependent role in respect to men and children, and to society in general. Two outstanding modes of behavior indicate the immediate dynamic situation. (1) All the female cases are classical examples of masculine protest reaction — a rejection of the feminine functions. The defense mechanism utilized by all of them is hostile masculine identification which produces the typical phenomenon of bisexuality. The rejection of the feminine role, the wish to be a man, is in many cases naively and openly expressed. In other cases it shows itself more in derivatives: being head of the house, controlling the environment and making the decisions. Interest in competitive sports is the most common manifestation of this pattern in earlier life. Some of the patients show their masculine identification in a predilection for the masculine posture in the sexual relationship. In the deeper psychoanalytic material, the masculine identification appears at times through the utilization of the neck or limbs, or of the whole body as phallic symbols. This identification has always a hostile connotation and is often linked with castrative impulses both in the form of grabbing with the hands and of oral incorporation. Such a competitive relationship with men serves as one means of discharging hostile feelings. (2) With few exceptions the cases show an excessive masochistic need to do for others, which serve both as a discharge of the hostility and as a denial of their own extreme dependent demands.

The general psychodynamic background of all these patients is a chronic, inhibited, hostile aggressive state, relieved by discharge through the two character trends discussed above.

A case illustrative of the first mode of defense is Mrs. S. G., 28 years old, who developed painful stiff muscles immediately after she found out her husband had had a love affair. After continued pain and stiffness of the muscles for a few months, she developed a fairly generalized arthritis. Her mother was a conscientious, but cold woman; the father had deserted the family when the patient was 2 years old. She was very competitive with an older brother and spent much of her childhood in outdoor activities. She felt that her mother's role and the position of woman in general was unbearable and said openly she would rather die than tell her husband she loved him, *even if* she did. "Then I could never be on top." She refused sexual intercourse for several months after marriage, had never had an orgasm, and agreed infrequently to sex relations. Although her husband had been a prize fighter of sorts and she was a frail appearing little woman, she always headed the household and made the decisions directing her three young daughters in assisting her excellent housekeeping. Her husband's infidelity was the first indication of his rebellion and of her inability to compete with him and control him. When frustrated in her competition the hostility increased, found no outlet and the muscle soreness and arthritis followed. During analysis she nightly refused to go out for recreation with him and finally he was unfaithful to her for the second time. This led to an acute exacerbation of the illness.

The masculine protest is far more subtle in such cases as Mrs. T. H. who developed acute arthritis of a severe nature four different times after lovers had abandoned her. Her unconscious hostile identification with men, envy of the brothers, interest in sports, and her competitive relationship to a weak husband were subtly integrated in a complicated character structure. Although she did not have orgasm, she had sexual relationships easily with her lovers as the terminal event in her machinations to overcome and control them. Primitive, destructive tearing, castrative dreams toward men were common, often associated with oral incorporative impulses.

An example of a patient who manifested the second type of character defense, the excessive masochistic need to serve, is

Mrs. E. S., 32 years old and mother of three children. She was the eighth of nine siblings. The following statement gives a succinct picture of her personality: "I am very anxious to get over my arthritis so I can finish having my family. If my mother had not had such a large family I would never have existed." As a young girl she not only did heavy housework and cared for her invalid mother, she also assisted the father with duties on the farm, although there was a younger brother. All the siblings went to college; after completing high school she went to live with her older sister to care for her and her many children. In her marriage she continued to display the same slavishly serving attitude toward her three daughters and her husband. Reaction to a miscarriage marked the onset of her arthritic symptoms. On entering analysis she said characteristically, "I have no emotional problems, but I am glad to do anything for science."

GENETIC RECONSTRUCTION

In respect to the pronounced bisexual attitude and the masochistic need to serve, associated with a chronic state of hostility, certain family situations have been found typical. There is usually a strong, domineering, demanding mother and commonly a more gentle, compliant father. Booth speaks of his patients having stern parents and Halliday found that the arthritic had at least one domineering parent, and that self-restriction began early in life. As little girls, our patients developed a dependence upon and fear of a cold aggressive mother and at the same time a great deal of rebellion which they did not dare to express because of that dependence and fear. This relationship with the mother is the source of their intense masochism; the female role becomes frightening to them at the oedipal period. Those patients who have brothers express their sibling rivalry in a hostile identification with the males. This attitude is subordinated to their dependent relationship on the mother since by assuming the masculine role they are more acceptable to her. A further component of their aggressiveness toward men is based on identification with the mother, whose dominating attitude toward a depreciated father they repeat in their own relationship to their husbands. There are indications that in their oral aggressive attitude toward the cold and rejecting mothers lies the earliest basis of the later grasping, aggressive attitude toward men. This often appears in castrative tendencies in dreams. One patient, speaking of jealousy and men, said, "I feel like grabbing what they have . . . I am so grabby, I feel I have to hold on tight." The masochistic, serving attitude stems also from the earliest mother-daughter relationship; it is designed to placate the mother and to resolve the guilt feelings toward her which originated in sibling rivalry and oedipal jealousy. In addition there is the wish to atone for the resentment against the mother because of her original rejection. The masochistic serving attitude allows the arthritic woman to express the hostility and at the same time to discharge it in a more acceptable fashion, in serving but at the same time also dominating the environment. Furthermore the suffering is aimed to win the mother's love in which the child never was secure.

DISCUSSION

The fact that these patients express and discharge unconscious emotional tendencies through the voluntary muscles puts their symptoms in the category of hysterical conversion. At least, the *modus operandi* is the same as in conversion hysteria — namely, the expression of an unconscious conflict by somatic changes in the voluntary muscles. Our present assumption is that these muscle spasms and increased muscle tonus under certain conditions may precipitate an arthritic attack.

In the majority of our cases the unconscious tendencies which find expression and discharge in the muscle system are chronic hostile aggressive impulses and the defense against them. Accordingly the character structure is of a compulsive nature. Two cases, for example, had definite washing rituals.

In a few of our cases the actual localization of the arthritic condition is in relation to a current conflict; the affected organs become the focal point in which the patient expresses unconscious tension, as we observed in their dreams. The sexual conflict was expressed in specific representations of the limbs or the whole body as a phallic symbolic defense against the masochistic feminine wishes. In some cases a nonsexual conflict was symbolically related to a specific bodily area.

These findings correspond to Halliday's assertion that arthritic patients show either hysterical or compulsive character structures. However, we question on the one hand Booth's belief that symbolic use of the body is true in all cases, and on the other hand Halliday's assertion that it never occurs.

In the light of these considerations the arthritis cases we have seen could be described as a series. At one end are those cases in which aggression and defense against attack are handled by discharge into somatic conversion with a symbolic expression of ideational content. In all gradations to the other end of the series we find those cases where the egosyntonic discharge of chronic inhibited hostility through muscle activity, hard work, and sports has been interrupted, and there develops an increased general muscle tonus which may precipitate an arthritic attack. Of the cases closest to conversion hysteria, we cite the following examples: (1) With the mobilization in analytic sessions of strong feelings connected with oral attacks on the mother's breasts, one patient developed an arthritic condition in the sternal-costal joints. (2) Another woman, who had been accused of infidelity by her husband (who finally asserted himself), developed severe arthritis in the ring finger which spread to all the fingers of both hands. Moving toward the other end of the series are such cases as: (1) A young woman, hard working since early childhood, who developed arthritis when a hated, dependent younger sister died. (2) Another patient with a strong masochistic need to serve her children developed arthritis shortly after a spontaneous abortion. Again if there is an interruption of the usual mode of expressing hostile masculine competitiveness, for example, by the husband's suddenly becoming much more capable and strong, we may see the muscular tension rise and arthritis develop. In quite a few cases, the patient cannot be held in analysis. Some women break off and run away because the analysis threatens their intense masculine protest, the loss of which would make their relationship to men intolerable and would throw them back on the dreaded mother.

In all these cases detailed studies of the widely varying precipitating factors of the disease process show in the psychodynamic factors of these patients a common denominator. As the most general psychodynamic formulation which can account for all our observations of precipitating causes and exacerbations as well as for fundamental etiologic factors, we postulate a general predisposing personality factor which develops as the result of excessively restricting parental (predominantly maternal) attitudes. In the little child the most primitive expression of frustration is random motor discharge. If, through punitive measures, this discharge becomes associated with fear and guilt, in later life whenever fear and guilt arise there results a psychologic strait-jacket. These patients try to achieve an equilibrium between aggressive impulses and control. They learn to discharge aggression through muscle activity in ego syntonic channels: hard work, sports, gardening, actively heading the house. They learn also to relieve the restrictive influence of the conscience by serving others. Whenever this equilibrium is disturbed by specific events which interrupt their adaptive mode of discharging hostility and relieving guilt, the chronic inhibited aggression leads to increased muscle tonus and in some way to arthritis. In the last analysis we always see an increase of dammed-up aggressive impulses resulting either from external obstacles such as a recalcitrant husband, or an increase of internal inhibition, such as guilt which increases when its atonement through service is interrupted.

In a small number of cases specific sexual conflicts are handled by the typical symbolic conversion mechanism. Whether this is superimposed on the same character structure as in the majority of our cases, or whether this can independently lead to the disease is an open question. The fact that in some of these latter cases we see a masochistic concept of sexuality rather than masochism in character structure makes the second assumption more probable.

As we progressed in our understanding of the psychodynamics of rheumatoid arthritis, we were able to explain many of the remissions as well as relapses which took place in patients during analysis.

If the old avenue of discharge for hostility is opened up again through sudden compliance on the part of the husband, the arthritis has been observed to subside. A woman with very severe arthritis had to be carried about by her husband. When he died suddenly, she got out of bed, assumed charge of everything, travelled across the country for the funeral and made an immediate recovery which continued for many months. The recurrence of arthritis when opportunities for masochistic service are diminished has been observed, followed by its subsidence when self-sacrifice is again demanded by family conditions. As the patients become more able to receive help in analysis, the disease diminishes.

In the study of arthritis one must bear in mind the fact that the personality picture of advanced crippled cases is overlaid by a chronic psychologic adaptation of the personality to the state of being crippled. Time does not allow us to go into details of cripple psychology. Naturally the pre-existing character has an influence on the behavior, but new features dominate the picture. Most authors who have studied such cases were impressed by the secondary features such as stoicism and optimism. In addition to the self-deceptive wish fulfillment, this type of adaptation can be easily understood by the fact that the diseased condition relieves the patient from guilt feelings and gives him the right to expect attention that was previously withheld or unacceptable. This was most clearly seen in a patient who had had to care for a demanding father for years. When her arthritis became advanced she said, "Now he will have to take care of me."

PRELIMINARY THEORETICAL CONCLUSIONS

In these cases the general psychodynamic background is a chronic inhibited hostile aggressive state as a reaction to the earliest masochistic dependence on the mother that is carried over to the father and all human relationships, including the sexual. The majority of these personalities learn to discharge hostility through masculine competition, physical activity, and serving, and also through domination of the family. When these methods of discharge are interrupted in specific ways, the persistent increased muscle tonus resulting from the inhibited aggression and the defense against it, in some way precipitates the arthritis. But these factors — rejection of a masochistically conceived feminine role with its typical defense of masculine protest, increased muscular tension or spasms due to inhibited hostile aggression — are found so commonly in patients who do not suffer from arthritis that additional etiologic factors, still unknown, must be postulated. The nature of these factors is probably somatic: inherited, traumatic, or infectious. Whether further studies of psychodynamics and physiology will allow the claim that certain cases may develop a pathologic joint change only as a result of chronic muscular tension without any predisposing somatic involvement remains to be seen. Be this as it may, recrudescence of the psychologic conflict situation, according to our view, is largely responsible for relapses; and improvement of the psychologic situation, for remissions.

The view that increased muscular tonus is involved in this disease is further substantiated by the extremely common observation that arthritis patients complain of muscular rigidity and tenseness upon awakening. Some of them report sleeping in overflexed positions. In many cases muscular stiffness and pain were the precursors of the first arthritic attack. We should refer here again to the common use of neostigmine by clinicians who believe relief of muscle spasm and pain can occur even in a burned out joint. In order to test the validity of this latter hypothesis we have begun a study of muscle tonus in arthritis patients and in control groups, with the help of a special apparatus devised by Dr. Ralph Gerard of the University of Chicago.

7

A CASE OF MIGRAINE

IT is not the aim of this paper to go into an extensive discussion of migraine and its etiology. The emphasis is rather on the more effective use of the transference in a therapeutic challenge.

In the past ten years there have appeared a fairly large number of excellent papers demonstrating the psychogenic factors in migraine. Contributions from Gutheil, Fromm-Reichmann, Knopf, Selinsky, Touraine and Draper, Slight, Wolberg and others give a great deal of evidence that conflict situations, such as hostile destructive aims toward a beloved person, set off the migrainous attack. Various concepts of the somatic component have been advanced, constitutional weakness or some physicochemical mechanism serving as the organic vehicle for the acting psychological factors. With some disagreements, clinicians generally describe the sufferers from migraine as frequently of the intellectual type, as conscientious to the point of an exaggerated sense of responsibility. They have a need to be independent; they are ambitious, highly sensitive to criticism and show, among women especially, considerable sexual maladjustment and a definite trend toward conventionality. Excellent therapeutic results are reported in many cases treated psychologically.

The patient under discussion is a 29 year old, married female physician, who has suffered from frequent and severe typical

Reprinted with permission from *Proceedings, Third Brief Psychotherapy Council*, pp. 69–120. Chicago Institute for Psychoanalysis, October 1946.

migrainous attacks since the age of 15. There was no other presenting complaint. She has been seen about 75 times over a period of 19 months. The treatment is not yet completed, but for the purposes of the paper, this is not pertinent.

The migrainous attacks, (blurring vision, right hemicrania, nausea and vomiting with occasional diarrhea) seemed to be related to various emotional stresses. They began at 15 when the patient was expected to take care of her three young stepsisters during the summer vacation at a time when because of economic stress the stepmother had to go to work. The patient had insisted instead on having a vacation with her girl friend, and while on this vacation the headache began. At nine years, the patient had had a fall when she saw stars and was in bed for two days with vomiting. The findings at that time were negative. Her stepmother had had migraine for years and during these attacks would have to withdraw to her bedroom for a day or two.

The patient impressed the admission interviewer immediately as being an attractive, flexible, mature woman of considerable brilliance and charm. Her parents were ambitious, professional people who had come to New Hampshire from Austria just before they met and married in this country. When the patient was two, her mother became ill and after several month's illness died of endocarditis. As she spoke of this the patient felt vaguely that she recalled her mother's illness, but could not be sure. She was confused as to where she lived for a year in New England before she came with her father to a town near Chicago where she lived with a maternal uncle and aunt until her father remarried. The patient was then four. She had been told that she was a feeding problem for a short time after she went to live with her father and step-mother. The patient spoke of her step-mother as "mother" and did so throughout the treatment. She maintained that this kind, warm-hearted, sensitive woman was like one's own mother and stated she had always felt that her three step-sisters were like real sisters.

Her fifth birthday was one of her earliest and most delightful memories. The patient recalled no feelings about the first stepsister who was born when she was six and a half years old. She thought that she took pleasure in the coming of the other two siblings in the next four years. She felt her step-mother had always been very warm and supportive and thought of her father as quiet, intelligent, cheerful and kindly. She recalled crying when she was twelve years old when her father told her that her own mother had died. At the time, the patient had cut him short saying she knew this.

The patient had had excellent group relationships and good intellectual adjustment through her high school and college years. Although hard pressed financially the family had made it possible for her to have an extensive education and had taken pleasure in this, never begrudging it. At the time the patient came to treatment, she had many friends of both sexes.

She met her husband in college when she was 18; she married him, a professional man, seven years later. He was said to be brilliant and attractive but inclined to be a little pessimistic. The couple had many engrossing mutual interests. Their sexual adjustment had been excellent; they were "about to decide to have a child" when her husband had to enter the service and go overseas. He was away when the patient came for treatment. It was decided that for a few exploratory interviews with the psychiatrist the patient was to be seen only once a week, after which a plan of treatment could be made.

In the first hour with the therapist the patient gave much of the above material. She was quietly friendly and talked easily. She stated she had had her worst migraine attack just before coming to the office. After much questioning she recalled she had just spent two days with a woman who acted quite friendly but whom she suspected of harboring much unconscious hostility toward everyone. She had never thought of resenting this woman until the therapist raised the question. Although the patient had dreamed little of her husband since he went into service, just before she came for treatment she had had two dreams in which she was meeting him as a civilian; details were lost. She had been conscious, too, of wanting him to be home lately. The therapist commented that possibly it was more comfortable to turn to him than to an unknown woman therapist. The patient laughed and went on to say, however, that she had mixed feelings about his return, for she was uneasy that he would ask her to cut down on her work and have babies. She also recognized that this feeling was due to some problem in her, for she was by no means ready to have children.

In the second hour she brought a dream in which her husband was stationed at an air field near her, but he appeared in a delapidated old Air Force outfit. The elements in this simple dream give the crux of much of the structure of this case. She associated with this her need for him rather than for women, but she recognized how annoyed she was with him that he had to do menial tasks in the Air Force. She discussed her fears for his emotional and work inadequacies. The therapist asked why she made matters worse for him in the dream by giving him a wretched uniform. She was not clear as to her motives. When it was suggested that possibly a fear of her identification with him in some emotional inadequacy led her to withdraw and depreciate him, the patient realized for the first time how she *had* avoided going to visit him in training camps in this country. Now she began to feel guilty toward him. It was pointed out that although she needed him, she immediately tried in the dream to deny that his strength was important to her.

Thus there appear three fairly definite elements in this patient's

A Case of Migraine

character structure: some serious anxiety about turning to women, greater ease in leaning on her husband, but a need to depreciate him. In spite of this, with the therapist the patient showed a real warmth. Since it was felt that too frequent hours would probably have threatened her need for independence in relationship to the therapist, she was given an appointment for one week later.

In the third hour the patient brought a dream in which she was competitive with a woman for an Air Force major; she depreciated the woman. The major was much older than her husband and by far his superior in rank. Associations led to the realization that in the last interview the patient had at first been a little annoyed that the therapist had not let the dream go by as a depreciation of the husband, but later the patient felt she had a wonderful husband after all and she would not give him up to anyone. The therapist replied, "As soon as I question your depreciating him, you feel I may compete with you?" The patient laughed and said, "I hope it's just your theory." The therapist went on to say that since the major was an older man, could there be some deeper significance to the dream? Possibly as a child the patient may have been quite fond of her father and jealous for all his attention. The patient was definite in her denial of this, and added that such theorizing was a little surprising. In the next hour she stated that immediately on leaving the office the week before, she had recognized her anger at being asked about jealousy of her father and had realized emotionally that the major in the dream had many likenesses to her father. Upon inquiry with regard to early feelings, she recalled that once at eleven while her step-mother was away, she tried to crawl into her father's bed, but he firmly said she should sleep in her own room. She recalled quite consciously she had felt "snuggly" on this occasion and had had actual sexual thoughts in her mind that night at the age of eleven. She was piqued and angry with him.

The patient then recalled that since the last hour she had had several dreams. These proved to be disguised dreams which on association led quickly to sexual fears of very young boys. She went on to say that she had thought for a long time that she would be very uneasy with a young son and had only thought in terms of a daughter. One saw in her fantasies also the same hostility to a son which she may have felt toward her rejecting father. Soon thereafter in the same hour the patient expressed fears of a competing daughter also, for if the father had not been firm, there would have been trouble. Now the patient voiced the fear that her husband might not be equally firm with a daughter.

Then the patient had her first severe headache in four weeks of treatment. At first she gave superficial explanations, such as just having seen her sister with her fiancé. Associations led to the realization of intense resentment in a competitive situation with a colleague. Now she began to think maybe there *was* some connection between headache and such competition.

The therapist's accumulated impression of the patient after five interviews corroborated the original impression: she was an attractive and brilliant young woman, reared in a home of good conventional standards. Discussion of her work and friends made it appear that she had a very good ego. She was not only intellectual but highly intuitive as well. That she had read widely and was acquainted intellectually with psychoanalytic theory was to the therapist an immediate warning that this patient might understand interpretations too readily and seem to accept dynamic explanations without emotional assimilation. All psychoanalysts are aware of the pitfalls in therapy with such patients. To use this patient's understanding, to capitalize on the flexible quality of her ego, and yet to strike at the depths of her feeling was recognized by the therapist as the challenge in this case. Fortunately the patient was endowed with keen psychological insight and with the capacity to use this insight not only in the presence of

A Case of Migraine

the therapist but also during the intervals between interviews. Unconsciously, she "worked through" the revelations and interpretations of each hour, producing in the next session deeper and always relevant material with appropriate feelings. Though she showed immediately a defensive attitude toward women, she had sufficient basic warmth to enter a rapport with the therapist, with whom it was easy for her to identify herself. This constituted the beginnings of a workable transference which had to be kept strong enough to bear her defensiveness against women and yet not so intensive that it would interfere with the analysis of this defense. (The importance of maintaining this equilibrium will be obvious as the therapeutic process unfolds.)

Since the treatment seemed to be moving satisfactorily during these first five sessions, it was decided to continue with weekly interviews for the time being. There was no indication that the treatment should not be conducted with the patient sitting up; indeed this procedure was found to be highly important as the treatment progressed.

The therapist found it striking in the early material that this young woman who had never had sexual relations with anyone but her husband was, as an eleven year old girl, quite aggressive with her father and actually conscious of sexual feelings at that time. Her father had been firm, but where was the girl's guilt? This was the therapist's first hint of what later turned out to be the traumatic nucleus of her neurosis, namely some interference with a wholly normal oedipal period through loss of her mother at two. Yet it was noteworthy that the patient had always had orgasm in her marriage and enjoyed sexual relations. It should be emphasized that these are indications of a much better emotional adjustment than one usually sees in migraine cases.

Following this material, for three sessions the patient produced dreams and associations having to do with jealousy over her siblings. She produced first an actual memory of jealousy of her beautiful step-mother who was able to have and nurse the babies, and later envy of the babies themselves. She recalled noticing especially the beauty of her step-mother's breasts as well as the feeling of envy for the baby, and she remembered feeling strange and far away from her step-mother at such times. The question was raised, what prompted this strange and distant feeling? During these three weeks the patient was quite depressed, but without headache.

At this point dreams of competing with women on a professional basis (friends and therapist) were common but when little twists in the dreams were pointed out, the patient realized that work competition and masculine identification were pure masks for her jealousy and competition with women. Dreams, as well as expressed resentments in dealing with her female patients, brought to light the patient's homosexual fears in relation to them and to the therapist.

At this time a patient of our patient, a young girl, developed a crush on her. Our patient dreamed that she avoided making a medical examination of her young patient and instead took her to a prayer meeting. As our patient began in the hour to realize how cold and abrupt she had been recently with the 15 year old child, she began to weep and grieve that her problems should hurt her patients. When the therapist suggested the recent anxiety with the girl might be related possibly to some uneasy feelings toward the analyst, the patient became uneasy and said, trying to be flippant, "Let us take it to prayer meeting." Later she said she felt anxious and afraid. When the therapist wondered if her fear did not indicate some guilt or anger, the patient burst out weeping, saying her step-mother was so kind she could never be angry with her and she wished the therapist would be "more mean" to her. The analyst commented, "You wish possibly I'd

A Case of Migraine

be cold and abrupt as you were with your young patient — then you would feel less guilty." The patient added quickly with just a shade of annoyance, "I think in the end I make her less depressed," and the therapist replied, "I think you do." Here her competition with the analyst came out on a professional level. Furthermore the patient was feeling she would like to be with the analyst but not in the position of suffering through an uncovering therapy.

The next defense that appeared was a shifting of her conflict with women in the direction of hostility toward men. First there were dreams of men fighting men. From material that had come into the interviews unwittingly, the therapist felt quite sure the patient's husband and father were kind and considerate men. With this in mind she raised the question as to whether the patient might be projecting her hostility toward men onto men. This soon was proved by multiple associations and further dreams. The patient realized now that when preconscious hostility to men was interpreted she would become angry at once, whereas when an interpretation about similar hostility to women was raised, she usually felt depressed.

For the first time the patient realized that unconsciously she had frequently been hostile with men in a subtle way. She spoke of competing with them intellectually and she knew she had unwittingly hurt her husband through frequently telling him of other men. Details related to these episodes showed her hostility to be unmistakable. She was for a time depressed over this. It became increasingly evident that her masculine protest and her profession were a defense against competition with women; that her hostility to men was a defensive intellectual disguise. The headaches became more severe as her resentment and criticism of her husband began to come to light. She finally came to feel warmer toward her husband and dealt with her young men students with more frankness and fairness. This was due, however, only to partial insight and to the transference effect, namely identification with the therapist, for the emotional insight into the cause of this hostility had not yet emerged. Then President Roosevelt died. The patient felt devastated by a sense of personal loss.

After the President's death an astonishing change was observed. The patient became strikingly more regressive: she had no interest in her work; she would not cook for herself but went to her step-mother's often for meals and felt uneasy and defensive about this; she had no interest in giving to her patients or students. This period had all the signs of a depression with mourning. Accordingly the therapist arranged for two or three extra interviews so that the patient might feel she was receiving something during this distressing period. The therapist finally commented that she believed the patient must have felt much greater than the usual dependence a little girl feels on her father because of her mother's early death, and wondered also if she may have blamed him for the mother's death. This elicited no response from the patient but that night she had a violent headache. She reported a highly disguised dream in which she hated men for their connection with birth of a baby. In associating she said, "Maybe I blame him for my birth to offset any guilt I may have toward my birth and mother's death." With this she associated new memories of the excitement connected with the birth of her first step-sister. She was then in a panic (and is angry now, as she recalls it) because she and an aunt had to take her step-mother to the hospital in the absence of her father. She was terrified that her step-mother would die. Her own unconscious ambivalent wishes here were not suggested, but the therapist felt it important to query again as to whether the patient might have felt that her father was responsible for her own mother's death. This recalled to the patient a dream from the night before in

A Case of Migraine

which she had made a nonsensical slip to her father indicating she was having psychoanalytic treatment. In the dream he looked hurt and the patient awoke. There followed several weeks of resentment toward her father. "It is his fault — not my mother's — that I am having to have treatment now. I can't tell him I am in treatment because I am so angry at him and am afraid I shall hurt him."

The therapist continued to be impressed with the patient's psychological insight. (18 interviews had now taken place). Since the transference relationship had mobilized the patient's confidence in the therapist, she continued to focus attention on her problems without too much resistance. It was therefore decided that nothing was to be gained by altering the transference at this point. It is important to emphasize again that although this material has to be greatly condensed and therefore seems schematic and intellectual, actually this patient recognized and worked with her feelings to an unusual degree. No interpretations were actually given until the patient was obviously dealing with emotions and had given many leading associations.

Since there was evidence that her father and step-mother were really consistently kind and tolerant parents, who gave little grounds for resentment, the proposition grew in the therapist's mind that the loss of her mother at two years was probably never faced and integrated by the patient and that she was living out a defense against this trauma, unable to receive freely from the good step-mother. It was as if she were saying, "I will have no one but my own mother." The patient tried to lean more on men than women, but seemed to be defensive about this for these reasons: (1) she was blaming Father, not Mother, for Mother's leaving her and, (2) if Father really mis-used Mother, then he would mis-use her; men are not to be trusted entirely, (3) also by projecting all the blame on Father she could avoid facing her own later repressed anger at Mother which, one speculated, would be terrifying to her. If men are mean, then that explains everything and she could thus avoid thinking of Mother.

About this time the therapist was to leave for a vacation about which the patient had been told some time before. She brought a dream in which she was at a museum looking at four stuffed birds, a mother and three little birds. The little birds came to life and the patient remarked to someone, "Why don't they fly away?" As soon as the patient finished recounting her dream she said, "Oh, I see at once my guilt toward my siblings; I have them dead. But maybe I have them come to life only to get them out of the picture and away from the mother." Now the patient became depressed. The therapist inquired if even more she were guilty over the dead mother bird? The patient wept a little and commented that she had no such wishes toward her step-mother. The analyst suggested the possibility of exploring why this was a museum. At once the patient replied, "The bird was stuffed — I could go on seeing it, though dead." She was asked if this could in any way be associated with her own mother, and the patient recalled now that the day before the dream a friend had been speaking of *her* dependence on her mother and at that time the patient had wondered if *she* (patient) were ever dependent on her own mother. In answer to this the analyst said that this was only natural. Since the patient was such a little girl, only two, when her mother died she could have seen her mother's leaving only as a desertion. Instantly the patient retorted, "I wonder if I held it against my father" and angrily she said, "We are going in circles, way back to my mother — we are getting no place." "On the other hand," the analyst said, "we might be getting too close to the mother and this upsets you." The patient could see at this time no connection between the therapist's leaving for her vacation and the dream just discussed.

After the analyst returned, for several sessions all the analytic material was defensive — hostile and destructive toward men.

A Case of Migraine

Women were always misused by men. The patient continued in this assertion for some time rather than seeing the therapist as mis-using her by having left her. Finally the real meaning of the displacement and projection to men of her being mis-used by women became somewhat clear to her intellectually, but as yet it had not been emotionally assimilated.

After nine months of treatment the patient often dreamed of wanting a baby but *headache would set in* and she would awaken with pain. In the dreams the patient felt guilty toward her stepmother, but why was not clear. Consciously she did not want a baby and felt no competition with women. She insisted she was guilty toward her step-mother over wishes toward her father on the basis of many associations and dreams at this time. The therapist suspected the patient's talking about babies and step-mother and "oedipal material" was actually a defense against her earlier experience with her own mother.

For instance the patient had a dream at this time in which Ginger Rogers was writing comic strips to say that incest is the greatest problem confronting the nation and in the dream the patient felt in some way she should help write these scripts. It is obvious that unconsciously the patient was laughing at the therapist and her silly ideas about oedipal conflicts. Still she was trying hard to inject the incest problem into the discussion as the cause of guilt toward mothers and seemed to want the matter dropped there. Although the therapist felt there was guilt here, it was regarded as a cover for an earlier, greater conflict with the mother. The defense and its guilt, however, had still to be analyzed. The patient again mentioned her overtures to her father at 11 years. To bring out her anger to the therapist it was commented casually that he *was* wise to have handled this matter firmly. The patient looked depressed, flushed and said, "Now for a headache." A fairly severe one was developing as she left the interview.

She slept through her next appointment and showed her anger

against the therapist later in dreams. The patient was unable to express anything but the slightest annoyance and said that the therapist "did not have to be *so* stuffy and blunt about it." A dull headache developed during this hour. Frightening homosexual dreams then emerged, among them one of extremely eerie quality. In this dream the patient had come stealthily to some public affair in a large park. She and her girl friend were hiding and watching what was going on. Suddenly they were both swept up in a parade of women in black who seemed to be fascists and all enemies of the patient. She felt that she should go along with them since that would be safest. Her associations were interesting. "Does this have to do with spying on my parents? Does this have anything to do with peeking at my mother's death and at the funeral? Could it be that I feel all women are my enemies because I felt they were on mother's side and I was angry at her for leaving. I go along with them and they think I am one of them." The patient became very depressed as she discussed this dream from the point of view of the mother's death. Again we see her mention the *oedipal conflict* before she associates to her *mother's death*, as if any guilt over Mother at the oedipal level were far less painful than something deeper. The therapist's problem was how to get at this suspected conflict with the mother which existed in the pre-oedipal period.

About this time, the patient heard her husband would be home soon. She dreamt of him as a homosexual. This was such an obvious projection that the therapist questioned it at once, wondering about the patient's anxieties about depending on women. In analysis of this projection the therapist brought the conflict into the transference and called to her attention that the patient had hinted before that they would be hard pressed financially for a time when her husband was discharged; that apparently she had not even thought of asking that the therapist might then reduce

A Case of Migraine

her fee. The patient confessed she had worried over this and she was *consciously* relieved when the therapist brought it up and the fee was reduced. Although all along in an inoffensive way this patient had shown a great need to be independent, it was with conscious relief she accepted this aid. Obviously, however, fear and defensiveness about this would certainly emerge. There followed dreams, highly disguised, that the therapist, not having children of her own, really did not like them and their dependence. It was pointed out that the patient feared greatly any dependence on the therapist lest in the end she would be let down. To this the patient protested, maintaining her strong confidence in the analyst. At last in one of these dreams the patient could see her own pattern of projecting all blame onto men transferred to the therapist. She had the therapist really liking children (and yet there was a twist in this), but the real fault for not having children was the analyst's husband who was too dependent himself to stand such responsibility. Everything is the men's fault, not Mother's or women's. It was clear by now that the patient's main lines of defense against anger and fear and guilt toward the mother's dying were "men are to blame — men misuse me — Mother is not to blame — my guilt toward Mother is oedipal — not terror or anger over her leaving me at two. Men are homosexual and dependent — I am not."

Just before her menses the patient had the following dream: She and another woman were involved. The patient was extremely anxious in this dream, whereas the other woman was calm, kind and objective. Before them was a foetal-like baby, crying and red with helplessness and anxiety, all bound up in a fish-net like covering. The patient was extremely concerned, whereas the other woman was not, and the patient tried to get through the net to help the baby. She saw herself as identified with the baby; the therapist was the woman, in whom unconsciously the patient had much confidence. She wondered if she could have felt anything like this baby in the first year or two of her life when her mother was ill. She was not sure whether her mother was in a sanitarium or whether the dream related to her mother's death. When asked if she had ever asked her father if her mother were in a sanitarium she said she had never asked him anything. The therapist was impressed that this ordinarily warm, anything but shallow woman, at this moment spoke flippantly and almost callously. She was pushed for the real reason why she had asked her father nothing and she answered, "I am afraid of what he might think." When asked what he might think, the patient said that he would wonder why she wanted to know and then she stopped, saying she felt "awfully depressed." The therapist commented, "It must be that you have a great fear of learning something since you cannot ask your father about your mother," and added, "Possibly you are more uneasy in a dependent relationship with women than with men." The patient said she had always been able to ask things of men but not of women.

It soon became clear that the headaches were related specifically to babies or Mother. If her friends mentioned babies or mothers, the patient was certain to have a migraine. "Babies" meant dependent demands on the patient. Once when the patient was depressed and the therapist asked sympathetically if she felt "sorry for herself," she became incensed. When asked why she had taken this as a criticism, the patient insisted that she should be grown up. The therapist took this up with her sympathetically, picturing what she might have wished as a little girl losing her mother. This made the patient depressed rather than angry and headachey. From this time, since it was clearer that the loss of her mother was highly significant for the patient, the therapist held her to analysis of the meaning of the mother's death. Resistance to this was intense, as will be seen, with over and over again

A Case of Migraine

a flippant callousness or stubbornness that indicated some fear underneath, for such an attitude was completely out of character.

Time after time she tried to elude the problem of her mother with all kinds of projections, fears for her husband's inadequacy instead of her own, men's homosexuality, etc. Any slight sexual inadequacy in her husband led to associations which showed her unconscious terror when she could not lean completely on him. Such a situation left her too aware of her own unsolved dependence. As she brought up these matters the therapist promptly indicated there might be some problems in the husband we should look into later, but that now the patient was only pushing them to the foreground as a defense. This would annoy the patient and though she laughingly agreed, she showed some sulkiness and developed a headache. The patient maintained strongly that her own mother had utterly no significance for her and that her stepmother was her mother.

About this time it was discussed with the patient how, through accepting her step-mother as her own mother, she could use this as a defense and would thus not have to face the painful fact that there were two mothers. At once the patient became deeply depressed during the hour and when the therapist persisted in asking her what she was thinking she became stubborn and angry and said she could think of nothing for she was developing a headache. In this interview the anger was more prominent and the headache not so severe.

For a week there were no headaches, no depression, but feelings of detachment, almost depersonalization. This was a better defense apparently than the headache, since the latter was wearing a little thin. Several authors mention that at times the migrainous patient may faint, when the headache as a defense is not sufficient. The therapist decided at this point she would push the patient hereafter to think, regardless of the headache and not allow her to escape through her migraine. When the analyst pushed her to more expression in one hour, a violent headache preceded by some anger developed. The patient said, "I cannot think with such a headache."

In a dream that night, a pair of spectacles appeared on a vague woman in the dream. The spectacles seemed the only clear thing. These were associated by the patient with a pair of the mother's that the father had, also a lapel watch of the mother's that the patient said just six months before the father agreed the patient might have. She had not taken the watch, thinking it unattractive. The therapist felt this was an excellent point at which to insist that the patient face emotionally that she felt she was different from her step-sisters. When the patient was asked if she would mind if her father gave the watch to one of the step-sisters, the patient became angry and burst into tears with, "It's mine — she was *my* mother." These were the first tears over her mother. It should be mentioned that this woman had rarely cried in her entire life, that she prided herself on this control.

The analyst now wanted to mobilize more feelings about the mother. These next steps are extremely important. First the analyst could honestly believe this woman's mother had been warm and loving because of the basic warmth she showed through the good positive transference — positive but never hungry. It must be kept in mind that a little child has to be assured of some love from her mother in order to dare face the full extent of her terror and ambivalence about the loss of a mother. The therapist decided to fantasy a little with the patient about the fact that the mother was probably a loving person since the patient had always seemed so basically warm. This fantasy was mixed with sympathetic comments about how sad and lonely and lost the patient must have felt as such a little girl. The therapist was exceedingly careful not to suggest too much loving by the mother in order to

A Case of Migraine

avoid stirring up too much terror over the loss. It should be remarked here that it was good the patient was sitting up. To avoid any misinterpretations of the therapist's profound sympathy for the patient, it was helpful that she could observe the analyst's facial expressions. It now seemed wise that the patient should have more frequent interviews — two or three a week. This seemed necessary to intensify the working transference, to enhance the feeling of confidence in the therapist.

The patient's reaction to such fantasying was to sob brokenly but quietly, and finally she recalled that long ago she was told many times that her mother had gotten up from her sick bed to buy a lovely doll for her when she was two. For several sessions the patient just cried brokenly. This weeping from loneliness and feeling sorry for herself, with no anger, was something strange to her. She sobbed many times, "I have never known such loneliness as I feel now — but I must have, at one time." With her husband, she realized she was acting like a leaning, lonely little girl and was inarticulate like a child in telling him of her grief. To see her sob in the interviews was extremely pathetic because of the peculiar child-like appearance and quality which came over her. There were no headaches now and none of the anger formerly associated with them. There was none of the remorse in the sobbing of the depressed guilty patient; it was just the sobbing of a lonely child. Only feelings came up — no content. These were feelings too far back to recall content, but there were many dreams in which there was a vague woman who just seemed to come in and go out. Each dream ended with her going. At this time sad and lonely as the patient felt, the analyst believed that since the anger toward the mother had not yet really been mobilized, she should not move too close to the patient in giving comfort through physical contact such as a pressure of the hand lest the patient become too guilty. The analyst's verbal comments and facial expressions, however, were deeply sympathetic.

The patient soon realized for the first time that she had always felt a certain defensiveness with her step-mother; she recognized that now she had become much more at ease with her step-mother. She remarked that her step-mother (who had migraine) had lost her mother as a little girl and that *she* had had a fine step-mother.

For the next three weeks the analyst continued to give the patient two or three interviews a week. For such a hidden mourning, where work and people outside make demands on the mourner, a few hours a week with the analyst seemed pretty barren at best. Much of this time she wept quietly with deep grief saying very little. Often her only comment was, "I only feel— I can pin it on nothing—just lonely." At first she regarded this as a humiliation since she was a grown woman. After she was able to accept the fact that it was natural she should feel sorry for herself, she wept in a heart-broken manner. The therapist knew it was then safe to be openly sympathetic with her.

With the patient the analyst fantasied the little child in an atmosphere of mourning where the adults close to the child are so burdened by their own sorrow that they cannot weep with the child. They withdraw and of course the little one withdraws. Having the whole burden of fear and despair to carry alone the child represses everything. Later when the less grieved adults try to talk with the child, it is too late.

The patient feared her husband would not understand her if she spoke to him of her grief and she said if it were not for hurting her step-mother she would feel much more at ease in talking to her; "she would understand." When the therapist commented that this was a real index of the patient's love and confidence in her step-mother's great warmth, she wept even more for her own mother. It was as if the reconciliation were coming first through

A Case of Migraine

the step-mother. It should be noted here that so far all the weeping is the patient's sorrow for herself; at no point did she express any sorrow for the mother that had to die. This, it was speculated but not revealed to the patient, meant that the anger toward the mother was still repressed and that no real reconciliation was yet possible. At the end of the hour the patient said, "I wish I could get this straightened out before I leave for Maine for my vacation in three weeks." The therapist said she understood for she knew that the patient was going to a locality close to the place where the mother was buried. The patient suddenly commented that she had wondered why she had chosen Maine this year. Several times in recent sessions a mention of resentment toward the mother for leaving had been made by the therapist but had elicited no response.

In the next three sessions when certain slips gave indication of negative feelings toward the analyst, the patient was made aware of this. Such minor resentments soon developed into very frank, sulky provocative behavior. At this point the therapist responded to the provocative adult with some impatience of tone as she questioned the patient. The patient sulked and said nothing. By the end of the interview she had a moderate headache. She reported next time that as soon as she got outside of the analyst's office, she realized she was extremely angry with the therapist; she laughed and cried on her way home and felt that the therapist did not like her. She realized that she had been more angry than she had been in years, and her headache disappeared almost immediately.

To the next interview the patient came depressed but with anger close to the surface. When the therapist said nothing, the patient gave a long, angry lecture to the therapist pointing out that an analyst should never be impatient, that it was a profound disappointment to find the therapist so sharp the last hour, that the therapist lacked subtlety when she failed to realize that the patient cannot talk when she sulks; that this had been true for years. The analyst listened quietly and finally the patient became uneasy and said, "I feel so scared, just panicky." The therapist, seeing the patient beginning to be tearful and anxious, said that she felt the patient was fearful the therapist no longer liked her. The patient nodded and then began to cry and was obviously in great misery. The therapist told the patient that her anger had been followed by fear that she was unloved, possibly because as a little girl she was terrified and angry that her mother had gone away and had never come back to reassure her that she was safe and loved in spite of the anger. If her mother could have come back, the mother would have realized the child's anger was because of her terror at being alone and would have loved her and not blamed her. This threw the patient into the most desperate suffering. Since she was obviously in great agony, the therapist moved closer to her, patted her on the shoulder, took her hand and openly sympathized with her.

Now for the first time the patient seemed to be letting go of her great grief with real abandon; she was no longer crying silently. This went on for a long period. The patient was obviously getting an increasing feeling of confidence from the therapist's sympathy and closeness to her. Suddenly she sobbed, "For weeks I have been weeping for myself and just now I feel so sorry for my poor mother — to die so young." She cried sorrowfully, saying repeatedly, "Poor Mother." When at the end of the hour she said that her husband was being very considerate of her lately, the therapist assumed that she would now feel more free about letting him see her grieve. The patient was sad because he would not be home until late that night. At this, the therapist asked if the patient took the *New Yorker*. Since she did not, the analyst gave her the copy in which there was a beautiful, subtle story of

A Case of Migraine

a young girl who lost her parents. In this story the child's weeping was inhibited by well-meaning relatives but the relief came when she was allowed to weep by her mother's old Mexican gardener who wept with her. The therapist suggested that the patient in privacy tonight might read this story and mourn with the girl.

We see now the recent phases of the patient's progress. She realized some of the loneliness and loss of her mother in mourning. Then when she had experienced intense anger toward the therapist followed by fear that she had lost the analyst, she was assured of understanding and affection. Thus with abreaction of the grief and fear came reassurance and final reconciliation.

Two nights later at her father's home she thought of her mother's watch, wanted it, but did not take it for fear her stepmother might notice and be hurt. In the next session she said, "So many times lately I have wanted to ask my father where the cemetery is, but it is not so easy." The therapist replied, "I know you want to go there, and are you afraid if you speak to your father you will weep, and make him sad?" She stated this was the case and was going to have her husband ask the father.

She still had mentioned no uneasiness in regard to leaving the therapist for three weeks' vacation. When she came in for her last hour, she said, "I don't think of my vacation — I only think of my work starting again." The analyst suggested that the patient seemed to be blotting out the vacation — could this be related to uneasiness regarding separation from the therapist? The patient commented she had not thought of this, but she *had* felt suddenly two days ago, "When this is over, my treatment will stop." The analyst added, "The little two year old girl still feels hurried, doubtful, and fearful that she must take care of herself." Then the patient sobbed desperately, "I want to go to her grave, for I know now what I have lost." To this the analyst replied, "And you almost feel as soon as you find me, I will be lost to you also. You see possibly there is still some fear toward your mother and me — I am not going to die." The patient cried brokenly, suddenly stopped and said, "I think she is in Richmond." The therapist was amazed and asked what the patient meant. She said, "I think she may be in the family lot in Richmond, Virginia — Oh no! I know that isn't true. I know she is in New Hampshire. I must still be afraid of her and the loss." The analyst felt the patient should not have to go through this visit to the grave too much alone, so she fantasied this trip and grief with the patient in the hour. The therapist said, "You must recently have visualized yourself often at the grave," and the patient abandoned herself to tears. "Often I have thought of it and I dread the tangibleness of the loss when I come to the grave." At the end of the hour she said she no longer felt isolated from her husband in this, that he was so kind and tender, and if they could possibly make transportation connections she was going to New Hampshire.

Two weeks later a letter came saying that the first few days in Maine she had a dull headache, until one morning she awakened after a dream and felt extremely angry at the therapist for letting her leave. At once the headache subsided and she was very happy. She had never enjoyed a holiday so much with her husband; he thought she was delightful. She wanted to get to New Hampshire if connections could be made without taking too many days of her husband's vacation since this was his first since he went overseas.

The patient returned from her vacation with the following account. She and her husband had the address of a friend who would show them the grave. The patient allowed a day for this stop-over. What occurred was in a sense tragic. The friend had moved. The patient finally reached him on the phone from the station as the conductor was shouting "All aboard." She heard from him that the cemetery was across from the railroad station, and she barely made her train. As she sat down in the moving train, the cemetery came into view. She was very sad for a time but consoled herself with her husband's assurance they would return some time. There was no headache.

She returned from her trip, radiant. She had never found her husband so tender and kind and he seemed delighted with her more casual serene dependence on him. She laughed, "My talk about his inadequacy was nonsense." She went on, "A few months ago when you pressed me to talk of my mother I felt that had nothing to do with me; in a few months a new world has come to light." With regard to further treatment the patient said, "In my last session with you I was feeling I would be thrown out soon — now I feel relaxed and know that you will give me what time I need. Right now I don't know what it could be, but I feel I at least have time to mull it over." This soon led to a discussion of babies and her fears. It became apparent that she had fused the idea of babies with death of the mother and her own fears of death at childbirth. When the analyst commented that because of her great fear of loving and losing she might hesitate to love a baby, the patient had a sudden emotional release. She talked rapidly of loving children of her friends, pets of her sisters, wanting to play with them, but always managing to remain an onlooker. She had dreaded seeing her sisters mourn over the death of pets.

Periods of sadness and mourning for her mother and longing to ask her father about her continued for some time. It was interesting to see the shifting and re-integration of new attitudes in the re-working of the oedipal conflict as a living experience and not just a defense. Her warmth and interest in babies became obvious. She now told people frankly she wanted a baby. She began to plan her career in such a manner as best to allow for the coming of a baby, and for a long period to be given to the infant's care. Her husband did not push her but joined eagerly in her thinking.

When an interruption of the analysis was suggested, the patient became depressed and worked through considerable fear and resentment toward the therapist for abandoning her. She had a severe generalized headache when her husband spoke somewhat impatiently of his wife's dependence on the analyst. Instead of facing her anger toward him immediately, she, contrary to her recent attempts to analyze her reactions, simply abandoned herself for a time to a pounding general headache. Later she responded to him with great anger and the headache subsided.

The interruption of treatment is now in progress and when she returns the degree of relapse can be determined.

DISCUSSION

The discussion of this psychotherapy falls under three headings: (1) The structure of the case, (2) Therapeutic accomplishment, (3) Speculations with regard to the future.

1. *The structure of the case.* We see in this case the effects of a serious trauma to a little child before there was much power of verbalization. It is believed that this basically warm woman was really loved as a little child and that she herself loved before the loss. Undoubtedly the child was terrified without her mother and with her fear came angry frustration. There was no return of the mother to relieve the terror and appease and forgive the anger. Gradually the intensity of such feelings must have been repressed. This left the patient unable to dare to receive fully the love from the really good step-mother — such loving and sudden loss and terror should never be risked again. Her great fear was fear of loss associated, of course, with the inherent frustration and anger.

Since she was unable to relate herself to the step-mother as a mother it would appear that the oedipal period did not have normal progress. Since there seems to have been no seductive permissiveness by the parents who can only account for the 11 year old girl's lack of guilt for her sexual feelings toward her father by the fact that she had never lived through the oedipal situation with an emotionally *accepted* mother.

Her headache developed in adolescence when demands were made on her for the first time to give to the younger siblings. Since her own receiving had been interrupted at two years, she could not give later without mobilizing that *early trauma* which was too painful to bear. An extension of this conflict is "Babies lose their mothers by death, and therefore babies are frightening. One dare not love babies too much, for they might die and the loss would be unbearable."

We see this basically warm child later making an excellent social, scholastic and marital adjustment, certainly not just superficially. Although this patient had a character neurosis with migraine as a defense against mobilization of the painful trauma, still the character involvement was far from a profound and crippling one. Sexual and group adjustments were good; this is not true in many cases of migraine which usually show serious sexual maladjustments. The question is why was her character not more dominated by the early trauma?

Counteracting factors were the thoroughly kind and consistent father and step-mother. Had the step-mother been less kind, the patient's trauma might have become less encapsulated and more negative behavior might have come out toward the substitute mother, with less inclination toward migraine but with a less healthy integration of the personality. The encapsulation of the trauma was further maintained by certain definite lines of defense:

a. "I will never allow myself to expect or to depend too much on a woman." We saw all through this woman's life a pseudo-independence which, however, was subtle and never offensive to those about her.

b. The other outstanding defense was the attempt to lean on father and husband. This, however, was far from totally satisfactory and she had a need to depreciate them subtly for the following reasons: someone or something finally had to become responsible for the mother's leaving, since it was too frightening to make the mother responsible and too guilt-producing to go on hating her. Thus the father was to blame. Mothers are innocent but fathers mis-use women. Yet for two years the little girl was left more or less alone with her father. She had to be dependent on him whom she mistrusted. Here again to atone for her guilt toward him and to convince herself she was self-sufficient, she depreciated what her father and husband did for her. Inadequacy was attributed to the men; hostility toward men was turned into hostility between men — the final projection of her problem with the mother to men. Still, leaning on men was far safer than turning to women. The remarkable thing, and this speaks for the kindness and strength of the men in her life, was that somehow this woman had been able to have a satisfactory sexual relationship with her husband.

2. *What was accomplished in the treatment?* During the process of analyzing these defenses the patient gradually lived through such a reintegration of her fears of loss and her hostile impulses that the migraine began to subside. But far more important are the character changes. Gradually in treatment the patient had observed that the analyst had understood her terror at the loss of the mother and accepted the small degree of the patient's annoyance. The final great burst of anger toward the analyst terrified the patient, for she felt she had lost the therapist, since "no one had ever returned to forgive me." Some real continuity with the past and reconciliation were brought about, ending with

sorrow for the mother herself and the wish to go to the grave. The corrective emotional experience had at last come through her relation to the analyst who stayed by her and forgave her. The patient feels a new security and serenity in depending upon her husband whom she finds is equal to it and delighted with it. Her relation to her step-mother which she *had* thought was perfect, is now — surprisingly to the patient — more relaxed and warm. She says she no longer has the old anxiety about children nor the feeling that people and her husband particularly are pressing her to have a baby. At last she feels she can take her time and do this when she wishes, and the wish is increasingly prominent.

Why was this case suitable for treatment on the basis described? First, this woman's character was not completely dominated by her early trauma, which seemed fairly well encapsulated. Although early in treatment the reasons for it were not clear, still one could see a good, workable transference develop in this patient though she was seen at weekly intervals. The optimal degree of the working transference is the ideal of any therapy. Although defensive against her good mother, she showed early an identification with the woman analyst who in many ways represented to her an ego-ideal — her forgotten mother. Furthermore this patient had a remarkable capacity to continue the therapeutic work between sessions through this identification with the analyst. She did not just sit back and drift. Every therapist must sense and gauge the correct balance between the problem to be mobilized and how much transference feeling is necessary to do this. In many cases, however, the cure can only be effected by fostering a more intensive transference neurosis.

Although the therapist could not know it until later in the treatment the patient usually worked in relation to the analyst as if underneath she felt women (mothers) were good — "I will do my best and the analyst will do her best." And because otherwise it would have been too painful, she went along in fairly good faith.

The analyst worked quite actively and consciously toward mobilizing her fear of loss and hostility; otherwise a much longer time and a more intensive transference neurosis might have been necessary. The activity in thinking and feeling by the therapist makes the patient feel less frustrated and angry toward the analysis itself.

3. *What is to be expected in the future?* The analyst can only speculate (and this will be interesting for discussion) since by the time the proceedings are published we shall no doubt have substantiation or disproof for some of our speculations. The therapist's feeling is that this woman needs some time at last to catch her breath and not feel rushed toward termination.

The real test will come when this patient must decide whether to become a mother means life or death, and becomes pregnant. This would involve any unresolved fear of her death as a mother and her fear of loving a baby since the patient could not at one time risk the possibility of ever losing such a beloved object. When she can accept motherhood with equanimity she will be cured without a doubt. No abrupt termination would be so effective as possibly a few interruptions for two or three months in order to allow more abreaction of the separation. In this way one can see how much anger recurs.

Although she will not be my patient at such a future date, still it would be interesting to speculate how she will handle her children during their oedipal period. It was to be expected that some unconscious shifting in the ego structure would come about with her reconciliation to her mother, and this was observed. When she has a son or daughter she would be able to guide them through the oedipal period without undue permission or anxiety.

During the interruption, the patient developed a severe headache. In a dream she saw herself as a very small baby "perfectly formed and healthy — not like that squalling, terrified little red monster caught in a net in one of my earlier analytic dreams." It was obvious that although her condition was greatly improved, she felt that "even though the baby was doing so well, it should not yet be left on its own." She reported that she had felt fairly intense anger and irritability with her family and her work and associates during the interruption. Such prolonged conscious anger was new to her. Furthermore, she had felt angry with the analyst and doubtful of her ability. She voiced this frankly when she returned to treatment. These reactions to the therapist are now undergoing further analysis. A follow-up report on this case will be given at the next Council meeting.

8

RECURRENT URINARY RETENTION DUE TO EMOTIONAL FACTORS

With George E. Williams, M.D.

> In the following report of a case of recurrent urinary retention, the therapist was Dr. Williams whose therapy was supervised by Dr. Johnson.

THE problem of chronic and recurrent urinary retention in women has been studied by a number of urologic workers (1–17) interested in this subject. Still unknown is the etiology in those cases in which no organic findings are present. In their scholarly paper Emmett, Hutchins, and McDonald state that these conditions are often diagnosed as "urinary retention of undetermined etiology" or "atypical cord bladder." They further state (5): "we are left, therefore, with the majority of cases of urinary obstruction and retention in which no contributing cause is apparent." In summary they conclude that "obstruction of the vesical neck and urinary retention occurring in women is of more common occurrence than is generally appreciated" and "that there seems to be no one predominant causative factor although numerous predisposing factors may be recognized."

The older methods of treatment in urology have been superseded by transurethral resection. Rather frequently, however,

---

Reprinted with permission from *Psychosomatic Medicine* 18(1956): 77–80.

such resections must be repeated, often several times. Acknowledging that there are many equivocal, accepted causes of urinary retention in a limited number of cases, we should like to add a well-documented case of recurrent urinary retention due to primary emotional conflicts. To the best of our knowledge no such case has been presented previously in the literature. Some outstanding urologists have encouraged us to publish such a documented case. This case is not offered in any sense as a profile study of a basic dynamic picture applicable to urinary retention in women. Rather this study is reviewed as evidence that urinary retention can be due to emotional conflicts primarily. A broader study of ego adaptations to incestuous experiences in many cases will be published later.

CASE REPORT

The decision to refer this patient for psychiatric study was made jointly by investigatively curious medical consultants. It was possible to observe repeatedly in this patient that emotional reactions to specific disturbing life events initiated retention of urine. A bout of retention could be predicted, during 3 years of intensive psychotherapy, when the emotions associated with such a set of situations appeared. Resolution of the emotional reactions fused with the events relieved the retention. During the last 18 months of psychotherapy there was no retention of urine.

The patient was a 28-year-old woman, a competent executive secretary in an advertising agency in a large midwestern city. When the internist saw the patient she was complaining of fatigue, vague abdominal and pelvic pains, and recurrent episodes of urinary retention which lasted from a "few hours" to 36 hours. One year previous to our initial examination the patient had been hospitalized with identical complaints. In that episode, as in the present instance, results of physical examination were essentially negative. Complete urological, gynecological, and neurological investigations were nonproductive. The original history contained a reference to numerous attacks of "kidney infections" occurring before the patient was 6 years old, with no subsequent episodes.

Personal History

The patient, 1 of 3 orphans, was reared as an only child from infancy by a paternal aunt and uncle. In the first psychiatric interview the patient appeared moderately depressed. The most recent instance of urinary retention requiring hospitalization had occurred after an extremely tense situation with a dishonest employer. In the initial interviews the patient tried in multiple ways to please the therapist with her answers and general demeanor, and denied categorically any feelings of irritation or anger toward anyone, including her employer. As she recalled traumatic situations, her reaction was to blame herself entirely. As therapy progressed, the patient was able to give a more nearly accurate account of her history. Early in treatment, the patient was quite unconscious of the truth with regard to the way in which she had been reared by her aunt and uncle. Since she had been trained to believe consciously that these adults were perfect, she had repressed through hostile identification all the disturbing facts.

Early Childhood

The evidence that highly pathological experiences centered around the patient's urogenital tract came to the fore gradually during the first year of several hours of intensive psychotherapy (4–7 interviews a week). Fortunately, the major facts operating in this case have been confirmed from sources outside the patient.

The aunt and uncle had evinced a pathological interest in the patient's urogenital tract from early years. The bathroom procedures were supervised frenetically by the aunt, who insisted that the patient be accompanied by the aunt or her husband whenever the child occupied this room. As a very small girl, when the patient made a guileless remark about her own genitals, the aunt in fury spanked her severely. The child was admonished never again to mention or to touch her genitals.

During the patient's first 6 years of life there were recurrent "urinary infections" associated with much pain, urgency, and frequency. When urinary accidents occurred both the aunt and uncle punished the patient. On a trip to town or when guests were present, the child, on asking to be taken to the bathroom, was met with enraged statements that she was not to mention such matters except when the family was alone. When the patient consequently wet herself, severe spanking followed. At such times the aunt berated the child that she was uncooperative and naughty when her "parents" were doing so much for her. The aunt deliberately obstructed the patient's many attempts to get to the bathroom. Each accident filled the patient with remorse and horror of the subsequent punishments which, with each occurrence, mounted in severity. These feelings contributed to the urgency and frequency, so that a vicious circle of "parental" obstruction, accidents, physical punishment, recrimination, fear, and tension developed. The patient was so terrified in this atmosphere that she dared not defend her hopeless position with the slightest verbal protest. Now, amazingly, the aunt admonished the patient to avoid sitting on the lawn because "her urine was poisonous and would kill the grass."

Until the patient was 5 years of age her aunt had bathed her and forbade her to look at or touch her genitals. When her aunt sustained a fracture of her arm, the bathing was entrusted to the uncle, who continued to bathe the child until she was 12 years old. When the patient protested feebly, the adults rejoined that bathing supervision was necessary to ensure that there be no playing with genitals. When the patient denied such activity, her aunt retorted that she knew the patient was at least "thinking about it."

Frank Adult Seductive Phase Toward Child

Frequently arguments between the patient's uncle and aunt soon involved the patient in another emotionally devastating dilemma. The uncle, fondling the child on his lap, declared that she was his "best girl," and derogated his wife. If arguments occurred between the uncle and aunt while the patient was away from home, upon her return the child was requested by her aunt to "love up" her uncle so that he would "not be angry at all of them." The patient reluctantly obeyed her aunt's perverse wishes and felt humiliated at the fondling, which her aunt was observing. Such seductive episodes always culminated in the aunt's then accusing the patient of trying to take the uncle's love from her. As the patient entered adolescence, the uncle's interest became unmistakably passionate, with fondling of the breasts and genitals. We were warned for several weeks of this behavior by the appearance of threatening incestuous dreams and gigantic urticaria over the face, breasts, and thighs of the patient. The uncle admonished the patient never to permit boys to do as he did.

Course in Therapy

Several months of psychotherapy, 5 hours a week, were necessary to elicit the above material, with the patient unaware of any rage toward her relatives. Our patient, until now, had assumed the full burden of guilt about the adults' behavior, complying with their attitudes. At this time, our patient complained of abdominal pain, and urinary retention developed. Psychotherapy was then directed toward bringing into consciousness the hostile revenge we know is always *unconsciously* felt by such a patient. As the patient finally became conscious of her violent anger towards the uncle and could express it to her therapist, the urinary retention subsided. Because of very early inculcation with the belief that her urine could kill, whenever the patint's unconscious murderous impulses toward the uncle were aroused, she unconsciously dreaded urinating for fear she could then actually kill him. However, when conscious of these feelings, she, as an adult, had no fear of murdering, since she knew she could control such wishes. These facts have been verified from concomitant sources.

Before the anger associated with the recall of traumatic incidents became conscious, we always could observe an attack of retention. Illustrative of such recalled traumatic experiences is the following. The patient's course in therapy became very stormy as with horror she began to relive consciously the first of several rapes by her uncle when she was 17 years old. Associated with this account was another bout of retention, which was alleviated as soon as the murderous rage appeared.

The symptom of urinary retention came and went, dependent upon whether the anger associated with the new memories was unconscious or conscious. It became increasingly less difficult to bring the anger into awareness and to alleviate the periods of retention. During the first 9 months of intensive psychotherapy, with recall of many traumatic experiences, the associated anger finally came so quickly into consciousness that retention in time no longer intervened.

It is unnecessary to include here all the details of the implications of events surrounding episodes of retention before the patient came within our purview. It became lucidly evident that contacts with men in a parent-superior position, such as an employer, were disturbing to the patient because the patient unconsciously had always feared some dishonest and seductive maneuver on the part of her employer. The tension associated with contact with any employer mounted and retention developed. It seems almost redundant to emphasize here that any therapy must take into account the patient's own instinctual intrapsychic impulses that operate in such an experiential milieu.

DISCUSSION

Here we see that the patient as a young child never was permitted for a day to escape from the hostile, suspicious, contradictory adult attitudes directed toward the patient's urinary system. All these intense feelings became invested in the operation of her sphincters and bladder. When we add to this situation the aunt's admonition that the patient's urine was poisonous, that the patient was a naughty, uncooperative child in every instance, we have a vicious circle that makes for a malignant neurosis. No expression of rage was permitted for an instant by the aunt and uncle, and yet unconsciously the patient wished to kill them. When there is superimposed on this early neurotic foundation such pathological incestuous impulses as were expressed toward this patient, who also has her own instinctual wishes, it is little wonder that her urogenital functions could not be performed with serenity. In contradistinction to the situation in the mind of this patient, in well-adjusted adolescents and adults there is a very clear emotional separation between urinary and sexual functions.

As in much of psychiatric treatment, one would like frequent systemic examinations with which to correlate the material obtained in the therapy hours. Since there were no infections, however, there seemed no justifiable reason for introducing examinations which would upset the balance psychologically. Furthermore, the usual uropathies had been excluded by previous cystoscopic examinations.

No generalizations from this patient's experience can be made with regard to etiologic factors in other cases. Only detailed investigation of many cases will justify any possible correlation of common denominators. Let us recognize that even though in time we might unmistakably demonstrate emotional factors as the specific stimulus in a large number of cases of urinary retention, this is still not to say that psychotherapy would be the treatment of choice. If intensive psychiatric treatment for a number of years were necessary to cure these patients, with all the storminess that might go with it, as in this case, the question will naturally arise, is this the treatment of choice? We would maintain, however, that in this particular case which we have reviewed, the urinary retention was only a small part of the total pathological process in this woman's personality which would have wrecked her life had she not had prolonged psychiatric treatment.

SUMMARY

1. In recurrent urinary retention in a young woman, several years of intensive psychiatric therapy revealed unmistakable evidence that early, highly pathological attitudes of the adults in the home directed toward the patient's urogenital functions were primary and specific etiological factors.

2. No dynamic generalizations are drawn from this one case, but after a body of clinical data was accumulated, predictability was seen to operate; it was possible on the basis of the psychological situations arising in the therapy to predict when an attack of retention would develop and under what circumstances psychologically such retention would be alleviated. Only research in a number of cases will justify the conclusion that emotional factors

often can be of primary specific significance in the etiology of cases heretofore baffling. It is emphasized that if and when such psychological factors present themselves as of primary significance, only considerable investigation and experimentation will determine the treatment of choice.

REFERENCES

1. Baurys, W. Bladder neck obstruction in the female. *Pennsylvania M. J.* 44 (1940): 206.
2. Cabot, H., and Shoemaker, Rosemary. The role of glands of the female urethra in the production of infection of the urinary tract. *Tr. Am. A. Genito-Urin. Surgeons* 29 (1936): 461.
3. Caulk, J. R. Contracture of the vesical neck in the female. *J. Urol.* 6 (1921): 341.
4. Caulk, J. R. Obstructions at the bladder neck in men, women and children. *Internat. Clin.* 47 (1937): 136.
5. Emmett, J. L. The surgical treatment of urinary retention. *Presented at the Fifth Annual Clinical Conference of the Chicago Medical Society*, March, 1949.
6. Emmett, J. L.; Hutchins, S. P. R.; and McDonald, J. R. The treatment of urinary retention in women by transurethral resection. *J. Urol.* 63 (1950): 1031.
7. Emmett, J. L., and McDonald, J. R. Proliferation of glands of the urinary bladder simulating malignant neoplasm. *J. Urol.* 48 (1942): 257.
8. Engels, C. F. Bladder neck resection in women and children. *Tr. West Sect., Am. Urol. A.* 12 (1944): 94.
9. Foley, F. E. B. Diagnosis and classification of the various forms of bladder neck obstruction. *Minnesota Med.* 12 (1929): 137.
10. Folsom, A. I. The female urethra: A clinical and pathologic study. *JAMA* 97 (1931): 1345.
11. Folsom, A. I., and Alexander, J. C. Referred pain from the female urethra. *J. Urol.* 31 (1934): 731.
12. Mirabile, C. Resection of the bladder neck for obstruction in women: Report of a case. *New England J. Med.* 228 (1943): 751.

13. Neff, J. H. Resection of prolapsed mucosa at the vesical neck for retention of urine in the female. *Tr. Am. A. Genito-Urin. Surgeons* 31 (1938): 263.
14. Nesbit, R. M. Vesical neck contracture in the female with urinary obstruction. *Urol. & Cutan. Rev.* 37 (1933): 291.
15. Thompson, G. J. Transurethral operations on women for relief of dysfunction of the vesical neck. *J. Urol.* 41 (1939): 349.
16. Winsbury-White, H. P. Two cases of retention of urine in women. *Lancet* 1 (1936): 1008.
17. Young, H. H. The pathology and treatment of obstructions at the vesical neck in women. *JAMA.* 115 (1940): 2133.

9

COMMENTS ON DISPOSITION OF AMPUTATED BODY PARTS

> I would also like to include in this section Dr. Johnson's discussion of a paper on "Treatment of Acute Painful Phantom Limb," by L. C. Kolb, L. M. Frank, and E. J. Watson presented at a Mayo Clinic staff meeting. The discussion contains some clinical observations on body image and amputation that do not appear elsewhere in her writing.

I HAVE been asked to say just a few words about the authors' suggestion that the surgeon might preoperatively make a considerate inquiry as to the patient's concerns about the disposal of the body part. I agree that the surgeon could do this and spare many patients great secret emotional suffering because most patients never even volunteer these sad concerns to a close relative — they fear it may seem too strange and feel that only they ever had such thoughts.

Let us consider the psychologic background for the authors' suggestion. The attitudes and thoughts of patients in the preoperative period with regard to the part of the body to be amputated are deeply personal and painful in the normal person. Many of us are apt to think the loss of a hand, leg, or breast is disturbing just because of the pride hurt by the mutilation and the functional handicap. All that is there, to be sure, in the normal person, but

Reprinted with permission from *Proceedings of the Staff Meetings of the Mayo Clinic* 27 (1952): 110–18.

also, to lose a hand or leg or breast arouses feelings of sadness and real mourning for the long familiar part that is to go away forever. I can only liken it qualitatively to the normal mourning over contemplated loss of a member of one's family. The mourning is over the hand to be lost, not over the stump. Hatred is the feeling felt toward the stump at first. When we have a patient's confidence, he will tell us preoperatively how he secretly looks and looks at the sick hand, trying to fix in his mind and memory all the old landmarks, every scar, the wrinkles, the form and color, and feels that it is qualitatively like a contemplated farewell to an old and dear friend. Therefore, since the part to be lost has this meaning, is it any wonder that the patient, almost with panic, fantasies about whether the amputated hand will be handled with respect and tenderness by the surgical team? This one question they fear to face in their own minds and they may secretly weep or become unduly anxious. They express it to us as almost a feeling of pity and protectiveness toward an old familiar something that is being cast out. Of course, it is the highly neurotic persons who have a need for any complicated ritualistic burial ceremonial and I am not referring to them.

The authors have suggested, therefore, that proper preparation of the patient about to undergo any amputation of a significant visible body part might include a considerate inquiry by the surgeon as to the patient's concerns with regard to the disposal of the part to be amputated. Such preoperative discussion should be a very simple gentle statement that the physician is well aware that the loss of the hand, for example, represents an unhappy occasion — that aside from any handicap or changed appearance it is sad to lose something that belongs to one and has been familiar for so long. The physician would then go on to say, "I want you to know, therefore, that we appreciate this and will handle it with all the consideration and privacy you would wish."

The patient may weep at this point which should be permitted quietly for a few minutes. The weeping means only that the patient feels close to and trusting of his physician. The patient may want to know then exactly what his physician will do with the amputated part, and the normal person can always, without trauma, accept thoughtful preservation in a fluid or cremation. Patients cannot bear the idea of their loved hand or leg being dumped into a can with all kinds of debris. It would certainly be reassuring if a patient could know that there has been a respectful private cremation of a limb by a special hospital attendant, if cremation is the form of disposal.

Some physicians may feel, "Why not let sleeping dogs lie — why stir up such questions preoperatively?" I can assure you it is not a question of stirring anything up — it is already there and our task is to reassure the patient in his lonely secret situation that his feelings and wishes are appreciated.

The normal person has no concern about disposal of internal organs since they are not part of the normal body image.

SECTION

III

Antisocial Behavior

If one had to choose *the* major contribution from all others made by Dr. Johnson during her professional career, the selection would most reasonably be in the area of her providing us with a wider understanding of antisocial behavior. As a child psychiatrist, her clinical observations encompassed several generations (child, parents, and often grandparents), whereby she could test out the hypotheses of depth psychology using the insights and methods learned in her extensive training in and practice of psychoanalysis. This longitudinal study was facilitated through her refinement of the technique of collaborative therapy. During her years at the Institute for Juvenile Research (1937–42) she also held an appointment as associate in criminology at the University of Illinois School of Medicine (1938–42). In 1942, she was promoted to assistant professor in criminology at the same institution. She held this position until 1946. The culmination of these years of study appeared in print in 1949 in her paper, "Sanctions for Superego Lacunae of Adolescents," first presented at the Chicago Psychoanalytic Society meeting of March 25, 1947, and appearing as a chapter in *Searchlights on Delinquency*, edited by K. R. Eissler (New York: International Universities Press, 1949). This paper is included in the following section in its entirety.

In the preparation of this section, the greatest bulk of Dr. Johnson's publications had to be reviewed to make appropriate selections and to avoid excessive repetition, since she wrote for many different audiences. The seven articles chosen span a decade of writing. Some repetition will be noted, since each article appeared as a complete and separate unit. The reader will observe shifts in emphasis reflecting both the varying audiences and the development of the ideas over time.

10

SANCTIONS FOR SUPEREGO LACUNAE OF ADOLESCENTS

THE problems discussed in this paper are not peculiar to adolescents, although most of the material will be drawn primarily from my experiences with that age group.

It is essential to define the character problems involved: those of adolescents in conflict with parents or some other external authority because of an acting out of forbidden, antisocial impulses. There is rarely a generalized weakness of the superego in the cases under consideration but rather a lack of superego in certain circumscribed areas of behavior, which may be termed superego lacunae. For instance, a child may be entirely dependable about regular school attendance or honesty at work, but engage in petty stealing or serious sexual acting out. Frequently, mild or severe neurotic conflicts accompany such superego lacunae.

I shall attempt to illustrate that the parents may find vicarious gratification of their own poorly-integrated forbidden impulses in the acting out of the child, through their conscious or more often unconscious permissiveness or inconsistency toward the child in these spheres of behavior. The child's superego lacunae correspond to similar defects of the parents' superego which in turn were derived from the conscious or unconscious permissiveness

Reprinted with permission from *Searchlights on Delinquency*, ed. K. R. Eissler (New York: International Universities Press, 1949), pp. 225–45.

of their own parents. These conclusions are the result of the collaborative study and treatment of the significant parent as well as the adolescent patient as reported briefly by Szurek in 1942 (17).

The literature reveals a variety of descriptions and discussions of the etiology of such superego defects. Reich (13) was the first to introduce the term "impulsive character" into psychoanalytic literature. Alexander (2) introduced the concept of the need for self-punishment as a motive for "acting out." Other authors stress the patient's receiving insufficient love and warmth so that a strong identification with the unloving parents is impossible. This lack of love is commonly considered the basic cause of superego defects.

Schmideberg (14) believed that people who act out their conflicts have a greater constitutional inability to tolerate frustration than the more inhibited persons. Greenacre (7) reported in some detail a number of cases of psychopathic personality but without concomitant study of the parents. She found that the fathers of such patients were usually ambitious and prominent, and the mothers usually frivolous and superficial, giving little attention to the home. She discussed the interrelationships of such parents with the child in respect to its superego development, but did not speak of defects in the parents' superego.

Aichhorn (1) and Healy and Bronner (9) stated that some antisocial children have identified themselves with the gross ethical distortions of these parents. These observers saw the gross pathological correlations but apparently did not stress the implications in the subtler cases with which we are concerned in this paper. Healy and Bronner attributed the child's inability to develop a normal superego to the coldness and rejection of the parents, so that one child in a family may steal and another will not, depending upon the one being unloved and the other loved. Even granting that unloved children may not develop a "normal superego," it does not follow that coldness of parents alone can lead to the superego lacunae under discussion. Some very cold parents create such great guilt in children that a punitive, hostile superego is developed. On the other hand there are warm parents whose child may act out antisocially.

At the Institute for Juvenile Research our collaborative therapy of purely neurotic children and their parents revealed certain unmistakable but subtle parent-child interrelationships in which one provided the other with an unconscious impetus to the neurosis. The confusing literature on delinquency and the dissatisfaction with our results in treating delinquent children stimulated a research into the subtle family relationships for a clue such as we had found in the purely neurotic cases. It seemed logical to seek some hidden links between the superego of the parent and the child, even in cases where the parent himself did not act out.

Szurek (17) stated the problem briefly and brilliantly in an understandable and simple way for both the gross *and* the subtler pathologies. Due to limitations of space he could not present the large amount of available evidence for his thesis. He saw the problem as a defect in personality organization — a defect in conscience:

> Clinical experience with children showing predominantly behavior which is a problem to others and *concurrent therapeutic effort with the parent* leaves the impression that the genesis of some of the human characteristics included in the definition of psychopathic personality is no greater mystery than other syndromes in psychopathology. Almost literally, in no instances in which adequate psychiatric therapeutic study of *both* parent and child has been possible has it been difficult to obtain sufficient evidence to reconstruct the chief dynamics of the situation. Regularly the more important parent — usually the mother, although the father is always in some way involved — has been seen *unconsciously* to encourage the amoral

or antisocial behavior of the child. The neurotic needs of the parent whether of excessively dominating, dependent or erotic character are vicariously gratified by the behavior of the child, or in relation to the child. Such — neurotic — needs of the parent exist either because of some current inability to satisfy them in the world of adults, or because of the stunting experiences in the parent's own childhood — or more commonly, because of a combination of both of these factors. Because their parental needs are unintegrated, unconscious and unacceptable to the parent himself, the child in every instance is sooner or later frustrated and thus experiences no durable satisfactions. Because the indulgence or permissiveness of the parent in regard to marked overt hostility, or to some mastery techniques, for example, is uncertain, and inconsistent, control over the former or acquisition of the latter by the child is similarly uncertain and confused. If a discipline of the parent is administered with guilt, it permits the child to exploit and subtly to blackmail the parent until the particular issue between them is befogged and piled high with irrelevant bickerings and implied or expressed mutual recriminations.

The astonishing observation emerging repeatedly in our studies was the subtle manner in which one child in a family of several children might unconsciously be singled out as the scapegoat to act out the parent's poorly integrated and forbidden impulses. Analytic study of the significant parent showed unmistakably the peculiar meaning this child had for the parent and the tragic mode in which both the parent and the child were consciously, but much more often *unconsciously*, involved in the fatal march of events. As therapists we could not avoid feeling sympathy for these consciously well-intentioned parents whose unconscious needs were unwittingly bringing disaster down on the family. This was strikingly illustrated in several families that had an adopted child as well as one or more children of their own. The acting out of the parent through the adopted child was always rationalized as inherited behavior.

Although not emphasized by Szurek, another fact that became obvious was that not only was the parent's forbidden impulse acted out vicariously by the unfortunate child, but this very acting out, in a way so foreign to the conscious wishes of the parent, served often as a channel for hostile, destructive impulses that the parent felt toward the child. In many cases, parents may reveal blatantly the child's acting out to schools, family friends and neighbors in a way most destructive for the child's reputation. This becomes one of the greatest sources of rage in the child. The press recently reported a young adolescent girl hanging herself because her mother, missing $10.00, telephoned the school authorities to search the girl's purse.

Thus the parents' unconscious condoning of the acting out of asocial impulses by the child may serve the two-fold purpose of allowing the parent vicarious gratification of forbidden impulses as well as the expression of hostile destructive impulses felt toward the child.

Similarly the child consciously but more often unwittingly exposes the parents to all degrees of suffering through acting out. This acting out may often be an exaggerated picture of the unconscious impulses of the parent.

We must first understand the behavior of a well-integrated parent, and the subtle conscious and unconscious ways in which this behavior directs the child's superego development in order to be able to recognize the evidences of such destructive sanctions in less integrated parents. To be sure, the dissolution of the oedipus conflict puts the real seal on the superego, but it is well to be aware of all the preoedipal and oedipal subtleties in the family which are part and parcel of this development. To the child in the early and middle latency period there may be alternative modes of reacting on an ego level, but when the superego is involved the child normally is reared as if there could be *no* alternative reaction in regard to the suppression of the impulses to theft, murder, truancy, etc. The well-integrated, mature mother issuing an order to a child does not immediately check to see if it has been done, or suggest beforehand that if it is not done, there will be serious consequences.

Such constant checking or such a warning means to the child that there is an alternative to the mother's order and an alternate image of *him* in the mother's mind. Identification with the parent does not consist merely of identification with the manifest behavior of the parent. It necessarily includes a sharing by the child of the parent's conscious and unconscious concept of the child as one who is loved and honest or sometimes unloved or dishonest. It is essential to appreciate this fact if we are to understand the etiology of superego defects and plan a rational therapy. Angry orders or suspiciousness or commands colored by feelings of guilt convey to the child the doubtful alternative image of him in the parent's mind. The mature mother expects the thing to be done, and later if she finds the child has sidestepped her wishes, she insists without guilt on her part that it be done. The mother must have this undoubting firm, unconscious assurance that her child will soon make her intention his own in accordance with her own image of him. This, however, produces a rather rigid and inflexible attitude in the young child. As Fenichel (5) says: "After the dissolution of the oedipus complex we say the superego is at first rigid and strict . . . and that later in normal persons it becomes more amenable to the ego, more plastic and *more sensible*."

In adolescence the superego is normally still fairly rigid and the child is greatly disturbed when adults express doubts about it. Nothing angers adolescents more than to be warned about or accused of indiscretions of which overtly they were not guilty. Such lack of good faith in them threatens to break down their repressive defenses and lowers their self-esteem and feeling that they would do the right thing. It suggests an alternative mode of behavior which at that age frightens them.

With these simple basic concepts in mind it becomes relatively easy to see what is happening in some rather simple cases of superego defect and to present the evidence for what Szurek stated in his article. It should be made clear that it is not within the scope of this paper to discuss the multiple determined types of character defenses which the child may evolve and use. Nor can the particular mode of therapy dealing with such character defenses be here included. These topics have been discussed in previous papers (6) (7).

Let us return to our simple cases of superego defect. How is truancy initiated? It is not just that parents are cold and rejecting as so many authors imply. How does the specific idea of leaving home originate? At six the little girl may say angrily: "You don't love me — nobody loves me — I hate you all." Quite often the child will receive such replies as: "Well, why don't you just pack your bag and go live some place else if you think we're so awful?" We know that some parents even follow this up by packing the little one's suitcase which at first may terrify the child. The suggestion to leave home comes more frequently from inside the home than outside, for not many small children tell others at school that their parents are mean or get suggestions from other children to leave home.

If little children (especially up to the age of eleven or twelve) let the thought that they are unloved come into consciousness at all, they then do not express that thought outside the family circle from feelings of both guilt and pride.

When we carefully examine the cases of a first or a repeated running away, we often find that it was the parents who unconsciously made provocative suggestions from a variety of motives such as hostility, or a need of vicarious gratification or both.

As, for example, six-year-old Stevie, who had been running away since he was four. His father seemed to know an inexplicable amount of detail concerning the boy's episodes of exploration. He reported that during these same two years he himself had been unable to continue his work as driver of a transcontinental truck, a job in which he revelled. Instead his present job confines him to the city. It was striking to observe this father with the little boy. He asked Stevie to tell of his most recent running away. When the child guiltily hesitated, his father started him on his way with an intriguing reminder. As the boy gave his account, his father was obviously fascinated — even occasionally prompting the child. Toward the end the father suddenly and angrily cut the child off saying, "That's enough, Stevie; now you see what I mean, Doctor?" Stevie could not help but see his father's great interest and pleasure when he told his tale each time he returned home, even though at the end of his account he received his whipping. The father was a kind, well-intentioned man who rightly feared for his little son's safety, but he was quite unconscious of the fact that the stimulus of his own thwarted need to travel was easily conveyed to the small, bright boy of whom the father said: "Stevie's really a good kid — he would follow me around the top of a wall 50 feet high."

No better example of how an adult can initiate such running away can be found than the story of how Aichhorn (1) deliberately resorted to such provocation as a technique of treatment. In handling the transference he consciously used a simple provocative mechanism to get a boy to run away from the institution, since he could not make any positive contact with the adolescent.

Sanctions for Superego Lacunae of Adolescents 121

This very narcissistic boy, with no positive feeling for Aichhorn, constantly complained about the institution. Aichhorn made subtle suggestions about the attractiveness of the outside world and an hour later the boy ran away. As Aichhorn had anticipated, some days later the boy returned, having found the outside world uninviting and then entered at once into a positive relationship with Aichhorn.

Let us now attempt to discover how stealing is initiated.

One of my patients, a woman, who had been in analysis for nine months, came in very angry at her nine-year-old daughter. The reason for the anger was that the child had been found stealing some money from the teacher's desk the day before. The patient stated that she knew Margaret had taken nickles from her purse off and on since she was six or seven but had said nothing, feeling that "she would outgrow it." When I asked why she had said nothing, she said it was never serious, so she had felt the less said the better. It was stated earlier in this paper that the mature mother does not anticipate trouble nor check up constantly on her child. On the other hand, neither does she let something amiss go by when she observes it, but instead handles it promptly without anxiety or guilt. She can neither be the nagging, checking detective, nor the permissive, lax condoner. During this hour, my patient told me a dream she had had over the weekend. In the dream she went into Saks and stole a beautiful pair of slippers. In the discussion I commented that I was struck with the fact that in her dream she did not even project the theft onto someone else and wondered if possibly her mother had been permissive with little thefts. Then my patient told me, for the first time, of numerous thefts all through her childhood and adolescence and that her mother had always protected her. For instance, during one year of her adolescence she had stolen at least two dozen lipsticks from stores. The prohibitions which had been so poorly integrated in her own life were unconsciously permitting and condoning her daughter's stealing. It was a revealing experience for my patient when three months later her mother came for a visit, to observe her mother's little deceptions and permissions with the two grandchildren, such deceptions as my patient had herself hitherto ignored. She did what she could to stop them and decided to limit long visits from her mother until the children were much older. In a very short time her daughter stopped all thefts as my patient, through her analysis, was able to make a definite stand without anxiety or vacillation. The child, formerly so unhappy and unpopular later became an outstanding pupil in her school.

We see in this mother's behavior an attitude commonly found among parents of children who steal. The parent whose own superego is defective is the one who will say "he will outgrow it," and often the parent who is not involved in the acting out is the one who finally insists upon bringing the child to treatment. "He will outgrow it" is the permissive protective attitude that keeps the problem active.

There are many such parents whose own poorly integrated prohibitions permit them to let slight offenses go by, only to react with sudden and guilty alarm at the first signs of criticism from outside the home by then angrily accusing and punishing their child. The child, confused and angry, in turn feels betrayed, and may in his own mind review his parents' similar deceptions. If he has the courage and is not too ashamed, he may point this out to the parent, and in this way the vicious circle of hostile, mutual blackmail and corruption is started.

The fantasies, hopes and fears which parents express in reaction to some behavior of their child is one of the commonest ways in which a child is influenced toward a healthy or a maladapted career. The horrified comments or anxiety over some behavior of the child are well-known to everyone. How commonly we hear the parent of the little child, caught in some minor offense, angrily say, "You are beyond me — I can't handle you any more — if this doesn't stop, you will end in the reform school." Or the child who is just beginning to misbehave is likened to his uncle who came to a bad end. We become "good" or "bad" depending upon our parents' fantasies about us.

A professional worker recently told me that seventeen years ago she visited her friends who had a nine-months old baby boy. The worker took the little boy on her lap and when he reached up and put his hands around her neck, the child's mother with a really frightening expression said, "I hope my son won't be a killer." The worker told me that by the age of fifteen years that boy had committed murder.

However, I do not intend to use evidence here of the more tragic cases, which have come to our attention, but will confine the discussion to fairly simple examples.

In *Psychoanalytic Therapy*, written by the Staff of the Institute for Psychoanalysis of Chicago, I reported the case of seventeen-year-old Ann who suffered from great anxiety and whose mother had written fraudulent excuses for the girl's absences from the school. The girl refused treatment and I treated only the mother. It was possible to analyze not only much of the mother's destructive hostility to Ann, but also in the transference, to manage and thwart the mother's attempts to corrupt the analyst and pull her into the vicious circle. Two years later, Ann is in college and making an excellent adjustment.

Another case is that of a sixteen-year-old girl who came to treatment because of several years of severe depression and the occasional idea that she was being poisoned at the school cafeteria. As her depression subsided and her anger toward me came out, she went home one day and told her mother she was so angry at the therapist, she was going to kill her. The mother said, with horror, "Oh, Marion, don't bring any more tragedy on the family." Marion rushed back to me greatly frightened saying, "My mother actually believed I would murder — what is wrong with her?" At that point I succeeded in also getting the mother into treatment with another analyst. It was forunate that I did so, for Marion's father had died psychotic, and the maternal grandmother had been promiscuous, so Marion's mother was acting out ominous impulses through this girl, and blaming them all on Marion's heredity from her father.

When one parent advises a child to keep something from the other parent, it is a frequent and destructive factor in creating deceptions and stealing. "Here, I'll give you $2.00, but don't tell your father." One could list an endless array of such sanctions. In treatment these children will always try to get the therapist to lie to the parents. The parents' "more sensible superegos" unconsciously overlook the fact that to the rigid superego of a six- or nine-year-old, this does not look "sensible" but dishonest.

If we break a promise to a child without a sincere statement of the facts and a regretful apology, we undermine his ability to identify with us as adults of sound integrity.

In work with neurotic adolescents and young people, all therapists at times unwittingly ask questions which the child interprets as a permission. For instance, one frequently hears of analysts in a consultation with a twenty-year-old ask, "Have you ever had intercourse?" One young colleague told me he learned only too well the unwisdom of such a question. In the initial interview he asked a nineteen-year-old college student if he had had intercourse and the patient said, "Yes." Several months later his patient confessed that at the time the therapist had questioned him, he had *not* had intercourse. He felt guilty that he had lied and ashamed that he was so unmanly, so he had sex relations to undo the lie and prove his manliness. Probably all therapists unwittingly make some of the same errors in the treatment of children which some of the parents make to a greater degree. It is just these errors that led me to consider carefully Freud's meaning and intention when he made his suggestion for offsetting "acting out" in analysis, by interpreting and warning ahead of time.

Some analysts, dealing with cases of perversions or even more serious antisocial behavior, warn the patients ahead of time that they may have the impulse to act out in some manner. Certainly, *this* was not Freud's thinking on the matter. When he spoke of revealing to the patient, at the correct time, the possibility of his acting out and the meaning of it, he had in mind the so-called "acting out" of the neurotic patient on the couch who was repeating in the transference the salient episodes of his earlier life. This is an entirely different matter from warning a patient about some antisocial impulsive behavior. In fact, if I understand Freud correctly, he warned analysts against mobilizing and interpreting too rapidly any impulses that might be dangerously expressed outside the analytic hour — particularly sadism. A loose and unclear concept of what is meant by "acting out" has led a number of analysts to carry over Freud's suggestions about transference "acting out" to the "acting out" in a serious antisocial way. A warning to a patient with defective superego can act as a destructive force, disrupting what one has attempted to build up, namely, the patient's belief in the therapist's ethical concept of him. Any warning or questioning without factual justification may be interpreted both as a humiliation and a permission.

There is an additional etiological factor in these cases which is puzzling. In work with adolescents from all social strata, I was impressed, as was Szurek, with the fact that sometimes the child's parents had a similar partial superego defect, that is, the mother was promiscuous or the father committed some thefts, etc. But there are other cases in which the parents had never actually done any of this acting out so far as we could find, and yet we could see them unconsciously initiating this with the child. These parents, let us say, had some neurotic conflicts about thefts, promiscuity, etc., like many of us, but why did such parents permit themselves to act these conflicts out through the child, while many neurotic parents do not? With this question in mind, whenever I had a parent in treatment, I explored the relation to her own parents very closely.

Where did the parent get the permission to act out through the child? Since the parent did not act out herself, she must have had a fairly strong conscience. Yet what caused this poorly integrated prohibition to appear in the next generation?

I frequently found that the present parent had gone along for years developing a good conscience, was secure about controlling her own impulses and then something arose that led her parents to surprising suspicions and accusations. Since the parent under treatment already had a good conscience, he or she could not respond to this permissive accusation by acting out, yet was enraged at the injustice and defamation. The rage and the permission would then come out unconsciously by being displaced onto the daughter or son. The parent's acting out through the child may also occur when the parent, with a well-developed conscience, *later* observed dishonesty, erotic acting out, or some other disturbing behavior in *her* parents and felt much pain and confusion about their actions. Our parent in question already had a good conscience and too much guilt to do likewise herself, but the confusion, anger, and permission cannot be normally integrated into her personality and appears later through her own child. For several years I have found increasing evidence to substantiate this statement, but I am not satisfied that this is the final answer.

With this understanding, it could be seen more clearly why at the Institute for Juvenile Research we had failed so repeatedly with even relatively mild cases of acting out, although we had seen some of them frequently (four to five times a week), for one or two years. We had given a great deal of consistent warmth and affection, but the child continued to steal or act out sexually. Any guilt developed toward us with regard to an act was met with unconscious permission at home and the child was only confused and frequently became more fearful toward us and finally stopped coming. We succeeded with even mild cases only if we could get the significant parent into treatment or could remove the child from the home during the therapy. Treatment of such parents whole role is so often unconscious, is a miserable ordeal for them and the greatest sensitiveness and skill is necessary in carrying them through. Many break away in spite of our best efforts to go slowly. Where the sanction was perfectly conscious on the parent's part, treatment of him was almost always futile. If neither treatment of the parent nor placement is possible, then any treatment in a severe case is not only futile, but often dangerous, because the parent can unconsciously act out through the child and make the therapist "responsible," just as parents make heredity the scapegoat in some adoptive cases.

My first experience with such a serious hazard came a few years ago. A young woman therapist who did not share our conviction of these dangers insisted on trying treatment of a ten-year-old boy who stole and had set a few fires three years earlier.

Neither parent had been interviewed with the idea of considering treatment. A few weeks later a serious fire occurred at the home. The mother particularly was enraged at the therapist. To relieve the tension and clarify the situation I talked with her. She told me that she had been downtown shopping; that she was a woman who trusted her premonitions and she had become uneasy about something vague and hurried home. A few blocks from home she heard the fire department and, "I just knew it was our house." When I asked her why she should have been so uneasy and certain, since there had been no fire for three years, she flushed, stiffened and maintained, "I always trust my hunches." I asked her if the boy had mentioned fires at any time recently. She thought for a while and then told me that he had become angry at his little sister a few days before. When the mother interfered, he shouted that he hated them all and would kill them or burn them all up. This is a frequent threat of many angry children and the average parent pays no attention to it. This mother had told him then that if he tried anything like that, he would end in the reform school. Like most of these threats by parents of antisocial children, they are not carried through and the child knows the parent will protect him until he does something far worse. I spoke reassuringly of our interest in helping in some way, but she angrily withdrew herself and child entirely from the treatment situation, blaming the child's therapist.

In treating younger children and adolescents with conscience defects, one of the great errors commonly made is that of too energetic attempts to liberate the child from the permissive parent, especially by telling the child that the parent is dishonest, or sexually unstable. These children often know these facts consciously, but it is a frightening and humiliating thing to the insecure young patient to be told such things. If he is not conscious of such facts, this knowledge early in treatment is devastating to the child and utterly cruel to the parent who is unconscious of the implications in his or her permissive behavior or attitude. When the children become more secure in handling their own impulses, these patients if they observe them, bring up these tragic facts themselves and they can be discussed at that time.

I wish to emphasize certain facts about the treatment of the young and older adolescents who are not too seriously handicapped. With the exception of one girl who lied and stole, all were able to develop a fairly *positive transference* within a month or two. To be sure some were seen five and six times a week for the first few months and were permitted many additional telephone contacts. I spent over a year developing a good relationship with one girl. There were two girls and one boy whom I never saw, but whose mothers I treated — one by psychotherapy for nine months and two in analysis. All of these cases were adolescents who in certain areas of behavior had excellent conscience formation but nevertheless showed other symptoms of defect such as stealing, lying, cheating, running away, or sexual acting out. I cannot emphasize too strongly that the successes I have had are not with very severe cases such as the highly narcissistic children with widespread superego defects. Also, when I have been successful, the parents have been cooperative and well enough to enter treatment themselves or allow me to place the adolescent in a school or a club.

To make for a simpler presentation of some of the principles of the direct treatment of an adolescent with a conscience lacuna, I shall confine the discussion more or less to one group, namely those children in whom stealing was the essential problem. I can think of none whom I have treated who did not also have neurotic conflicts which likewise had to be resolved when the time was propitious.

In the literature such brilliant therapists as Aichhorn and

Schmideberg speak of more or less long periods of education and re-education of such children preparatory to analysis or along with analysis of their neurotic symptoms. This preparatory "educational" phase apparently has to do with strengthening the superego, but I have always wished they would write in more detail of the therapeutic technique which brings this about. Aichhorn deals rather extensively with the need to change the urge for living by the pleasure principle into a more realistic attitude, but there are few specific details of the ways and means he employed.

Aichhorn never began by asking a child to give an account of his misdemeanors because he felt quite sure he would only weaken the relationship by forcing the child into more falsifications. Many therapists, however, approach an adolescent boy who steals by trying to get him to give an account of his misdemeanors and difficulties. When they are asked why they force the child to recount these facts, they reply that it is to see if he has "insight" into why he is brought for therapy. Usually he would not give a frank confession, but even if he did, this has nothing to do with "insight." If he were deeply deprived early, then the therapist might say he hopes to help the patient to see some connection between the consciously or unconsciously permitted stealing and his emotional deprivation. But by proceeding this way their patients' thefts usually increase for reasons which will soon be clear.

How does the patient react to such an approach? By evasions, rationalizations and outright falsifications and the ensuing anger, fear and humiliation will now present an even greater obstacle to therapy.

The primary difficulty is a partial superego lack — a lacuna. If a normal superego is developed through identification with mature parents who automatically believe in and are certain their child will have integrity, then it would seem logical that the correction of such a lacuna (even at so late a period as adolescence) must proceed by having the therapist assume that there are the same potentialities for identification with himself as he would see in his own child. This attitude is essential or all the warmth in the world will not repair a conscience defect in the child. I cannot emphasize too strongly that this attitude and a deep feeling of respect for the adolescent are absolutely basic in the treatment of these cases.

I have no great optimism about success with a very severe superego defect, but with the milder lacunae, the success of our treatment depends on our understanding of the child's relationship to the therapist.

At the initial interview, regardless of the transference, I do take into account a factor which Aichhorn does not elaborate. Since the adolescent for a long period probably has been consciously or unconsciously protected and his conduct ambiguously condoned by his parent or parents, he has therefore developed a definite pattern of expectation of some degree of whitewashing from other adults. As soon as the therapist gives in to that, the vicious circle of blackmail begins. Therefore, at the initial interview I merely say I know he has had these misunderstandings and difficulties about money which we need not go into but that I have the feeling as he becomes more sure of me, and we understand each other this will eventually subside. I feel that the child must be spared humiliation and given hope for the future without burdening him by excessive standards of good behavior. His past must not be held against him yet too great a whitewashing of his conduct would be permissive.

Let us remember that the battle at home has gone on through mutual corruption and blackmail, albeit often subtly. This is true in stealing, having the parents write false excuses, lying, etc.

Keeping this in mind, if the therapist begins by asking for an account of past misdemeanors, the patient will at once be humiliated and angry. Every patient soon tests the analyst over and over to see if he is corruptible, and if the therapist begins by humiliating him, that testing out will come much more quickly and often more seriously and the whole case may get out of hand before it is well started.

The first thing that should be verbalized casually to the child is the therapist's confidence that with the growth of mutual understanding, all of these old troubles in time will subside. Doubts, accusations or warnings that the child may be tempted to steal will rapidly destroy any possible identification with the adult's superego, the therapist's good understanding of the patient's potentialities notwithstanding.

If a therapist cannot sincerely feel that this child can eventually become thoroughly honest in relation to her without at the same time burdening the child with therapeutic expectations, no improvement will occur no matter how hard she strives to follow the suggestions given here. Many workers will say: "How can I have confidence in the child when he has stolen for years or set several fires? I shall feel duped if after months of treatment, I find he was pulling the wool over my eyes all along." This is a very real counter-transference problem. The therapist, without conflict in this area, would not mind if he finds he has been fooled for a time. Resistance and relapse are to be expected in the analysis of a neurosis, and similar lags and relapses are to be expected in treating superego defects. If despair or annoyance overwhelms the therapist at these points, all is lost. Misdemeanors should be neither overlooked nor whitewashed but be frankly discussed with the patient.

In several instances I have come into the picture after a crisis when the parents were terrified by the risks of the child's future and the child knew this. Feeling that for once an adult had to express to the child a sound expectation of him, I have casually but definitely and in the child's presence, expressed my complete assurance of success.

I remember the cases of a boy and a girl who precipitated near tragedies in the home by setting fires just before they were to leave for summer camps. I think the fact that the parents expressed their doubts in the children's presence and that I answered promptly and with conviction, made it possible for the children to feel safe. There was little time to develop strong contacts with these adolescents before camp, but the summer was successful. This is not to say that the task of the treatment had gone beyond a mere beginning. Many therapists may feel that in such a situation the child may "call your bluff" for his parents have usually threatened him with punishment for future misdemeanors only to give ground when the child put them to the test. The difference in these two cases was that I made no threats and said nothing to invite a threat.

Treating these cases calls for the greatest flexibility. At the beginning I may see them five or six times a week and answer their telephone calls every night for months. Especially with the narcissistic child it may need many hours a week to stir up any positive feeling. Broken appointments are frequently followed by a friendly telephone call from the therapist, and this may go on for weeks and months. So much flexibility and time for unpredictable calls and appointments are necessary that I avoid carrying more than two or three of these adolescents at a time on my schedule.

All analysts know how carefully and frankly they must deal with the ego problems of a paranoid patient. Similarly, a great amount of care must be taken with these patients, to avoid any possibility of the patients seeing the therapist as deceptive or evasive in any way. I make it clear that if anyone should ever talk of him to me, I shall tell him at once and if possible get his permission before talking to anyone about him. As an adult in these matters, I do not display the "sensible superego" of Fenichel but to many of my colleagues may give the impression of being child-like in my care to have everything above board. I am extremely careful about promises since to a small child a promise is part and parcel of the whole matter of superego development. Some of these adolescents will beg you to promise they can go home in three months — but I use great care in never over-promising just to ease temporary pain.

I make it a point to catch little off-color dishonest things immediately, even though a good positive transference may not yet have developed. The child so often, consciously and unconsciously, makes these little slips early to test the therapist's corruptibility. I try to do this before many of these events have occurred or before the child has too much tension about seeing where I stand. This has to be done in a very comfortable and friendly manner. During the war the commonest technique was to offer to get me extra ration stamps. My own response was to smile and comment that I guessed I could stand the government regulation without dying. At first the patient may be wary about lying and cheating since he knows that is the reason for coming, but often he unwittingly lets slip some matter about cheating because there is little guilt.

Twelve-year-old Jerry had been in to see me about four times and had quickly developed a strong attachment. One day as he was leaving he said, "Well, I'm off to the movies. Sure lucky I'm little and can get by at half price." I laughed and said, "It isn't the size you know, Jerry. When you are twenty-one years old, whether you are six and one-half feet tall or five feet tall, you will get to vote. The law goes by age, not by size. But, by the way, speaking of age, when you became twelve, did your Social Worker increase your allowance since at twelve, by law, you have to pay more for movies and street cars?" Jerry said, "No, should she?" I replied, "I'm sure she would have if she had thought a minute, for it's the only fair arrangement for boys and girls when they become twelve. Let's try to telephone her about it now and get her O.K. to my lending you the extra today and when she sees you Saturday, you can repay me." He was eager to call her and, of course, she agreed. A few weeks later Jerry said, "The kids think I'm a sucker to spend double for movies." He was silent a while and then said, "I crashed the gate last Saturday with the kids, but it's no go. No more of that."

I never moralize nor act too grave about the matter but comment casually and good-naturedly that I guess we had better stick fairly closely to the rules of the game. Very early, they watch you closely for any slip. I recall a young social worker, just beginning treatment of an adolescent girl who stole. The worker parked her car by a "no parking" sign. When she stepped out of her car and saw this, she commented that she would have to move the car. The girl said, "I noticed the sign and wondered what you would do." There is often a decrease in anxiety and increase in positive feeling when one of these small episodes has been handled definitely and good-naturedly. Complicated character defenses magnify the therapeutic problem greatly, but a therapist's own guilt or anxiety in dealing frankly with the child can frequently greatly intensify the child's defensiveness.

In her second hour, an adolescent girl who had been stealing and who lived in a boarding club, showed me $5.00 which she had just received from her mother and said, "I'm not going to turn this in to my Club Mother." I asked her to describe the set-up at the club, and she explained that the girls turned in their money and then asked for it when they wanted to spend it. I merely commented that it sounded similar to the arrangement I have with the bank which I found very satisfactory and safe. The girl said that she was going to spend 50c and not report it, to which I replied the rules probably irked her somewhat, but that it was a simple matter to report spending the 50c. She then asked if I would report it, and I casually answered, "Why should I, you will report it, and let's drop the subject." The next hour she asked if I had checked up with the Club Mother; I appeared rather blank for I had forgotten the incident. She reminded me and then added: "Well, I turned in the report."

But suppose the child returned and defiantly told the therapist she had not reported the fifty cents? What is the therapist to do then? My own experience has been that if I then became an accomplice, in the end the child's need to test me further would drive him to increasing excesses and I would lose the patient. Therefore, my own procedure is again casually to try to work with the patient toward making a collaborative report as well as talking over her basic uneasiness about whether I will protect her in small or large misdemeanors.

A twelve-year-old boy once said to me, "That new foster mother of mine won't work out." When I asked why, he replied, "She has no respect for me — she's a snooper. I told her I was going to the Y and that I would take the bus. When I was waiting for the bus, I saw her following in her car, so I slipped into a building and later went out and got my bus to the Y. She told me I didn't go to the Y and when I asked her how she knew, she said she had a seventh sense. She's just tricky and it won't work."

I would rather be deceived for a time than raise such doubts of my belief in the child. I have seen foster mothers give great warmth only to ruin it all by such doubting.

As soon as the patients consciously or by a slip give me facts of misdemeanors or facts come to me by other routes I take them up with the patient frankly at once. When the therapist lets little things go by, and this is observed by these patients, their anger at the seeming treachery of being severe only when a serious misdemeanor arises, is justified. This is exactly what happened at home in their past experience where they were protected in small deceptions. If the first attempts to corrupt the therapist are handled correctly, then very soon one may begin to see more superego strength in the patient. I find that handling such attempts along with warmth makes for a more rapid, confident and positive transference. I think that this has been one of the greatest obstacles and pitfalls in the therapy of these patients. Either its real meaning is overlooked at the beginning or it is mishandled. I have had to deal with several mothers with relatively good superegos in certain areas who nevertheless made attempts to corrupt me. It took only a few hours to work through these attempts with firmness. The change in their child, whom I never saw, was striking enough for others as well as the mother, to report it.

It is important when a relapse occurs that every effort be made to help redress a wrong to someone else, but at the same time to maintain the patient's confidence in his growing strength. I usually help the patient to see that some lack of security may still be leading him to thoughtless and impulsive behavior but that a large part of him would prefer to avoid this. In returning stolen goods or adjusting some wrong, I make it clear to the adolescent that we must return the article with as little fuss as possible, for I do not want the patient to suffer unfair and exaggerated criticism. It is important to help the patient with regard to correcting any injustice done to someone. No young child and usually no adolescent should have to go back to the store alone to return some stolen article or to adjust some serious infringement of a rule with the head of a boarding school. However, if the therapist is willing to help in such situations, the child might take it as suspicion on the analyst's part that the child will not carry through and this must be watched for and reassurance given. The therapist's position has to be one of helping to make amends to the injured party even though punishment may still come about in contrast to the parent's attitude. Yet the therapist should make clear to the patient that she will do everything possible to help the authorities to understand the plan of therapy. Many times the young child or adolescent will agree to do this. What if they do not agree? The therapist may feel afraid that the patient will turn against her if she exposes him. If, however, she maintains silence, she certainly has laid herself irrevocably open to blackmail by the patient and may never undo this. This course would be similar to the vicious family circle of mutual evasion and permissive protection where the parents give in to the child's promises or threats of suicide. Aichhorn writes in detail of this giving in by the parents and of his own capacity to avoid being overwhelmed by such threats. If the therapist is frightened of taking a stand here out of self-protection sooner or later she will lose the patient who will try to push her into a worse situation in his vain attempt to find someone who has the courage to set limits to his forbidden impulses. I believe that the craving to have limits set to their forbidden impulses is often why children and adolescents arrange things so they will be caught. This reason, I believe, to be more often determining than the motive of guilt.

By this time it has become clear why any questioning of the patient or any accusation without facts, or any warnings of possible impulsive acting out of antisocial nature will weaken that confidence the patient achieves from the therapist's confidence in him. If this occurs, then the adolescent for instance, feeling hurt and spiteful will react rapidly and try to enmesh the analyst quickly in the old family net of attempted corruption. Unless he is alert the therapist very soon can be pulled into an embarrassing and destructive situation by the angry child. Then the less experienced therapist is apt to be corrupted by his own anxiety and guilt and the fat may be in the fire.

I recall one gifted social worker who had been making splendid progress with a sixteen-year-old girl who had been stealing for years. No stealing had occurred for nine months. The girl was on a clothes allowance. One day the worker irritably told the child she should not have bought an article of clothing without asking her. They were walking in the suburbs and in two minutes the patient had the worker picking some flowers inside a private yard. The worker soon got hold of herself and said it was not the thing for them to do. Now the girl pitifully tried to excuse the worker, for she wanted her worker to be honest and said there were not any "no trespassing" signs. The worker, however, made it clear that she had been doing wrong even if there were not any signs forbidding trespassing. The girl agreed, "That is right — people do not have signs in their homes saying 'do not take the furniture.' " The worker also made it clear to the patient that she (the worker) had no justification for being so incensed about the articles of clothing, since the girl had her own budget for clothes. Actually the worker had for a moment succumbed to the girl's spiteful corrupting influence because the worker was guilty over her irritable outburst toward her patient.

After a therapist has put a great deal of effort into the treatment of one of these difficult patients, one can see how she might overreact to a report that the child has been stealing for months while the therapist had believed things were going well. Some therapists are so hurt and humiliated that they see themselves as "duped." One young man therapist said to me: "I feel like a soft fool taken in by that kid." We usually do not react with any such feeling of abuse in the analysis of a neurotic if our patient has a serious relapse after long and hard work with him. This male therapist had overlooked many small signs of ominous import before this major evidence shattered his self-esteem. His personal need to do so had been sensed by his patient, who had been well aware of the small ways in which he was getting by before he acted out more dangerously. This is one of the great hazards in treating such patients, namely, to avoid accusations without good evidence, but to see little off-color things when they *do* arise and to handle them immediately with frankness and without anxiety on the part of the analyst.

It is important to stress again the adolescent's reaction to feeling that his therapist has a deep respect for him. He must gradually see himself as a personality endowed with the many facets which his therapist has spread before him. A ragged eleven-year-old boy came in beaming one day. I asked him why he was so happy and he said, "I love my new teacher, she respects me." Therapists must not overlook the many small opportunities for stressing their confidence in their neurotic or delinquent patient's sense of good taste and correctness. That adult who can sincerely make an insecure adolescent feel that his ideas have significance, can hope for success in his treatment.

Handling transference and countertransference problems involved in treatment of the partially developed superego is extremely complex and relatively little explored. I have touched on only a few aspects of our experience with such cases.

In most of these cases there are also neurotic problems that must be analyzed. One should analyze only that transference neurosis which interferes with therapy until the particular defect in the superego has been strengthened. If the latter is not achieved before the therapist begins intensive analysis of the neurotic conflicts, the acting out of the mobilized deeper impulses will get out of control. While our experience in treating these cases was still limited, this mistake occurred often.

Suppose one is dealing with a sixteen-year-old girl who stole and who had too much responsibility for the care of younger siblings. To begin analyzing this girl's dependency needs before the superego had been strengthened with regard to property would lead to such a flood of stealing as to defeat any therapeutic efforts. After this patient's intense guilt about her hatred of her younger siblings had been analyzed, we could see how the mother's unconscious condoning of the stealing had made possible this less painful mode of expressing both her hatred and her own needs. When stealing is an acting out of the oedipal conflict, if one starts to analyze the conflict before the prohibition about stealing is fairly firm, the problem will certainly get out of hand as I saw happen all too often in my early IJR days.

This is the sort of "insight" I think many therapists have in mind when they begin therapy by saying "let us see why you take things," and the more they probe, the worse matters become. But it is true that these conflicts often boil up too rapidly even before the analyst made any attempt to mobilize them, so that treatment is extremely difficult if not impossible outside of a controlled environment. Treatment of the adolescent always involves his total family and environment relationship. When he is secure enough in his own self-esteem he will, himself, come to the more painful aspects of his parents' personalities which confuse and shame him. When this happens, the therapist must avoid both permissiveness and any moralistic condemnation. I usually stress that this seems to be the parent's problem, that it is not an innate defect, but that had the parent had an easier life and been more secure with his own parents, and had had a helpful counsellor outside the home, matters might have been different. I speak of my regret that one of us could not have helped long ago to make this parent's life a little easier. Although this approach makes the young patient more guilty toward the parents and more neurotic, in such cases this is better than to cut him off from the parent.

In summary I should like to state briefly the significant features in this paper:

1. I aimed to elaborate on the evidence for the etiology of conscience defects as presented by Szurek in 1942.

2. More detailed clarification of the subtleties involved in preoedipal and oedipal and latency superego formation was given with the emphasis on the child's seeing the parent's concept of himself as part of the mother with whom he is identifying.

3. Using this concept as the basis for treatment, the doubting, accusations and policing of the child's developing superego were seen as illogical to any rational therapy. I have emphasized the difference between the warning given in the analysis of a neurosis, the acting out of the transference and the effects of warning a patient about antisocial behavior involving a superego defect.

4. I have enlarged upon the therapist's role in setting the limits of permissible behavior as soon as test situations arose in the treatment. I have pointed out that his own unanalyzed guilt feelings can prevent him both from quick recognition of such situations and deftness in meeting them. It was stated that it is necessary to set definite limits regardless of threats by the patient in order to avoid repetition of the mutual blackmail and permission of the family constellation. An attempt has been made to depict a few of the details of how certain incidents in the relation-

ship with reference to the superego were handled. This represents only a limited amount of material, should not be accepted dogmatically, and represents possibly only the manner in which certain therapists might operate.

5. The cases reported where the treatment was successful were not severe maladjustments. They were patients who were able to develop some positive transference, fairly soon, whose superego defect was not widespread, and whose significant parent could cooperate by also entering treatment or by permitting the child to be removed from the home during treatment.

REFERENCES

1. Aichhorn, August. *Wayward youth.* New York: Viking Press, 1935.
2. Alexander, Franz. The neurotic character. *Int. J. Psa.* 11 (1930): 292.
3. Alexander, Franz; French, Thomas; *et al. Psychoanalytic therapy.* New York: Ronald Press, 1946.
4. Bromberg, Walter, and Rogers, Terry C. Authority in the treatment of delinquents. *Am. J. Orthopsych.* 16 (1946): 672.
5. Fenichel, Otto. *Problems of psychoanalytic technique.* New York: Psychoanalytic Quarterly, Inc., 1941. Chapter 5, p. 71, Comments on the analysis of the transference; chapter 6, pp. 80–81, Working through and some special technical problems.
6. ———. *The psychoanalytic theory of neurosis.* New York: W. W. Norton, 1945, pp. 468–69.
7. Greenacre, Phyllis. Conscience in the psychopath. *Am. J. Orthopsych.* 15 (1945): 495.
8. Hacker, Frederick J., and Geleerd, Elisabeth R. Freedom and authority in adolescence. *Am. J. Orthopsych.* 15 (1945): 621.
9. Healy, William, and Bronner, Augusta. *New light on delinquency and its treatment.* New Haven: Yale University Press, 1936.
10. Johnson, A.; Szurek, S.; and Falstein, E. Collaborative psychiatric therapy of parent-child problems. *Am. J. Orthopsych.* 12 (1942): 511. (Reprinted above, p. 26).

11. Johnson, A.; Falstein, E.; Szurek, S.; and Svendson, M. School phobia. *Am. J. Orthopsych.*, 11 (1941): 702. (Reprinted above, p. 14).
12. Orgel, Samuel Z. Identification as a socializing and therapeutic force. *Am. J. Orthopsych.* 11 (1941): 119.
13. Reich, Wilhelm. *Der triebhafte Charakter.* Wien: Internationaler Psychoanalytischer Verlag, 1925.
14. Schmideberg, Melitta. The mode of operation of psychoanalytic therapy. *Int. J. Psa.* 19 (1938): 314.
15. ———. The psychoanalysis of asocial children and adolescents. *Int. J. Psa.* 16 (1935): 22.
16. ———. The treatment of psychopaths and borderline patients. *Int. J. Psychotherapy.* 1 (1947): 45.
17. Szurek, Stanislaus. Genesis of psychopathic personality trends. *Psychiatry* 5: (1942): 1.

11

THE GENESIS OF ANTISOCIAL ACTING OUT IN CHILDREN AND ADULTS

With Stanislaus Szurek, M.D.

> In 1952 Dr. Johnson and Dr. Szurek published a summary article for the adult psychiatry literature in *The Psychoanalytic Quarterly*, vol. 21, no. 3. To provide elaboration on the first paper included in this section, "Sanctions for Superego Lacunae of Adolescents," and at the same time to avoid repetition, the following paragraphs have been extracted from that article.

PARENTAL ATTITUDES

WHAT constitutes "love" and "warmth" needs definition. If these include *rationalization* by a parent of guilt about his own sadomasochistic impulses, and appear as "gentleness" or "indulgence," the child experiences them as condoning, as acceptance of his impulse. Firmness with respect to the *form* of expression of the child's egocentric or revengeful impulse is to be distinguished from sadistic suppression. Firmness bespeaks a parent who has learned how to gratify all his essential egocentric impulses *nondestructively* to himself and to others; such firmness may be devoid of masochistic or sadistic coloring and distortion. The stable parent has learned how his own interests may either eventually be gratified in some measure, or how to choose which

---

Reprinted with permission from *Psychoanalytic Quarterly* 21 (1952): 323–43.

interest is pre-eminent, while clearly recognizing and accepting the consequences of his choice. He may even have learned how all of his major goals may be reached in some creative course of action. He may have the capacity to experiment before committing all his energies to any goal, and continue flexibly to search out the way to satisfaction of his major needs and wishes.

Such parental attitudes provide a child with various experiences encouraging the child in turn to anticipate: (1) that his basic impulses are gratifiable, at least eventually; (2) that his disappointment, rage or revengefulness at delays to his satisfactions are understood and accepted as natural reactions, but that their *form* of expression may invite retaliation from others; and (3) that the parent will patiently respect such reactive feelings, prolonged though they may be. In short, there are, most generally, ways of obtaining sensual and other satisfactions at appropriate times and places, with appropriate people. Pertinent and amplified discussions of the concepts of "love," "guilt" and "restitution" have been presented elsewhere by one of us (Johnson [1]).

SELECTION OF THE SCAPEGOAT

The subtle manner in which one child was unconsciously selected from several children as the scapegoat to act out for the parent was striking. Analytic study of the significant parent showed unmistakably the unique significance of this child to the parent, and the tragic pattern of parent and child moving inexorably in a fatal march of events, usually unconsciously. A profound sympathy was evoked for these consciously well-intentioned parents, whose unconscious needs were unwittingly inviting disaster upon the family.

A striking illustration of "scapegoat selection" occurred in several families whose children included an adopted child. The common pattern was a parental acting out through the adopted child, which conveniently provided the rationalization of inheritance to account for the delinquency.

In other instances, parental guilt, born of unconscious hostility toward one child, made firmness and fair-dealing difficult. Parental vacillations appeared to be critical factors in the genesis of specific superego lacunae.

The sources of such hostility of the parent are varied. The child may have become unconsciously a rival for the indulgence of the other parent. The child may represent a parent's sibling with whom the parent has unresolved sibling rivalry. The child may be born or reared at times of high tension between parents. Numerous other factors and combinations of factors operate.

Another illustration was seen in the adopted adolescent son of the head cashier in a large manufacturing concern. The son was brought for treatment because of stealing. The thefts were revealed when the mother surreptitiously secured, actually stole, the key to the boy's diary and discovered a well-ordered bookkeeping system of amounts extracted from guests' purses balanced against his own expenditures. The mother's duplicity was exceeded by the father's who, scrupulously honest in business, had for two summers confiscated checks the boy received in payment for employment by the father's firm. To the boy, such behavior was not only an outrage, but an obvious sanction for his own predatory behavior.

Many have observed that children and adults with severe compulsive neurotic symptoms, such as intensive handwashing, may also steal repeatedly. Such stealing, or the cleptomania of adults, again denotes the existence of one defect in the superego through which the patient may act out tension. Detailed study of such stealing in our adult patients with a compulsive neurosis shows clearly whence this permission stemmed.

Perhaps the concepts in this section may best be epitomized by the words of a nine-year-old girl who asked the therapist, "When is my mother going to do her own stealing?"

SEXUAL ABERRATIONS

Sexual aberrations also have become more understandable to us when viewed in the light of the concepts described. In several cases of long-standing overt homosexuality, search has revealed an unwitting fostering of some aberration by one of the parents. If this be true of patients in conflict and seeking treatment, one can but conjecture how great is the superego defect in cases in which the overt homosexuality arouses little or no conflict and no desire for treatment.

Little boys and girls in the œdipal or earlier stages may insist on being of the opposite sex and wearing the clothes of the opposite sex. Detailed collaborative therapy reveals a fostering influence by one parent, such as that of the mother who gave her six-year-old boy all her cast-off clothes. Interestingly, the boy's desire to be a girl dated from the birth of a favored little sister three years earlier.

A young man of great professional talents had been an overt homosexual for several years, since the age of eighteen, when his mother told him that his father was not her husband. The mother's hostile motivation was clear. The youth's unconscious rage was the immediate potent determination of his homosexual turning to men as a protection against murdering a woman. The precipitating event occurred in a confused family setting, characterized by distorted adjustments and undue maternal permissiveness since our patient had been a child. His rage at rejection by his real father was rapidly erotized.

We have recently treated two men whose mothers were grossly

maladjusted maritally and extravagantly seductive with their sons. The mother of one, twenty years old, said to him when his father was dying, "Jim, I'm madly in love with you; you are so handsome." This was but the culmination of years of varying degrees of seduction. The major factor in the patient's passive homosexuality had been the protection afforded by his father against the patient's murdering his mother, even transcending in importance the factor of fear of the father, tremendous as it was. This young man refrained from overt homosexuality only with a great struggle, and came to analysis very disturbed.

A colleague (2) treated a homosexual young man whose mother had the adolescent son escort her clandestine lovers home, "to make things look better." The boy, aware of everything, erotized his rage toward these men, spiting his mother as well.

The unconscious sanctions of parents and their seductions of sons and daughters into homosexuality are revealed by their guilty, anxious, angry interrogations into the children's early conscious or unconscious homosexual play and explorations. Thereby may be stubbornly fixed what otherwise might have been a transient stage of normal growth. The heterosexual or homosexual acting out of a child is thus parentally guided.

A depressed, forty-two-year-old woman came to consultation complaining primarily of the sadistic promiscuity of her twenty-year-old son. Since his adolescence, the mother had intently absorbed the minutest details of his accounts of intimacies with girls. The patient's husband was a beaten and submissive man. The sources of her ambivalent seductiveness with her son were easily adduced. Her own father was a Don Juan. From her early adolescence he came to her bedroom nightly to fondle her and even made attempts to enter her bed. At the first such instance, the patient sought protection from her mother. But the mother did not dare reproach the father, "lest he kill her." From the father, to the patient, to her son, sanctions of the forbidden are evident in three generations. The son, refusing treatment, will provide still another generation toward the biblical ten.

Among adolescents, whose parents we have also been able to study, we have seen no exhibitionism or voyeurism that has not revealed indubitably from which parent the necessary sanction stemmed. Admittedly, the opportunity to study such parents is limited; they refuse or soon discontinue treatment. Undoubtedly, multiply determined neurotic conflicts contribute to exhibitionism and voyeurism. We have been concerned here only with the immediate mechanism which precipitates acting out.

SANCTIONS FOR ACTING OUT

The fantasies, hopes and fears expressed by parents regarding some behavior of a child is a common and powerful influence toward healthy or maladapted living. Horrified parental anxiety over some behavior is expressed to the child: "You are beyond me; I can't handle you any more; if this doesn't stop, you will end in the reform school." Or, "You are just like your uncle; he came to a bad end." Parental fantasy guides the child's course of action.

Mothers who have seriously erred premaritally frequently betray acute anxiety regarding their daughters' behavior on dates. Accusations, detailed questioning and dire warnings, rather than preventing undesirable behavior, constitute unwitting permissions. The overly anxious mother with poorly integrated promiscuous impulses or reaction-formations against sex may function similarly, even though she may never have acted out. The father also may contribute. Exasperating rigidity about dating, with a casual provocative suggestion, often upsets the balance. Only close collaboration between the two therapists of the parent and the child can reveal the unmistakable mutual provocation.

One mother, early in analysis, glossed over an account of sexual acting out as a girl, in which there had been no conscious fear of pregnancy. A year later in her analysis, anxiety developed lest her young daughter "may go with a fast crowd, drink and get into trouble. All adolescent girls do too much sexual playing. One eggs on the other. I will worry about her getting pregnant. A girl cheapens herself. It's degrading. I don't know how to warn her but I must." The mother's poorly integrated masochistic impulses, partially repressed, were projected to the child. Not consciously fearful of pregnancy herself, she nevertheless feared her child's being cheapened and becoming pregnant. Her fantasies implied both destructiveness to the child as well as vicarious gratification for her own repressed impulses. Eventually, it was revealed that the patient's stepmother, as glamorous as she was unstable, frequently discussed sex, and suggested, "You will probably be more highly sexed than your stepsister — *and have more trouble!*" The stepmother was subsequently entranced with lurid accounts of the patient's dates. The patient's analysis fortunately progressed, so that the heritage from the stepmother was not transmitted to the daughter, whose dates no longer aroused undue anxiety.

THE ROLE OF GUILT

Guilt, and a need for punishment, have been advanced by Alexander (3) and others as a major etiological determinant of antisocial acting out, citing as evidence the frequency with which such acts are rigged to facilitate detection. While examples are numerous, our experience has not borne out this concept of etiology. It is our impression that the desire to be caught is a groping for protection against committing even worse offenses which might bring down extreme retaliation, even destruction. The sequence does not appear to be guilt causing acting out so as to be caught, which assuages guilt. Rather, it is unwitting parental prompting which caused acting out, with a fostering of detection aimed at checking more serious future acting out with major dreaded penalties.

The fear displayed by an apprehended delinquent child only simulates the genuine anxiety of an internalized conscience — neurotic guilt. On the contrary, we have found that such fear frequently stems from anticipated punishment, with no guilt coloring.

Failure to appreciate the distinction by the analyst impressed with the apparent guilt of the offender may even foster further offenses by an immediate search for sources of unconscious guilt. There is unconscious guilt in abundance in the cases under discussion, as in all neurotic personalities. A tide of welling hostility against a young sibling may be effectively dammed by defenses. A rent in those defenses, created by unconscious parental permissiveness for a specific form of acting out, may provide an outlet for the emotional energy. Thus forbidden impulses derived from a variety of neurotic conflicts may find expression in stealing, arson, truancy or worse, depending upon the nature of the sanctions. Very commonly, great guilt about sex is acted out in stealing, given appropriate parental permission.

These concepts indicate the error of probing for hidden guilt as the first approach to delinquents. With the rent in the defenses unsealed, the immediate result may be an increased impetus to act out with even greater seriousness through the permitted, though antisocial, channel. The first therapeutic efforts should be directed toward repairing the superego lacuna. In an adolescent who has great guilt about hostility toward siblings, and who unconsciously feels permitted to steal, unless the superego defect of stealing has been adequately managed, it is dangerous to mobilize the neurotic conflict with siblings, for the acting out may then increase. Only later is it safe to proceed with a thorough analysis.

THE "CAUSE" OF ACTING OUT

Science can seldom ascribe any phenomenon to a single cause. Our goal has been to emphasize a major cause of antisocial behavior while still recognizing that the antisocial child reared in a family is the product of a multiplicity of variables of mixed quality and quantity.

Scientific proof of causation is not satisfied by demonstrating the invariable presence of the suspected cause (unwitting parental permissiveness) whenever the effect (antisocial behavior of children) is observed. It must also be demonstrated that the suspected cause does not occur unless the effect is also seen. This, too, has been our experience. Parental permissions have never been revealed without ultimate antisocial behavior in at least one "scapegoat" child. The superego lacuna of the child has always been traceable to a specific parental permission. Our thesis is not *post hoc ergo propter hoc*. The enmeshing interplay of parent and child in the affected area bespeaks more than a fortuitous time sequence.

SUMMARY AND CONCLUSIONS

In this paper the authors have assimilated material from their experience and publications since 1942, dealing with the etiology of acting out antisocially. The observations apply equally to the young "delinquent" or the "psychopathic personality" of later years, who is etiologically a delinquent grown older. By means of collaborative therapy of children and parents the authors have observed that the parents may unwittingly seduce the child into acting out the parents' own poorly integrated forbidden impulses, thereby achieving vicarious gratification. A specific superego defect in the child is seen as a duplication of a similar distortion in the organization of a parent's own personality. The outcome is doubly destructive toward the child's and the parent's ego organization, unless adequate therapy of both is provided.

REFERENCES

1. Johnson, Adelaide M. Some etiological aspects of repression, guilt and hostility. *Psychoanalytic Quarterly* 20 (1951): 511–27. (Reprinted below, p. 333).
2. Kolb, L. C. Personal communication to the authors.
3. Alexander, Franz; French, Thomas M.; *et al. Psychoanalytic therapy: principles and application.* New York: Ronald Press. 1946.

12

PARENTAL PERMISSIVENESS AND FOSTERING IN CHILD REARING AND THEIR RELATIONSHIP TO JUVENILE DELINQUENCY

With Edmund C. Burke, M.D.

> The following paper was written with a Mayo Clinic pediatrician for presentation at a general meeting of the Mayo Clinic staff and for subsequent dissemination to the medical profession in the "Proceedings." Dr. Johnson hoped that through education of professionals, perhaps there might be some preventive forces mobilized. In short, this represents an attempt at preventive psychiatry.

RECENTLY pediatricians, child psychiatrists and others engaged in family counseling have become aware of the growing number of parents seeking advice in matters of family discipline. Mothers exclaim that they are unable to cope with a child's misbehavior, saying, "I can't do a thing with him." Perhaps a child has become a problem in management at home or at school. Vandalism, truancy or theft may have occurred, and parents seem at a complete loss as to how to cope with the problem.

Oftentimes a parent may say, "I never could do a thing with

Reprinted with permission from *Proceedings of the Staff Meetings of the Mayo Clinic* 30 (1955): 557–65.

him; he isn't like my other children at all." Some mothers, having been confused by the flood of conflicting opinion on child management, may indicate that they have allowed Johnny to do pretty much as he pleased, lest he become frustrated and neurotic. "After all," the mother says, "all the books say I shouldn't spank him."

Since ours is a society which has definite prohibitions against transgressing the rights of others, the child must be acquainted early in life with the rules of living. The primary unit of society is the family; hence, all such learning should begin there.

Lack of spanking or punishment is not the explanation for emergence of delinquency. Rather, the explanation lies in the deep-seated attitudes and unconscious feelings of the parents toward a child's actions. Delinquency is a problem as old as society itself. In all probability the press, radio and television have magnified and distorted its proportionate growth. For centuries spokesmen have deplored the increases in delinquent behavior. It is true that antisocial behavior among children is increasing moderately, but at little, if any, greater rate than misbehavior in the adult population. Although the goal in counseling parents is to stem the increase of juvenile misbehavior, we are among those adults who do *not* feel that adolescence is a volatile age when anything can happen just because of that age. In fact, we subscribe to the opinion that adolescence is a very conservative age unless misguided adults interfere with or disrupt a fine balance. One of us (Johnson) (1) has written extensively elsewhere of adolescent conservatism.

Our thesis is that a large share of individual antisocial behavior today stems from an unwitting sanction or unconscious encouragement of such antisocial behavior by one or both parents, so that the parent achieves vicarious gratification of his own poorly integrated forbidden impulses. The delinquencies under consideration are those arising in *apparently normal families of good reputation* unassociated with the influence of sociologic gangs.

Let us reemphasize that fact of unconscious sanctioning and fostering by parents. Consciously, most parents are deeply concerned with the child's misguided behavior, but have no idea that he or she, the parent, is actually promoting it. How could this be? We must lay some basic groundwork of understanding before we proceed further with our thesis. In order to do this, we shall quote frequently from the report made in 1954 by Szurek and one of us (Johnson). (2)

THE CONSCIENCE

A child's conscience is not inherited ready-made but is developed, especially during the first 6 years of life, through identification in great detail with the total behavior of parents. To an equal extent, conscience develops from the parents' conscious and unconscious image of the child and from their concepts of and hopes for a child. Until recently, pathologic aspects of the conscience were considered only in terms of its being too punishing to the patient. For years, any antisocial behavior was explained in terms of a patient's being excessively guilty about conflicts or being driven by uncontrollable, instinctive drives. The attitude of many parents has been to avoid drastic repression of the child, lest he become neurotic or behave in an antisocial manner. Such reasoning has been a grave error. In neurosis, the conscience has been developed so that it is too severe and rigid, but this is not an adequate explanation for antisocial behavior.

Psychiatrists, as well as parents, have erred in assuming that prohibitions in all forms lead to too much guilt and thus neurosis. Prohibitions in themselves do not lead to unhealthy guilt; rather, they are an important aspect of a child's security. So far as the prevention of neurosis is concerned, the prohibition of antisocial activity merely requires the presence of a parent sufficiently mature to manage the resentment expressed by the child over the limit-setting that society demands.

It has become increasingly clear that many parents, particularly those with poorly integrated impulses, have become uneasy about setting limits, even concerning matters which are specifically destructive to society, such as stealing, sexuality or even murderous intent. Yet it is evident that certain specific acts, such as stealing, setting fires, murder and sexual destructiveness, cannot be tolerated in our society. They must be prohibited completely and definitely. An act of specific antisocial behavior should arouse guilt in everyone, but the guilt alone is not unhealthy.

Prohibitions against antisocial activity may provoke anger in a child, but such a child is not likely to become neurotic if he can express his anger in a legitimate way. In psychiatric therapy sessions this child may angrily hammer nails into a board or knock down his castle of blocks. His rage is thereby expressed, yet his actions have not been antisocial.

In our work with children and parents, we have observed that problems arising as a consequence of a strict conscience usually are easier to manage than is delinquency emerging as a result of a laxity or defect of conscience.

THE "BLACK SHEEP"

The reader now immediately asks, "How do you explain that one child may steal, whereas all the other children in the family are completely honest? They all have the same parents." Indeed, they have the same set of parents, but parental attitudes differ toward each child, depending on multiple influences in the parents' own pasts. Some variables are the sex of the child, position of the girl or boy in the list of children, feelings of the parent toward certain of his or her brothers, sisters or parents, and feelings in the marriage at the time of each pregnancy. The tragic fact remains that one child is selected unconsciously as the victim or "black sheep" to live out the loophole in the parents' own conscience with their unconscious drives toward antisocial behavior.

It may be that there is only one victim-child in a family. Again, we have observed that one child steals, another becomes truant and a third engages in very destructive behavior. Careful study elaborates how each child is selected to live out a particular need in one or both parents. Observations in such families become highly complex patterns of multiple formulas determined by the parents' pathologic needs from their own past experiences.

An all too common example is the 12-year-old who lies continuously. How this comes about is no longer difficult to decipher. Every little child must learn what truth is — this requires a kindly, very consistent training. A mother recently said of her 12-year-old son, Mike, "He has always been a liar — the truth is not in him — beatings do no good. I tell his father that that child was born a liar like his father's brother. I try to shame him, but it does not work. Since he was 4 years old I have shamed him and told him he was not like his brothers, and I warned him that I did not know what would become of him."

This mother could easily see that her other children needed training in what constitutes the truth, but in the case of Mike she assumed, when he was 4 years old, that he could not be trained like her other children. Careful study of the mother revealed that from his birth the mother had identified Mike with his father's brother, whom she thoroughly disliked, as an "unreliable liar and braggart." This mother had not wanted the child when she knew she was pregnant, being at that time quite unhappy in her marriage.

Here we observe a mother, hostile and unhappy, selecting a victim, Mike. The choice of misbehavior was *lying*, fostered by frequent references to unreliable Uncle George and statements to Mike that the mother had no confidence in her ability to engender respect for the truth in Mike. The child then sees that his mother's image of him for the future is one of falseness and unreliability.

The great educator of 300 years ago, John Locke, was keenly aware that parents get much gratification from their children's successes. He also recognized that an antisocial child was reared by inherently antisocial parents whom the child was imitating. During the years of research, which it took some of us to see how a child becomes delinquent, we were unaware of Locke's pungent observations. The mystery was gradually unravelled scientifically through studying the parents as carefully as the child. It became unmistakably clear that parents not only enjoy children's successes, but also derive unconscious gratification from children's failures, such as failure to go along with society's mores. Hostile toward a particular child, the parents foster antisocial behavior in keeping with their own unconscious impulses toward similar misbehavior.

In time, investigators were able to see precisely how parental impulses toward a form of an antisocial act are communicated to the child. These modes of communication of society's forbidden activities, consciously approved by the parents, are well known by investigators today.

If, within themselves, parents are confused about impulses, these parents are never straightforward with a particular child. Such parents vacillate, evade, befog issues and thoroughly confuse the child. The interested reader will wish examples of how this behavior shows itself. First, one detects in the parent two opposing forces operating; namely, prohibition on the one hand, and in the next breath, unconscious permission. Examples of these transactions are multiple and, when looked for, easily discernible. Although we have described some of these operations before, (2) they cannot be repeated too often.

1. We are all familiar with the parent who tells the child it is wrong to steal, but who covers up for the child when he does commit a theft. The child immediately learns the significance of this maneuver. Tommy takes 50 cents from his father's dresser. When the father tells Tommy that the money must be returned, the mother assures the father that she spent the money. Children have told us recurrently of this cover-up technic. Such a parent does the same thing with regard to thefts outside the home; namely, covering up and consoling herself with the thought that eventually Tommy will outgrow his thieving propensities.

2. Children observe at an early age little dishonesties in the parents with regard to short-changing tradesmen. The approving smile of smugness, when such a deception has been successful, conveys to the child the impression that honesty can be short-circuited in favor of opportunism.

3. Integrity with regard to the truth and money should hold in every relationship. It is no more approved to steal from mother than from the lady next door. Recently, a mother said to her 10-year-old daughter, "If you *had* to steal, why couldn't you keep it within the family?" It is easy to see the hedging and flimsy prohibition in such a remark. Stealing under all circumstances should be forbidden.

4. Entering movies or riding buses at rates based on other than one's true age cannot be condoned. Yet, we often encounter parents' encouraging undersized 12-year-old George to pay only half-rate at the movie.

5. Whenever parents allow themselves to write illicit excuses for Mary's absence from school, such parents have truly begun a train of untenable situations for themselves. "If they did it once, why can't they do it again?" Temper tantrums often add force to the child's demands. In many such cases we have treated only the parents. These are the same parents who make and break promises lightly. The child soon learns that at home "one's word" is of shallow significance.

6. Parents tell us of Johnny's destructive behavior at school with an interested smile, obviously achieving some delight from such vandalistic behavior. A child sees the parents' interested and eager smiles as they extract details of some misadventure on the child's part. Since the parents have betrayed such vicarious gratification through the eager smile, the punishment at the end of the discussion is of little value. The child will repeat his misdemeanor whether it is vandalism, truancy, or stealing, in order to observe his parents' smiling approval. The interested smile is also one of the common modes of conveying unconscious, parentally approved sanction for sexual acting-out, as will be discussed more fully later.

7. Some parents, in their own unconscious vacillations about integrity, are all too inclined to accept flimsy stories about where Peter found the dollar or the new trinket. The child observes the conflicting play of prohibition and permission on the parents' face, and the train of tragic events begins.

8. In every family investigated for antisocial behavior, be it stealing, truancy, vandalism or fire-setting, easily detected is the hypertrophied degree of deception practiced in the families. "Do this, but don't tell so and so." Tricks and ruses are employed to achieve desired ends by adults and children. Such tricks are employed frequently to get the child to the psychiatric clinic, in spite of the pediatrician's advice of the direct approach.

It is not difficult to detect pathologic features in the foregoing illustrations. What, however, is the situation in the more normal and healthy home? Here we observe that certain prohibitions and taboos are absolute, with no alternatives. Furthermore, these prohibitions are enforced in a calm, earnest atmosphere. There is no call for parental hostility in this training atmosphere. The parent knows that this loved child will, with training, become a thoroughly reliable child, and has as the only image for the future a child who will become a fine person. Such a normal parent, adhering consistently to training, does *not* let little things go by, and if such a parent discovers that her wishes have been circumvented, she takes it up with the child at once. In the early years of training, when the little one appears with a toy belonging to another, the mother immediately and calmly goes with the child to return the property to the rightful owner. The mother does not conclude that this child will be a thief, but rather, knows that careful training is necessary at all points to instill a regard for ownership in the child.

The well-adjusted parents have an equal respect for the child's property, and would not open the child's mail without permission or consider reading a child's diary unless so requested. Parents likewise do not open a child's purse without permission. A rigid setting of limits and taboos applies to old and young alike. This ensures that the young have a teacher who deserves to be copied in all facets of social behavior.

PERMISSIVENESS AND SEXUALITY

Freud was the first investigator to recognize the curiosity of little children with regard to nature, birth, growth and development. He recognized the child's interest and concern with sexual differences, and observed the jealousy with which the child competes with parents for each other. He advocated that all children's questions be answered simply and without evasions, but advised against going beyond the child's single question for that time. Freud felt that evasions and anxiety in parents in the face of children's biologic curiosity are unfortunate, and he hoped to dilute the atmosphere of such tension. He was a very conventional and moderate person who never condoned the exhibitionistic family nudities in some of the so-called progressive homes today. Freud knew such spurious frankness only increases children's tension.

In the atmosphere today of misguided "modern frankness," unstable parents go far beyond the arena of good sense in their compulsive drive to make sex and bathroom functions an open book. The children sense the parents' tension, eagerness and lack of tranquility in this setting, and the child's attention becomes far too fixated for healthy emotional development. Any child of 5 or 6 begins to give little indications of a wish for privacy. Too often these wishes are overridden by the parents, and finally the child complies with the atmosphere about him. Children go through phases of not wanting to be hugged too closely, but this desire also is often disregarded. In such supercharged environments the children achieve no real tranquility in their emotional adjustment to father and mother.

Under the guise of motherliness and fatherliness, children far too old for such actions are in the bathroom with parents of the opposite sex, and are taken to bed, even into their adolescence, with inappropriate embracing and kissing. Only parents poorly adjusted in their own marriage have such a need for pathologic closeness with the child. The child cannot defend himself successfully against these parental emotional demands, and the child unconsciously and angrily complies.

It is no longer any mystery to some of us as to how the child's emotional life becomes distorted into perversions and sadistic sexual practices. These are all unwittingly cultivated in the atmosphere briefly elaborated above. No son can sleep with his mother, while father sleeps in another room, and hope to develop into anything but a highly hostile, destructive person sexually. In those families in which we have the opportunity of studying parents as well as the delinquent child, there is no longer any mystery about the etiologic development of the personality capable of committing a sexual crime. Less pathologic is the condition of those children who grow up and marry, but who can never love the spouse. Unconscious hate ruins the marriage, all stemming from a childhood of being overly stimulated emotionally by a parent. Undue embracing and closeness physically with a parent through a child's adolescence only arouse great quantities of unconscious hatred. This hostility carries over into a later marriage.

In the sexual area, delinquencies are largely unconsciously generated and fostered in the home. Undue interest and smiling eagerness, suspicious questions or dire warnings obstruct a child's identification with a parent tranquil about sex. No lessons can be taught an adolescent when avid parental interest is evinced over sexual misbehavior. Punishment is then of no validity or use. Children behave sexually in accordance with the parents' conscious and unconscious image of the child.

THE PROSPECTIVE

We are proposing, then, that the absolute cultural prohibitions still hold and must be rigidly inculcated at home, where the first 6 or 7 years of life and training are utterly basic to development of character. Absolute rigidity about the taboo against murder, arson, theft and sexual destructiveness prevents individual delinquency in the nongang sociologic areas. Such rigid prohibitions usually do not lead to neurosis. Other factors come into play to cause neurosis. If anger is not permitted legitimate outlet, such as verbalization, it is repressed, and emotional conflict and neurosis could ensue. A child need not be prevented from voicing his resentment of prohibitions, but the cultural prohibitions of our society must stand. Treatment of a child who is indulging in antisocial behavior in the home and is subject to parental sanction and influence involves treatment of the parents as intensively as, or more intensively than, treatment of the child. This is a long and very expensive procedure, but the best so far known.

Since parental sanction of antisocial behavior usually is unconscious, it is legitimate to question whether widespread lay knowledge of the role of parents in delinquency promises to limit the phenomenon. The mischief perpetrated by the poorly integrated parents of "respectable status" might well be curbed if it were generally conceded that delinquent behavior is not usually ascribed to heredity, bad companions, poor schools or divorce. The poorly inhibited antisocial impulses of adults then may not so readily find expression in the encouragement of scapegoats. Perhaps such adults might become neurotic, evidencing emotional conflicts in which conscience has prohibited direct expression of an urge to antisocial action. Troublesome as such neuroses may be, in the form of phobias, compulsions, conversions, or a hundred other neurotic expressions, they are preferable to antisocial behavior, with its threat of perpetuation through generations. In most instances, a neurosis, with a strong conscience, is more amenable to therapy than delinquency in which the conscience is too weak. The psychiatric therapist affixes no blame, but prefers to interpose a degree of understanding that would divert conflicts of parents toward individual neuroses rather than toward vicarious gratifications through the misbehavior of children. (2)

SUMMARY

Factors responsible for antisocial behavior and delinquency in families of "respectable status" have been presented. A multiplicity of variables enters into the family rearing of any child, but the specific stimulus for a child's antisocial behavior is the unconscious, or less often conscious, sanction from a parent. This specific behavior of the child is causally related to a specific defect in the parent's own conscience in this aspect of behavior. It is advocated that knowledge of such origins of delinquency be made widespread with the aim of erecting parental conscience barriers against the fostering of vicarious misbehavior, since such behavior may be transmitted from generation to generation through interpersonal living. Individual neuroses that might result, even though severe, are more amenable to treatment than is the delinquency complex.

REFERENCES

1. Ross, Helen, and Johnson, Adelaide M. Psychiatric interpretation of the growth process: part 2, latency and adolescence. *J. Social Casework* 30 (1946): 148–54.
2. Johnson, Adelaide M., and Szurek, S. A. Etiology of antisocial behavior in delinquents and psychopaths. *JAMA* 154 (1954): 814–17.

13

PARENTAL INFLUENCE IN UNUSUAL SEXUAL BEHAVIOR IN CHILDREN

With Edward M. Litin, M.D., and Mary E. Giffin, M.D.

> The following paper was written collaboratively with
> Drs. Litin and Giffin, colleagues who worked with Dr. Johnson
> when she directed the Child Psychiatry Unit at the
> Mayo Clinic.
> The section of the paper on therapy has been deleted
> in the interest of conserving space.

INTRODUCTION

OUR research suggests that unusual sexual behavior evolves by adaptation of the ego to subtle attitudes within the family, a process that distorts the instinctual life of the child. Perverse sexual acting out and many unusual heterosexual patterns result from unconscious permission and subtle coercion by adults. The parental influences operate reciprocally with the needs of the child, so that eventually each participant stimulates the other.

Parents unwittingly seduce these children into the expression of the parents' own forbidden impulses, thus affording the parent unconscious vicarious gratification. This gratification usually is

Reprinted with permission from *Psychoanalytic Quarterly* 25 (1956): 37–55.

associated with revenge, displaced from old insults. A specific defect of the superego in the child duplicates a defect in the superego of the parent.

Other studies (6) showed that fixations in children occur for two major reasons: because some specific stimulus frightens the child and inhibits growth or causes regression; or because parental gratification from the child's behavior perpetuates the behavior. Occasionally, of course, a fixation may result from a dramatic incident such as sudden death of the mother.

Many patients have strong latent homosexual, exhibitionistic, and transvestite trends but do not act out these impulses, just as many neurotic persons show latent tendencies to set fires, steal, or destroy, yet never carry out such fantasies. Precise analyses of these latent tendencies have been graphically described by many authors since Freud's early work. But what gives the impetus to overt expression? In his paper, "Confusion of Tongues Between the Adult and the Child," Ferenczi (2) sensitively described the child's awareness of parental ambivalence. Of a child subjected to adult seduction he wrote:

> The most important change, produced in the mind of the child by the anxiety-fear-ridden identification with the adult partner, is *the introjection of the guilt feelings of the adult* which makes hitherto harmless play appear as a punishable offense. When the child recovers from such an attack, it feels enormously confused, in fact, split — innocent and culpable at the same time — and its confidence in the testimony of its own senses is broken. Moreover, the harsh behavior of the adult partner, tormented and made angry by his remorse, renders the child still more conscious of its own guilt and still more ashamed.

Such a child has no choice but to introject the confusion, guilt, fear of detection, anxiety, hostility *and sanction* which it has just observed in the parents.

DISCUSSION

When it is possible to study parents and child with sufficient accuracy, a tight symbiosis is found, a process that is serving the needs of both. From study of this symbiosis, we have learned the following facts about unusual sexual behavior in children.

1. The child has suffered during its development the confusion and dissatisfaction that result from its parents' poorly integrated marriage.

2. One parent has been consciously or unconsciously seducing the child; usually the other parent has unwittingly condoned the seduction.

3. The seduction may or may not be followed by genital frustration.

4. Concomitantly, the parent subtly defines a pattern of unusual sexual behavior. This behavior may be genital, or it may be pregenital and perverse. The child regards it as partially condoned and acceptable and therefore carries out the act. It may feel very little guilt and shame.

"Seduction" refers to a pathological parental tempting of the child. Unconsciously, in the guise of tenderness, or consciously by jostling passion, the parent imposes upon the *young* child an adult form of ambivalent sexuality completely inappropriate to the child's age. To the *adolescent*, such passion and genitality may be more appropriate physiologically, but the psychological response stimulated by it cannot be integrated with the child's ego. Collaborative therapy also makes it possible to answer the following questions.

1. Why is one particular child chosen for the parental sanction out of all the children in a family?

2. Why is a specific kind of sexual behavior permitted to the child, and what in the parents' histories and married life permits it?

3. How is the parent's need for this kind of unconscious gratification communicated to the child? How is tacit permission granted either for regression to a pregenitally disguised, perverse response, or for hostile, antisocial sexuality?

French (3) corroborates our observations; he has observed a comparable process in cases of perversion in adults. Similar observations have been made on adult homosexuals by Kolb and Johnson (7).

We are chiefly concerned in this study with the adaptive reactions of the ego. We do not deny the importance of the unfolding instinctual phenomena or of the constitutional endowment. We are attempting to delineate the effects of personal relationships upon the basic instincts in the course of adaptation of the ego.

The process of unconscious communication between parent and child is the clue to understanding. The parent's continuous revelation of his ambivalence perpetuates the child's perverse or antisocial behavior. If he knows how, the therapist can learn the cause of the child's trouble and can discover how to begin therapy; he must find out the exact words and specific activities by which the parent encourages the child's deviation. The parent's words to the child are by no means the only influence the parent uses; his ideas, hopes, interests, fears, and frustration are also perceived by the child in the parent's gestures, intonations, bodily movements, provocative smiles, and manipulations of events.

Time and again "double talk" instead of a firm direct statement is employed by the parent. The comment of the mother of a fourteen-year-old transvestite is typical. This boy enjoyed smelling and wearing his mother's discarded underwear. When this became obvious to her, she said, "For heaven's sake, if you must do that, at least take some of my clean things." The father also condoned the behavior. When the boy was eight he appeared before his father wearing some of his mother's discarded clothes and her lipstick and earrings. The father was at first shocked, but then said, "Teddy, you would have made a pretty girl. It's a shame."

Frequently the parent has encouraged the child's deviation by his behavior rather than by words. An adolescent boy in difficulty because of his sexual activity remembered how his very attractive mother repeatedly paraded nude before him. He recalled with rage her provocative smile when he became embarrassed by his erections in her presence.

Under the guise of being "modern" and "hiding nothing from the child," many ambivalent parents show little or no modesty with respect to their children, go about the house in all degrees of nudity, sleep and bathe with the child, allow no privacy in the toilet, play with a two-year-old's genitals, permit close physical examinations, and disregard the child's feeble attempts to have privacy. After a time, the child for its own good reasons complies with its parent's wishes; thus child and parent stimulate each other. In such a peculiarly permissive family, talking about sex is often rigidly prohibited. Or far too much discussion of sex may occur, producing an unconscious gratification of parents and child.

The mother's behavior during the child's pregenital and early genital period is especially important. At these times the guileless, polymorphous sexual interests of the child may be given a particular direction by the nature of the mother's conflicts. In the pregenital period the mother's problems are the greater determinants; the father's influence is stronger during the oedipal and later periods. This may be an important cause of the greater incidence of certain types of perversion among boys. Equal attention must be paid to the problems of mother and father, since in some cases the father is the major factor.

CLINICAL DATA

The first four cases illustrate hostile sexual acting out by adolescents.

Case 1

An obese twelve-year-old boy was brought for consultation by his mother because of convulsive seizures for the past year. These seizures began during a period when the patient was daily witnessing vicious charges and countercharges between his parents; the mother often screamed that she would kill the father and his women. Medical examination of the boy pointed to the hysterical nature of the seizures, as did the remarks of the mother. She was beginning to fear that the boy might hurt her. "For the past six months," she said, "he's been getting awful sexy. When I lay with him in bed he gets an erection. He's crazy about women and I have to watch him more and more. . . . Some day he'll hurt some woman; maybe kill someone."

This mother still bathed her son and maintained no privacy in bathroom or bedroom. Her fantasy of the boy's future was shown by her further comments, "Doctor, I want to have a book for him to read about sexual disease. Yesterday in a show he put his arm about a little eight-year-old girl. This little girl moved and he followed her. I told him later, 'You're a sex maniac. If you want intercourse you need a woman of seventeen.'" As she recalled this, the mother remarked that the patient used to attempt to choke her in his seizures.

This mother and son were mutually seductive, both verbally and physically. The mother was indicating to the boy that he was unmistakably sadistic in his sexual approach toward women. The boy had vicious fantasies about them. Unfortunately for the boy and for society, it was clear that he was moving not toward psychosis but rather toward acting out. Permission for such behavior was clearly being given repeatedly by his disturbed mother, and condoned by the actions of his philandering father.

The following three cases emphasize the fact that incest frequently occurs in severe neurosis and is often associated with acting out through a child. The experiencing of incest does not make inevitable the development of either psychosis or promiscuity, as has been so frequently said.

Case 2

A sixteen-year-old severely neurotic girl felt a compulsion to cover her body. She tied her nightgown so tightly that it caused cyanosis of the face, and she could not rest unless the bedclothes were pinned tightly around her. This compulsion suggested incest. Proof was unobtainable, for therapy was not permitted, but her father was later arrested for molesting young girls.

Case 3

A twenty-two-year-old girl came for help because she was concerned about her uneasiness with men and her wish to get away from them, even in her work. Actual incest had occurred, but her relationship with her mother was essentially good. She revealed the experience to the mother, who believed her statements rather than assuming that they were childish fantasies. Had the mother refused to believe the girl, a more serious psychiatric illness undoubtedly would have developed. Such a willingness to believe was recommended by Ferenczi. He pointed out that it is important to consider carefully the statements of those patients who can hardly believe their own senses; we thus give them a better means of assessing reality. Incest between father and daughter is far more common than we formerly believed. We can see now that in years past patients were lost or driven into psychosis by our failure to believe them because of our conviction that much of their accounts must be fantasy.

Case 4

Occasionally drug addiction and pain are the symptoms presented by a patient who has been subjected to sexual assault by the father. One thirty-three-year-old woman, depressed and anxious, complained of severe pain in the back for which three laminectomies and a spinal fusion had been performed. Only after many weeks of therapy did she discuss her recent practice of self-flagellation. After months of treatment she recalled her subjugation in early adolescence to her father's flagellations, during which his orgastic pleasure was made apparent to her.

The following cases illustrate the principal factors in the development of perversions. Frequently we find that young children engage too exclusively in some particular one of the many forms of sexual behavior characteristic of this "polymorphously perverse" period of life. Although at such an early age there is no orgasm, and therefore many persons would not call this a "perversion," yet the hypertrophy of one form of sexuality can be so profound and organized that we cannot accept it as merely the unorganized sexuality of the child.

Case 5

Bobby, aged five, was brought because of transvestitism of two and a half years' duration. His mother was a highly ambivalent woman with strong envy of men, and his father was very passive and feminine. The mother said the symptoms began when Bobby commented on how pretty she looked and noted particularly her new shoes. She was much flattered and told Bobby, as she hugged him, that she had some old shoes he could use. He began to wear her shoes almost all day, and she remarked,

"How cute you look." Bobby's grandmother also fostered this interest. Generous neighbors continued the practice. They supplied a startling quantity of old shoes, hats, and purses. In a short time Bobby was dressing up in his mother's clothes, complete with cosmetics, jewelry, and accessories.

The mother became somewhat uneasy about Bobby's masquerading when he was four but never took a really firm stand. The behavior continued, despite occasional feeble protests by the father. Bobby's play at five was almost completely feminine; he pretended he was the mother washing dishes, cleaning the house, and ironing. He asked to be called Beth, a name suggested by his mother when he asked her what she considered a pretty name for a girl. He became fascinated with weddings and fancied himself the bride. The family accepted these fantasies: his grandmother even sent him his mother's bridal veil. It is not surprising that the child asked his mother when she was going to divorce her husband so that he, Bobby — or Beth — might marry Daddy.

After his appearance before a group of her friends in his feminine attire, the mother remarked, "You must never dress like that in front of company; only in front of the family." When the mother's doctor pointed out the permission implied in this statement, the mother became bewildered and angrily described the seductive behavior of her father toward her, behavior still expressed by her sitting on his lap. She recalled her insistent demand for a football and helmet, at the age of five, instead of the suggested birthday present of a French doll. Her son had requested a washing machine on his fifth birthday in spite of his father's timid suggestion that a football might be more appropriate.

The mother had always been hostile to her father; she expressed similar hostility to her son by destructively fostering his transvestitism. She had been extremely seductive with Bobby, appearing nude before him even during menstruation. She not only bathed Bobby but herself bathed with him, and she continued to sleep with him in spite of his erections. Typical of the attitude of the family was the father's remark, "His dressing up is just a phase. I went through it myself."

This boy would not have been brought to psychiatry had it not been for a chance remark picked up by an astute pediatrician during medical evaluation, so repressed were the "trilateral" emotional conflicts perpetuating the disturbance.

Case 6

A twelve-year-old boy was brought for treatment because of an episode of exhibitionism. His mother, a very forceful, domineering woman, was seductive with the patient. The father was insecure and sadistic. The patient, in contrast to the other members of his family, was extremely modest and always tried to cover himself when either parent burst in on him in his room or at the toilet. His father's response to the boy's modesty was, "What's the matter with you? Why are you covering up? You haven't anything I haven't got — only smaller." The mother's great interest in the boy's genitals was shown by her histrionic reporting of such remarks as this.

The boy finally complied by gratifying the unconscious voyeuristic impulses of his parents. After the episode of exhibitionism, the mother insisted upon taking full charge of questioning him, leaving the father completely out of the incident. She finished her questioning by saying, "There are only two possibilities for you. If you are insane there are special institutions for such people: if you are just mean there are places for criminals too." The boy was thus given no alternative to antisocial behavior.

Case 7

A thirteen-year-old voyeuristic boy slept until the age of ten in his parents' room. He was removed then only to make room for a baby brother. The patient's mother was highly seductive with him; she exhibited herself, embraced him, and talked far too freely. When at the age of six the boy asked to see the mother's vagina, she allowed him to look. She did this a number of times in response to the boy's increasingly anxious inquiries. When at the age of eight he became "too sexy" and said, "Why can't we make a baby?," she scolded him severely, maintaining that such an idea was very wicked and that he must never even think of such a thing. She then discontinued her very close embraces, but continued to dress in the boy's presence and to maintain no privacy in the bathroom. When the patient was twelve a maid complained of his peeping when she bathed, but the parents did nothing. A few months later a neighbor saw the boy on a ladder, peeping into the bedroom of the neighbor's eighteen-year-old daughter. Again, nothing was said. Not until the police found the boy again peeping from a ladder did the parents bring him for help. In this case, the mother seduced the boy by showing him her genital, refused physical consummation, and encouraged his peeping by doing nothing to prevent it.

Case 8

A minister, forty years of age, with a severe anxiety neurosis had been dressed as a girl in childhood, had slept with his mother throughout his adolescence, and had been tacitly encouraged in bestiality by his mother (case reported in [*Psychoanalytic*] *Quarterly*, 22 (1953): 491–92). The minister brought his ten-year-old son to us for treatment because the boy had trouble in school and because his parents feared the child was homosexual. As the minister discussed his own past, his role in his son's problems became clear to him.

In cases of fetishism we have noted ambivalence in the mother, who seduced her child, withheld gratification, and then encouraged its use of the fetish as a substitute for parental affections.

Bak (1) also describes seductive and permissive attitudes in the mothers of fetishists, but interprets the clinical facts differently. Overt homosexuality was stimulated by parents in a similar way.

Case 9

A sixteen-year-old girl was brought to treatment by her mother because of a "very homosexual" relationship with a teacher. From the time of the girl's birth her mother had been ambivalent; she lay on the bed with her, encouraging mutual stroking of the breasts and other affectionate play. Violent physical fights alternated with hugs of reconciliation. It became obvious that the child would not have been brought to treatment had it not been for the mother's jealousy of the teacher.

SUMMARY

Perversion and antisocial sexual behavior in children and adolescents results from adaptation of the child's ego to subtle attitudes of its parents which distort the instinctual development of the child. Parents of these children unwittingly seduce them and encourage their aberrant behavior. Clues obtained from the parents are useful in treatment of the child. One or both parents and the child must be treated concurrently by therapists who collaborate. Often the child must be briefly separated from the parents at the beginning of treatment; the aberrant behavior, and its encouragement by the parents, must be prohibited by the therapist. After treatment is accepted by the child, its pregenital fixations and castration anxiety can be analyzed in the usual way.

REFERENCES

1. Bak, Robert C. Fetishism. *J. American Psa. Assn.* 1 (1953): 285–98.
2. Ferenczi, Sandor. *Confusion of tongues between the adult and*

the child (The language of tenderness and of passion) (1932). *Int. J. Psa.* 30 (1949): 225–30.
3. French, Thomas M.: Personal communication to the authors.
4. Johnson, Adelaide M.; Falstein, E. I.; Szurek, S. A.; Svendsen, Margaret. School phobia. *American J. Orthopsychiatry* 11 (1941): 702–11. (Reprinted above, p. 14).
5. Johnson, Adelaide M., and Szurek, S. A. The genesis of antisocial acting out in children and adults. *Psychoanalytic Quarterly* 21 (1952): 323–43. (Reprinted above, p. 145).
6. ———. Factors in the etiology of fixations and symptom choice. *Psychoanalytic Quarterly* 22 (1953): 475–96. (Reprinted below, p. 353).
7. Kolb, Lawrence C., and Johnson, Adelaide M. Etiology of overt homosexuality and the need for therapeutic modification. *Psychoanalytic Quarterly* 24 (1955): 506–15.
8. Zilboorg, Gregory. Discussion of reference 1, at the meeting of the American Psychoanalytic Association, May 9, 1952 (not published).

14

THE SEXUAL DEVIANT (SEXUAL PSYCHOPATH): CAUSES, TREATMENT AND PREVENTION

With David B. Robinson, M.D.

> Having worked out a theory of causation from her clinical observations on antisocial behavior, Dr. Johnson felt that attempts should be made to educate the medical profession as one means of possible prevention. Toward this end, the following article was published in the *Journal of the American Medical Association.* I was coauthor of this article at a time when I had just completed my psychiatric residency training. In her usual encouraging and generous style, I was to have been senior author. At the last minute, however, the order changed and she became senior author. Dr. Johnson felt that such an article would be picked up by the popular press and result in controversial and, perhaps, heated debate. She felt that she was in a more secure professional position than I to absorb any ensuing "heat." Indeed, the article was reported in *Time Magazine*, August 12, 1957.
>
> Occasional letters still arrive from readers who "learned something worthwhile" from this article published more than ten years ago.

THE sexual deviant poses a problem of tragedy to himself, distress to his family, and concern to society at large. Although sexual deviations are emotional disorders of individuals

Reprinted with permission from *Journal of the American Medical Association* 164 (1957): 1559–65.

that require correction by a psychiatrist, the prevention of such disorders is largely at the command of the family physician and the pediatrician. The outlook for eradication or even significant curtailment of the incidence of sexual deviation is as gloomy to the psychiatrist operating unaided as is the prospect of treating individual patients with smallpox in the absence of prophylactic vaccination to a family physician. Actually, the family physician and the pediatrician, working in concert, can "vaccinate" large segments of the population against the "virus" of sexual deviation.

At the outset, it is essential that there be an end to the use of terms of hostile connotation toward the patient and to visions of the deviant as inhuman, predatory, incurable, and inevitably destined to pursue his present course. The older and too common terms of "psychopath" or "sexual psychopath" or "psychopathic personality with pathological sexuality" should give way to the more objective designations of "sexual deviant" or "sexual deviation," as recommended in Standard Nomenclature of Diseases and Operations. Under the term "sexual deviation" we include (1) any hostile, destructive sexual behavior manifested toward others (sexual sadism) or accepted from others (sexual masochism) of the opposite or of the same sex, and (2) all such unacceptable forms of overt sexual behavior as exhibitionism, voyeurism, fetishism, transvestism, homosexuality, and bestiality.

Considerable variability characterizes the degree of hostility and destructiveness toward others or toward the self. Furthermore, attributes incorporated into the total personality of the sexual deviant vary tremendously from patient to patient. Some have a well-developed conscience in all other areas of social behavior, while others may possess multiple conscience defects and display such additional antisocial activity as lying, stealing, firesetting, and vandalism. No consistent personality pattern is exhibited. The concept of a uniform constitutional inability to establish warm, meaningful human relationships or to learn by experience is by no means universally applicable. Such personality defects may certainly accompany hostile sexual behavior or perversion, but they are not at all specific for this group of patients. Such traits often occur in many neuroses and psychoses and in instances of delinquency.

DEVELOPMENT OF CURRENT CONCEPTS

Fortunately, in recent years, a better understanding of such sexually deviant behavior as the foregoing has removed the stultifying shackles of old theories of genesis, based upon constitutional defects, which promised little for therapy or prevention. The early work of Freud (1) and Ferenczi (2) emphasized abnormal but modifiable psychological development in contrast to inborn and intractable drives. Subsequently, much serious research has been pursued by many physicians to achieve a better understanding of the pathogenesis of these conditions. Only an increased comprehension of the causation of the disorders can provide a guide to intelligent treatment, help for the patient, and the protection of society. More important, an appreciation of causal factors fosters alertness to incipient manifestations of trouble ahead and suggests measures for prevention, which must be the primary concern of the psychiatrist, the pediatrician, and the family physician.

The research on causes of "individual delinquency" carried out during the past 15 years by Szurek and one of us (3, 4) suggested a new approach to the problem of the sexual deviant. By means of intensive treatment of parents of the non-gang-member delinquent child, we demonstrated that repeated stealing, arson, and vandalism are stimulated by unconscious or rarely conscious antisocial impulses in the parents. The parents derive unconscious but real gratification from the enactment by the child or adolescent of impulses socially forbidden the parent. In very large numbers of the cases studied of serious conscience deficiencies in children of "good families," parental fostering of the antisocial behavior was discovered in every instance in which an adequate search was possible or was permitted.

Parallels between delinquencies related to property or truth and delinquencies pertaining to sex were displayed in the early investigations of Szurek and one of us. (4) Extensions of findings linking parental fostering and sexual deviations were presented by Kolb and one of us (5) and were still further elaborated by Litin and co-workers. (6)

PARENTAL SEDUCTION

To understand the pathogenesis of antisocial pathological sexuality, the physician must face a disquieting but demonstrable fact: examples of all degrees of parental seduction of the child occur more commonly than it is comfortable to contemplate, regardless of the socioeconomic status of the family. The seduction may be as subtle as a caress or as blatant as actual incest. Seduction in any degree is the pathological sensual tempting and sexual stimulation of the developing child — the future sexual deviant.

Rather generally, people, including physicians, reared as they are in our culture of healthy taboos, are likely to react initially with anger and repulsion to accounts of seduction, especially the more obvious forms. Increased understanding of the backgrounds of these patients and of their parents tempers the natural emotional response, which gives way to sympathetic but grave medical concern.

The simplest unwitting seductions occurring in a family often reflect confused parental efforts to be "modern" and hide nothing from the child. The conventional restraints of common modesty respected outside the home are ignored when the children are concerned. The parents parade about the house in all degrees of nudity, sleep with the child, bathe with the child, and respect no bathroom privacy. The child's normal but tentative efforts at privacy are disregarded. The behavior may extend to such more frankly seductive practices as playing with the child's genitals or permitting an intimate physical examination of the parent. Initial reluctance by the puzzled child gives way to compliance in the climate of permissiveness, and the parent and child stimulate each other.

In such families, no consistent attitude toward conversation about sex is displayed. A vague sense of guilt may rigidly proscribe all mention of sex, or "freedom from prudery" may foster excessive discussion of sex, providing unconscious gratifications to parent and child, with supercharged, unhealthy but exciting tension.

The pathological aspects lie less in the overt behavior of the parent than in the age of the child involved. In infancy, nudity, bathing, inspection, fondling, sleeping together, and virtual absence of privacy are appropriate and even necessary. The entire coloring of these phenomena changes as the infant becomes a young child. Persistence of such distortions of kindly parental affection into adolescence is frankly pathological, destructive to the child, and dangerous to the parent and to society.

Under the guise of "motherly" or "fatherly" affection, boys and girls may be bathed by parents, often of the opposite sex, until adolescence. Children sense at bathing whether a mother's close inspection of the genitals is an honest, brief, physical necessity or an anxious, seductive maneuver. The bathroom may be as devoid of privacy as a railroad station. Habitual undressing, with startling abandon, occurs before the eyes of children. Sleeping with children of the opposite sex is prolonged into the teen-age period. The mother may still continue to lie with the son, despite awareness that erections occur. Study reveals that such mothers achieve from these experiences a gratification admixed with hostility and anxiety.

Stimulated by this parental behavior, the child finds no outlet for his aroused sensual impulses. Eventually, mounting frustration and anger force him to follow one of two courses. One is regression to the relative safety of more infantile attitudes and behavior patterns. Such a retreat quiets the immediate conflict. The other is physical aggression toward women. Unfortunately, neither course resolves the rage nor dissipates the overstimulated unconscious sexual drives.

Transgressions beyond the legitimate parental embrace of affection and into the sphere of frank bodily petting and intimate palpations of adolescent children by fathers or mothers are much less uncommon than is suspected by the average person. Often these seductive maneuvers of varying degrees of intensity by one parent are condoned by the other parent. Our patients have included members of families of all economic and social levels who have engaged in frank incest or its close approximation with the sanction of the second parent.

It is incumbent upon the scientific investigator to distinguish clearly, especially in his own mind, between observation and speculation, between objective phenomena and subjective hypothesis, and between an event recorded and a theory propounded. The observations set forth in this section on parental seduction are neither speculation, hypothesis, nor theory. They are events that occur, not uncommonly, and they are events to be observed and recorded, if the observer possesses an open mind and the knowledge, persistence, patience, skill, and experience to uncover these stubbornly elusive facts.

PARENTAL FOSTERING BY EQUIVOCATION

Antisocial behavior of almost any kind may be fostered by vacillation, ambiguity, equivocation, or "double talk" on the part of parents, such as the following examples show: "Fire-setting is prohibited, but, if you must light a fire, let us burn papers in the sink," "You must not steal, but, if you do take money, take it from my purse instead of the neighbors'." "Do not lie," but a half-hour later the parent will say, "Perhaps we should tell teacher you were sick that day we went riding."

A spurious admonition to right behavior, prompted by a fragile parental conscience, is rendered futile by the permissive, "but if you must. . . ." (7) Such ambiguities occurring in individual delinquency have been reported extensively elsewhere.

These techniques are also employed in the fostering of behavior oriented toward sexual deviations. A request to "sonny" to wear his bathrobe becomes ineffective when coupled with mother's "cute" reference to the charms of the boy's nudity. Orders to "stay out of the bathroom until dad has finished" are more appropriate in a family than open doors.

A transvestite boy of 14 years of age, at the age of 5 had been found smelling assorted laundry items belonging to his mother. Instead of an unequivocal prohibition, the mother urged only that the boy substitute her clean underclothing.

Children sense the anxious, vacillating permission and seduction in such parental double talk. Another manifestation of double talk is the parentally expressed concern for imagined future misdeeds by the child — the imagination deriving from the parent's mind but taking root in that of the child. There may be dire warnings of future sexual misconduct quite foreign to the child's conscious inclinations. A consciously guileless adolescent who is subjected to suspicious, suggestive, unfriendly quizzing angrily apprehends the destructive lack of faith on the part of the parent. The child senses that he is expected to misbehave sexually. The parents' fantasy that their small child will probably get into sexual trouble during adolescence provides a compelling guide. Unconsciously, the parents gradually maneuver this child into adolescent sexual acting-out.

CONCEPT OF PATHOGENESIS

Our investigations testify to the origin of sexual deviations in pathological permissions or even coercions of the child by adults within the family. Direct, hostile sexual misbehavior usually derives from conscious overt parental fostering, while perverse sexual aberrations result from unconscious or, more rarely, conscious stimulation by a parent. In either case, it is clear that parents who so distort their child's psychosexual development are emotionally very confused, badly maladjusted, and definitely sick, belying every outward appearance of their stability in the community. All such parents reveal an unsatisfactory marital sexual relationship.

Establishment of a cause-effect relationship demands that parental pathological permission or coercion (a causal factor) be always present when the child displays deviant sexual behavior (the effect). Also, it is required that such parental sexual sanctions always be absent in a control series in which children do not display the sexual deviations and perversions under consideration. These cause-effect relationships have always emerged from the intensive studies by Mayo Clinic research workers in parents and children with sexual abnormalities and in the control group displaying many nonsexual emotional disorders. So constant are these findings that perhaps we may be warranted in the tentative judgment that alternate concepts of the pathogenesis of sexual deviations held by other competent psychiatrists are derived either from unfamiliarity with the concept described herein or from failure to search sufficiently, diligently, and intensively for the casual relationships described.

Direct Hostile Sexual Acting-out

When the parents consciously foster and sanction deviant sexual behavior in children and adolescents, what happens is plain enough. Adolescents who are allowed to know that their parents indulge in illicit sexual affairs will angrily incorporate the defective parental standards and be guided accordingly, essentially in imitation. Family illegitimacies that are condoned and brought to the children's attention provide sanctions for illegitimacies by the children. Similarly, children's hearing and observing hostile sexual behavior between parents lead the children to identify with this parental fusion of viciousness and sexuality and later to behave in like manner themselves.

The mother may continue to sleep with an adolescent boy, despite awareness that he is experiencing erections. The mother may permit or encourage the fondling of her breasts by boys into the age of adolescence. Fathers may sleep with daughters and engage in all degrees of caressing and genital stimulation. Actual incest, particularly of the father-daughter variety, occurs far more commonly than we formerly knew. Such experiences provide the child with a sexual excitement, coupled with a baffling frustration that arouses an anger that is intense but often repressed for a time. This is the soil from which stem all degrees of promiscuity in girls. The counterpart, maternal seduction of the son, is the environmental heritage for sadistic, direct sexual acting-out by the boy, who will soon become the adolescent and later the man. When the parent compounds the injury by projecting all blame upon the child, as often occurs, the sense of guilt is overwhelming, the conflicting evidence of the senses is incomprehensible, and a flight into frank psychosis may be the alternative to sexual acting-out.

Case 1. — We recently studied an 11-year-old girl of a middle-class family whose mother had known for years that serious genital seduction was being carried out by the father. The mother, frigid and very disturbed, for a time had been glad to be relieved of sexual marital "obligations," but eventually her mobilized anger and jealousy demanded that something be done to correct the family situation. The father, himself the product of a distorted background, openly confessed his behavior with the daughter and agreed to a program of long intensive treatment for the child and both parents. Without long inpatient treatment, this child faced not only probable pregnancy as a result of her father's actions but the virtual certainty of promiscuity. A complication in this case, magnifying the therapeutic difficulty, was the almost complete absence of shame or guilt on the part of the child because of the apparent approval of the mother.

Whatever may be the obvious superficial stimuli to seductive behavior provided by parents, there is also a hidden, usually unconscious, hostility toward the child and a compelling motivation concealed even to the parent, to destroy the developing personality. It is essential for the physician to appreciate that these parents behave in this manner because of emotional traumas administered by their own parents. Such parents are in as pressing need of treatment as are the children. Too commonly, the uninitiated physician becomes so angry at the parents that he may encounter difficulty in treating them. Awareness and understanding of the experiences suffered by these parents in their past enable the psychiatrist to treat the parents objectively and sympathetically.

Case 2. — Another instance of direct sexual acting-out was that exhibited by a 19-year-old man arrested for grasping women's breasts. Here, again, conscious fostering predominated in the confused family. The father of the patient frankly fondled the mother's breasts in the presence of the children. Noisy, sadistic sexual altercations between the parents were common. For three years, the young boy knew of his mother's sexual escapades with a lover in the family living room while the father was at work at night. The son was permitted to touch his mother's breasts until he was 12 years of age.

At that age, to the utter incomprehension of the boy and to his further undoing, he was shouldered with blame. "The touching of the mother's breasts must stop." Told that he was a "sex maniac," he was warned that "boys like you go around attacking women when you grow up." The mother told us of her apprehensions from when he was 7 years of age that the boy was "over-sexed" and would be "one of those sex fiends." The unfolding story, freely but tearfully recounted, leaves almost nothing to the imagination in the sequence of fostering by overt example, permissive sanctioning of imitative behavior, and the devastating picture of the boy portrayed by the mother's hostile anticipation.

This was no "other-side-of-the-tracks" narrative; it was no family of dubious reputation and whispered rumor. This family was an asset to the community, a strength in the church, and an example of industry, stability, and friendliness.

Perverse Sexual Aberrations

In contrast to the instances of direct hostile sexual acting-out, stemming from conscious parental behavior, the perversions, such as exhibitionism, voyeurism, and transvestism, are traceable more often to unconscious parental sources. These unconscious aberrant sexual impulses of the parents, distorting the instinctual sexual development of the child, may easily defy detection. The origin and nature of the forces operating in the perversions differ significantly from the factors responsible for direct sexual acting-out.

In the adolescent — later the adult — searching taking of the history always reveals the following contributing factors:

First, the child develops in a climate of confusion and frustration resulting from a poorly integrated marriage of parents who never even approximate a mature or gratifying marital relationship.

Second, one parent unduly stimulates the child, usually unconsciously, but occasionally consciously, by behavior of a sexual coloration; such as kisses or embraces just a measure too lingering or too intimate, lying on the same bed with the child, displays of nudity, and performance of bathroom functions quite unhampered by the amenities of privacy. Usually, the second parent condones the seductive stimulations.

Third, and critically different from the etiological sequence in direct, hostile sexual acting-out, the stimulation, however sexually charged, is aborted short of genital or even breast contact between parent and child. Consequently, the relationship is particularly heavily burdened with genital frustration.

Fourth, the parent deftly deflects the child toward unusual sexual behavior of a distinctly immature nature, carrying no uncomfortable threat to the parent with a limited commitment to seduction. Unconscious capital is made of such normal physical and sensual childhood expressions as peeping, which becomes voyeurism, "showing off," which becomes exhibitionism, and bisexual play, which becomes transvestism or homosexuality.

At an early age (about 2½ or 3 years), when a little child is emotionally rather bisexual, it is very easy to foster a boy's turning to girl's play and dress. Litin, Giffin, and one of us (A. M. J.) (6) have described in detail a case in which a mother, with the father condoning it, instilled transvestism in her 5-year-old son. This masculine woman had been seduced by her father and subconsciously hated men, including her son. She was excessively sexually stimulating to her little boy, short of genital contacts, and maneuvered him into completely feminine behavior. The child was not brought for psychiatric treatment by the parents, to whom the behavior was entirely acceptable, but he was referred by the pediatrician, who detected the unusual behavior in the course of an examination for a hearing difficulty. We have encountered numerous instances of the early stages of a mother's guiding a boy toward fetishism.

If a mother unduly shows off her body to her male child and inadvertently but obviously reveals enjoyment of the child's displaying his own body, the normal but limited exhibitionism of a little child may gradually increase to an abnormal extent. Thus, overly stimulated by a seductive mother who frustrates any genital contact, the child observes that his parents permit and encourage him in exhibitionistic behavior. The mother is stimulated by this increasing display. Since his actions are at least partially condoned by and are acceptable to the parents, the child carries out the acts with very little guilt or shame.

Yet, it has become abundantly clear to us that the child harbors a great anger, arising from the contradiction of an initial sexual stimulation culminating only in a subsequent genital taboo. All exhibitionists we have observed are consciously or unconsciously very angry at women. We have seen many instances of this same parental background in exhibitionistic adolescents, and, in every instance in which we have had the opportunity to study the parents as intensively as the child, we observed the same interplay of parent-child forces in operation. In all male sexual deviants involved with perversion, we always seek and invariably find (1) the sources of hostility toward a woman and (2) the stimuli for the specific sexual behavior evolved. The following typical case vividly depicts the tragic train of events responsible for an adult male's exhibitionism.

Case 3. — A 36-year-old married man was committed to a state hospital for the mentally ill because he had repeatedly exhibited his genitals to women in his home community. Warned by the police in his home town, he was subsequently apprehended in a neighboring town for the same offense. On the day he was admitted to the hospital, a 45-minute interview conducted by an experienced psychiatrist elicited the following revealing information from the patient.

One and a half years earlier, this patient first had the urge to exhibit his genitals to women and had since carried out the impulse at irregular intervals. He said that, preceding the exhibition, he felt "weak all over" and was aware that the impending act was wrong, but he was irresistibly driven to expose himself. When he exposed his genitals he placed his hand on his penis and experienced both an erection and orgasm. He vigorously denied fantasies of intercourse or of aggressive sexual activity at the time of the exposure. Devices, such as saying the rosary when the impulse toward exhibitionism gripped him or having more frequent intercourse with his wife, were of no avail. Authoritarian warnings from the local police were ineffective. The patient was quite aware that his uncontrollable impulse was destroying his life.

At birth this patient had been abandoned by his parents. For the first nine years, he was reared in a state orphanage. During this time he rarely had social contacts with the girls at the orphanage, since rather strict segregation of the sexes was enforced. No cruelty or seduction was directed toward him by any of the employees at the orphanage.

At the age of nine years, the patient was adopted by a farming couple who had two children of their own, a boy and a girl. In this home the patient was permitted no manifestation of normal anger under threat that he would be returned to the orphanage. Verbal references to sex were strictly taboo; the patient never dared request information about sex. Characteristically, however, certain forms of sexually oriented behavior were not only exempt from taboo but even fostered and encouraged. The mother bathed the patient's back from the time he was nine years old until he was 30 years old. In those years, during this bathing experience, the patient often experienced erections, which he knew his foster mother observed.

When the patient was 30 years old, the foster mother, by that time a widow, became a cardiac invalid. She demanded that the patient take over her household duties as well as the total care of herself. Since there were personal needs to be met at night, the patient slept in the same room with the foster mother. The foster mother would permit none but the patient to bathe her ("to the waist only") and to administer to "sores" upon her body. During this entire time the patient dressed and undressed in front of the foster mother, quite aware of a degree of accompanying sexual excitement. Obvious erections were recurrently observed by the foster mother, who neither protested nor averted her gaze. At this point in the interview, the patient said, with some feeling, "She should have told me the first time to dress somewhere else."

Recollection of other episodes about which "she should have told me it was wrong" included an incident of peeping at an outdoor toilet that was being used by girls. When the patient was detected in this act, the foster mother merely exclaimed, "Oh, you boys!"

These years of inordinate seductive stimulation, coupled with genital sexual frustration, aroused in the patient a vast anger, a rage of enormous intensity. The emotional traumas delivered by the irregularities in the sexual sphere were multiplied by an admixed financial niggardliness of no mean proportions on the part of the foster parents. From 9 to 27 years of age, the patient worked on the farm with no compensation other than his room and board. When his foster father died, the patient, then 27 years old, became responsible for all the farm work, including care of the stock. He then began to receive a mere $100 monthly, in addition to his room and board. The final insult came when, after the patient had spent three years in caring for the foster mother under the circumstances described, she died, leaving a will completely excluding the patient from benefits. Instead, the foster mother bequeathed her farm and all other possessions to her natural son, who had never given her help and who had always derogated and criticized the patient. Consciously seething with rage at this monstrous injustice, the patient feared he was having a "nervous breakdown."

Let it not be thought that the foster parents of this patient were queer recluses who saved old newspapers on a run-down farm. They were successful farmers, respected members of the community, and altogether "nice people" in the eyes of their friends and acquaintances.

Ultimately, the patient left his former "home" and secured work that would provide appropriate pay. He saved money, fell in love, and married a young woman. In the marriage the patient encountered considerable difficulty from impotence, a scarcely surprising sequel to the antecedent psychosexual experiences. The young couple bought a farm and worked hard together to retire financial obligations.

When the wife became pregnant, the exhibitionistic symptoms began to assail the patient. At this time he was utterly unconscious of anger or hostility toward his wife. On the contrary, he insisted there had never been a difference of opinion between the two of them.

ETIOLOGICAL DETERMINANTS

This narration requires no technical or professional embellishment for definition of the nature of some of the factors responsible for the sexual deviation. The seductive stimulations, the appalling frustration, the parental fostering of exhibitionism, and the evolution of rage and hate are abundantly clear. Less clear to the uninitiated is the reason for the eruption of these forces into the overt practice of exhibitionism just at the time when the life circumstances and outlook of this patient "appeared" most favorable. At that time, for the first time emancipated, he could live independently, purchase his own farm, and make a home. Consciously, he was quite happily married. A baby was coming, and a good family was in prospect. What, then, was profoundly wrong?

Recall, in the life of this patient, the almost total absence of any compulsion to assume real responsibilities, until the death of the foster mother. The sheltered life of the patient while he was in the orphanage was followed by a protected — although otherwise harrowing — existence on the farm. As long as he remained passive and dependent, his basic material needs were met. The fact that he stayed on the farm in a setting of such submission identifies his basically passive-dependent character. Commonly, such a dependent person, seeking a mate, may search out a "mother-figure" upon whom he can continue to be dependent. This is the pattern of life that is familiar and comfortable. It is sufficient as long as it lasts. The anticipated arrival of the baby, however, posed a subconscious but definite threat to the patient's familiar, comfortable, sufficient existence. A rival newcomer might displace him from his position of dependency. Twice before he had been abandoned — at birth by his true mother and again by the death of his foster mother, who left him absolutely nothing from her estate.

As the pregnancy progressed and the imminent appearance of the rival approached, the patient's anxiety and resentment mounted. The subconscious fear of abandonment was coupled with a mobilizing of the rage born of his previous desertions and frustrations. Hostility toward women, usually unconscious, is an invariable ingredient of male exhibitionism. In its origins, the patient's rage was fused with sexual emotions, conditioned by the repeated seduction and frustration in his life with the foster mother. Exhibitionism was the specific accepted channel for the expression of the hostile-sexual urges that he had learned so very well from her through 24 long years.

We may well inquire how and why was it possible to obtain the illuminating, painful history of this patient in one relatively brief interview. Such an unfolding of the past, in our experience, by adult patients with behavioral disorders of an antisocial nature commonly requires a rather long treatment period to engender the necessary complete trust in the therapist. In adolescents and children such accounts often are obtainable only in repeated, persistent simultaneous interviews with both parents and child. (8)

In the case under discussion, the vivid memory of the profound insult of disinheritance and its attendant fully conscious anger favored an early revelation of the past. But, however close to the surface this material lies, the conduct of the interview by the physician is the determining factor in bringing the truth to light. The psychiatrist and physician must be aware, by means of previous research, experience, or training, that the bare facts recounted proceed from an underlying pattern and that there is a high degree of specificity in the causal antecedents of sexual deviations. In this instance, the experienced psychiatrist knew what to seek and how to find it by indirect questions "flanking" the central episodes.

THERAPY

Definitive psychiatric therapy of the overt sexual deviant is a prodigious task. The adolescent requires active and prolonged treatment by a skilled therapist. A few dynamic psychiatrists are becoming aware of the etiological aspects of sexual deviation and are gradually developing increasingly effective techniques in the treatment of both the child and parents.

In the light of our newer knowledge, we can interview parents and adolescents more intelligently. When the hidden sequences are uncovered in all their significance, the patients comprehend the origins and unfortunate rationale of their unusual behavior. A degree of understanding effectively penetrates the barrier between them and the therapist, and they may become ready and willing to enter into serious treatment. It must be repeated that treatment is an arduous, time-consuming process for the parents, adolescents, and therapists; consequently, it is very expensive. Treatment of a child or young adolescent while he or she is still living with untreated parents yields disappointing results. If the parents do not cooperate, it may be necessary to treat the child in a residential center removed from the parents. Unfortunately, such centers are far too few to meet the needs.

Treatment of the adult sexual deviant is indeed a formidable undertaking. A highly trained therapist is essential, and often the patient must be placed in a protected hospital environment for many months, especially early in treatment. Again, too few psychiatric facilities are available for adequate treatment of such patients. The problem is further complicated when there are a wife and children to support.

Therapy probably should never be commenced if there is no compelling motivation for treatment. Such instances are not uncommon, despite grave difficulties threatening dire consequences. Such sexual deviants are often devoid of guilt and conscious anxiety and seek only to avoid detection. This lack of guilt may be traced to the permissiveness of the parents during the early years of the formation of conscience. If adequate specific treatment is not available or if the patient cannot be motivated for treatment, the most charitable action for the patient and for society may be commitment to a state hospital for protective custody. Threats or punishments have been generally ineffective in compelling or helping the patient to control his or her pathological impulses.

Many of these patients have a very strong conscience in areas other than the sexual and are therefore dependable in most spheres of social behavior. However, without highly definitive and extensive therapy, it is never safe to predict that the patient will not indulge in a later repetition of his sexually deviant behavior. Individual psychiatric evaluation is necessary for assessment of the total personality structure and the future potentials of each patient.

It is entirely clear that the mere elucidation of etiological factors in the genesis of his sexual deviation and the subsequent intellectual discussion of them with the patient do not effect a cure. In the adult and in the adolescent, there are complex phenomenologic elaborations and extensions into the entire fabric of the personality, affecting all phases of interpersonal relationships. These complexities must be analyzed intensively and extensively; they are familiar to psychiatrists and psychoanalysts and are more appropriately discussed in other contexts.

PREVENTION

What we wish to stress in this paper is prevention by the family physician and pediatrician rather than treatment by the psychiatrist. The goal is prophylaxis, based upon an understanding of etiological aspects. When the psychiatrist encounters the sexual deviant as an adult, recognition of the etiological factors often requires long analysis. In the case of the child and adolescent, we readily observe the strategic pathological emphases at their inception. The sexual deviants constitute a social problem of a magnitude beyond the reach of the limited numbers of highly trained psychiatrists. Behavior physically dangerous to others and of major concern to the courts and to society is primarily to be anticipated from the group of openly hostile, sexually destructive deviants. The deviants, however, ordinarily displaying the less physically harmful perversions, such as exhibitionism or voyeurism, may unpredictably break through into more directly destructive sadistic action. Since hostile seduction by parental figures underlies all the sexual deviations and hate and anger are prominent, any deviant impelled by that hostility may become dangerous physically.

Although we know more today than formerly about the genesis of sexual deviation as it develops within the family setting, we are still woefully deficient in properly trained personnel and facilities for the treatment of these complicated conditions. It then becomes of paramount importance to embrace the strategy of prophylaxis and detection of early danger signs. This is the domain of the pediatrician and the family physician. It is these physicians who therefore must be alert to the multiple possible manifestations of all degrees of seduction and sexual stimulation within the family confines.

A first approach consists of education of the parents. Many well-intentioned parents, influenced by the misinterpretations of Freud's theories, do not observe proper and healthy rules of modesty in the home. Dangerously little knowledge has led them to believe that "neurosis is based on repression of sexual curiosity and interests," and, therefore, it is erroneously believed that an open approach to sexuality provides an emotionally healthful climate. The resulting multiple forms of bodily exposure may result in unwitting and excessive overstimulation of the child.

Second, pediatricians and family physicians must squarely face the unequivocal truth that all degrees of seduction and sexual stimulation occur all too commonly and in families which exhibit every outward aspect of respectability, decency, and conformity with convention.

There should be a few simple but pointed routine queries by the physician. Who sleeps with whom in the family? Which ones bathe together, and do they bathe themselves? What are the family habits regarding bathroom privacy? Are dressing and undressing communal functions? Is there a healthy degree of modesty in the home? What are the children's chief interests at play and habits in dress? Too often, such interrogation reveals unmistakable signs of an unhealthy atmosphere. When encountered, such tendencies should be met with an uncompromising counsel of prohibition.

If the parents are unhappily married and their hostile sexual impulses strain for an outlet, a physician's simple education of the parents, admonition to proper behavior, or direct prohibition of the seductive behavior may be of no avail. In such cases, combined psychiatric treatment of parents and child is indispensable. However, instances amenable to a forthright relatively simple management are sufficiently numerous to warrant a rather general effort by pediatricians and family physicians. Such a program holds genuine promise for prophylaxis, for sparing many children a miserable life outlook, for strengthening the fiber of the public character, and for preserving society from an unhappy quota of hurt and violence.

SUMMARY

Clinical research reveals that destructive direct sexual acting-out and perverse sexual behavior are forms of sexual deviation that develop, in most instances, from unconscious or, less frequently, conscious pathological fostering of deviant sexual behavior early in life within the family settting. Investigation further demonstrates that, engrafted upon this framework, direct and overt sexual seductive behavior inclines the child toward later direct sexual, destructive acting-out, while indirect, disguised sexual stimulations engender the sexual perversions. Since therapy of the full-blown sexual deviant is long and difficult, prophylaxis is the preferred attack on the problem. Equipped with understanding and employing relatively simple procedures, the family physician and the pediatrician may well reduce significantly the incidence of sexual deviations.

REFERENCES

1. Freud, S. Three essays on theory of sexuality, 1901–1905, in Standard Edition of *Complete Psychological Works* (London: Hogarth Press, 1953), 7:135–71; Instincts and their vicissitudes, in *Collected Papers* (London: Hogarth Press, 1915), 4:60–83; 'A child is being beaten': Contribution to study of origin of sexual perversions, in *Collected Papers* (London: Hogarth Press, 1919), 2:172–201; Psychogenesis of case of homosexuality in a woman, in *Collected Papers* (London: Hogarth Press, 1920), 2:202–31;

Fetishism, in *Collected Papers* (London: Hogarth Press, 1927), 5:198–204.
2. Ferenczi, S. Confusion of tongues between adult and child (The language of tenderness and of passion), *Internat. J. Psycho-Analysis* 30 (1949): 225–30.
3. Johnson, A. M., and Szurek, S. A. Genesis of antisocial acting out in children and adults. *Psychoanalyt. Quart.* 21 (1952): 323–43.
4. ———. Etiology of antisocial behavior in delinquents and psychopaths. JAMA 154 (1954): 814–17.
5. Kolb, L. C., and Johnson, A. M. Etiology and therapy of overt homosexuality. *Psychoanalyt. Quart.* 24 (1955): 506–15.
6. Litin, E. M.; Giffin, M. E.; and Johnson, A. M. Parental influence in unusual sexual behavior in children. *Psychoanalyt. Quart.* 25 (1956): 37–55.
7. Johnson, A. M., and Burke, E. C. Parental permissiveness and fostering in child rearing and their relationship to juvenile delinquency. *Proc. Staff Meet. Mayo Clin.* 30 (1955): 557–65. (Reprinted above, p. 155.)
8. References 3, 4, and 7.

15

ETIOLOGICAL FACTORS IN FIRST-DEGREE MURDER

A brief study of six convicted first-degree murderers was reported in the *Journal of the American Medical Association* in 1958, by Duncan, Frazier, Litin, Johnson, and Barron. The final summary only is included here to represent this additional area of investigation pursued, again with her junior colleagues.

SUMMARY

Six prisoners convicted of first-degree murder and their parents consented to undergo investigation by the collaborative technique in a pilot study. White male prisoners were selected who were of at least average intelligence, from middle-class families, not members of a gang, not alcoholic or epileptic, and with neither organic disease of the brain nor a history of psychosis.

Remorseless physical brutality inflicted through the childhood and adolescence of the prisoner at the hands of parents was a common factor in four cases. The other two prisoners proved to have been psychotic at the time of the murder, and these two had not been treated with such gross brutality.

Unconscious fostering by parents, such as has been described frequently in individual delinquency, was not observed in these cases. Rather, the prisoners learned to behave like their brutal

Summary reprinted with permission from *Journal of the American Medical Association* 168 (1958): 1755–58.

aggressors and learned by conscious example that violence was a solution to frustration.

The need for family physicians and pediatricians to be aware of, and to intervene in, such brutal family patterns is emphasized with a view to preventing possible tragedy. (Dr. Johnson).

16

JUVENILE DELINQUENCY

> As the final representation of Dr. Johnson's highly developed thinking in the area of antisocial behavior, her chapter on "Juvenile Delinquency," written for the *American Handbook of Psychiatry* (1959), is reproduced by permission of the publisher. Significantly, this was the last work of Dr. Johnson's to be published before her untimely death in 1960.

DELINQUENCY has been with us from the time man began trying to civilize himself by establishing certain social codes of behavior. John Locke, (20) the great English educator, three hundred years ago deplored delinquency in the same vein as we do today. Six thousand years ago an Egyptian priest carved on a stone, "Our earth is degenerate. . . . Children no longer obey their parents." What do we mean by the term "delinquency"? We refer to that behavior which is opposed to those tenets held by society and the law in our particular culture. The major offenses are stealing, truancy, fire setting, vandalism, and cruelty of all degrees up to murder. Even though the jurist calls delinquent that behavior which deviates from society's code, today, increasingly, such antisocial children and people are not considered capable of responsibility for such behavior. Just as the individual's responsibility for neurotic or psychotic symptoms has been repudiated by most modern psychiatrists, so has the delinquent's re-

Originally published as chapter 42, volume 1, in the *American Handbook of Psychiatry*, edited by Silvano Arieti, © 1959 by Basic Books, Inc., Publishers, New York. Reproduced with permission.

sponsibility for his acts been considered. Although the superego, the conscience, the moral part of his personality is affected, still, as we proceed with a consideration of the etiologic factors in all forms of delinquency, we shall see that the patient is involved in experiences beyond his capacity to make choices and which obstruct his normal development.

"From many sources comes the cry that the Juvenile Court is coddling young criminals and that children should be punished for their offenses," says Judge Winnet (31) in a recent address to the American Medical Association. The Judge sees no evidence that punishment has ever ameliorated the situation and believes that "punishment does not reach the causes of delinquency . . . public punishment . . . can only increase resentment and rebellion and the sense of being outcast." Similarly, Judge Winnet feels that evidence shows that punishment of the parents has been so impracticable as to be worthless.

In the young child we are prone to speak of his having a behavior problem when he defies law and order. When the child reaches pre-adolescence and adolescence and opposes society's tenets, we call his misbehavior "delinquency." When authority is circumvented by the older age groups, the term "psychopathic personality" is assigned.

Since the first juvenile court was established in 1899, in Illinois, over 3,000 such courts have emerged. Why has this growth been so vast? The answer is found in the previous irrationality of following a criminal procedure as applied to children.

That delinquency is increasing steadily seems undeniable, if the observer considers a statewide area and not some special locality. Many authorities think there is a national trend toward increased delinquency above what we might expect from increased population. This is said to be particularly true among girls. In some fairly representative cities authorities state that, considering the increase in population, there has been no increase in delinquency over the past years. In some cities, and especially in suburbs, the figures are rising, but many investigators correlate such a rise with better police work and record keeping. More delinquency or not, no one can doubt that it is on the increase as a practical problem that we encounter, and one that must be met. With the exception of specific circumscribed areas, few contend that delinquency is on the decrease. The juvenile courts fail in approximately 50 per cent of their cases. Such problems lead to certain conclusions: One is that our agencies and resources for helping children are inadequate in number, or that we do not offer the right kind of psychiatric and community service in dealing with the problem. Both factors, of course, may be operating. To offer the appropriate kind of service, we must first arrive at an understanding of causes.

CAUSATION OF DELINQUENCY AND THE DIFFERENTIATION OF GROUPS

In discussing causation of delinquency, there are two common pitfalls. Either a discussant sees causes as too complex and manifold to unravel, and one feels hopelessly discouraged listening to him, or another discussant creates uneasiness by oversimplification of the entire issue. There have emerged, however, some fairly clear concepts of causes related to this challenging problem. The central thesis of causation, as viewed by many students today, leads us to see two large categories of antisocial behavior — the unconsciously driven individual delinquent from the so-called "good or normal" family, and the gang or sociologic group operating at any economic level. It may be well, for the moment, to forget about overlapping of these two large groups. What operates causally in the individual delinquent is, to a large extent, different from what propels the gang or sociologic form of delinquency, and this, in turn, dictates different treatment measures for the two groups. Fifteen years ago — and even widely today — many investigators telescoped all delinquents into one category. This has led to vast confusion in understanding etiology and personality structure and in prescribing treatment. Some years ago many psychiatrists talked as if all delinquents had problems that only the psychiatrist should treat. Sociologists maintained a similar position for themselves as the therapeutic agents. As research progressed, it became clear that certain cases could only be relieved in the psychiatrist's office, while large numbers of other delinquents would be helped only by the sociologic-community approach. Everyone will not agree with the author, but many students of the problem today see the validity of the concept, etiologically, of the two great categories of delinquency.

Let us consider the individual delinquent about whom we know far more today and about whom many are more in agreement as to etiology. Vast areas are still to be explored with regard to personality structure and treatment.

THE INDIVIDUAL DELINQUENT

For treatment to be rational, etiology must be explicit. Arrival at our understanding of clinical evidence for etiology has necessitated drastic changes in our previous understanding of traditional psychoanalytic theory. The psychoanalysts' first interest was in the neuroses, and for years, with few exceptions, research was concerned largely with this aspect of psychopathology. In understanding the neuroses, one conceives of a too-punitive superego. Until recently, pathology of the superego was viewed only in terms of its being too punishing to patients. For many years any antisocial acting out was explained in terms of a patient's being excessively guilty about conflicts or being driven by constitutionally unmanageable instinctual drives. Alexander (2) conceived of the need for self-punishment as a motive for acting out. It is granted that the individual delinquent frequently suffers from neurotic guilt, yet the question that Alexander did not answer was why the resolution of guilt was sought specifically in acting out. The reflected preventive attitude for all patients had been, "Do not repress the child so drastically or he will become guilty, neurotic, or act out." Therapists, as well as parents, have become greatly confused, thinking that prohibitions in all forms lead to too much guilt and thus, neurosis. Some therapists unwittingly permitted and fostered acting out in, especially, the sexual sphere. Prohibitions of a culture in themselves do not lead to unhealthy guilt; rather, they are an important aspect of security. As far as the prevention of neurosis is concerned, the prohibition of antisocial activity merely requires the presence of a parent sufficiently well integrated to accept in legitimate ways the hostility expressed by the child over the limit-setting that society demands.

It has become increasingly clear that many parents, particularly those with poorly integrated impulses, have become uneasy about setting limits, even concerning matters which are specifically destructive to society, such as stealing, pathologic sexuality, or even murderous intent. Yet it is evident that certain specific things, such as stealing, fire setting, murder, and sexual destructiveness, cannot be countenanced in our society if the child is to develop comfortably in that society. Freud (8) himself said:

Let us get a clear idea of what the primary business of education is. The child has to learn to control its instincts. To grant it complete freedom, so that it obeys all its impulses without any restriction, is impossible. It would be a very instructive experiment for child-psychologists, but it would make life impossible for the parents and would do serious damage to the children themselves, as would be seen partly at the time, and partly during subsequent years. The function of education, therefore, is to inhibit, forbid and suppress, and it has at all times carried out this function to admiration. But we have learnt from analysis that it is this very suppression of instincts that involves the danger of neurotic illness. You will remember that we have gone into the question of how this comes about in some detail. Education has therefore to steer its way between the Scylla of giving the instincts free play and the Charybdis of frustrating them. Unless the problem is altogether insoluble, an optimism of education must be discovered, which will do the most good and the least harm. It is a matter of finding out how much one may forbid, at which times and by what methods.

As most of us clearly recognize, there is, then, specific behavior, the expression of which should arouse guilt in everyone. The guilt alone is not unhealthy. Neurosis need be feared only if rage has been harshly repressed, along with the prohibition of such antisocial activity.

Concern in more recent works is with the development of that form of pathologic superego which permits antisocial behavior. Clinical evidence (19) shows it to be lacunar, weak in some respects, punitive in some, and normal in still other areas. Many people have strong latent antisocial impulses, yet never act out such fantasies. In recent years students have been concerned with defining the specific stimulus, if any, to the acting-out behavior with lucid definition of possible secondary causes. We wish to consider the problems of the direct acting out of forbidden antisocial impulses: namely, stealing, truancy, fire setting, and direct sexual acting out in the individual delinquent.

HISTORICAL CONTRIBUTIONS AND ETIOLOGY

The provocative contributions of Reich, (21) Alexander, (2) Alexander and Healy, (3) Healy and Bronner, (13) Schmideberg, (22) and many others have long been known to the student of delinquency. It was Aichhorn (1) whose contributions first unquestionably moved delinquency out of the nihilistic depths of constitutional inheritance, into the realm of dynamic understanding.

August Aichhorn, friend and associate of Freud, published the first real milestone on the road to an understanding of the problem of delinquency. *Wayward Youth* (1) has been a stimulus to students of the problem since the publication of this readable and challenging approach. Actually this was almost the first attempt to study the baffling problem of antisocial behavior in a manner that stimulated a fundamental treatment approach. Although today we see more clearly etiologic specific stimuli, know more of the pathology of the superego and ego in these children, still any student must concede that Aichhorn raised this baffling problem from the gates of the reformatory to a level of dynamic understanding and challenge. Not only did Aichhorn open up a new field for psychoanalytic inquiry, but the warmth, optimism, and imagination of this man have for decades stimulated the personal growth of many students in the field. *Searchlights on Delinquency*, edited by K. R. Eissler (5) and published by International Universities Press in 1949, was dedicated to Professor Aichhorn on his seventieth birthday. Any student of delinquency will refer to the brilliant introductory chapter, "General Problems of Delinquency," by Eissler. Although there have been notable advances on many fronts relative to understanding and treatment since the publication of this work, reference to it will suggest a storehouse of provocative concepts as well as known facts. In fact, this work is the only reference to date in which so much can be learned. Aichhorn did not, however, make any differentiation between the individual and sociologic delinquents — a distinction which many students believe is necessary to more basic understanding.

Any student of delinquency will find himself indebted to

Healy and Bronner (13) for their fundamental contributions. Although, like Aichhorn (1) and Alexander, (2) they made no distinction etiologically between the individual delinquent and the sociologic form, they contributed much to our understanding of secondary causes in the individual delinquent and much that is primary in sociologic delinquency. These workers noted clearly such gross pathologic distortions as forging in the parent and stealing in the child. They did not note the subtle unconscious etiologic correlations to be described by later research workers. Healy and Bronner attributed to coldness and rejection by the parents the child's inability to develop a normal inhibiting superego, so that one child in a family may steal and another will not, depending upon the one being unloved and the other loved. This is a part of the truth. Even granting that unloved children do not develop a healthy superego, it does not follow that coldness of parents alone can lead to the superego lacunae we observe. Some very cold parents can create such great guilt or need to make restitution to a needed object that a very punitive superego is developed in a child. This is one of the settings from which stems the masochistic child. (18) It is equally true that there are also relatively warm parents whose child may act out antisocially — especially in some of the sociologic delinquents.

Schmideberg (22) takes us back to a more nihilistic view in that she suggested that people who act out their conflicts have a greater constitutional inability to tolerate frustration than do the more inhibited persons.

There is frequently confusion regarding the use of the phrase "acting out." The expression "acting in the transference" was first used recurrently by Freud to refer to the phenomenon which was seen during psychoanalytic therapy in which the neurotic patient repeated in the transference, without insight, certain salient episodes in his earlier life.

Eduardo Weiss (30) aptly described it in the following way:

> By acting-out is meant the behavior of a person who repeats without insight an unconscious psychic situation out of his past in terms of current reality. A man, for instance, repeats intense feelings of hostility towards his brothers and sisters by quarreling with his fellow workers. . . . Freud considered transference as a form of acting-out. According to Freud one acts-out instead of remembering. However, psychoanalytic experience teaches us that patients in analysis often act-out emotional situations which they have already remembered. . . . Freud's formulation can be modified by saying that one acts-out instead of remembering fully with the appropriate attending emotions. . . . While acting-out is a substitute for recall, it does not have the therapeutic effect of the latter. The patient who acts out has still to acknowledge that *his present behavior is a reproduction of past experiences.* . . . I fully agree with Anna Freud who says that the patient who acts-out *exclusively* cannot be analyzed.

In most recent years the phrase "acting out" has come to be used almost exclusively in referring to that behavior against authority which is specifically forbidden by our society. Actually, except for the moral issue, there is no sharp line of demarcation between the acting in the transference and the kind of phenomenon expressed by the unconscious acting-out problems with which we are dealing. This is in keeping with the view commonly held today: that ego and superego are not separate entities, but merge imperceptibly on the spectrum of reality testing. At one end are observed highly moral aspects of the ego — that there can be no alternatives to conforming morally. Proceeding to the opposite end of the spectrum, increasingly complicated alternatives and choices become obviously permissible, since ethics is not involved; it is more in this latter area that acting out during analysis occurs.

Since the early work of Johnson and Szurek, (19) collaborative studies by other students on antisocial acting out have continued.

From the initial studies emerged the thesis that antisocial acting out in a child is unconsciously fostered and sanctioned by the parents, who vicariously achieve gratification of their own poorly integrated forbidden impulses through a child's acting out. In turn, the child's behavior stimulates the parents to added need for this gratification. One or both parents, in addition, unconsciously experience gratification for their own hostile and destructive wishes toward the child, who is repeatedly destroyed by his behavior. It is possible, in every case adequately studied, to trace the specific conscience defect in the child to a mirror image of similar type and emotional charge in the parent. The focus of these observations has been not on the activities of the kind seen among deprived and other sociologically determined gang groups but rather among individual children of poor or of privileged class, frequently from families of "good" reputation and high social standing.

The superego defects in these children are frequently in only one or two areas and are rarely widespread. A child may steal but never be truant. Another may set fires and do nothing else that is antisocial. In another, only the sexual sphere will be implicated through the acting out. To be sure, like other people, these patients have neuroses with conflict and guilt, but they have also the superego weakness in one or more areas, permitting discharge of tension.

As early as 1942 Szurek (24) described the psychopathic personality as being only a delinquent grown older, as an individual defective in personality organization, specifically in the individual's conscience. Szurek distinguished those individuals from the sociologically stimulated gang lawbreakers, and presented one of the earliest contributions to the dynamic understanding of these problems. He wrote:

Clinical experience leaves the impression that the definition of psychopathic personality is no greater mystery than other syndromes

Juvenile Delinquency

in psychopathology. Almost literally, in no instance in which adequate psychiatric therapeutic study of both parent and child has been possible has it been difficult to obtain sufficient evidence to reconstruct the chief dynamics of the situation. Regularly, the more important parent, usually the mother, although the father is always in some way involved, has been seen unconsciously to encourage the amoral or anti-social behavior of the child.

As time has elapsed, we have observed that fathers are probably as frequently implicated as mothers.

CONSCIENCE

It is impossible to understand the dynamic concepts behind the behavior of these individuals unless one has clearly in mind the development of the normal superego. One must understand the reaction of the well-integrated parent, and the subtle conscious and unconscious ways in which this behavior directs the development of the child's superego. Identification with the parent consists of more than incorporation of the *manifest* behavior of the parent; it necessarily involves inclusion of the subtleties of the parent's conscious and unconscious image of the child. The healthy parent fantasies his child as capable of becoming law abiding. The well-integrated, mature mother does *not* immediately check on a child following an order or request; she unconsciously assumes that the order will be carried out. The neurotic mother, who immediately checks or warns that if the job is not done dire consequences will follow, merely conveys to the child that an unstated alternative exists in the mother's mind. It is frequently with this alternative image in the mother's thoughts that the child more strongly identifies. This is true because the child senses the peculiar parental emotional need conveyed in the anxious, vacillating tone of the parent's expression.

The child internalizes, then, not only the positive, socially consistent attitudes of the parent but also the frequently unexpressed, ambivalent, antisocial feelings. We cannot agree with those who state that the child identifies only with idealized aspects of the parent. The child identifies with all facets of the parent, repressing those parental characteristics which cause conscious confusion, anxiety, and shame.

INDIVIDUAL DELINQUENCY

An Etiologic Theory of Unconscious Individual Delinquency

The patients with whom we are specifically concerned in this section are those manifesting what are frequently called "superego lacunae." The apparent "punched-out" aspect of this kind of superego is misleading except from the point of view of society. (10, 19) From the point of view of the patient, there is a positive, undeniable drive toward acting in the manner in which the parent unconsciously wishes, even though it is antisocial in direction. The conception of a deficit within the superego structure must be elaborated to include the overwhelming parentally determined dynamic push toward antisocial behavior which the child senses, and with which he necessarily complies. Although we are not here concerned with sociologically delinquent gang members, there is frequently overlapping of the individuals who act out antisocially, these latter often moving into gangs.

If the thesis is correct that parents unconsciously initiate and foster antisocial behavior in order to experience gratification for themselves, accurate documentary evidence must be defined in answer to two basic questions: (1) How is sanctioning communicated to the child? and (2) Why is one child implicated in a family in which all of the other children are quite conforming?

Not only is it possible by careful questioning and observation to define the process by which a specific child is chosen and the dynamic factors behind the choice of a particular form of socially disapproved behavior, but it is also possible to detect the highly personal technique by which the parent transmits the double talk, interest, permissive tone, or structured situation by which the activity is fostered.

During the process of definitive treatment, it is clearly seen why one child becomes emotionally chosen to be the outlet of expression for those forbidden impulses. An adopted child, whose behavior can be blamed on heredity, becomes a natural victim through whom to express antisocial trends, with simultaneous expression of hostile feelings in the parent toward this child. Sometimes the only son of a woman who is disturbed by unresolved, hostile, dependent problems with her own father, and permitted by her own mother to carry on petty stealing, may become the means of expressing both her unconscious anger and her poorly integrated stealing impulses through her fostering such socially destructive activities in her child. Ruth Eissler (6) has lucidly written of the scapegoat child in *Searchlights on Delinquency*.

Proper understanding of case material is impossible unless one is aware of the many innuendoes of communication which occur without conscious awareness between parents and child. Such communications take place by all conceivable means of approach — sometimes errors of omission, frequently ones of frank commission. Knowing *what* to listen for, and how, the diagnostician, listening to the spontaneous communications of the parents, defines these operations from direct quotations, double talk, facial expressions, and often through histrionic portrayal by some parents who dramatize the actual interchange between themselves and the child. In the more subtle cases the casuistic, disingenuous rationalizations of these parents can reduce the whole spirit of an ethical principle to a quibbling absurdity.

The specific manner in which, for instance, the truancy from home was handled on a particular day must be obtained; frequently, when this is done, one finds that the mother met the girl with the comment, "If you don't like us and our house, find another; we can get along without you."

The entranced parental facial expression apparent to the child describing a stealing episode, a sexual misdemeanor, or a hostile attitude toward a teacher conveys to the child that the parent is achieving some pleasurable gratification. No amount of subsequent punishment will act as a deterrent against the recurrences of the acting out. A child wishes to do the thing which he senses gives the parent pleasure, even though he may be punished. We frequently see parents who describe the child's delinquent behavior with obvious pleasure. Plainly, the child's antisocial behavior is stimulating that parent. Suspicious questioning often conveys the parents' unconscious wish that the child comply by doing the thing *verbally* warned against.

Frequently, parents verbalize evasions and deceptions such as, "Here is an extra quarter, but don't tell your father"; "You can get into the movie for half price, since you certainly don't look twelve years old"; "Fires are dangerous, but if you must get it out of your system, then we'll set some in the sink."

A mother can make such a suggestion, yet she would never recommend that her child take a trial run in front of cars on the street. The mother of a fourteen-year-old girl was not genuinely interested in prohibiting her child's stealing; she said to her daughter, "Why did you take the money from your *aunt's* purse instead of from mine?"

Children hear their parents gloating about shortchanging the grocer; naturally, they sense the parental pleasure. We cannot cheat a child or anyone else and expect the child to overlook it. Some parents do not follow through when the facts of stealing are perfectly clear. For instance, they hesitate to go with the child to the dime store to make proper restitution for a stolen trinket.

Paralyzed consternation may overtake a parent whose seven-year-old has just taken a dollar from the dresser or displayed a trinket pilfered from the dime store. Why this anxiety, confusion, or even undue hostility? Why not manage the matter firmly and directly? There is a reason. An impulse in the parent, alternative to complete honesty, compels vacillation and hedging rather than the establishment of a clear limit. That impulse may explode into a rage, with threats of the reformatory. Such a parental reaction suggests to the child that his impulses to steal really may get out of hand. In his unsophistication and dependency, he is inclined to accept the painting of Dorian Gray as a true image of himself.

The mature, normal parent neither anticipates impending disaster nor dismisses monetary transgression as trivial. Instead, the problem is resolved promptly without anxiety or guilt. The mother says, "Susie, you took the dollar from the dresser; please get it for me at once. No one may take another's money without asking permission." She insists that the money be returned promptly. Of the dime store trinket, she tells Johnnie firmly and without anxiety that it is wrong to take things without paying for them. She accompanies Johnnie to the dime store to return or pay for the article. Storekeepers are accustomed to parents coming on such errands and usually accept the proper restitution. Such a parent is neither the nagging, checking detective nor the permissive, lax condoner. She does not dismiss recurrent minor thefts with the rationalization "Oh, he will outgrow it," only to bring the child for treatment when the school complains of theft.

Many parents, whose own poorly integrated prohibitions permit them to overlook recurrent slight offenses, suddenly react with guilt and alarm at the first suggestion of criticism from outside the home. They respond with righteous accusations and punishment. The child is confused and angry at what now appears to be parental betrayal. If the child is not too ashamed or frightened, he may give voice to his recollections of similar parental deceptions, initiating a vicious cycle of hostile blackmail and mutual corruption. A mother who has poorly integrated prohibitions concerning her own hostile sexual impulses may fantasy that her eight-year-old daughter will "get into sexual difficulties" as adolescence approaches. With her provocative warning accompanied by anxiety, she is a predictable stimulus to vacillating sexual behavior in such a child.

Truancy concerns everyone. How does truancy originate? Parental coldness and rejection are insufficient causes, contrary to some authors; these are nonspecific stimuli. The child of six, sensing coldness and rejection, may say angrily: "You don't love me — nobody loves me — I hate you all." Then, and not infrequently, the specific stimulus may be applied by the parent: "Very well! Why don't you just pack your bag and go live some place else if you think we are so awful?" We have observed some parents who even went so far as to pack the child's suitcase — a terrifying experience for the child. The suggestion to run away comes more frequently from inside the home than outside, for rarely do small children tell their friends that their mothers are "mean," or get suggestions from other children to leave home.

How an adult can initiate running away is found in the illuminating account of Aichhorn (1) who deliberately resorted to such provocation as a technique of treatment. In managing the transference, he purposely used a simple suggestive device to provoke a boy to run away from the institution. His aim was to establish a positive contact with the adolescent, in which he had been unsuccessful. This very narcissistic boy, with no positive feeling for Aichhorn, constantly complained about the institution. Aichhorn made subtle suggestions about the attractiveness of the outside world, and an hour later the boy ran away, as Aichhorn had anticipated. In keeping with the therapist's predictions, some days later the boy returned, having found the outside world uninviting. He entered at once into a positive relationship with Aichhorn.

We frequently have patients whose parents tell the child to ask the physician for permission to do something they already well understand to be forbidden. Parents complain of *children's* breaking family rules when the parents themselves, consciously or unconsciously, break rule after rule and promise after promise without apology or comment.

The process of vicarious gratification now becomes clearer. The antisocial behavior of the implicated child becomes a means of parental expression by which poorly integrated antisocial impulses of the parent are expressed through the child. As Emch (7) lucidly stated it, the child is "acting out the caricatured reproduction of past parental behavior." In addition to this use as a mode of expression for parental impulses, such a child is the recipient of a hostile destructive drive in the parent; in close relationship lie vicarious gratification through the child and the wish to destroy this same child. Such family behavior, in the end, is destructive to both the child's ego organization and that of the parent, who is constantly being stimulated by the acting-out child. It is a mutually adaptive transaction.

In so complex a setting as family life, a multiplicity of variables operates, so that no single secondary cause for delinquent behavior can be isolated. As already mentioned, it is the contention of Johnson and Szurek (19) that unwitting permissive sanctioning by parents is a major and specific cause for children to live out antisocial impulses. Scientific proof of causation is not satisfied by demonstration of the invariable presence of the suspected cause (parental sanction) whenever the effect (antisocial behavior of children) is observed. It must be demonstrated also that the suspected cause does not occur unless the effect is also seen. This has been the experience of many students today. Johnson and Szurek (19) have never observed these parental permissions without antisocial behavior in at least one child who had been chosen as a scapegoat. The thesis is not merely reasoning based on *post hoc, ergo propter hoc*; the enmeshing interplay of parent and child in the affected area bespeaks more than a fortuitous time sequence.

Phenomenology and Treatment of the Individual Delinquent

Many authors feel that they were never able to grasp etiologic factors in individual delinquency until they had treated and thereby studied the parents as carefully as the child. Similar collaborative treatment makes it more readily possible to understand what is going on phenomenologically. Because of research in the last fifteen years, much is known of the normal development of, as well as the pathology of, the superego in children.

One of the most lucid accounts of the normal child's moral development is that of M. Woolf. (32) Carefully developed are such matters as truth and lying, the sense of property, and sexuality in the young child in a normal family. However, there is a remarkable lack, so far, of research concerning the ego distortions in these children other than those facts well known to cause neurotic distortions. What is less frequently described are the ego distortions and adaptations closely related to the specific superego pathology and the hostility of the parents. Almost nowhere in the literature is there a *detailed* account of the psychoanalysis and treatment of an individual delinquent. The author has heard two recent papers of this nature, but they have not yet been published. Szurek (25) and Johnson (17) have published very briefly how some of these cases resolved their problems in treatment, but most of these were rather simple cases and not published in sufficient detail.

Confusion arises immediately when studying ego distortions in delinquents, for in early papers no distinction was made between the individual delinquent and the sociologic delinquent. Be that as it may, a few concepts seem current since the work of Aichhorn. (1) He always maintained that the first step in understanding and treatment of delinquent personalities was the establishment of an object-relationship, and he drew attention to the difficulty of doing so because of the delinquent's inherent inability to form relationships that can endure frustrations. Van Ophuijzen, (29) Friedlander, (9) and Szurek (25) held the view that in cases of antisocial behavior the treatment plan consisted in the establishment of a relationship with a child. Some workers speak of a process of reeducating the child by means of an emotional relationship to an adult who represents a parent substitute. All agree that treatment is more effective before or at the beginning of the latency period, regardless of whether treatment involves parents or child or both, or whether it is done with the child in residency outside of the home.

Pertinent questions arise relative to the above statements. Many of the delinquent children, individual or sociologic, can and have formed strong object-relationships. This too often, however, involves relationships with an object whose superego ideals consciously or unconsciously differ from those of society at large. The author cannot emphasize too strongly that great confusion exists from the telescoping of all delinquents together in one category. If we are dealing with the individual delinquent unconsciously sanctioned by permissive destructive parents, the phenomenology is special for that disorder, and treatment must be psychiatric and quite different from that child who is a sociologic delinquent.

Kate Friedlander (9) says, "We are familiar with the picture of the anti-social child during late latency period and puberty, with his narcissistic self-evaluation, his impulsiveness and his inability to establish object relationships which endure frustrations." This description cannot be accepted as evaluating vast numbers of delinquents. Many of them have established strong object-relationships with parents and other adults, but these are relationships which do not conform with society's codes. Many delinquents can endure frustrations having to do with those prohibitions long consistently demanded by the family, but they cannot endure frustration associated with what has been permitted by the family. We know countless individual delinquents who do not have the narcissistic, self-evaluation observable in others. We must be discriminating in describing the character structure of delinquents as a total group. In each individual case a careful evaluation must be made of the healthy personality structure, conflicts, and defenses. Sometimes limit-setting has been excellent and effective in many areas but defective in another. To be sure, in certain cases, vast areas of limit-setting have been overlooked, and then we see the generally impulse-ridden child.

Much research is being done on the so-called predelinquent personality. There seems little doubt that, with careful study of the family, such forerunners in behavior should be detectable early, particularly in the individual delinquent. In sociologic or gang delinquency, the manifestations of impending difficulty may appear at a later age in the child. The soil for such sociologic outburst, however, is often well known in certain city areas. The child, neglected, mistreated, or subjected to overt misbehavior on the part of parents, may well move into a subculture group to resolve his insecurity, degraded self-esteem, and anger.

Once the diagnosis of individual unconsciously sanctioned delinquency has been clearly made, in *general*, treatment needs are now rather well known. If the child remains in the home, not only the child but the significant parent or parents must be treated by the psychiatrist as much or even more intensively than the child. Residency treatment for the child with little or no work done with the parents demands a long therapy if, when the child returns home, his treatment is to remain a stable integration. The availability of residency treatment of a dynamic nature is sadly lacking in America as well as elsewhere in the world. Depending upon the age of the child and the severity of the pathology at home, such residency therapy can be expected to run into years. Many times, parents are so disturbed and so destructive toward the child that they resist help for themselves in the dilemma. It has been the experience of the author and many others that treatment of the child in the home, without the parents in therapy, usually leads to greater acting out in the child. It appears that, with the child only in treatment, the unconsciously sanctioning parent feels he can shift the responsibility for the outcome onto the psychiatrist and is unconsciously motivated to act out his poorly integrated impulses even more so through the child. Ruth Eissler (6) has written brilliantly of the threatening of a family equilibrium by any therapeutic success with the acting-out member. This, therefore, necessitates concurrent help for parents.

Almost no intensive residency therapeutic cases of individual delinquency have been published. Rudolf Ekstein, then at the Menninger Clinic, gave, at a national meeting, a detailed partial treatment of such an adolescent boy, and it is to be hoped that this document will be published in great detail. In his paper on character synthesis in adolescents in general, Gitelson (11) deals with many valuable ideas on the therapeutic task and technique in treating the delinquent.

Many therapists have found that analysis of unconscious neurotic conflicts before the fairly good establishment of a solid superego led to disaster. As long as the child has no guilt about acting out in some area, such as stealing, anxiety aroused by uncovering an unconscious guilt about sibling rivalry, for instance, only leads to further acting out.

There are many valuable pointers on treatment of the individual delinquents by several authors in *Searchlights on Delinquency* that should be carefully scrutinized by all therapists in the field.

Hacker and Geleerd, (12) treating aggressive acting-out delinquents in a residency setting, found that there was a need for definite limiting-setting in successful treatment. They showed that, lacking internalized controls, the children became victims of unbuffered drives: "His demand for freedom thus becomes a denial of vulnerability which he feels consciously or unconsciously."

Treatment of parents and child outside the residency setting, to be most effective, must be of a collaborative nature. Intensive analysis and close collaboration of all parties concerned must be conducted in order for all participants to gain insight into the unconscious pathology and its genesis. This kind of therapy was the means through which Johnson and Szurek (19) arrived at their understanding of the genesis of unconscious, individual, antisocial acting out. In conjunction with an understanding of the genesis of the problems went, hand in hand, the necessary therapeutic changes. Parents are appalled as they gradually become aware that they are instruments in their child's misbehavior, and the greatest sensitivity and wisdom are necessary to help them analyze their role and conflicts. The author has treated many parents of very young delinquents (stealers, truants, fire setters, misbehavior in school) where the child was not treated at all. In such young cases it is often amazing to see the change in the child as the parents work through, in the transference, the problems associated with their poorly integrated impulses. Again we see parents whose destructiveness toward the child is so grave that it is easily apparent, from dreams and fantasies, that they can never be satisfied until the child arrives in reform school or prison.

There is not space in this chapter to discuss the multiple factors inherent in refined collaborative therapy. Szurek, Johnson and Falstein, (26) Johnson, (16) and others have written extensively of this elsewhere. Certainly, to see an adolescent five times a week and parents only once a week, the latter only in a supportive therapy, will never be effective. An analytic uncovering therapy for all concerned is mandatory. The parents who have poorly integrated antisocial impulses arrived at this level of operation with their child because of similar difficulties with their parents, albeit less blatant oftentimes. Necessarily then, their superego code and ego distortions must be meticulously analyzed in the transference. The author, with Szurek and other associates, has conducted such collaborative treatment over long years and knows that it is effective. Let us consider, however, the vast numbers of individual delinquents and the paucity of well-trained dynamic therapists. The only answer seems to rest with the earliest detection of difficulty, and we shall owe our gratitude to those research workers now engaged in such studies.

SOCIOLOGIC DELINQUENCY

What differentiates the individual delinquency just discussed from that great mass of sociologic or gang delinquency? In the individual delinquency from "acceptable" families, we emphasized that there developed a conscience defect *unconsciously* fostered by the parents. This fostering is the specific stimulus, with a great variety of secondary stimuli. So far, there has been no evidence of such a one-to-one specificity of stimulus in the gang or sociologic delinquency. It is the author's impression that arrival at telling etiologic factors in sociologic delinquency is a much more complex and difficult problem than has been true with the unconsciously fostered individual delinquency. Time and great open-minded collaboration between all research groups will be necessary to solve this formidably baffling problem. Fortunately, men and women with such characteristics have been working for years toward a greater lucidity of understanding. This author, having studied the individual delinquent with collaborators for twenty years, feels on fairly familiar ground there. It is difficult, however, for me to do full justice with clarity to the problem of sociologic delinquency.

Etiology of Sociologic Delinquency

Much has been written by way of explaining sociologic delinquents. It is safer at this time to suggest that only partial answers have been given, as most workers themselves would agree. A survey of some of the major views held to explain subculture sociologic or gang delinquency are the following: Some have asserted that the disorder is "traditional" and handed down from generation to generation. There is a hard core of truth in this, but additional factors seem to be involved, as will be reviewed. The so-called "social disorganization theories" maintain that sociologic delinquency flourishes in "interstitial areas" of our great cities, where not only is the area economically depressed but the population is mobile and never achieves a solidarity of community spirit or social organization. Observers with differing data in such areas maintain, however, that the social organization of the area as a whole may not be chaotic and without cohesiveness. As

Cohen (4) says, "the social organization of the slum may lack the spirit and the objectives of organization in the 'better' neighborhoods, but the slum is not necessarily a jungle. . . . The qualities and defects of organization are not to be confused with the absence of organization."

The so-called theory of "cultural origin," which has enjoyed considerable vogue, is supported by a great deal of challenging data. A classic statement of the cultural-transmission theory of sociologic juvenile delinquency is that of Shaw and McKay. (23) Certain well-known delinquency areas in Chicago were described, with the persistence of the delinquency attributed to the persistence of a delinquent tradition. The principal conclusion of a monumental storehouse of research by Shaw, McKay, and their associates was that sociologic delinquency was a subcultural tradition in the areas of the city inhabited by the lower socioeconomic classes. Such delinquent groups were not correlated with any national group. Thus, regardless of whether Poles, Norwegians, or Italians had taken over the area, the rate of delinquency would continue. At no time did Shaw and McKay maintain, however, that economic factors were the whole answer to the problem. Hewitt and Jenkins' (14) studies found, like Shaw and McKay, that sociologic delinquents were likely to come from lower-standard homes. Many statistical studies tend to confirm the popular impression that gang delinquency is primarily a working-class phenomenon. This is not to say that gang delinquency does not arise in upper-class areas. It is, however, far less common, and, where it exists, as yet has not been subjected to careful study. Tannenbaum (27) and Ruth Topping (28) have also been serious exponents of the cultural-transmission theory.

Any areas of high mobility and conglomerate composition lack a unity of culture, or certainly one consistent with the codes of those representatives of the larger society. Some authors maintain that the adult world presents no clear-cut authoritative models to the child, and he is confused and lacking in respect for any code. Others maintain there is in his group a subcultural unity with codes, but that it is incongruent with the larger society. It is "their" world against our world. Their subculture avows it is all right to steal or betray the other world. In war our culture says it is acceptable to fight and kill the enemy. The gangs and subcultural groups from which they stem may have little guilt about stealing or manhandling those outside their culture.

Hirschberg, (15) speaking from much the same point of view, has said:

In certain city areas, "the blighted areas," delinquent groups are a significant part of the social organization. Many of the people who live in these areas, regardless of their personal morality, have a strong subgroup sense of rejection by the larger and wealthier society on whose outskirts they live. Tremendous feelings of frustration and resentment ensue, and group attitudes condoning hostility, rebellion and destructiveness come into being. As a result, a mother and father in such a society may raise their child with the conventional emphasis on honesty, respect for property, etc., while they simultaneously express their bitterness, criticism and hatred of the larger society with which they struggle. As an individual the child *may* have no serious internal emotional problems. Again he may be deeply disturbed by personality conflicts. He then becomes a member of a subculture and freely joins with others into an aggressive group with whom he can identify and which is capable of anti-social activity. Nor is this problem confined exclusively to the poor. Many people who have struggled hard for years to accumulate a large fortune have powerful wishes for a hedonic way of life which they verbalize to the child but do not act out themselves, but which their children proceed to realize. Wanton indulgence of sexual impulses, of desires for "high living," or of "madcap" activity, may all be acceptable values in the parental culture, although as individuals these same parents may at times be reasonably conventional people. Their group antisocial ideal, however, achieves concrete form in the behavior of their children when the latter come together and form a clique, a set, a club, or whatever. Fundamentally the subgroup phenomenon is the same and the outcome in either case, rich society or poor, is a delinquent group. From the point of view of our society, however, the major problems arise with the groups and gangs that come from the more marginal economic societies.

What makes the sociologic delinquent group is that it is largely moulded by community and home forces more or less *consciously* in opposition to the whole other social world. For example, a youngster growing up in a gypsy society might have certain values and standards about stealing which would be very difficult from those of the villagers among whom he wanders. He would have incorporated a conscience which was "defective" in at least one area, in that it held stealing to be an acceptable way of obtaining money. This would be both his family's teaching and the way of the group. Once having incorporated the values and images of his parents and his culture, this gypsy youngster would then not only be able to steal without conflict, but would steal as an activity of his sociological group. There would be no *conscious* pressure brought to bear on him when he stole. Nor would he have guilt about what he did. Stealing would be an easy and natural act. On the other hand he might have a great deal of fear of reprisal and he might experience much reality-based anxiety in connection with his act. But it is important to realize that the conflict he experienced would be a conflict between himself and external reality, not between him and his own conscience.

Albert Cohen (4) says of the culturist view that the delinquent is said to develop

no respect for the legal order because it represents a culture which finds no support in his social world. He becomes delinquent. . . . From the recognition that there exists a certain measure of cultural diversity it is a large step to the conclusion that the boy is confronted by such a hodge-podge of definitions that he can form no clear conception of what is "right" and "wrong." It is true that some ethnic groups look more tolerantly on certain kinds of delinquency than others do; that some even encourage certain minor forms of delinquency such as picking up coal off railroad tracks; that respect for the courts and the police is less well established among some groups and that other cultural differences exist. Nonetheless, it is questionable that there is any ethnic or racial group which positively encourages or even condones stealing, vandalism, habitual truancy and the general negativism which characterizes the delinquent subculture. The existence of culture conflict must not be allowed to obscure the important measure of consensus which exists on the essential "wrongness" of these activities, except under special circumstances which are considered mitigating by this or that ethnic subculture. Furthermore, if we should grant that conflicting definitions leave important sectors of conduct morally undefined for the boy in that delinquency area, we must still explain why he fills the gap in the particular way he does. Like the social disorganization theory, the culture conflict theory is at best incomplete. The delinquent subculture is not a fund of blind, amoral "natural" impulses which inevitably well up in the absence of a code of socially acquired inhibitions. It is itself a positive code with a definite if unconventional moral flavor, and it demands a positive explanation in its own right.

Cohen (4) attempts a new view of accounting for the delinquent subculture — why it is there in the first place, why it is located where it is, and why it has a peculiar content. In his theory of any subculture's genesis he maintains that people with similar problems tend to draw together in a community. Depending upon the problems, collective solutions are elaborated with mutual support and identification. He believes that being reared in social worlds quite different from the middle-class standards of schools which he must attend leads to status frustration and loss of self-esteem in the child. Sharing such conflicts, children tend to draw together in little groups or gangs. Depending upon their private needs and tailored accordingly, the delinquent subculture represents a rewarding of any who attack or assault the middle-class status system. In other words, the delinquent subculture is thus seen to be the logical response to the frustration inherent between their early rearing and the middle-class standards they encounter in school and elsewhere.

Many students accept such views only in part. For instance, in severely delinquent areas, we find many children who are well-behaved and stable citizens even though poor economically, because they are being reared in families where the parents are truly normal, setting limits effectively, guiding their children consistently and affectionately. A famous educator in this country told the author that he was reared in a highly delinquent slum area. Six of his early friends had already been sent to the gas chamber. The educator, however, had been reared by economically poor but affectionate, consistent parents who emphatically set limits about all behavior that tended to get out of line. Cohen himself says that the explanation he has offered assumed that the delinquent subculture stems from conditions of the working class. He suggests that, could such delinquency flourish independently of those conditions as found in the middle class, "it would strongly suggest that those conditions are not necessary even in the working class. It would suggest we may have overlooked some other constellation of circumstances." As with the works of Shaw and McKay, there is not the space here to do justice to the distinguished contribution that Cohen has made to the study of sociologic delinquency. Their theoretical formulations and data should be considered carefully by any student open to challenging inquiry and suggestion.

Many students feel that in sociologic delinquency a multiplicity of variables enter the picture, with no single one asserting itself as the specific stimulus. In sociologic delinquency, not only do clashes of class and poverty enter in, but there are child neglect, lack of consistent supervision, adult antisocial example, and all degrees of cruelty and rejection; they all create their own personality problems, the solution of which may be sought in identification with common problems of the gang. Fortunately, no one seriously concerned with such delinquency is satisfied with any answer, and excellent research continues on many fronts.

As has been said, many psychiatrists and sociologists have long confused the issues of etiology and treatment of delinquents by condensing them all into one group. The unconsciously fostered individual delinquent scapegoat child is seen by many students as being different etiologically and often phenomenologically from the sociologic subculture gang delinquent. There are students, however, who today do not agree on such a distinction, so further research, education, and clarification seem necessary. Long ago, Shaw and McKay, (23) in Chicago, recognized that the gang delinquents, in large part, could not be helped in the psychiatrist's office. Albert Cohen was careful to make the distinction as suggested above. He said, "Although the 'delinquent subculture' is not a category of delinquency statistics, there are a number of studies which distinguish group or gang delinquency from other delinquency." Cohen goes on, "These studies furnish us with an important kind of evidence about the distribution of the delinquent subculture, for it is a hallmark of subcultural delinquency that it is acquired and practiced in groups rather than independently contrived by the individual as a solution to his private problems." It is this latter group who can only be treated by the psychiatrist.

Because of the confusing condensing of all delinquencies as if belonging to the same category, there are no reliable statistics of the ratio of the individual unconsciously sanctioned delinquent to the sociologic group. Except for a particularly blatant or vicious individual delinquent case, we more frequently read in the press of the sociologic delinquents. Because of this confusion also, it is impossible to talk of the ratio of girls to boys in either group. Taken as a whole, however, practically all published figures from many sources conclude that male delinquency is at least four times as common as female delinquency. Authorities seem fairly well agreed that female delinquency is more likely to be sex delinquency than other forms. Although girls at times may be involved, as Cohen says, " 'stealing,' 'other property offenses,' 'orneriness' and 'hell-raising' in general are primarily practices of the male." As one observes in a large diagnostic clinic, probably in individual unconscious delinquency, girls steal almost as much as boys. This is certainly not true of the sociologic group.

We come now to the overlapping of the two large groups of delinquency. Oftentimes, the lone individual scapegoat delinquent of the first group, with his deeply personal conflicts, gravitates to a gang in the sociologic areas. When such an individual, internally driven by antisocial impulses and the hostility of the parents, enters such a gang, he is often far more of a problem than are the others. He may be driven unconsciously to steal, destroy, or kill in a manner far more vicious than do other members of the gang that emerged in a culturally antisocial area. This is because of the generated hostility in the unconsciously aroused delinquent.

Treatment of Sociologic Delinquency

To set about a rational treatment, certainly first we must settle whether we are dealing with individual delinquency, initiated as previously described, or sociologic delinquency. The individual delinquent and his parents, as discussed above, are problems for the psychiatrist. Treatment of sociologic delinquents demands a broader and frequently entirely different approach. To be sure, such children, in part, may have internal conflicts demanding psychiatric treatment, but the acting out, often in large measure, is the product of the subculture into which they have drifted and often of living with direct adult examples or lack of any guiding supervision.

In the years of the late thirties and forties at the Institute for Juvenile Research in Chicago, recurrently, social agencies and the courts referred children to us psychiatrists for treatment — children who were not the personally involved individual delinquent but rather the sociologic delinquent. These were not cases appropriate for psychiatric treatment. The sociologist, with his appreciation of group mores, of presence or lack of community leadership, of traditions of delinquency in an area, of economic imbalances and pressures, of community resources that lead to cohesiveness or its lack, is fitted for leadership in directing a therapeutic attack. Long ago, in Chicago, Shaw and McKay (23) and others gave impetus and direction to the multiple community approach that seemed pertinent to a basic modification of the pressures in a delinquent area. Not alone was economic improvement significant, but leadership that would bridge the chasm between the ego-ideal of the delinquent area and that of larger society was necessary. Individual leaders, religious resources, recreational opportunities, police and court cooperation, social agencies — all must contribute to a broad-base community therapeutic attack. All sociologists and psychiatrists interested in this problem should study the truly pioneering work of Shaw and his colleagues. This work not only portrays their data and theories of the inception of "area" delinquency, but it includes the therapeutic measures.

The sociologist, in his enthusiasm for a therapeutic attack on a gang area, should not overlook those delinquents who have internal conflicts not susceptible to the techniques of therapy drawn upon from the community. It is necessary, therefore, diagnostically and therapeutically, that the sociologist and psychiatrist work together very closely. Too often, one gets the impression that psychiatrists maintain that what we need are more psychiatric clinics and residencies — that this will solve the problem. Again too often, newspaper reporters at least get the impression from sociologists that their approach will resolve all delinquency. Both kinds of therapeutic treatment are necessary, depending upon the correct diagnostic evaluation. Many times, careful diagnostic procedures will indicate that, for an individual child or family, both approaches are necessary, possibly not concurrently but in time, to resolve the problem.

EDUCATION

We cannot leave the problem of treatment of either category of delinquency without some reference to the possible efficacy of education. Many of us are often inclined toward pessimism on this score, but only time will show how much can be achieved through the avenue of bringing pertinent data to parents and adolescents involved in delinquency.

Whether parental sanction of antisocial behavior is conscious or unconscious, it is legitimate to question whether widespread lay knowledge of the role of parents and other adults in delinquency promises to limit the phenomenon. Nothing can be lost by such an approach, and the thesis might be defensible that the mischief perpetrated by the poorly integrated parents under consideration might well be curbed if it were generally conceded that delinquent behavior should not, without searching scrutiny, be ascribed to heredity, bad companions, poor schools, or divorce.- The poorly inhibited antisocial impulses of adults may not then so readily find expression in the encouragement of scapegoats. It is true that such adults might then become neurotic, evidencing emotional conflicts in which conscience has prohibited direct expression of an urge to antisocial action. Troublesome as such neuroses may be — in the form of phobias, compulsions, conversions, or a hundred other neurotic expressions — they are preferable to antisocial behavior, with its threat of perpetuation through generations. In most instances, a neurosis, with conscience holding the fort, is more amenable to therapy than is delinquency, in which the conscience is too weak or is in abeyance. The psychiatrist and sociologist apportion no blame but prefer to interpose a barrier of understanding that might divert conflicts of neglect or cruelty of parents toward their own individual neuroses rather than toward the misbehavior of children.

Educationally, we must consider the meaning of the juvenile court to parents and children. Both the general public and children continue to be unable to divorce the juvenile court from the criminal court and delay use of the juvenile court when it could be most profitably employed. Judge Nochem S. Winnet of Philadelphia points out that continental countries have tried to offset the criminal odium by placing the delinquency problems in the Department of Welfare, as in Sweden, or in the Department of Education, as in Russia. Judge Winnet (31) suggests that we use the designation "family court," which removes the emphasis from the child.

There is no doubt but that widespread knowledge among healthy citizens is the fundamental lever through which to enlist their aid and support for clinics, courts, civic therapeutic work, and an attack on a broad front for the amelioration of both categories of delinquency.

REFERENCES

1. Aichorn, August. *Wayward Youth.* New York: Viking, 1935.
2. Alexander, Franz. The neurotic character. *Internat. J. Psycho-Analysis* 11 (1930): 292.
3. ———, and Healy, William. *Roots of crime.* New York: Knopf, 1935.
4. Cohen, Albert K. *Delinquent boys: the culture of the gang.* Glencoe, Ill.: Free Press, 1955.

5. Eissler, K. R., ed. *Searchlights on delinquency: new psychoanalytic studies*, pp. 3–25. New York: Internat. Univ. Press, 1949.
6. Eissler, Ruth. In Eissler, K. R., ed., *Searchlights on delinquency*, pp. 288–305.
7. Emch, Minna. On the "need to know" as related to identification and acting out. *Internat. J. Psycho-Analysis* 25 (1944): 13.
8. Freud, Sigmund. *New introductory lectures on psychoanalysis*, pp. 203–4. New York: Norton, 1933.
9. Friedlander, Kate. Latent delinquency and ego development. In Eissler, K. R., ed., *Searchlights on delinquency*, pp. 205–15.
10. Giffin, Mary E.; Johnson, Adelaide M.; and Litin, Edward M. Specific factors determining anti-social acting out. *Am. J. Orthopsychiat.* 24 (1954): 664.
11. Gitelson, Maxwell. Character synthesis: the psychotherapeutic problem of adolescence, *Am. J. Orthopsychiat.* 18 (1948): 422.
12. Hacker, Frederick, and Geleerd, Elisabeth. Freedom and authority in adolescence. *Am. J. Orthopsychiat.* 15 (1945): 621.
13. Healy, William, and Bronner, Augusta. *New light on delinquency and its treatment*. New Haven, Conn.: Inst. Human Relations Publication, Yale, 1936.
14. Hewitt, Lester, and Jenkins, Richard. *Fundamental patterns of maladjustment*, pp. 94–104. State of Illinois, 1946.
15. Hirschberg, Cotter. Sociologic delinquency. Paper given at the San Francisco meeting of the A.M.A., July, 1954.
16. Johnson, Adelaide M. Collaborative psychotherapy: team setting. In Heiman, Marcel, ed., *Psychoanalysis and social work*, pp. 79–108. New York: Internat. Univ. Press, 1953. (Reprinted below, p. 245.)
17. ———. Sanctions for superego lacunae of adolescents. In Eissler K. R. ed., *Searchlights on delinquency*, pp. 225–45. (Reprinted above, p. 113.)
18. ———. Some etiological aspects of repression, guilt and hostility. *Psychoanalyt. Quart.* 20 (1951): 511. (Reprinted below, p. 333.)
19. ———, and Szurek, S. A. The genesis of antisocial acting out in children and adults. *Psychoanalyt. Quart.* 21 (1952): 323. (Reprinted above, p. 145.)

20. Locke, John. Some thoughts concerning education. *Harvard Classics*, 37:9–195. New York: Collier, 1910.
21. Reich, Wilhelm. *Der triebhafte Character*. Vienna: Int. Psa. Verlag, 1925.
22. Schmideberg, Melitta. The mode of operation of psychoanalytic therapy. *Internat. J. Psycho-Analysis*, 19 (1938): 314.
23. Shaw, Clifford R., and McKay, Henry D. Social Factors in juvenile delinquency. Vol. 2 of *National Commission on Law Observance and Enforcement, Report on the Causes of Crime*. GPO, Washington, D.C., 1931.
24. Szurek, S. A. Notes on the genesis of psychopathic personality trends. *Psychiatry* 5 (1942): 1.
25. ———. Some impressions from clinical experience with delinquents. In Eissler, K. R., ed., *Searchlights on delinquency*, pp. 115–127.
26. ———; Johnson, Adelaide M.; and Falstein, E. I. Collaborative psychiatric therapy of parent-child problems. *Am. J. Orthopsychiat.* 12 (1942): 511. (Reprinted above, p. 26.)
27. Tannenbaum, Frank. *Crime and the community*. Boston: Ginn, 1938.
28. Topping, Ruth. Treatment of the pseudo-social boy. *Am. J. Orthopsychiat.* 13 (1943): 353.
29. van Ophuijzen, John. Primary conduct disorders. In Lewis, N. D. C., and Pacella, B. L., eds., *Modern trends in child psychiatry*. New York: Internat. Univ. Press, 1945.
30. Weiss, Eduardo. Emotional memories and acting out. *Psychoanalyt. Quart.* 11 (1942): 477.
31. Winnet, Nochem S. Legal aspects of juvenile delinquency. Unpublished address to A.M.A., Philadelphia, December, 1957.
32. Woolf, M. The child's moral development. In Eissler, K. R., ed., *Searchlights on delinquency*, pp. 263–72, 1949.

SECTION IV

Collaborative Psychiatric Treatment

17

COLLABORATIVE PSYCHOTHERAPY: TEAM SETTING

From the chronological point of view, the first paper in this chapter would logically be the 1942 paper on collaborative psychiatric treatment written with Dr. Szurek (as senior author) and Dr. Falstein. Since this paper has already been included in the Introduction, I have chosen a later work to open the present section.

Whereas, the 1942 paper referred only to collaboration of two psychiatrists in the limited context of treatment for parent-child problems, the 1953 paper extends the definition of team participants and elaborates on wider clinical and research applications of the method. The paper closes with several conjectures and questions attesting to the breadth of Dr. Johnson's scope of interests. Later papers pursued some of these conjectures. Examples include questions about the etiology of psychosis and combined organic-psychodynamic factors in the genesis of epilepsy.

IN this chapter I intend to describe a highly refined procedure of therapy so far not widely used or understood, I shall be concerned, for the most part, with collaboration between two therapists. Two psychiatrists, or one psychiatrist and a social worker, may participate, as a minimum. At times three therapists may be intimately concerned. In this kind of therapy, the procedure no

Reprinted with permission from *Psychoanalysis and Social Work*, ed. Marcel Heiman (New York: International Universities Press, Inc., 1953), pp. 79–108.

longer is limited to the psychiatrist interpreting the structure and needs of a patient and advising the social worker to do thus and so, with occasional conferences to understand the movement of the case.

THE FUNCTIONS OF THE MEMBERS OF A TEAM

The concept that the psychiatrist always has the greater knowledge and experience is purely academic. Actually, the extent of one's knowledge depends only upon training and experience. It is no academic matter, however, that legally the psychiatrist must bear the final responsibility for the therapeutic task undertaken.

In this team procedure as I have experienced it for many years, every therapeutic hour by each therapist is reviewed fully with the other and the dynamic interplay of patient with patient, and each with her or his therapist, is fully discussed. Although this procedure first evolved where a child was concerned, it has been extended just as carefully in certain cases where the two patients are adults. By such collaboration in psychotherapy, the psychiatric social worker at times may contribute any of the multiple functions she fulfills in case work. Such activity would be in addition to the highly refined psychotherapy in which she participates in the office. Collaboration of the kind described can be a part of case work, then, and I can see no reason for sharp lines of demarcation between the prerogatives of workers in certain cases.

In observing clinically the mutual therapeutic responsibility, several features become evident. The question immediately arises as to the rationale for, or benefits accrued from, such a collaborative procedure. Such benefits cannot be observed in all cases — in fact in many cases only damage might evolve from the introduction of two therapists into the life of one patient or into the lives of two members of a family. This is a problem that warrants careful diagnostic scrutiny in every case.

Furthermore, the earlier procedure whereby the psychiatrist always treated the child, and the social worker treated the mother or father, has been greatly modified in a more rational direction. The needs of the patients — in a family those who need help might be only the two parents or some other two adults — and the training and experience of the members of the team should decide the question of procedure. I hope that the earlier dubious concept that the child needs a more dynamically experienced and trained therapist will go by the board as a generalization. The new direction has evolved along with increasing knowledge of how intricately the parent-child pathologic condition intermeshes in an etiologic symbiosis. The age of the patient cannot decide the issue of the introduction of a dynamic therapy.

Likewise, the sharp demarcation between definitive uncovering therapy and supportive therapy, limited respectively to the psychiatrist and the social worker, seems obviously untenable. At present it is believed that good supportive therapy demands as thorough a knowledge of dynamics as does uncovering therapy. Even in interviewing a mother or father or spouse on a so-called "simple reporting" level, real skill is required to maintain the tempo. Similarly, if the curative process requires fairly definite uncovering therapy by the psychiatrist, together with extra-office calls by a woman social worker who will explore the patient's social or recreational life, the role of this latter person, to be effective, demands the keenest understanding. This is true in an institution or outside of one. It may be that the roles of the participant therapists are reversed in a particular case, especially if the psychiatric social worker participating in such close teamwork is experienced. I encourage social workers to work with the transference and resistance as the case demands, and as the capacity of the workers makes possible, just as I encourage any senior resident in psychiatry. Needless to say, many residents and many social workers never will be able to work with transference and resistance, and never can become successful members of highly sensitive collaborative psychotherapy teams. It is a fact, however, that the social worker has to do much of the taxing leg work in dealing with the environment, such as court work, interagency contacts, making housing and housekeeping arrangements, conducting home studies, and so forth, largely because she has had the training and experience in many of these areas which usually the psychiatrist has not had. When she does psychotherapy, whatever the approach to definitiveness of it, this is only part of her function in case work.

I have covered sketchily only a few of the problems which arise concerning a collaborative team. Now, however, it is possible to consider fundamentals and I think it has been made evident that what I am about to discuss applies equally to both situations regardless of whether the team consists of two psychiatrists or a psychiatrist and a social worker.

THE NEED OF RESPECT AND FRIENDLINESS WITHIN THE TEAM

It is impossible to achieve much for the patients if, within the team, respect and mutual friendliness are lacking. The patient or patients soon sense competitiveness, narcissism and defensiveness or overprotectiveness in the therapist and further progress is prevented. For instance, two parents may be put at loggerheads or they may be led into apologizing for one another; under such circumstances it is impossible to get very far with their child. If there were no unresolved blind spots in either therapist, to speak hypothetically, then there would be no clinical need for the two members to get together to discuss their cases or case; only for research would this be necessary. However, there *are no* thera-

Collaborative Psychotherapy: Team Setting

pists without blind spots. The benefit achieved, therefore, from frequent discussion of cases is, in addition to research, the assistance one gives another to see what he might not see because of countertransference difficulties. In the course of discussion, resistance frequently springs from overidentification with one's patient. Therefore, collaborative conferences, to be of clinical value, must transpire, as has been said, in an atmosphere of friendliness and respect. In many instances benefit may accrue to the patient from my colleague's suggesting a point of view of which I have been unaware. At times I may be rendered very uneasy or irritated by his or her suggestion. The latter is characteristic of every collaborative enterprise, but the persons concerned must be so friendly and conscientious that they will be willing to explore the sources of such irritation. Such exploration obviously involves no confession to one's collaborator — such insight is one's own personal affair — and the collaborator should be concerned only with the renewed progress of treatment. Every good therapist grows somewhat in the course of each case even if working alone; he grows even more with each successful collaborative experience.

The psychiatrist, because of his own problems or inexperience in an enterprise in which he is collaborating with a social worker, may be anxious and hesitant about the social worker's therapeutic efforts. This feeling quickly is conveyed to the social worker and, whether she becomes irritated or not, the fullest use of her skills will be jeopardized unless she is a highly stable and experienced person. The reverse likewise is true. Tensions of the sort described should be aired mutually as soon as they are sensed by either partner. The psychiatrist, who for so-called philosophical or empirical reasons feels uneasy about collaborating with a certain other psychiatrist or with a certain social worker, should avoid entering upon such an enterprise. In other words, each member of the team *must* become aware of his own and of the other's assets, skills and limitations and the two must be able, as has been said, to deal with these openly, in a friendly atmosphere, or the procedure is doomed to failure. Often each must search for some time to find the collaborator with whom he can do the best work. The limitations otherwise can be too destructive on either side.

In my first attempts to advance the useful technique of collaborative therapy, I was most fortunate that an old and valued friend from medical school days happened to be in the same child guidance clinic. Thus, S. A. Szurek and I were able early to deal frankly with each other and to work in a friendly atmosphere. Having achieved real gratification and confidence thus, it has been relatively easy since to establish similar relationships with a number of social workers and with other psychiatrists.

I do not wish to be overly optimistic but, by and large, I have encountered circumstances wherein social workers and I have functioned with mutual pleasure. I have had the good fortune to teach in a number of the leading schools of social work and thus have had the opportunity, on the spot, to observe with the greatest respect their excellent and difficult educational and training programs. Therefore, because I was not ignorant of the philosophical concepts and clinical training imparted in such schools, I did not become anxious about the aptitude of their graduates. Furthermore, I had no fear of their attempting to maneuver me into a position of sanctioning their assumption of clinical responsibility for which they could not take the final legal responsibility. This I have never experienced. Social workers have taught me much about law and agency functioning; I have taught them something of the dyanmics of the personality. In research there is no qualitative line of demarcation in mutual psychotherapy even though, in research, both partners cannot always be highly experienced.

THE SETTING FOR COLLABORATIVE THERAPY

As for the situations for possible employment of such a team, I can be brief. Such collaborators could work in children's agencies; family agencies; public health agencies; guidance clinics; medical, surgical and psychiatric hospital settings, and under the purview of the psychiatrist in a private setting. I have worked on teams with social workers and psychiatrists in every one of these settings and with real comfort.

At the risk of appearing to repeat myself, I must make clear a conviction which applies especially in the private setting. I am completely opposed to nonmedically trained persons doing psychiatric therapy, even though it involves only so-called environmental manipulative therapy, without the supervision of a psychiatrist. The shortage of psychiatrists is a spurious argument for this practice. The more that is known generally by the public of emotional disorders, the more complicated become the defenses (as the conflicts are pushed deeper). Thus, psychosomatic symptomatology of a deeper and more complex nature is increasingly seen. Grand hysteria has largely disappeared in the more sophisticated urban areas and more complicated psychologic and somatic solutions are apparent. Many new organic diseases are likewise recognized from year to year and the interrelationships with psychogenic factors are so complicated that even the medically trained psychiatrist is in for trouble if he does not recurrently turn to the internist or surgeon for help in the proper evaluation of the symptomatology presented by his patients. Just the routine of sending the patient who is receiving psychiatric treatment to an internist once a year is no guarantee of safety, although it is better than nothing. Thus, as I said, no matter how highly gifted or experienced in psychotherapy a person without medical training may be, I am opposed to his undertaking care of a patient without the closest collaboration with a psychiatrist. On the other hand, if a gifted and experienced psychiatric social worker is functioning under my supervision, I set no more limits to the extent to which she treats her patient than I would set for a senior resident or a colleague of my level of experience.

I wish to reiterate that collaborative therapy does not imply occasional review with the psychiatrist of the status of the social worker's patient but regular conferences covering their mutual therapeutic hours in detail. This should be emphasized, since the procedure I have in mind has little in common with a tendency which I question although I do not condemn it; namely, referral of a patient by a psychiatrist to a psychiatric social worker who conducts treatment and who only occasionally consults with the psychiatrist.

SELECTION OF PATIENTS

Selection of patients best adapted to collaborative psychotherapy demands careful diagnostic study. Generalizations do not apply. Much of what I shall discuss below is still open to question. Some declarations, however, can be made with considerable confidence. In three large groups of cases intensive research has been done and for these collaborative therapy is to date easily the most effective procedure. This is not by any means to maintain that it works in all such cases, but nothing else seems so nearly adequate.

1. All little children or adolescents who are acting out seriously, in an antisocial manner, and who are living at home, are hazards to others and usually it is futile to try to treat them unless the significant parent [1] also is being treated. If placement of the

---

[1] In any case, one or both parents may be concerned in the pathologic state. For convenience, however, I generally shall use the singular. Moreover, because the parent who needs treatment more often is the mother,

child or treatment of the parent is out of the question, then it is less damaging to the family situation if a therapist does not undertake treatment of the child. Etiologically many of us who are in this work believe that the child acts out because the parent has a need to achieve vicarious gratification through the child for his own poorly integrated, forbidden impulses. This is more often unconscious than conscious on the parent's part. At the same time, the destruction of the child's stability in his society is also an unwitting expression of the parent's hostility to that child. Often just one child in the family is selected to be the scapegoat, and the reasons for his selection must be understood in each case. If the parent is consciously or unconsciously condoning the child's behavior and brings the child for help only to avoid his expulsion from school or to propitiate or beguile the law, through the therapists, treatment of any nature is practically hopeless unless the child can be removed from the home. If a therapist succumbs to the situation of unconscious sanctioning by treating only the child, then the acting out often becomes far worse. Increasing acting out on the part of the child may occur because the therapist has been unwise in his technical handling of the case but often another potent factor is that the parent, for multiple reasons, unloads the responsibility for any deviation into the therapist's lap, thus giving increased rein to his own pathologic sanctions of the child's acts. This is not the place to go into this matter in detail, but such unloading never fails to happen if only the child is treated. Case material later in this chapter will illustrate

usually I shall use a feminine pronoun to refer to "the parent." Likewise, I generally shall use a feminine pronoun to refer to the psychiatric social worker because this worker almost always is a woman. On the other hand, usually I shall employ a masculine pronoun to refer to the psychiatrist because, thus, the task of distinguishing between psychiatrist and social worker will be simplified.

this concept. Further relevant discussion also is to be found in *Searchlights on Delinquency*, wherein Szurek and I have written chapters (7, 1), and in a more recent paper of ours (5). Collaborative therapy seems a necessity in cases such as have just been described.

2. Another large category of patients whose condition some have found difficult to alleviate except by collaborative effort is composed of those troubled by prolonged fixations. In these cases, diagnostically, a child seems fixated at some instinctual level for a long time — either having regressed to such a point or never having moved beyond it.

In a normal family, if a child regresses after the death of a member of the group, or in the course of the child's own organic illness, or with the advent of a new sibling, support and kindliness at home, with or without therapy, usually restore the child relatively rapidly to his previous more mature level of adaptation. When, in the face of such reality, or beset by fantasy, a child remains obstinately fixated, my experience indicates that search should be made for what, in one or both parents, may be fostering the fixation. When a child remains arrested in his growth, or, when older, becomes unable to reach adjustment with his parents and regresses, it is important to search for something in the parents which frightened him at the higher level, but also to determine whether, at the fixation level, something may be giving the parent unconscious gratification. To illustrate this point the following might be described:

Johnny, aged six, gets a new baby sister. Soon Johnny begins to soil his clothes and this soiling continues. Finally he is brought for treatment by the less involved parent. Intensive analysis of the child alone may fairly well clear up the rivalry with the sister — the double oedipal conflict — so that Johnny is co-operating fairly well with parents, school and friends. The soiling, however, obstinately remains. It looks as if he has considerably by-passed this pathologic characteristic of his growth for the time being.

How is this explained and what can be done about it? Close scrutiny almost always reveals that at least one parent, for multiple reasons, has continued through the child an instinctual gratification and it takes the form of condoning arrested or regressive development as exemplified in soiling. The child feels a powerful obligation to the parent to continue to supply this gratification and case analyses reveal clearly what he sees in the face, hears in the voice, and observes in the behavior of this parent that conveys to him what he must do. A child so involved in a parent's guilty demand and sanction of the child's antisocial acts feels as guilty and frightened about modifying his behavior as would a normal child who was being seduced by an outsider to steal. Often such a pathologic situation can be observed and successfully treated only if treatment of both child and parent is undertaken. Again, case material will help to clarify these claims, which I originally incorporated in a paper read before the American Psychiatric Association in May, 1952.[2]

The most difficult cases the therapist encounters, except those which exemplify actual psychosis, fall into the foregoing two numbered categories. Until, in both groups, the details of the pathologic symbiosis were perceived and resort was had to mutual concomitant therapy, often the attempt at cure failed miserably.

---

[2] The paper was entitled "Collaborative Psychotherapy as a Research Tool in the Study of Fixation"; it has been expanded and will be published soon under the title "The Etiology of Fixations." [The paper was eventually published in 1953 under the title of "Factors in the Etiology of Fixations and Symptom Choice." It is reprinted below, p. 353.]

3. Something of the third category, namely, psychoses, will be discussed later under more theoretical implications.

These, then, are the three types of situation in which treatment is most difficult. Cases in group 1 require immediately tactful identification of which parent is unwittingly fostering the acting out. Cases of group 2 necessitate detailed scrutiny into what enrages the parent about the child's achievement at a normal level, plus what instinctual needs the parent is gratifying, through the child, at the fixation level or levels. And, as has been said, comment on cases of group 3 is deferred.

Many cases do not require the intensive uncovering and special therapy that have been described. On the other hand, in many cases, benefit results from collaborative efforts directed toward a different goal and geared to a different form of operation from those described. For instance, a neurotic woman or man may live inextricably in a miserable reality situation. After all, therapists cannot change the world and must often attempt to help patients so immured. Such a situation is familiar to any family agency. The best that the psychiatrist can do with it is to employ some degree of uncovering and supportive therapy and the best that the psychiatric social worker can do is to give more or less environmental manipulative help. Even in the selection of a housekeeper, the social worker should act on the basis of a great deal of dynamic understanding. Sometimes an adolescent girl whose mother is dead or ineffective may profit from definitive psychotherapy, but only if it is accompanied, at a certain phase, or throughout, by the peripatetic resources of an experienced and trained real mother figure. A worker who can function as such a figure will be called on many times to handle, verbally or not, many dynamically pertinent factors that are bound to form a part of even the most distinctly extra-office relationship.

Another group of patients of whom there are all too many are either adolescents or adults who suffered great physical brutality as children but whose mistreatment was of such a nature that, instead of acting out, they submitted masochistically. Analysis of such intensity and depth as would free these patients can be made only if there are available the economic and geographic resources to hospitalize them at various phases of their analysis when they become suicidal or act out. If such resources are not available, chaos may result. Therefore, in many such cases my goal is a limited one as far as cure is concerned. A collaborative setup, highly flexible and uncontaminated by narcissistic ambitions of either therapist, often can operate fairly successfully for years, making life less destructive for these patients. Only the team and the particular assets of its members can control the decision as to who might be seen by the psychiatrist or the social worker. If a very masochistic parent, physically misused early, has a disturbed child, the child might be accessible for highly definitive therapy, whereas only support for the parent, dynamically comprehended, may be — and I think should be in many cases — the instrument of choice. In a situation such as has been described, if two therapists are working concomitantly, the most careful collaboration is necessary to cope with the hostile envy of the parent while, at the same time, care is being taken not to endanger the defenses that are successfully damming back the parent's homicidal and suicidal impulses. Social workers and psychiatrists know from experience that environmental help, some degree of abreaction and so on, can carry such a parent, *if* the therapist knows how to limit every possible cause for regression. Many highly masochistic egos can be kept working if the therapist gives his treatment in careful doses, not too frequently, and if he has no need within himself to foster the patient's undue dependence and regression. Many therapists working intuitively get into such a tangle. Also analytic therapists — especially the very young or the very old — lose for a time or forever their confidence in bringing to bear on the issues what resources intuitively they used to employ with real sensitivity and success. The net result is that their patients frequently regress more easily than do many who are handled by the sensitive, intuitive, nonanalytically trained man.

Actually, the cases that lend themselves especially to collaborative therapy are some of the most difficult ones. When I analyze either an adult or a child, and no one else in the family needs serious help, the case usually is not so taxing as some others are. Take an example similar to one I used earlier in this chapter: A child or an adult has lived in a normal family but has had long organic illness, or early in the life of the family a crucial member of it has died, such as a mother. The analysis may be long and stormy and may cause the patient the greatest misery; still it presents a problem that is far easier dynamically than if the pathologic state of a family is genetically significant.

When the question of collaborative therapy arises after careful diagnostic study, an immediate practical problem is: How can the significant parent be brought into treatment? This entails a brief discussion of the degree of insight of the parent.

1. Some parents have insight and ask for help for themselves as well as for the child.

2. Some parents pay only lip service to the idea that they may need help, having heard lectures and read many articles.

3. Some parents can accept the fact of psychologic aberrations in the child but are extremely resistant to seeing their own role in the neurotic symbiosis.

Those of the first category come relatively readily into treatment. Those of the second group often will accept the proposition that the therapist see them as well as the child, to evaluate better their feelings in the whole situation and the extent to which such feelings may be clarified. It may not be necessary to say to such a parent: "You are a patient also." This type of parent will be likely soon to recognize this himself.

It is with the third category of parents that, in the beginning of their clinical experience, many therapists seem uneasy as to just how to proceed. Many questions arise which to them seem difficult; they believe that they are involved as therapists in a question of ethics and procedure.

Let it be remembered that in many cases, when the parents complain about the child, the motive for their coming is involved with their own pathologic state. Such parents, in their symbiosis with the child, have come to the point at which the ledger of gratification no longer balances equally or in the parents' favor. This is really the complaint and the motive for coming. Thus, the therapeutic responsibility is disrupted by any overidentification with child or with parents. Yet the following confusions arise in the minds of therapists.

Suppose the parent comes complaining of the child. The therapist knows that in time work must be done with one or both parents. Should he be silent about the role of the parent then, and start with the child? Later, when he tries to include the parent in treatment for one or more reasons (jealousy of the parent, resistance of the parent to losing the gratification she obtains through the child, blocking by the parent of the child's new attempts at growth), what will be the result? Many parents then feel that to draw them into therapy for which they never asked is to betray them. Their sense of being cornered may or may not be successfully analyzed. If the attempt at analysis in this direction fails, whether the parents remove the child from therapy or permit him to remain, the therapist, feeling that it would be a blow to the child to dismiss him, is saddled with a situation which never will be successfully resolved. This sequence of events has been part of every therapist's experience. The following has been observed, and can be correctly maintained: After the preliminary diagnostic evaluation has been made, and the mutual, or common, pathologic state has been briefly but frankly discussed with the significant parent, and it has been suggested that treatment for child or parent or both would be helpful, but the parent is not ready for such an approach, she will withdraw the child from possible treatment. The child, then, possibly will be deprived of treatment for years — because the parent was frightened by the proposal made to her.

I have raised many of the difficulties that may arise from the opening discussion with a particularly resistant parent. How can resolution be achieved, to the benefit of all? When a therapist encounters a difficult situation in which neither of two technically possible approaches seems feasible, it is frequently helpful for the therapist to concentrate on a question: May there be some problem of countertransference which makes the difficulty seem insoluble? In my own experience, much improvement in my technique in dealing with a highly resistant parent has come about through resolution of some countertransference resistance in myself. In a case involving a highly resistant parent, the therapist could, of course, take the attitude that if the parent is going to feel tricked or betrayed, the child may have to suffer and be deprived of treatment until the parent comes to her senses. Or, if the therapist overidentifies with the child, he may feel it is justifiable to allow the parent to feel concerned and betrayed so that at all costs the child may be rendered safe from a destructive symbiosis. But neither of these attitudes really solves the difficulty.

It will be profitable in this connection to think further of what transpires in the course of an adult's analysis. This will entail some review of what has been said. The patient, in his anxiety, may ask for a blueprint of what is going to happen. After a few interviews with him it can be perceived that he will have many terrifying and miserable periods. He will rage at the therapist for not having warned him of the severity of the ordeal. He will charge that he was trapped and so on. Yet this is not explained to him ahead of time because he might not believe what he was told anyway, or he might be frightened away from treatment. In time, transference to the therapist will carry him through his ordeals whereas, at the beginning of treatment, he could not possibly know of this transference and its strength to help him. It is part of the therapist's job as a physician to accept the patient's feelings. In time the patient knows that the therapist's conscience is clear, for later the patient realizes the strength of the transference and how it makes his ordeal bearable. *If*, however, an inexperienced therapist has not the fullest emotional appreciation of what he was obliged to do to save his patient, he will be so guilty and frightened by the accusation of trickster or traitor, that only chaos can result. Tricks are tricks when the perpetrator uses a technique for a selfish or narcissistic reason or out of ignorance.

Thus, in dealing with parents who obviously are without any insight, I feel perfectly guiltless about not telling them at the outset that they must be patients. The mother, for instance, at first may talk only about the child. Soon she may be talking more about herself. When, however, resistance develops, then she protests that she never asked for treatment; it is then that she charges betrayal and so forth. Here again the skilled therapist counts on the development of transference as a support when resistance has to be analyzed. The plan may not always work, but the technique is increasingly fruitful as experience increases. Parent and child both are likely to continue with treatment.

As time has gone on, then, it has become increasingly clear to me that much of what, in my early work, I called frankness with patients or frankness with resistant parents, stemmed from my fear that some day I would be called to account and that, should the day come, feelings of guilt might spring from many sources which had no rational bearing on the issue at hand. The therapist can feel very guilty about his ignorance or lack of experience, or about his purely selfish wish to set up a treatment situation as he wants it, so that it will be easy on him and things will work out "his way." If he is conscious of these sources of his guilt and admits as much to the patient, order takes over where chaos reigned.

Thus, today, rather than frightening parents into withdrawing from all help for their child and themselves, I can without guilt tell a highly resistant parent that I will try to help the child if the parent will join in the therapeutic enterprise and will see a colleague who will add, in the case, whatever knowledge she can acquire of how things move at home. An experienced colleague soon will have the parent talking more and more about herself or himself. I do not emphasize that the parent is to be a patient too. When, later, the parent becomes anxious and angry her therapist helps her to understand what is frightening her and why she doubts my good intentions. This recalls my earlier statement that the parent's real motive in bringing the child for help is that the mutual neurosis (when it *is* that) is shifting the balance of gratification so that more pain than gratification is being felt by the parent member.

There are varied points of view of this single set of problems which I have briefly covered with regard to the diagnostic and planning responsibilities of the team. Undoubtedly my thinking, as well as that of others, will change with greater experience and study.

In the cases now to be discussed I am concerned primarily in elaborating how a team can actually function in the therapeutic task at hand. In this presentation, in limited space, it will be impossible to attempt to describe the variations in technique that are necessary in cases of all the large categories wherein collaborative therapy is advantageously applicable.

ILLUSTRATIVE CASES

Let it be said that a child apparently has been fixated for a long time at a certain instinctual level. This level, say, is more malignant than that at which a child might be fixated who by death or illness had been deprived of a member of his normal family but who had received intensive therapy alone or else splendid support at home.

Case 1. — Four-and-a-half-year-old Eddie was brought for treatment because he wanted to be a girl and because, with the exception of a few months when a housekeeper was in the home, he continued to soil. For the previous year and a half his soiling had been according to a ritual; he had to defecate into a diaper when lying on the bathroom floor. Eddie abhorred odors and had to be cleaned immediately. He was the terror of the neighborhood and had no friends. He had a sister, two years old, who was much more the mother's favorite, as she spontaneously admitted. Realizing that the mother was a very neurotically ill woman who would need long analysis, we decided to start intensive analytic treatment for the boy, leaving the mother untreated for the time being.

The boy was permitted to regress to the infant level, to a pre-ambivalent state. The therapist was permissive of the boy's dependency needs, and Eddie soon realized that he did not wish to be a girl but a baby. Without pressure to grow up, and with indulgence, he became rapidly satisfied; he no longer wished to be a baby or a girl, and began to grow up to the level of a child five years of age with a five-year-old's problem of ambivalence toward both parents. Within a year and a half, Eddie was a happy child, possessed of friends, progressing well in kindergarten, competing normally for his age with his father, no longer victimizing his sister and so on.

One island of trouble, however, remained absolutely fixed — the soiling ritual in the bathroom. On a simple reporting level the mother told how Eddie had said, "What would you do if I used the toilet?"

She told him, "I don't know."

When Eddie said, "When I'm six, I'll probably use the toilet," she said she could think of nothing to say.

This woman was paralyzed, so to speak, concerning an appropriate response. Nevertheless, the fact that Eddie now was asking such questions, and in play was insisting that Hopalong Cassidy and all his heroes go to the bathroom after breakfast, showed that he was beginning to try to solve his problem. About this time his sister, then three-and-a-half-years-old, was reported to be developing the same soiling difficulties.

For research reasons and to avoid another long course of treatment, it was decided to try to engage the mother in treatment, but of as limited extent as possible. At first she was excessively sweet and ingratiating. After a time she talked regularly to her therapist about the children's bathroom habits, recurrently asking advice but discarding it before ever it was given. One day her therapist commented that the mother seemed troubled about being at all definite or firm about these functions in the bathroom. The mother then told that when her little daughter had seemed hesitant to urinate in the bushes with the neighborhood children, the mother had gone out and showed her how to do as the other little ones did. When the therapist asked the mother if she knew why she did this, the patient became defensive and very angry.

The mother then talked at length of many Pacific tribes "who can soil all their lives." She gave a considerable anthropologic summary. When the therapist then suggested that possibly the mother had some feeling, not fully known to herself, about the soiling impulses of people, the mother vehemently denied this. Immediately, however, she recounted, with many angry tears, that from her early childhood through late adolescence her own mother had permitted the family home to be unclean. The patient's father, a passive, inadequate man, and the mother, had allowed the latter's alcoholic father and three alcoholic brothers to live with the family and the house was "constantly smeared with, and smelling of, vomitus and urine." The patient had been humiliated so often by this that finally she had ceased to bring friends home. To condense the material drastically, she had not been conscious of her rage at her mother for permitting all this "mess" and, making an identification with her mother so that she would be relieved of her feeling of hostility toward her mother, was finally achieving ambivalent gratification through the soiling habits of her son and now of her daughter. Of course, she was crippling them as well.

In other words, the mother, having repressed her rage toward her own mother, was trying to solve the problem in this way: "I don't have to hate my mother for permitting that outrageous mess made by my uncles and grandfather, if I can be messy too — through my children." Fostering this in the children also gave vent to much of her hostility; it was transferred to the children and was destroying their adjustment with everyone concerned.

Finally, when Eddie *did* begin to sit on the toilet to defecate, it was soon clear to his therapist that the heckling by his mother persisted — that he still was far from pleasing her. The mother awarded him a large candy bar for a big "B.M." and a small piece of candy for a small "B.M." Arguments, of course, ensued over size of "B.M." and the merited award. His therapist found Eddie confused and angry. She first of all had to clarify the realities for the child; namely, that nobody can decide to have a large or a small "B.M.," which was counter to the mother's assumption. The anger against his mother, the anger against the therapist as a transference figure and also as a person having a different view from his mother, had to be analyzed. The mother's therapist, apprised of this new form of unconscious attack and disapproval at home, could quickly identify it in the mother's vague and extremely distorted material. Undoubtedly the mother's therapist, having been warned by the child's therapist, could see through the mother's disguises more rapidly than she could have done if she had been working alone, and could accelerate the mother's progress. The mother volunteered the story of the awards and bickering about the size of the stools and of course the therapist encountered intense maternal resistance following inquiry as to why the awards had been given.

There were many indications of great confusion in Eddie's mind about realities, promises and deceptions. It became increasingly clear to the mother's therapist that her patient might tell three different stories about one incident. The therapist never could be sure when the mother was falsifying outright, so she took this up directly with the mother. The patient went on to tell how her own mother frequently would lie to spare her daughter from having to face definite and inevitable painful realities.

Gradually the patient became able to deal with realities and to avoid deceiving herself, her therapist and her children. The immediate effect on Eddie was evident. It was gratifying, from that time on, to see this mother work sincerely at her treatment and to observe a real personality emerging from the previous mist and fog of vagueness, isolation and anxiety. Her treatment continued long. Eddie became well long before the mother's therapy terminated.

It might be interesting to discuss the work of a collaborative team in an acute emergency situation.[3]

Case 2. — The service was asked to send someone to see a boy, twelve years old, who was in a hospital and who had regressed to the level of a two- or a three-year-old. He was soiling, was eating only a little fluid and was whining like a baby. The history included the information that the boy had been brought to the hospital partially blind. One evening an orderly had begun to shave his head. The boy had protested and the orderly had told the boy that his brain was to be operated on. Next day, in fact, a brain tumor had been removed. The boy had recovered all his neurologic faculties. There was no possibility that injury to the brain or edema of the brain was a factor in his state by the time the psychiatrist saw him and heard from him about his terror concerning the operation. While the boy was still in the hospital, his therapist bent all efforts toward comfort and mobilizing the anger which was associated with his terror and with his sense of having been betrayed. In the course of the second hour of treatment the boy said spontaneously, "Maybe the doctor will come back and cut off my diddle (penis)."

3. [This case is presented in an expanded version in paper 22, p. 361. *Editor.*]

The anger came out in rages against doctors and nurses. The terrifying experience through which the boy had passed was particularly destructive in his case because he had been reared by a passive father and a tyrannical mother who had good reason to despise her own father; moreover, from the time of the boy's birth, she had consciously not wanted him and had hated him. He was considered a sweet boy who "never once talked back." In other words, this child had tremendous castration anxiety and doubts about any consistent love from the mother before what he considered his betrayal in the hospital. The boy's therapist hoped to gain his confidence and to help him back gradually to his previous adjustment while he was in the hospital away from his mother. This was not possible, however, since the parents were abjectly poor financially although the mother's father was wealthy. The parents left the hospital telling all the physicians they were returning home where help for the boy was unavailable.

Six weeks later, however, the parents called, saying that they were living in one rented room in the town where the operation had been performed because they had been too anxious to go home. The boy was then in worse condition than when he first had been seen in the hospital. He threatened to kill his mother, displayed a complete sleep reversal and refused most food since his mother insisted that he eat specific things and amounts. The father was exhausted. He had been afraid to sleep for fear that the boy would become violent against the mother. At this point the collaborative team began to plan and operate.

What were the possibilities of breaking into the vicious circle of anxiety and rage that was paralyzing this family? The mother was far too ill and inaccessible to enter even the most superficial therapeutic relationship. The father, extremely dependent and feeling very guilty for not having brought the boy to the hospital before the blindness was far advanced, seemed the only hope.

It seemed imperative to get the boy out of his regression and to preserve his ego. This was impossible with the mother heckling him constantly. It was decided that one therapist would be most sympathetic in an interview with the father and would give him a mild sedative to enable him to relax a little. In the interview, a strong immediate dependent transference and the father's sense of guilt about the boy were utilized. The father then was strongly advised that he must take a stand with the mother and send her home to rest while one therapist worked with him. Another therapist was to work with the boy, seeing him in his room at first, utilizing only a few simple interpretations and, for a time, responding to his needs mainly with great indulgence on a preverbal level. The father was advised to cater to the boy's whims about eating. If the boy wished only popcorn for two days, popcorn he should have. And he should be allowed to eat when, what, and only as much as, he wished. If the boy did not care to walk outside, if he wished to scold and swear, he was to have his way. Real destructiveness or physical battles were to be prevented if at all possible.

The father quickly put into effect all of the foregoing. Typically, he went out at midnight to get a radish sandwich which the boy requested. He carried the child to the bathroom as demanded; he urged nothing. The boy once swore and shouted for thirty-six hours straight. The next day he did this for an hour but it never happened again. The father, with his sense of guilt and his strong belief in his therapist, was extraordinarily flexible. No attempts were made to analyze the father's conflicts toward the boy and wife. After about five weeks the boy had grown up considerably. He was eating well and spontaneously. He was walking to the bathroom and outside. Nevertheless, he remained angry and said very little. His therapist, therefore, went to his room and repeated firmly and definitely the interpretations given in the hospital pertaining to his shock and terror, his rage against the doctors, his fears of real castration, his rage at the parents for abandoning him to the doctors without discussion and his rightful feeling that no one in the world at that time had protected him or seemed to love him. The boy was furious during all this discussion, but the next day the patient walked into his therapist's office smiling and behaving more like any boy twelve years old. Certainly he was more jaunty and more free of hostility, although he was adequately aggressive, than he had been, according to reports, before the operation.

When the mother returned to town, the father and the boy were far better able than they had been to stand firmly against her. Fortunately, moreover, her father had capitulated and gave all necessary financial help. Follow-up letters from the parents have indicated that the boy was like any twelve-year-old and talked up to his parents regardless of his mother's resentment.

Undoubtedly an experienced single therapist could have treated both father and boy. However, fairly young therapists were working on the case and it seemed better all around if each patient had its own therapist. Needless to say the father was completely won over to the idea that the boy was not losing his mind because he behaved as he did. Additionally, the landlady was most understanding to permit the shouting and cursing for the necessary six weeks of rehabilitation.

Presumably, the boy eventually will die of the malignant tumor. The frightful predicament of the mother as she sees him finally growing helpless can easily be imagined. Her bitterness, sense of guilt and depression will be tremendous and, at that time, possibly a therapist can enter the situation sufficiently to help her to ward off some psychotic break directed toward herself and possibly against the child.

Such an acute emergency situation as developed in case 2

lends itself well to management by a collaborative team. The father received, largely, dynamically understood support. The child received, for the longest period, largely nonverbal contact, rationally used by his therapist and tremendous indulgence on the part of his father. Only later, when a base line of confidence in the world again had been established in the boy, were the interpretations of his predicament offered and constructively accepted.

I should like to describe another challenge to a collaborative therapy that many therapists will encounter and which I believe cannot be handled otherwise. Both patients come for therapy because of an acute, hazardous state. To be sure, one very experienced therapist might be able to do the task alone but two therapists certainly can salvage many more patients than are being saved now by only one partner of the symbiosis being treated.

The following case typifies a hazardous undertaking unless careful collaborative planning is given, especially if both patients are to remain in the home. The case falls within the category of acting out but could move in the direction also of psychosis if given the right balance of forces.

Case 3. — The parents brought their son, fifteen years of age, for help. The boy came willingly for he was very anxious. He had had episodes of extreme panic contingent on the fear that he would kill his mother. Such episodes had been especially terrifying at night, when his destructive impulses also had been directed, to some extent, against his thirteen-year-old brother. The boy was a fine student but had no companions. His mother was "his girl," he said.

The mother was very apprehensive about her son's impulses and was easily observed to feel guilty. To condense the material drastically, she fostered his getting into bed with her and her husband and often alone with her, even though she observed her son to be uneasy about his erections. She unwittingly encouraged his isolation from colleagues, and, in one interview, the experienced therapist could observe the sadistic sexual gratification which the mother achieved from her relationship with her older son. In a few interviews, the background of her behavior became obvious.

It was believed that this boy, in one of his recurrent episodes of panic, could act out or break down, depending on the direction in which the mother might swing the balance of her power. The father, a most ambivalent man, could not be trusted to help. It seemed wise to have the boy live in the medical section of a hospital for a few days, where his therapist could see him. The boy would sleep in the hospital but would go out to school. At the same time the mother would begin treatment with her therapist. It seemed dangerous to have the two living together until some strengthening transference had been aroused in both. During the days that the boy resided in the hospital, his therapist found that he talked readily about his mother's being "his girl" and that he needed no other. The therapist was direct in telling the patient that as long as he remained so close to his mother he would be angry toward both parents, since his father was in the closest relation to the mother. It was explained to the boy that he had tried to solve this problem by being less grown up than he really was. It was added that this kind of solution also angered him. The therapist stated that there was another solution; namely, to stay out of the mother's bed and to work with the therapist about matters that worried him. In fact, the therapist was emphatic that getting into bed with his mother must stop at once. Soon much anger emerged toward the therapist, but gradually the boy became more relaxed and, the mother having been similarly prohibited by her firm therapist, the boy was sent home after five days of residence in the hospital.

The boy made rapid strides with his therapist, many defenses were analyzed, while necessary educational measures were introduced. The mother, a typical hysterical personality with all her sadomasochism toward males very close to the surface, developed a strong ambivalent transference to her therapist, a man. Her son, feeling freed of obligation to her neurotic emotional needs, soon worked sincerely at his therapy, and quickly acquired many male and female friends. When, finally, the boy wanted to interrupt his treatment since he was enjoying life, this was permitted — for years there had been too much demand on him that he be regressed and obligated to an adult. We knew he would need further therapy later, but with many adolescents interruptions for experimenting in growth are helpful and lead to ego change. At the same time, both collaborators agreed that great vigilance must be exercised by the mother's therapist to ensure her not using the boy again to escape her problems with her male therapist. In spite of such vigilance, for a time one could see her attempting to use the younger brother for her purposes, and he, formerly an outgoing popular boy, was quickly pulled into an anxious, regressed state. Increased therapeutic hours for the mother, and greater activity in analysis of her motivations, gradually freed this second boy. She then began to turn her destructiveness toward her husband, a more equal match, as her problems were further analyzed. Needless to say, this type of woman would need long treatment with variable amounts of help for her husband.

The foregoing case (case 3) is typical of the background in many of those relationships that lead to tragic acting out and homicide. The brutal murder of a mother by an adolescent son was spread all over the newspapers in the country about two weeks after our patients began therapy. Their anxiety as they identified with this tragic outcome was prominent. With the boy, his therapist emphatically professed no concern that his patient would ever act on his impulses. The mother felt so guilty about her destructiveness toward her son that, of course, she considered that she deserved to be destroyed by him and unwittingly fostered destruction. To understand where the mother received the unconscious sanctions for her behavior with her son, took only a short time to discover in her relationship with her parents.

Case 4. — A boy, two and one-half years of age, was brought to the clinic because he was constantly clutching his genitals. Even the most cursory observation of the child showed that this was not any masturbatory consideration but obviously protective. Analysis of adult males often reveals that, fearing their own hostile sexual impulses, they experience distressing contraction of the cremasteric muscles and upward retraction of the testicles. One interview with each of the parents demonstrated clearly the mother's tremendous unconscious hostility toward males. At the time they came to the diagnostic clinic, the marriage, at least consciously, was working moderately well. It was clear, from the fantasies inadvertently expressed, that the husband was being spared the wife's hostility, since it was being directed toward the child, subtly but potently, all overlaid with sweet reasonableness on the part of the mother. The little boy's own fantasies demonstrated clearly that his unconscious knew what was going on and he was greatly confused and frightened.

This mother showed sufficient flexibility and insight during the diagnostic interviews to warrant our advising the parents that we might be able to help by seeing Jimmie, and also the mother with regard to some of her feelings. Collaborative therapy was begun.

Jimmie immediately loved his play hours and the therapy, although it was obvious that he was fearful and inhibited about any aggressiveness. Every hour with each patient was reported in each seminar so that the significance of each patient's problems, as they impinged on the problems of the other, could be understood clearly. Jimmie's clutching was associated with any fearful situation in which he found himself with the therapist and it subsided completely, or worsened, as the mother's ambivalences manifested themselves in her own treatment. Of course, as in any such case, when she analyzed her conflicts with men, the husband began to experience her hostility; this was not always directed toward her therapist. As her negative transference was understood, she let up on her husband and Jimmie except when, to punish her therapist, she disturbed her husband to the point where he was furious and, hating her and psychiatry, wished often to terminate therapy.

As matters developed, it seemed important that Jimmie continue in treatment, since his inhibition against standing up for his rights, in even a small nursery group, was marked. Furthermore, as time went on it became clear that although the father's ambivalence toward him was far less than that of the mother, it was of such degree that he could not be depended on suitably to support the boy. The child continued, then, with his male therapist. The mother always called the child's penis his "good girl." The boy's confusion relative to this was profound, and his sense of obligation to the mother to think in terms consistent with her term long was obvious, although intellectually for a time she refrained from using the word. The major therapeutic task obviously became that of long-time dynamic therapy for the mother.

The last case which I wish to include here is a dramatic and tragic illustration of what can happen when awareness of the suitability of collaborative therapy, or the facilities to carry it on, are lacking. Before reporting the case I wish to mention briefly that not only can the destructiveness of parents and their thoughtlessly expressed fantasies weaken a child's ego integration and defenses but, also, a physician's fantasies and statements or predictions about a child can be devastating to a parent's ego defenses against destructiveness toward the child. Many end results of this mechanism are encountered.

Case 5. — The case in point was that of an identical twin, a boy three years of age, named Dick. The child had been in a frightful automobile accident when he was a year and a half old. A physician had told the parents that even if he lived, "he would be only a vegetable." The mother then wished he would die and, realizing that she always had disliked him, she felt relieved that he might die. These feelings, however, were unknown to the therapist until much later. The boy lived to become the terror of the neighborhood; he was utterly impulse ridden.

When he was brought for study, his intelligence and aptitudes were found to rate a trifle higher than those of the "well" twin. In a few play hours with him, during which he was the object of a degree of friendly, definite firmness with regard to acting out, he appeared to be a charming, active, fine little boy. The neighbors then found him to be so, but he was his old self with his mother.

The boy's problems were not organic and the parents were told that in time he would be well. It is known, however, that a neurotic parent cannot safely be robbed of hostile and vicarious gratification such as this mother was achieving through Dick's acting out, unless help is given her. This mother required assistance to resolve the need which had boiled to the surface when the surgeon substantially had given her permission to *believe* that her son was to be a psychotic vegetable. She should have had a collaborating therapist early in the picture, but one was not available just at the time and the family was planning to move away in a few months. To open up the woman's problem until after the move seemed unwise.

Actually, as events proved, it was unwise not to do so. For two weeks, her vicious attacks on the boy were interspersed with long periods of dreamy withdrawal, in which she seemed to be out of contact, even to the point of failure to feed the children, and in the course of which she was depressed and entertained suicidal thoughts. The development of these symptoms was not brought to my attention. Still, I should have foreseen their development, because I knew from long experience that the mother would be much disturbed to receive a hopeful (from the therapist's point of view) diagnosis about the boy. Such an event is as predictable as a colorimetric end point in a chemical determination.

In a few weeks the mother had broken so completely that she had to be hospitalized on a closed ward. Protected in the hospital, the mother relaxed, and study made it clear we were dealing with a highly sadistic woman. For years she had been very successful in a career and she had done fairly well with her family until the drastic diagnostic prediction about her twin son, which sanctioned her acting out through him and toward him. She had been ruthlessly treated by her father; she hated and mistrusted men, and she had been hostilely seductive toward many in her past. It became clear that hers was a malignant, hysterical personality, that she was not schizophrenic, and that she would be easily accessible to treatment, stormy as it would be. Actually this woman, before her break, had asked for some therapy if possible and probably the unfortunate break in her ego adjustment could have been averted by a second therapist.

THE COLLABORATIVE TEAM IN RESEARCH

The possibilities of the collaborative team as a research instrument have been explored only in the past twelve years. Many of us who have been interested in this matter have found that not only was the curative process catalyzed, in collaborative therapy, but that our observation of etiologic factors observed at their source of operation made for far greater scientific accuracy than we could attain by reconstruction of what might, or must, have happened. It was detailed observation of what operated in the parent-child symbiosis that led some of us, ten years ago, to question seriously many theoretical ideas such as those of "death instinct," "instinctual anxiety," "phylogenetic imbalances in opposing instinctual strengths," and so forth. Szasz, in his recent article (6), has brilliantly offered evidence from biologic sources — tissue cultures, for instance — which seems definitely to discount a death instinct. This is in line with what many of us have observed clinically and have questioned.

A group of us at the Institute for Juvenile Research, more than ten years ago, aware of the tool which social workers were sparingly, but effectively, using as a kind of collaborative psychotherapy, decided that we should study the parents as closely as the child relative to the baffling problem of so-called school phobias. Our observations eventuated in clear-cut understanding of the etiology of such neuroses in the child and the parents. This had far-reaching results and led to our use of collaborative therapy and to our research on "acting out." Reports of all of this work have been published (1, 3, 4, 5, 7, 8).

CONJECTURAL IMPLICATIONS DRAWN FROM COLLABORATIVE EXPERIENCE

Many child analysts have maintained, as did Anna Freud, that many children were not accessible to cure by analysis. The explanations for failure have never been definitive. If a child is in the course of analysis, some child analysts have maintained a parent should not be disturbed by being treated at the same time. In selected cases I have seen the necessity of doing this, however, and results have been beneficial, as is evident in this report. Accordingly, I am unimpressed with flat statements, unsupported by evidence, that the close type of collaboration of which I am writing should not be utilized.

Research in collaborative therapy has netted much advance in understanding of the dynamics of fixation. As Szasz has so correctly stated, in work with higher biologic forms such as man the investigator is not dealing with "closed systems" as he is in simple physics or chemistry; he is dealing with "open systems"; namely, with "symbioses."

Some of us who are working in child psychiatry today are observing lines of similar evidence for the etiology of psychosis. For instance, an eight-year-old daughter maintains that her mother is trying to poison her. Analysis of the mother's denial of her wish to destroy the child leads rapidly to the child's relaxation and freedom from the belief that her mother wishes to destroy her. This illustration can be multiplied over and over, but detailed careful studies of this kind of case must be made and are in progress all over the country.

Many syndromes certainly are composed of varying quantities of etiologic factors some of which are outright organic factors and some of which are emotional. These factors constitute a spectrum, one end of which is largely organic and the opposite end of which is largely emotional; between the two ends are variable mixtures of the organic and the emotional. Epilepsy, or so-called "convulsive disorders," furnish an apt illustration. Detailed studies by neurologists and psychiatrists, together with the collaboration of two or more psychotherapists if the emotional component is large, undoubtedly will furnish much more scientific evidence than is available now; such evidence is much needed. Automatically to give drugs to *all* persons with convulsive disorders, without further neurologic or psychiatric research, would lead to a dead end.

Collaborative research is as thrilling as a refined detective story, and nearly everyone who has ever been a part of a collaborative team, or engaged in group research, will bear this out. Fitting the pieces together, gathering hints as to what to watch for in the material of the two or three patients, is a fascinating experience that goes hand in hand with the gratification of realizing improvement in the patients. It is my impression that subtle observations in the home setting recurrently would enrich our understanding in ways heretofore largely unexplored. For this, psychiatric social workers experienced in intensive collaborative work are ideal members of a team. I am convinced that such home observation has been relegated too much to the category of early diagnostic exploratory studies. Possibly great secrets, therefore, have remained undisclosed. Anyone who reads many of the best detective stories can see in what infinite detail every lead is explored.

CAUTIONS ONCE MORE

Herein I have aimed to emphasize some of the benefits which I believe can be derived from the careful type of collaborative therapy that has been my experience. In closing, it seems important to reinforce cautions against certain hazards which I have suggested earlier. The closest communication between psychiatrist and psychiatric social worker must be maintained. The personal relationships between the collaborators of necessity must be kept continuously clear. More than a casual diagnostic study needs to be conducted to evaluate critically which patients would or would not be accessible to the collaborative approach. Lastly, until both collaborators are highly experienced, the psychiatrist certainly should be a highly trained and experienced member of the team, for the final responsibility, clinically and legally, is his.

REFERENCES

1. Johnson, A. M. Sanctions for superego lacunae of adolescents. In *Searchlights on Delinquency*, ed. K. R. Eissler. New York: International Universities Press, 1949. (Reprinted above, p. 113.)
2. ———. Factors in the etiology of fixations and symptom choice. *Psychoanal. Quart.*, 22 (1953): 475–96. (Reprinted below, p. 353.)
3. ———; Falstein, E. I.; Szurek, S. A.; and Svendsen, M. School phobia. *Am. J. Orthopsychiat.*, 11 (1941): 702–11. (Reprinted above, p. 14.)
4. ———, and Fishback, D. Analysis of a disturbed adolescent girl and collaborative psychiatric treatment of the mother. *Ibid.*, 14 (1944): 195–203. (Reprinted below, p. 282.)
5. ———, and Szurek, S. A. The genesis of antisocial acting out in children and adults. *Psychoanal. Quart.* 21 (1952). (Reprinted above, p. 145.)
6. Szasz, T. S. On the psychoanalytic theory of instincts. *Psychoanal. Quart.*, 21 (1952): 25–48.
7. Szurek, S. A. Some impressions from clinical experience with delinquents. In *Searchlights on Delinquency*.
8. ———; Johnson, A.; and Falstein, E. Collaborative psychiatric therapy of parent-child problems. *Am. J. Orthopsychiat.*, 12 (1942): 511–16. (Reprinted above, p. 26.)

18

ANALYSIS OF A DISTURBED ADOLESCENT GIRL AND COLLABORATIVE PSYCHIATRIC TREATMENT OF THE MOTHER

With Dora Fishback, M.D.

In this paper, the first of two reports of collaborative therapy included in this section to illustrate the method, Drs. Johnson and Fishback report their collaborative treatment of an extremely disturbed adolescent girl and her mother.

IN a paper by Szurek, Johnson, and Falstein, (1) attention was called to observations derived from a study of therapy of a number of children of varying ages. The authors stated a fact commonly known: that neurotic adolescents who are not too ill can often be treated without special therapy of the parents at the same time. However, treatment of profoundly disturbed neurotic adolescents would probably be ineffective within the home situation unless the significant parent or parents were also treated at the same time.

In the present paper the authors present an analysis of an extremely disturbed sixteen year old girl and the collaborative

Adelaide M. Johnson, M.D., and Dora Fishback, M.D., Analysis of a disturbed adolescent girl and collaborative psychiatric treatment of the mother, in *American Journal of Orthopsychiatry* 14 (1944): 195–203. © American Orthopsychiatric Association, Inc. Reproduced by permission.

psychiatric treatment of her mother. Although still unfinished, the case is presented because it illustrates several points: (1) The daughter, so ill at the beginning of treatment that one feared for her sanity, is now well on the way to recovery, while the mother, previously not considered ill, is now seen to present a complicated psychiatric problem. (2) Because of the psychopathology in the family, the girl's illness had been attributed to heredity rather than to her life experiences. (3) Treatment revealed the astonishingly distorted, at times gravely annihilatory, but mutually gratifying, attitudes of the mother and daughter toward one another. This, more than the immaturity of the ego and great strength of the instincts in adolescence, makes treatment difficult and dangerous. (4) Study of the case revealed that this girl could only be treated — or even allowed by the parents to remain in treatment — with the aid of the most detailed collaboration between the therapists.

A year ago the girl's mother, Mrs. B, came to Dr. J seeking treatment for her daughter Marion about whose condition she was very much alarmed. At the age of eleven Marion had become less and less tomboyish and increasingly seclusive, until she now had only one social contact, and that with another boyish girl. To Marion's and her mother's grief, the child had lost her former ability to draw and to play the flute. She was defiant toward her teachers and growing increasingly panicky about her very poor school work. When she entered treatment she was making only a pretense of attending school occasionally and after a time stopped altogether although she needed only one semester's work to graduate from high school. She attributed some of her frequent gastro-intestinal upsets to deliberate poisoning at the school cafeteria. Suicidal and homicidal thoughts were constantly expressed. For two years the girl had been crying almost constantly at home, reproaching herself for being so much trouble and expense to her mother, and eating and sleeping very poorly. Mrs. B had many friends and appeared to be making a good adjustment in her marriage and in the community.

Marion's maternal grandfather had been a gifted doctor but a morphine addict since Mrs. B was a baby. He died when she was seven. She had always feared him and had been aware of serious conflicts between her parents. His numerous siblings were "queer": a sister committed suicide; a brother's daughter developed a severe neurosis during adolescence.

After her father's death Mrs. B became extremely oversolicitous of her own mother (patient's grandmother) and had very disturbing fears that something terrible would happen to her. These fears subsided immediately when Mrs. B began to menstruate. The maternal grandmother supported herself and two daughters by taking in roomers. She was a cold woman who gave very little of herself to her daughters. Shortly after Marion came to treatment, the grandmother, who had lived with them for some years, was removed to a nursing home where she died of cancer. We shall learn more about her later.

Marion's father, a brilliant faculty member of a professional school in a large university, was known to have been afflicted for years with a paranoid psychosis. He not only carried guns which he brandished against imaginary conspirators, but succeeded in getting his wife to carry one also. She lived in terror of his suspicions and rages. Until the age of six he had believed he was a girl. He openly hated his mother against whom he made paranoid accusations. His mother suffered from depressions and had made several suicidal attempts. He had a horror of germs which, coupled with his wife's anxiety, led to unusual and peculiar precautions in the physical care of their children. Only recently has Mrs. B told her therapist of his sexual promiscuity, before and during marriage, with the impregnation of several women.

After graduating from high school Mrs. B worked first as a bookkeeper and then as a vaudeville dancer. Her first love was Marion's father whom she had met when she consulted him professionally. She was twenty-two and he a divorced man of forty-three. She fell in love with him at once and courted him, dancing for him her specialty, an oriental dance. She maintained naively that it was not "sexy." From the age of four, for several years, she had screamed in terror when she saw little boys and insisted that they cover their faces. The unusually large number of sexual overtures she had experienced or witnessed from early childhood seemed to her entirely accidental. Sexual relations had always been distasteful to her.

During both her pregnancies Mrs. B developed peptic ulcers and vomited so severely that she required bed rest. She nursed both children for six weeks, the exact length of time her mother had nursed her. Jimmy, three years older than Marion, was a very quiet, obedient, "good" boy who, it was revealed later, had at his father's insistence always urinated in the sitting position.

When Marion was a year old people said there was something strange and remote about her. She fought a great deal with passive Jimmy, accusing the mother of favoring him. After Jimmy's death from pneumonia when Marion was three, Mrs. B was deeply depressed and admits being withdrawn from Marion for months. The child became unruly and defiant, ate very little, and at age four threatened to kill herself because the mother had loved Jimmy more. In treatment the mother was able to admit this was true.

From the age of two Marion had insisted that she was a boy, wore boys' clothes, and called herself "Jackie" or "Bobbie." She hated dolls, to the dismay of her mother who was so unusually fond of them that she still made special trips downtown to fondle dolls at toy counters. Her daughter thought this silly and preferred the gun section. It was only at the age of eleven, when her breasts began to develop, that Marion gave up this apparent wish to be a boy. She hated to grow up, as had her mother, who at a similar age had strapped her breasts down tightly to prevent their development, whereas her sister, two and one-half years older, had massaged her breasts to stimulate growth. The sister died of tuberculosis when Mrs. B was nineteen.

When Marion was one and one-half years old her father died of a cerebral accident. She was six when her mother remarried. Mother's second husband was a professional man fifteen years her senior. He, too, had been divorced. His three half-grown sons lived with them at first, but returned to their own mother because of the violent quarrels with their stepmother. Shortly after her second marriage Mrs. B had a pregnancy aborted, after which her husband, "on his own initiative," had himself sterilized. According to the mother, Marion had at first loved her stepfather very much and he had been demonstrative of his affection for her. At about the age of eleven, however, she became antagonistic, striking out at him violently if he so much as touched her, and defending the mother against him in even minor disagreements.

When Marion came to Dr. J for treatment in February 1942, she appeared younger than sixteen and a half, but was an extremely well-built, attractive, brilliant, and sensitive girl. She was depressed, spoke of her feeling of isolation, of her dependence on her mother. She hated her school teachers and fellow students. She told of her intense jealousy of her dead brother, of her guilt for hating him and her resentment against her mother for having preferred him. She had been humiliated by her mother when, as a child, she had shown her love for her stepfather. She expressed hostility to him and felt that he, as well as other men, thought her second rate. During treatment her quarrels with her stepfather increased and were associated with adolescent sexual dreams. When she saw her therapist with a man Marion acted out her anger and suspicions against her, reacting to men as sibling figures.

As her depression decreased she began to defy her mother. The latter became panic-stricken when the girl angrily threatened to knife her teachers, and the girl was terrified by her mother's belief that she would really murder someone. At this point, a few weeks after Marion's treatment began, it was suggested to the mother that she see another psychiatrist who would be able to reassure her about these mutual hostile feelings. It was felt that the mother would require treatment, since her intense fear that the girl would kill someone seemed to spring from impulses within the mother herself. After this the girl was seen five to seven times a week, instead of twice weekly as before. The mother was seen once a week, later twice, and recently three times weekly.

Mrs. B was quiet, gracious, and nice looking, although rather obese. She impressed her therapist, Dr. F, as being very sweet, gentle and submissive. She felt inferior to her friends and feared to assert herself or to disagree with them about anything. She denied feeling hostile to her sister who had stolen all her beaux; to her narcissistic mother; to her daughter who was such a problem.

Early in treatment Mrs. B had the following dream. She and Marion, while walking along the street, met six handsome college boys. She seized her daughter and fled to a convent, the boys following. She cried to the priest, "Save us!" and rushed in, but the boys pushed the priest aside and ran into the convent after them. At this point the mother awakened. She saw in connection with the dream how she had imparted to her daughter her own ambivalence toward sexuality and how she wished to keep her a nun like herself.

While the mother was under anesthesia during Marion's birth, she had had a strikingly prophetic dream. She saw herself and her ancestors walking in a long, straight line. "The little stranger," just born, refused to follow them and despite the mother's desperate efforts, went off by herself in the opposite direction. We see clearly here her wish to have a child who would act out the mother's own forbidden impulses.

Both patients reported many dreams and fantasies, not only to their therapists, but also to each other. It was amazing to see how the unconscious of each spoke to that of the other. By close collaboration the therapists were able to understand the changing situation and to save time and discomfort for their patients who were acting out against each other, often very subtly. The girl, frequently ahead in treatment, often pierced her mother's rationalizations. She could, however, be thrown into depression by the most subtle obstruction on the part of the mother, which was discovered only in the girl's dreams or transference reaction to her therapist.

The central theme appeared early, and treatment was aimed at gradually making both patients aware of it, and of the defenses erected to maintain it, namely, their intense ambivalent dependence on one another based on deep-seated frustrations. The mother could not let her daughter grow up and achieve the sexual maturity and gratifications which had not been permitted her by her own mother, and the girl could not give up her infantile dependence.

Although the girl talked a great deal about her sexual interests, and the mother was constantly fearful that her daughter would become promiscuous, it was plain that Marion's sexual language was merely the cloak for pre-genital strivings, based on a profound need for love. The girl became extremely demanding of her therapist and her erotized ambivalent dependence came out in homosexual dreams in which the girl was the active, boyish partner.

Early in treatment the mother dreamed of the therapists as two monsters, one (Dr. J) who was taking Marion away, and the other (Dr. F) who was blind. She could not accept the fact that she wanted her own therapist to see and to help her. She was fighting to hold the girl and to avoid recognizing her ambivalent relationship with her therapist and with her own mother. She dreamed that the girl was coming between her and her husband and retaliated with dreams in which the girl was murdered, and with fantasies of beating Marion to death with a hammer. She then feared her daughter's murderous feelings, called her "crazy" and told her, sadistically, of her father's psychosis.

When the mother became aware of her need to tie the girl to herself and her fear and envy of the girl's becoming sexually mature, the girl came in wearing lipstick for the first time and described how she had passionately kissed her stepfather. Then the really serious feud began. All the deeper hostilities were expressed by each to the other in terms of sexual competition. The girl told her mother a dream in which she had been approached sexually, and the mother promptly dreamed of herself as being passionately pursued while wearing a red dress and red panties. This rivalry for men has alternated throughout treatment with prolonged homosexual orgies. The mother would allow Marion to pinch and kick and pound her for hours at a time and exhibit herself in the nude. The mother would tickle her daughter. After this they would lie on the bed exhausted, cuddle and "make up." The girl recognized much earlier than did the mother the sexual gratification and the passive and masochistic elements in this behavior. After assuring herself that despite violent threats to her therapist the latter would not harm her physically, Marion finally brought out with great anxiety her frequent fantasies since the age of eleven of being beaten over the buttocks by an older woman, just as her mother had beaten her in rare rages when Marion was a little girl. She recalled that when she was six, and her mother remarried, she had asked her stepfather to "beat me, beat me."

Mrs. B also began to see the homosexual implications in their behavior and spoke of her fears of homosexuality in the girl and in herself. At sixteen, although she had never had sexual feelings toward boys, she had become aware of such feelings toward a motherly girl of twenty-six. For the first time, she talked to her therapist of her longing for food and her fondness for sweets. In each patient the homosexuality is seen to be the expression of a deep need for love from her mother.

The mother was very hostile to her daughter who was growing up and would marry a young, unsterilized man. During this time the mother's dreams were of Marion dying or being kept a baby, of herself driving a car though Marion sat in the driver's seat, of cutting off the girl's fingers, etc. But on the conscious level she was protesting her wish that the girl grow up and go out with men. As time went on, however, the mother developed more insight into her own deeper feelings.

Marion's ego became progressively more mature, the sexual dreams about both her stepfather and therapist's husband became more disguised, and real guilt developed. The mother now dreamed of running to the girl for protection from men. The girl disliked playing the protective active role with the mother. She now recognized that her activity in the homosexual relationships had merely been defense against passive wishes. She became calmer and less demanding. The relationship between her and her mother improved. But now the mother developed a strong, unconscious wish to interfere with the treatment. It came out in a dream in which the girl became psychotic and had to be institutionalized; it showed in her insistence on Marion's going to a Divine Science practitioner; she wondered if insulin treatment would be more beneficial than psychoanalysis. Dr. F had to work through with the mother her many unconscious attempts to have

Dr. J corrupt the girl and get her to do some serious acting out of the mother's forbidden impulses and so sabotage the treatment.

The mother's own oedipal feelings began to emerge, with fears of the sexual father and hostile mother. Dreams indicated clearly that maternity was for her a defense against homosexuality and an exoneration for heterosexual activity. She felt dependent and immature. Now both patients began to tell of the grandmother's greed and narcissism. Mrs. B's mother had not allowed her to go to college. She described how grandmother had given more food and attention to her roomers than to her daughters. Grandmother had had sexual relations with her roomers, which Mrs. B, an adolescent girl at the time, had sometimes interrupted by feigning illness. Mrs. B had almost submitted sexually to a married man once; she felt no man could be trusted.

Her sexual competition with her daughter became even more evident, however, when Marion began to have dates at the end of the summer with Jack, a fine young man of twenty, who fell very much in love with her. The mother now dreamed that Marion was killed, that Jack was hurt, that she herself was wooed by a tall handsome man while Marion had only a small unattractive boy. When Jack left for college in the Fall, Mrs. B was able to admit envying her daughter for having treatment early in life which would enable the girl to have pleasures she herself had never dared have. Until this time she had tried to maintain that she was seeking the psychiatrist's help only for her daughter's sake. She was still very fearful of any marked dependent relationship to her therapist.

As the Christmas vacation and Jack's return drew near, hostilities flared into the open. The girl provoked the mother with boasts of the sexual relations she would have with Jack and the mother retaliated with much talk of her own marital intimacies. Thus each roused the other's homo- and hetero-sexual jealousies. Envy of her daughter's beau brought out the mother's dissatisfaction with her own husband, much older than Jack, and a blustery, dependent person who was financially a failure and, although she did not mention it in this connection, had been sterilized. The realization that her daughter could have a baby while she could not made her jealous, yet she was fearful that the baby would be left on her hands. After some discussion of these feelings Mrs. B suddenly realized that for the first time she no longer had the need to play with dolls and that many of her old fears had disappeared. Her intense interest in children and dolls had obviously been a defense against her own deep passive wishes. She now had passive homosexual dreams and was able to express greater wishes for dependence on her therapist, but still with great fear.

For weeks Marion had needed food from her therapist; wanted to be her baby. She feared that having a baby of her own would rob her of dependence, but expressed the narcissistic wish to bear children in order to triumph over her therapist who had none. Marion's menstrual periods, formerly irregular, now became regular but were accompanied by increasingly violent cramps. After ten minutes' analysis of some matter in which she felt at that time thwarted by her mother, the cramps would subside, whereas if she stayed at home they would continue for hours. The occurrence of the first menses at the age of eleven had terrified her. She had not wanted to be a girl. The next menses did not occur until she was fourteen years old.

Marion became progressively more mature, her ego stronger, her appearance even more attractive. She was talking now of returning to finish her high school work so that she might be ready for college in the fall. The mother, who heretofore had berated the girl for talking of wanting to marry and not go to school, now began to say that many people married and were happy without having gone far in school. In other words, now that she found herself unable to obstruct her daughter's sexual growth, she was turning to another battlefront.

In the final emancipation of the girl from her mother in this regard, one sees the same dynamics as in the school phobias described in a previous paper on this subject. (2) Because of her dependent wishes and her mother's need to exploit them, Marion had resisted returning to school, using every loophole in her mother's armor to do so. The mother, however, having received some satisfaction of her own dependent needs from her therapist, was now less hostile to her daughter and needed less gratification from her. When neither mother nor therapist would play into her wish to stay out of school and mother enthusiastically took a job outside the home, Marion returned to her classes.

Several times during the treatment, removal of the girl to a foster home or boarding school had been considered but could not be effected because neither patient was ready to give up the mutual gratifications in the existing set-up. The girl will be encouraged to go away to college as soon as possible even though more analysis may be necessary at the time of marriage or childbearing. The mother is less anxious now and more sure of herself in many ways, but needs more intensive treatment as the girl moves away.[1]

SUMMARY AND CONCLUSIONS

Briefly, the problem has been one of emancipating an adolescent girl from a highly ambivalent and erotized attachment to a mother who was herself extremely deprived of warmth by a very immature mother. The symptoms disappeared when they were no longer needed for mutual gratification.

This case serves as a basis for a better understanding of the

---

[1] One year has elapsed since this paper was presented. Mrs. B has made an excellent adjustment in her work and seems to continue her marriage with relative equanimity. Marion has matured very well in a university far from home.

genesis of some of the psychoses and severe neuroses developing in adolescence. In this case, where there is so much psychopathology on both sides of the family, the faulty heredity could have been used as a facile explanation of the girl's illness. The material illustrates the necessity of avoiding such explanations until the family interrelationships have been studied intensively and collaboratively.

This case shows also that intensive or analytic therapy of the disturbed adolescent is highly dangerous, not so much because of the child's instincts and immaturity of ego, as others have stated, but because she may be the channel through which the parent achieves, unconsciously, her own forbidden and thwarted impulses. For this reason seriously disturbed adolescents often cannot be treated without treatment of the significant parent, particularly in so far as the nature of the mutual gratifications binds the child to the home. The search for the parent's role requires far more than an occasional advisory interview. Intensive psychiatric treatment of the parent is needed, not only to obviate interference with the child's treatment and make it possible for the parent to accept changes in the child, but also to help the parent find new gratifications for herself.

The paper points up the necessity for evolving improved techniques for getting parents into treatment.

DISCUSSION

George J. Mohr, M.D.:[2] This paper has an important place among the many papers on therapy presented at A.O.A. meetings. Problems of need for treatment of parents when children are disturbed have long been discussed. There has been much expe-

[2] Institute for Psychoanalysis, Chicago.

rience in the collaboration of psychiatric social worker and psychiatrist in meeting the treatment needs of parents and children.

On the other hand when very intensive, or particularly psychoanalytic treatment of an individual has been undertaken, this has usually been relatively free of intimate contact with the problem of possible therapy of others. The most extreme view, e.g., that of Melanie Klein, was that children should be treated on the basis of being so strengthened that they should be able to meet the strains imposed upon them by normal or even a disturbed or disturbing environment without the therapist particularly concerning himself with modification of attitudes of the important persons in that environment. Generally speaking, however, child analysts have taken the more realistic attitude that in greater or lesser degree, depending upon a particular case, the parent too needs aid, ranging from occasional orienting and advisory interviews to intensive treatment.

In the treatment of adults it has long been recognized that often the individuals closest to the patient emotionally may need treatment, e.g., if one of a married couple comes into analysis, the likelihood is great that the spouse will eventually undertake analysis, or that in any event so doing would facilitate the solution of the problem. This is similar to the case just given by Doctors Johnson and Fishback.

There has been a tendency on the part of psychiatrists to feel, in intensive treatment situations, that they should rely entirely on information or insights derived from and through the patients themselves, eschewing contact with or even intimate awareness about the other emotionally involved persons except through their own patient. On the whole, this is understandable, and in some instances unavoidable or even essential in the treatment situation. But if the particular therapeutic situation calls for so doing, as Doctors Johnson and Fishback have demonstrated to be true for their case, a therapist should be able to feel free about sharing his experience with a collaborating colleague. Thus far this has been rather common at least in child guidance clinics between psychiatric social worker and psychiatrist. Doctor Stanislaus Szurek, in a discussion of this problem before the Chicago Psychoanalytic Society, pointed out one aspect of the particular treatment situation dealt with in this paper, namely, the necessity on the part of the therapists to divest themselves of any competitive attitudes in relation to one another during the course of treatment. We perhaps take it for granted that therapists do and always would do so, but it is worth while having this consideration properly appreciated. In the case just presented, it is seen that the patients progress at different rates, one seems for the time being to become more of a problem while the other improves. Here, there will have to be perspective about the total situation by both therapists so that they may both comfortably continue to address themselves to the problem.

I would be interested to have Doctor Fishback comment upon the sex of the therapists in such joint ventures. Was it just accident, perhaps under the exigencies of wartime, that the two female patients are being treated by two women psychiatrists, or was this deliberate design? In this particular instance, it is obviously an excellent arrangement, but one can readily see that whether one patient was dealt with by a woman and the other by a man might have important bearing upon the development of a case.

A final word about this paper as a contribution to the problem of therapy in adolescence. We all know that severely disturbed adolescents offer great difficulties in treatment dependent upon their tendency to "act out" under the influence of treatment. The degree of control offered in the present instance where the patient is so seriously disturbed makes possible the conduct of therapy in a situation which otherwise might well be out of hand.

REFERENCES

1. Szurek, Stanislaus; Johnson, Adelaide; and Falstein, Eugene I. Collaborative psychiatric therapy of parent-child problems. *Am. J. Orthopsychiatry* 12 (1942): 511. (Reprinted above, p. 26.)
2. Johnson, Adelaide M.; Falstein, Eugene I.; Szurek, S. A.; and Svendson, Margaret. School phobia. *Am. J. Orthopsychiatry* 11 (1941): 702. (Reprinted above, p. 14.)

19

PSYCHOTHERAPY OF A MOTHER AND DAUGHTER WITH A PROBLEM OF SEPARATION ANXIETY

With David B. Robinson, M.D., and Glen M. Duncan, M.D.

In this second example of collaborative therapy included in this section, treatment was carried out by two young psychiatrists in training under the supervision of Dr. Johnson. The text of this report was prepared for presentation to a predominantly non-psychiatric audience at a Mayo Clinic staff meeting.

SEPARATION ANXIETY, as the name implies, is a pathologic degree of anxiety experienced by one or both of two people when separation is imminent or actual. When two emotionally mature people take leave of one another, no problem arises, since each has enough respect for the other to permit his release, and each has enough self-confidence to turn elsewhere for his own emotional needs. In fact, in taking leave, each is fortified by the love of the other and by the memory of mutual friendship as each goes on to new life experiences.

This concept may be clarified by using a specific example: the ultimate in mother-love and father-love is seen in the ability to

Reproduced with permission from *Proceedings of the Staff Meetings of the Mayo Clinic* 30 (1955): 141–48.

nurture first and then to *release* a child appropriately to pursue his own independence and maturity. This release or separation can be accomplished without anxiety by a mother who has experienced satisfaction of her own dependency needs, and then has been permitted to grow into an independent life by her own mother. When a mother has experienced early emotional deprivation at the hands of her own mother, she cannot give to her daughter without much resentment and anger. She is then in the awkward position of hating one she also loves. It is not surprising that the mother then experiences anxiety and guilt as a result of her hateful — even destructive — thoughts toward the daughter. Such a mother will *subconsciously* wish to be rid of her child. As long as the child is kept physically close to her, these feelings are kept under control, but any separation causes much anxiety. We are all familiar with the anxious mother who is afraid Johnny will break his neck if he plays football, or be run over if he rides his bicycle in the street.

When these mixed feelings of love and hate are extreme (a high degree of ambivalence), there develops a hostile-dependent bond so *close* that the child is not permitted out of the sight of the parent. The child readily perceives his parent's ambivalence, and responds in kind. When the parent feels anxiety, the child experiences anxiety. Many problems of this type are seen in child-guidance centers to which the child is brought because of a so-called school phobia. In actuality, the problem is not fear of school or anything pertaining to school, but is the child's separation anxiety activated by leaving the mother on going to school. These problems occur in varying degrees of severity, ranging from transient abortive problems to those requiring intensive treatment. When the condition is severe and is left untreated, a seriously crippling condition may result.

REPORT OF CASE

Dr. Duncan: A 14-year-old schoolgirl, Barbara X, was admitted to the pediatrics hospital service on September 23, 1954, on a stretcher. After an acute febrile illness early in 1954, she had begun to *miss school* for long periods — 2 to 3 weeks at a time — complaining of weakness, aching limbs and back, fatigue and low-grade fever in which temperatures ranged to 100° F. By direct questioning a history was obtained of an increased intake of salt and water. Her parents noted her increasing awkwardness in helping with dishes and in eating. Her gait became altered. She had been seen by her local physician, who entertained diagnoses of brucellosis, rheumatism and "constitutional inadequacy." In fact, the home physician had forcefully urged the patient to return to school last spring. When her difficulty persisted, he had suggested an evaluation at the Clinic. The family delayed this for several months in the hope that summer vacation would see the condition clear up by itself. When the re-opening of school became imminent, the girl's parents were concerned lest she be unable to return.

Pediatric evaluation here did not reveal any organic cause for her incapacity. Emotional factors were suspected to be present, and psychiatric evaluation was commenced. Meanwhile, trichinosis, brucellosis, Addison's disease and electrolyte imbalance were considered and ruled out.

Dr. Robinson: For the initial psychiatric interview I saw Barbara in her hospital room. She was pale, tall, thin, reticent, tense, inhibited, fatigued and confined to her bed. She was very anxious to please the examiner and promptly suppressed any feelings that might have been stirred up during the interview. Similarly, in the history of her dealings with her parents the same pattern was present; that is, one of being "good" and compliant, with no show of antagonism.

As a small girl Barbara had been energetic and active. She had preferred outdoor activities and liked to be with her father at work on his farm. After an infection thought to be sinusitis, she began to have more trouble, with frequent colds, temperatures up to 100° F., fatigue, backache and generalized aching of muscles. There was also a shift in her interest from outdoor to indoor activities and pursuits. At the same time, she shifted her chief loyalties from her father to her mother. Significantly, these changes occurred soon after the menarche.

Dr. Duncan: As is done in all problems in child psychiatry, a detailed psychiatric evaluation of the mother was made.

The mother was a small, slight, timid and anxious woman who said she had been tired all her life. Her condition had been diagnosed at the Clinic in 1947 as "chronic nervous exhaustion."

She was an only child whose mother had died when she was 4 years old. Her father was a distant sort of man whom she adored from afar, but he sent her off to live with a succession of relatives. She had had a most miserable time with them, and was so flagrantly neglected by some that her father several times had to rescue her from them and send her elsewhere.

When she was 9 years old, her father had remarried, and her stepmother dominated her life from that time on. The stepmother was a demanding, domineering, grudging woman who made the child feel very obligated for what was being done for her. Even now Mrs. X says of her stepmother: "There is a strong bond between us. The only way you can get along with her is to give in to her."

When Mrs. X was 16 years old her father died. The same year she became pregnant by her first boy friend, whom she then married. The stepmother was very resentful of the husband, "because he took me away from her." She insisted that the young couple live with her, but after a few weeks the husband decided he had had enough and they moved out. Mrs. X was very much torn between her two loyalties, and even 5 years later her husband had occasion to say, "You will have to choose between me and that stepmother." Mrs. X declares: "My stepmother took my affection from my father . . . she was a very selfish person . . . I owe her a lot."

Mr. X appeared to be a rather dominating, sarcastic man who left his wife no doubts as to her inferiority in most respects and rode roughshod over her more sensitive feelings.

The other member of the patient's family is her sister, Elizabeth, aged 13 — a rather bright, energetic and outgoing girl who is subject to headaches and is rather attached to her father.

Dr. Robinson: It becames apparent that Mrs. X had never had a warm, sustained relationship with any mother or mother-substitute in the past. It will be recalled that her own mother died when she was 4 years old.

Now, a child 4 years old does not distinguish death from desertion. Hence, there is a response of primitive anger toward the mother for deserting her. But this feeling frightens the child, who after all loved and depended on her mother, so she blots out the anger from awareness in order to maintain emotional equilibrium.

Such a situation is especially damaging to a girl of this age, because she is involved in a competitive contest for her father's love and attention, and her mother is her competitor. The unequal struggle leads to primitive, fearful hopes that the mother will disappear, perhaps die.

Accordingly, in the future it will always be dangerous for such a child to entertain any hostile wishes toward a female person, and for her any separation or threat of it will revive the old, unresolved feelings of fear and anger about death and desertion.

As is apparent in Mrs. X's history, she not only lost her mother at the age of 4 years, but also the subsequent mother-substitutes mistreated her very badly. It is clear that she must have had tremendous, unconscious unresolved anger toward women. It is a common observation in psychiatric practice that such individuals are bound to have difficulty in parenthood if they must raise a female child. The reason is that in the child they unconsciously find a scapegoat against whom may be unleashed their subtle, retaliative fury.

Therapeutic Approach. — It was recognized that there must be a tight bond between mother and daughter. A therapeutic plan was devised. Two male therapists were chosen so that a workable relationship could be established more quickly. Speed was essential, since school was to open soon. It seemed to us, however, very unlikely that the patient would be able to return to school. It was decided that I would treat Barbara and that Dr. Duncan would treat the mother, both on an intensive schedule, twice daily at first, to be continued after the opening of school on a 1-hour-a-week schedule.

Accordingly, mother and daughter were asked to leave the hospital and to report at the Clinic the same afternoon. The mother, who previously had shown interest in the psychotherapeutic approach, telephoned to ask that the daughter remain in the hospital another day, and she offered many spurious reasons why the daughter should do so. We were insistent, however, that both mother and daughter appear at the Clinic, and they arrived — 45 minutes late — with Barbara in a wheel chair.

When Barbara was seen she obviously was sullen and angry, behind a façade of pleasantness. She complained of a headache and fatigue. The first session was spent giving her an opportunity to discuss her feelings about leaving the hospital so precipitously. At first she had nothing to say, until I pointed out that actually she was angry, and I told her it was all right to feel angry and to tell me about it. She was then able to agree, weakly, that she had been able to see no reason for rushing to the Clinic as they had done.

I then proceeded to tell her briefly and simply how emotional tensions can produce physical symptoms such as hers. When I told her I felt she was an angry person, she was close to tears. Before she left I told her she had no need for a wheel chair, and that I would expect to see her without it when she returned the next day. At this she stood and walked to the elevator.

Dr. Duncan: I interviewed the mother, and since I was by then familiar with the details of her upbringing, I was able to convey to her that I was rather more interested in and sympathetic with her difficulties in living than she had expected anyone to be. She responded to this approach, and continued to tell of the difficult times she had had with her stepmother and of the obtuseness and sarcasm of her husband.

Dr. Robinson: The next morning I encouraged Barbara to reflect upon and to discuss any irritations of the past few years. Significantly, she could more readily discuss angry feelings toward her father than those directed at her mother. She told of her father's hypercritical attitudes and double standards; for example, one standard of neatness for himself and a more rigid one for her. With some encouragement she then related a recurrent, distasteful practice on the part of her mother. This was her mother's insistence on squeezing Barbara's pimples, about which Barbara commented, "I don't like her to — she has her own face scarred from it. I tell her so, but she insists."

The hostile and destructive drives of the mother toward Barbara are clearly shown in this example. Here the mother is doing something to Barbara that in the past has marred and scarred her own face. This can mean only that she begrudges her daughter her complexion, and that hostilely she is setting about to scar Barbara's face — and over the daughter's protests. I allowed

Barbara to see my own disapproval of this practice, thus giving her tacit permission to feel her own anger and resentment toward her mother.

During the course of the next 3 hours of therapy, preparatory to the patient's going home, my efforts were directed toward increasing the bond between the patient and myself, to facilitate a loosening of the bond between the mother and the patient. The patient's resistance to treatment appeared in the recital of her first dream, in which she dreamed of missing her appointment with me. Dr. Johnson will mention the significance of dreams briefly in her discussion to follow. Suffice it to say now that dreams reflect unconscious thinking, and that in dreams we always look for a hidden wish. Therapeutic gains were apparent in the patient's open recognition of the connection between past irritating events and consequent somatic symptoms. Also, at the last interview, she reported taking her first stand against her mother. The mother repeatedly had coaxed her to go shopping with her. Barbara held her ground and refused to go, *but* on returning her mother commented, "I'm so glad *you* didn't come — it was so tiring" — implying that, *of course*, the outing would have overwhelmed Barbara.

Dr. Duncan: In the last hour before she left the city, Mrs. X asked, "What if my daughter can't start school on Friday?"

I told her quite emphatically that there was no reason why the daughter should not return to school on that day. (It is worth reiterating at this point that separation anxiety in which children chronically remain at home from school — one of Barbara's presenting symptoms — formerly was referred to in the literature as "school phobia." Of course, it has nothing to do with fear of school as such but is rather a maternally fostered pathologic emotional attachment to the home and the mother.)

Dr. Robinson: One week later we were elated to hear that

Barbara had been able to return to school when the term commenced. True, she had experienced tremendous anxiety; she had felt as if she were dreaming at times; she had even fallen down some stairs at school, and had wanted to go home — *but she had stayed in school.*

At this particular session Barbara's repressed feelings of anger toward her mother were seen to be approaching consciousness. She reported a dream in which she had been going to the hospital to visit a boy. There in the hall she met her mother, who "has a scar on her face, her head is swathed in bandages, and she is to have surgery on her brain."

Dr. Duncan: At the same time the mother reported that Barbara was going about according to her own inclinations, putting up her hair her *own* way (not mother's way), and brushing her teeth her *own way* (not father's way).

The next week, when both returned, the mother remarked how well *she* had been sleeping, and incidentally, that *Barbara had not been to school that week.* . . . because of a cold. By discreet questioning it was brought out that the mother had said the previous day: "If you are still sniffling, you'd better not go to school tomorrow."

Dr. Robinson: The patient's version of the incident just mentioned emphasized the mother's suggestive direction of this relapse even more forcefully. The patient reported that on Monday morning the mother had said to her, "Probably you won't feel well enough to go back to school until Wednesday." By Wednesday afternoon, when we saw the mother and daughter, there had been no move toward returning to school nor any plan for a return.

Dr. DuShane very kindly consented to examine Barbara's chest and respiratory tract so that together we could *insist* that she return to school the next morning.

At the same time the patient's attention was effectively focused

on the mother's role in encouraging her in this hypochondriasis —
and how actually destructive this could be in the long run in
stunting the patient's emotional growth and enjoyment in life.
The patient responded with additional examples from the past
to reaffirm the general pattern now becoming clear to her.

Dr. Duncan: At the next session the mother remarked how
fine Barbara had been, especially after the last day, when they
had seen Dr. DuShane. "*He* impressed us both very much," she
said to me, "he must take to children."

She went on to remark casually that *Elizabeth, the patient's
13-year-old sister, had been home from school for 3 days*, with
a headache. On inquiry it was learned that Elizabeth had decided
not to go to school, but that the mother had said, "Go — but you
can always come home if it's too much for you."

Apparently, the mother could not be content when both girls
were in school, and this idea was pointed out to her.

Since that time, therapy with the mother has centered largely
on her hostile dependency on her stepmother and the way in
which this has shown up in her relationships with her daughter.
Two of the mother's dreams highlight the wish fulfilment of the
hostile feelings she harbors toward her daughter. In one, Barbara becomes illicitly pregnant, just as Mrs. X had done; in the
second, Barbara wearing a pretty new dress, is being smothered
in the sloppy mud of the chicken yard. As a matter of fact, Mrs. X
exhibits the same hostile dependency on me as she did with her
stepmother, and this at present is being analyzed with her.

Dr. Robinson: Since the time of Barbara's returning to school
after her relapse, her interests and activities have been expanding
steadily. She has been doing well in school, has arranged and
conducted a family expedition to a basketball game, has shown
more sociability with classmates of both sexes, and is becoming
increasingly aware of her own neurotic methods of dealing with
life.

Before it will be safe to release the patient from treatment, without risk of early relapse, it will be essential for her to learn emotionally that she can feel anger toward me (the therapist) and express anger toward me (the therapist) without drastic results.

SUMMARY

Dr. Duncan: In summary then, we have seen the collaborative psychotherapeutic management of a case in which separation anxiety involved a mother and daughter to such a severe degree as to require the hospitalization of the daughter. This pathologic state was successfully resolved despite two relapses, and the mother gained insight into the use she had been making of the daughter to satisfy her own neurotic, dependent needs. The daughter similarly came to see her mother's role in the affair as well as her own contribution to it.

DISCUSSION

Dr. Adelaide M. Johnson: Since the major cause of neurosis in a child is his life with neurotic parents, it has seemed that the most effective method for observing what happens between them daily is to treat and study the parent and child concomitantly. The two or three therapists compare notes after each hour, and the fact that they do so is not keep secret from the patients.

This enterprise, however, will be productive only if the two therapists are equally interested in *both* patients' getting well. This in turn means the two psychiatrists must not be competitive with each other, for if they are, the patients will sense it at once. Only chaos results from such competition.

Any teacher or supervisor of two or three young therapists working collaboratively in a family with their patients immediately observes, then, whether the therapists are competitive with each other or are guilty about the possibility of such competition. We cannot play one patient off against another nor against a therapist. To do effective collaborative therapy and research, the therapists must be good friends consciously and unconsciously.

In the second supervisory conference with Drs. Robinson and Duncan I observed the excellent camaraderie that existed between the two men. This was a happy realization. Conducted in such a favorable atmosphere, collaborative psychotherapy has proved to be an invaluable therapeutic and research technic; more patients get well and the therapists perceive the fact far more clearly than could be possible otherwise.

Having suffered, we all unconsciously or consciously seek revenge — often against one as helpless as we were when we initially suffered. This usually means that the adult's revenge is directed toward his child, if there is a child. If the therapist succeeds in blocking his chain of events through removal of the child from the home or by treating the child so that he is no longer vulnerable to the neurotic parental attitudes, then the parent's first neurotic revengeful move is to turn against another child. In the case just presented, the sister of the patient became the scapegoat until the therapist intervened and dealt with this turn of events in the mother's treatment hours. Thus, we carefully watch *all* children in a family even though at the time we may be treating only one child and one parent or both parents. In my earlier days in psychiatry we did not realize these matters, and as soon as we began to get a child well, the parents often took him out of treatment. Today, with the parents in treatment, when the child begins to be freed of the neurosis, a new scapegoat is selected unless the parent's treatment has progressed as far as the child's.

SECTION V

Psychoanalytic Therapy

20

PSYCHOANALYTIC THERAPY

Dr. Johnson's paper "Psychoanalytic Therapy" is reprinted from *Twenty Years of Psychoanalysis* (New York: W. W. Norton and Company, Inc., 1953), edited by Franz Alexander and Helen Ross. The paper is one of four summarizing training and research activities at the Chicago Institute for Psychoanalysis for the period 1932–52 written by staff members of that Institute.

A VITAL part of the research program of the Chicago Institute for Psychoanalysis has been a study of psychoanalytic techniques.

We proceeded with the empirical knowledge that all psychologic diseases arrange themselves along a spectrum of therapeutic challenge. Those at the extreme right might react best to dynamic, highly supportive therapy. Those far to the left might be best helped by an extensive uncovering treatment as defined by Freud for the transference neuroses.

Psychoanalytic Therapy (New York: Ronald Press Company) published in 1946, presents a report of a systematic study of therapeutic techniques which covered approximately ten years.

In general the research of the Institute resolved itself into an exploration of the following:

1. What is a diagnostic dynamic formulation of the problems and assets of every individual patient?

Reprinted with permission.

2. What diagnostic criteria are valid in determining the treatment choice?

3. What are the treatment methods from which to choose, and may they be interwoven as the necessity arises?

4. What are the essential psychodynamic factors in any psychotherapeutic process?

5. Is there a qualitative distinction observable in those psychotherapeutic factors from case to case?

6. If we can objectively decide the foregoing, can we, and have we the right and responsibility to anticipate certain goals in the treatment process?

These research questions in time appeared to be subsumed under two major categories:

1. What is the best dynamic procedure for masses of cases along the spectrum that are not suitable for the classical analytic approach or do not require such extensive therapeutic management?

2. What reformulations might emerge in our experimental approach of postulates and beliefs purported to be sound which we have accepted as the best means of conducting classical analysis?

The possibility suggested itself that this exploration might reveal such additional knowledge as would make an uncovering therapy effective more often than Freud and many of us had experienced.

DIAGNOSTIC FORMULATION OF ASSETS AND PROBLEMS

Alexander and French and others of the Chicago group wrote explicitly and in detail about the need for careful diagnostic formulations and tentatively planned therapy — the need for some semblance of a grand strategy, an idea of the main goals and approaches necessary for treatment with the tactics always subject to change, with complications dictating a profound modification of the original comprehensive plan.

We were aware of the possibility that a great deal of the judgment which enters into a diagnostic formulation, as well as the decisions about what might be best for the patient, was subject to the personality of the physician. Awareness of this danger undoubtedly was one factor fostering the violent criticism of the Chicago group for attempting a careful diagnostic formulation and planning a therapy with certain reasonable goals before commencing therapy. The criticism was: "How can you presume to decide how far this patient should go in achieving mental health?" The criticism continued: "Any diagnostic exploration tampers with and distorts the potentials of the transference neurosis."

The alternative to such a preliminary determination of goals was a trial analysis. Many of us thought that trial analysis for all nonpsychotic patients smacked of the old shotgun prescriptions in medicine: give the patient "the works" for a time and see what happens. If the trial analysis (artificial as it is) is unfavorable after three or four months, and is abandoned, has no damage been done? Is it worse to interfere with the natural evolution of the transference by such careful diagnostic study as we advocate, or is it more injurious to tell a patient at the end of three or four months that he should not be analyzed? Have follow-ups been made on the ultimate outcome in such patients? Who treated them later and how?

Many of the group felt that it was not possible to plan or undertake a therapy without a thorough diagnostic formulation. The Chicago members believed that in the past psychoanalysts had not been willing to assume the responsibility of making a careful diagnostic evaluation initially because of their limited experience. Greater experience and knowledge today make it possible to define more clearly what might be safest and best for a patient. In fact, advanced knowledge makes us responsible for such a preliminary appraisal of each case. We have been keenly aware of the difficulty of this task. We readily admitted that the original appraisal must be subject to continuous reevaluation as the treatment progresses. On the other hand, to encourage every patient to engage in a trial analysis constitutes an unwarranted failure to assume our responsibility as physicians.

DIAGNOSTIC CRITERIA FOR DETERMINATON OF CHOICE OF TREATMENT

Our next concern logically was what diagnostic criteria, if any, are valid in determining the treatment choice. Such extrinsic factors as limitations in time, money, distance, and personnel available become matters of consideration in planning therapy. These, however, are not nearly so difficult to judge as dynamic criteria for treatment choice. The dynamic treatments to be considered consist of varying degrees of support and uncovering. Also the intensity of the treatment and particularly of the optimal transference must be considered. Each case must be evaluated individually from many points of view: is this an acute neurotic disturbance in a patient heretofore well stabilized; is this an acute neurotic decompensation in a patient suffering from chronic neurosis; is this a mild or severe chronic neurosis; was the childhood background malignantly distorted although the present acute disturbance appears relatively well encapsulated and mild; have the work and social relationships previously been relatively gratifying and productive regardless of the apparent seriousness of the acute picture; is the current external life-situation seriously collapsing or is it relatively stabilized; is it compatible with an improvement of the neurosis; do the patient's assets provide a significant counterbalance to the pathologic features in a given case?

Most of the members of the Chicago group became increasingly alert to sensing the assets in a patient, so that the focus of consideration was as much or more on the assets as on the pathology. Other considerations must be defined and evaluated in each case to decide a plan of therapy. Even if for extrinsic reasons the patient can come for treatment only once or twice a week, the choice of therapy may well be a long, searching, largely uncovering analytic therapy. It would seem there is no end to the necessity for continual exploration and clarification of this subject of criteria for judging treatment of choice. Many more studies by groups should be undertaken to find out how to minimize or eliminate the unconscious uncommunicable subjective factors operating in the physicians' evaluations.

Every effort was made initially to gain a broad perspective of the total terrain of the patient's personality so that the analyst might decide what limitations of goal, if any, should be exercised in treatment. French felt in all cases that this view from the mountaintop was necessary at the beginning lest the participants (analyst and patient) in treatment soon become lost in the gulleys and ravines.

GOALS IN TREATMENT

In planning treatment it was easier in some cases than in others to decide that the analysis of some relatively circumscribed problem might lead to restabilization of the patient; that a complete working through of the infantile neurosis seemed uncalled for in a patient heretofore productive and relatively happy in his relationships. In other cases the experimenter decided a fairly thorough analysis of the infantile problems seemed necessary, but attempted to use new and more flexible techniques to achieve a healthy ego expansion.

Goals of treatment might be far reaching in one patient and very limited in another; decisions were based on evaluation of the strength and structure of the patient's personality, on extrinsic factors, and on the special skills and limitations of the therapist. Evaluation of the correctness of certain diagnostic hypotheses and predictions could be made in some cases. Other cases were evaluated retrospectively — this made them less valuable in the actual experimental part of the program, but invaluable in furnishing data for further experimentation.

Of course, today, much more is known about dynamic supportive (anaclitic) therapy in phases of such illnesses as serious organic conditions with psychogenic etiologic factors, of schizophrenia, and during some periods in the treatment of adolescents.

In the Chicago work, and all over the country today, many therapists highly trained and experienced in the methodology of classical analysis begin their treatment with careful dynamic formulations and some tentative strategy for achieving certain goals which in their judgment the patient can achieve. The analysts so concerned in this work feel that they not only achieve more for more patients but also at times arrive at better results in the cases treated long and intensively but more flexibly.

THE ESSENTIALS OF THE THERAPEUTIC PROCESS

With regard to the essentials of the therapeutic process, a number of fundamental principles in analytic therapy were considerably clarified. In general, it is a sound basic analytic rule that no important changes in the life-situation should occur until after the completion of treatment. There were excellent reasons for such a view; especially the fear that a patient would "act out." However, such a rule can become nothing but sabotage in treatment of certain cases where the patient really should marry or make some important job change as part of his growth in treatment. Alexander has formulated this by saying that there probably should be no important basic change in the life-situation of the patient "unless both the therapist and patient agree."

It is clear that the goal of any uncovering therapy is to make irrational attitudes conscious and recognized by the patient as irrational through increased reality testing by the ego. Even in dynamic supportive therapy the aim is to help the ego of the patient to some such equanimity. In purely supportive therapy one cannot avoid development of the transference neurosis; and it must be analyzed. Certain technical devices are known, however, for obviating as much as possible resistance resulting from intensive transference involvements.

In all uncovering therapy the main instrument is analysis of the resistances arising through the development of the transference neurosis. Believing we had a considerable knowledge of psychodynamics, the Chicago group experimented with controlling the intensity of the transference. It was found that the therapist can consciously direct the intensity and depth of the transference in order to achieve a projected goal. What is interpreted, and the timing and form of such interpretation provide a potent instrument in determining, in part, direction and range of transference feelings. Also the frequency of contact, the distribution between the emotional changes in daily life and transference are means of raising or lowering the intensity of the transference involvement.

These important therapeutic instruments were the subject of

a great deal of scrutiny in the Chicago research, and no other part of the study created more violent criticism. This seemed like a real befogging of the one sure pilot light of rational therapy. While insisting on the validity and possibility of such management, it may be admitted that the fears and doubts of many of our colleagues were understandable in some measure because at the time we conducted our research, analysts were not nearly so aware of and frank about countertransference problems as is true today. However, a physician who has little bias *consciously* controls the depth of the transference and restricts its range and direction to achieve the projected goal earlier.

The Chicago group thought that this was a justifiable experimental procedure, that it became the responsibility of the therapist to use it consciously in maintaining the optimal transference level for the best progress in each particular case, no matter whether we dealt with psychoneuroses, organic cases with psychogenic factors, small or adolescent children, or near psychotics.

To be experimental and to avoid the hazard of the therapist's "acting out," the total dynamics of the treatment situation must be consciously managed. Retrospective rationalization of what was done is not in keeping with the scientific spirit of investigation or experimentation.

During our work it became well established that the intensity of the transference and the regression can be increased or minimized by use of certain technical devices such as frequency of interviews, use of the couch or not, the regularity of interpretation of transference resistance and of dreams. How well these devices can be utilized depends much on the flexibility of the well-trained, highly experienced analyst. In anaclitic therapy the therapist consciously chooses to "act with the patient's unconscious needs" if you will, but this is quite different from unconsciously allowing oneself to be maneuvered by the patient into "acting out."

The classical thesis that the emotional experience is the main factor of therapeutic change was re-examined. Formerly the emphasis was on the fact that a transference experience is a less intensive repetition of early pathogenic experiences (Freud). Also it was stressed by Freud that in adult analysis the mature ego is exposed to conflicts which the child's ego could not solve. According to the classical theory, these two factors are primarily responsible for the therapeutic effect of the transference experience.

In our formulation we added a third factor, namely that the therapist does not respond as the original father or mother did. It was not assumed that parents never react to their children in a healthy manner, but that they are always to some degree emotionally involved in their children and therefore not completely objective. The patient's discovery of this difference was called "the corrective emotional experience." The aim to foster this experience was consistently maintained throughout our work. Alexander stresses that every analysis has an emotional climate, depending on the patient's transference and the analyst's countertransference. He proposed that this emotional climate should become a conscious concern of the analyst and not be left to chance. The traditional aloof psychoanalytic attitude is by no means spontaneous but is highly studied. "The blank screen" can never be realized and the patients often complained of the artificiality. When a therapist has become aware that a patient needs warmth or firmness, the therapist can respond appropriately, qualitatively and quantitatively as seems wise. This is very different from any studied, unspontaneous so-called objectivity or artificial "role-playing."

Many patients, such as adolescents and the very ill, may need support, educational procedures, and guidance to avoid breaks. The analyst who has an unconscious need to make the patient in his own image and the analyst who cannot give up the rigid technique of the so-called classical analysis are both unqualified to treat patients who need supportive advice and educational information. Such therapists would be guilty of "acting out" because of their own unconscious conflicts.

In attempting to distinguish between analytic psychotherapy and classical analysis some have maintained that the distinction rests on two points: (1) The classical analyst works with the infantile neurosis entirely as it unfolds in the transference neurosis. (2) The classical analyst is passive, whereas the psychotherapist is more active, at times interfering with the evolution of this process and its potential.

This is an oversimplification of the problem. The terms "passivity" and "activity" need clarification. Actually either behavior, if unconscious, may constitute an "acting out" on the part of the therapist and interfere with the transference potential in an unsuspected way. Certainly, ground rules laid down at the beginning of classical analysis immediately distort the direction and intensity of the transference potential. Transference is one expression of regression, and every analysis of the resistance in the transference leads to deeper regression and greater dependence on the analyst. The analyst with his knowledge and experience exposes the meaning of the resistance, so that the patient consciously makes a new choice.

In analyzing the resistance and exposing new feelings to the patient, the classical analyst does not make the choice for the patient, but only reads or translates the road signs for the patient, who then chooses his direction. We do recognize, however, that the analyst may omit or include mention of certain road signs depending upon his judgment or timing, and so forth. A dynamic psychotherapist, in judging what goal might be possible of achievement by the patient, should, when the ego is working safely, function similarly. That is, he should analyze the resistances that arise in the enterprise and leave it to the patient to make his choice. However, the choice of what part of the resistance he interprets and the form and the timing rest with the therapist seeing his patient two or three or six times a week. Every analyst influences the direction and depth of the transference in this way. When he does it unconsciously, then he is in danger of "leading" or "acting" for his own sake rather than the patient's. Likewise, any good analyst, whether seeing patients two times or five or six times a week, becomes active, supportive, and educational and intervenes with a decision when that patient is dangerously confused and frantic.

Classical analysis as clearly defined by Freud for psychoneuroses is unnecessarily limiting. Anaclitic therapy in the severe organ neuroses, schizophrenia, and the many disturbances of children operates according to rational psychoanalytic principles about human behavior. However, in such therapy, the same degree of passivity by the analyst as is usual in the analysis of psychoneuroses would be nontherapeutic. Likewise, insight achieved by interpretation is virtually useless in certain phases. Analysis of some of these profoundly sick people may be prolonged and extremely intensive. Literal distinctions of "passivity" versus "activity" or interpreting versus not interpreting are spurious criteria of whether or not the therapist is employing rational psychoanalytic concepts and principles.

Some people consider psychotherapy as merely preparatory for classical analysis. That may be the case, sometimes. In many instances therapy may initially be one or two hours a week, without tampering with the transference potential; after a year the intensity of the transference may become so great as to be unbearable without more frequent interviews. This sequence does not constitute a preview followed by a full performance; it is a continuum. Qualitatively there is no distinction whatsoever in the successive phases. Many patients in deep depressions, able to verbalize almost nothing, are only made more guilty by frequent interviews. They may begin far better on one or two hours a week with no qualitative distinction in the two phases. Oversimplified concepts such as "activity" and "passivity" in such treatments have little validity in defining dynamically what transpires. *Is there a qualitative and quantitative distinction in content and affect in dynamic therapies?*

Many physicians who are experienced in classical analysis but have not treated patients one or two hours a week maintain (1) that such infrequent hours will not expose pregenital conflicts or (2) that anything short of classical analysis *should not* penetrate such pregenital areas: that if such material does appear, the ego defenses are probably weak and it may be dangerous to proceed, or that the therapist has made a mistake in the direction of "wild analysis."

The Chicago group found in many patients, treated one or two hours a week over a long period, that much pregenital conflictual material did appear, but not because of unpredictable wild analysis or enfeebled egos. Others have since found the same to be true and have agreed that the distinction is not qualitative but quantitative in those cases where the therapist in no way interfered with the evolution of the transference. Some of the classical analysts, inexperienced in dynamic psychotherapy, have felt that the appearance of pregenital material was evidence that the therapist had made a mistake. It seems logical to us that in focusing on current relationships and analyzing resistances at the genital level the patient will move in one of two directions; either toward facing some new phase of the Oedipal conflict or toward regression to some safer pregenital atmosphere. If he does the latter because of unbearable tension, it would seem necessary to follow his lead and deal with such fundamental difficulties as arise, to provide a firmer foundation from which he may finally return to face the genital conflicts with less fear. This concept refers to those cases where the original plan was to effect as thorough a reintegration as the patient could master. Throughout, the number of necessary hours per week will vary.

Our research group conceived of no sharp lines between levels of the personality to be explored, but consciously restricted the extent of the analysis depending upon what seemed necessary for a given patient, whether by long, short, profound, or superficial psychotherapy.

The Chicago group maintained that the plan of treatment in many cases may constantly change; that is, with supportive psychotherapy initially, transference complications may so develop that the whole therapy moves into a much more uncovering type of analysis with varying degrees of emphasis in dealing with the transference neurosis. Classical analysts who have no experience in dynamic uncovering psychotherapy often maintain that one can never achieve the intensity or depth of the transference neurosis in psychotherapy if hours are varied during different phases. On the contrary, those of us doing psychotherapy two hours a week have frequently had the experience that the transference neurosis may become so intense as to be unwieldy, that progress could be made only if the hours were increased greatly to "work through" the transference neurosis. It depends upon the patient and upon what is happening in him as well as in the therapist, whether decrease or increase of hours will modify the intensity of the transference reactions. For instance, patients with strong dependent needs, knowing that they can remain in analysis for a long period, five hours a week regularly, certainly will procrastinate about facing the anxiety connected with the dependency conflicts. Decreasing the frequency of the sessions may facilitate awareness of the tension connected with these conflicts and force the ego into greater effort at exploring this problem. We know that regression and indulgence at levels where the patient was formerly greatly deprived is of therapeutic value and often must be granted. Later or concomitantly, however, and with proper timing, the early repressed hatred must be brought to consciousness in an atmosphere of relative frustration.

THE VALUE OF FOCUS ON THE CURRENT SITUATION

We all know how important genetic material is for the therapist's understanding of what is happening in the treatment. But we know also that treatment becomes much more significant to the patient when he is continuously made aware of what goes on in current relationships, especially in the transference, because that is the proving ground for reality, past and present.

Since our purpose in treatment is to strengthen reality testing, we focus more on the actual problems and turn to the past only to reveal motives for the present irrational reactions. This search into the past is not only necessary for the therapist's understanding but at times is essential for clarifying the behavior of the patient.

Since the best results are achieved when the ego is working optimally, there seems no point in the analyst's overburdening an ego in its reality testing by being so "mysterious" that the transference neurosis becomes far too intense.

GROWTH OUTSIDE TREATMENT HOURS

It is common to conceive of analytic hours as oases of progress in a desert otherwise inert. The assumption that only in treatment interviews will problems be solved can become a dead end. It may constitute an effective defense against facing anxiety which may be painful. Freud himself came to the conclusion that in some cases, such as phobias, a point is reached when the analyst must encourage the patient to engage in activities formerly avoided. Many of the group in Chicago emphasized that the therapist should be aware that a great part of the patient's experience in working through an understanding of his problem transpires outside the therapeutic hour. These relationships therefore should be scrutinized continuously in the interview. This is *not* to say that feelings which should be worked through in the transference should be allowed free drainage into outside channels. This alone will never resolve the conflicts with the therapist. However, what happens outside the hours provides clues and constitutes a proving ground for what is developing with the therapist.

INTERRUPTIONS IN THERAPY

Alexander and some other members of the group have been particularly interested in experimenting with interruptions (other than vacations) to facilitate mobilization of conflicts and testing of the patient's growth, especially in the later phases of treatment. Alexander has emphasized the plateau on which a patient may rest as a defense against the anxiety of moving on into exploration of other problems. It certainly is true that interruptions over a long period will mobilize conflicts in some cases, whereas in others this procedure may serve as proof to the patient that he can now manage many new situations. This technical device, as indeed all techniques, useful in experienced hands, can be misused. It certainly should not be employed to cover up the therapist's shortcomings.

CONTINUING STUDIES OF THE PROBLEM

The Chicago group chose to define its research with the view of (1) modifying the plan of classical analysis so that it was employed as a highly flexible approach to cases across the total spectrum, and (2) re-examining certain "accepted" classical analytic techniques in those specific cases where we definitely had decided upon thoroughgoing resolution of the infantile neurosis.

Another point of departure for research in this subject was elected by the standing committee on Psychotherapy and Psychoanalysis of the American Psychoanalytic Association whose work has been proceeding for the last five years. The view of many of the panel members is that analytic psychotherapy involves a different terrain from classical psychoanalysis, a terrain to be explored and mapped, using the wealth of psychoanalytic concepts as a compass to facilitate exploration and as a blueprint to construct some rational communicable frame of reference for treatment of masses of cases not suitable, extrinsically or dynamically, for classical analysis. The research is proceeding with the hypothesis that dynamic psychotherapy may be an approach as effective as classical analysis with increasingly greater range of applicability, and that it is more inclusive theoretically and practically than classical analysis as literally conceived for the psychoneuroses.

It is apparent that many of the views of members of the Chicago group are gaining wide acceptance. The need for a diagnostic formulation, a flexible plan of therapy, and the dynamic essentials of the therapeutic process in analytic psychotherapy and classical analysis is becoming more clear. The enthusiastic re-exploration of certain concepts previously taken for granted in Freud's original copyright proceeds comfortably in the search for dynamic principles of therapy. It is noteworthy that the American Psychoanalytic Association appointed the standing study committee to explore the therapeutic process because of the national interest and concern emerging from the Chicago research.

SECTION VI

Theoretical Papers

THEORETICAL PAPERS

While recuperating from one phase of her final illness, Dr. Johnson once confided to me that she felt she was not highly "esteemed as a theoretician" by many of her psychoanalytic colleagues. I think this both amused her and troubled her. However, she considered herself first and foremost a clinician. By this, she meant that she preferred to derive factual patterns from clinical observations and *then* to theorize from the data. Mental gymnastics without direct supporting data were less appealing to her, undoubtedly because of her early doctoral training in physiology. Most of her papers are rich in clinical data. I have selected four papers which I feel are representative of the "theoretical" facet of Dr. Johnson. The 1952 paper, "Factors in the Etiology of Fixations and Symptom Choice," is not strictly theoretical in that the text includes several clinical case studies. However, I know that Dr. Johnson considered this to be one of her "important" papers as well as the 1949 paper, "Some Etiological Aspects of Repression, Guilt and Hostility," which appears first in this section.

21

SOME ETIOLOGICAL ASPECTS OF REPRESSION, GUILT AND HOSTILITY

It is becoming increasingly clear that our concepts of the relative roles of biological inheritance and the environment in character development have been sharply challenged by the striking observations of collaborative psychiatric therapists working with parent and child and by the provocative findings of the anthropologists. As all are aware, new light has been shed upon the mechanisms operating in the early development of the psychic apparatus, calling for a re-evaluation of certain of these concepts. Collaborative therapy and repeated discussions with Dr. S. A. Szurek provide much of the background for this paper.

The collaborative therapist and the anthropologist may be overly tempted to depreciate the role of biologically inherited patterns of behavior. Contrarily, these factors may be assigned undue emphasis by some psychoanalysts. To such internal drives as primary masochism and sex are ascribed a volcanic intensity which overwhelms the weaker influences of parental attitudes. It goes without saying that both categories of influences determining character development must be assigned their true weight eventually, although a final answer cannot be attained at this time.

Reprinted with permission from *Psychoanalytic Quarterly* 20 (1951): 511–27.

There is no intent to review the entire complex of early development, but rather to explore certain facets of the problem. There is need for a reevaluation of our concepts of (1) repression as a dynamic mechanism in psychic development; (2) the meaning of restitutive behavior in the child; (3) the genesis of hostility in man.

REPRESSION AS AN ADAPTIVE MECHANISM

Let us explore the classical concept that repression is a normal reaction of the infantile ego, as a consequence of what Freud thought were the extreme limitations of the integrative capacities of the young ego. Alexander (1) stated "in the last analysis repression is a primitive device of the ego to maintain its integrity." Anna Freud (2) said, "the significance of repression is reduced to that of a special method of defense." This was considered by her and by Freud as one of the psychic processes which served the same purpose: "the protection of the ego against instinctual demands." It is freely granted that repression is a necessity in the world of today. Fleeing from an overpowering enemy and fighting another on equal terms are likewise necessities. What more beyond necessity may be truly ascribed to repression?

Anna Freud considered repression as a defense against instincts, in three distinct categories: (1) superego anxiety in the neuroses of adults, related essentially to strictness in the education of the superego; (2) objective anxiety in infantile neurosis, which originates because the infant or little child "does not combat the instincts of its own accord . . . [but] . . . regards the instincts as dangerous because those who bring the child up have forbidden their gratification . . ."; (3) instinctual anxiety, or an innate dread of the strength of the instincts.

It is difficult to see any genetic distinction between Anna Freud's superego anxiety in the neurosis of adults and her objective anxiety in infantile neurosis except as regards the stage of development during which external influences operate. However, a major issue emerges from her concept of instinctual anxiety. She states, ". . . the human ego, by its very nature, is never a promising soil for the unhampered gratification of instinct. I mean by this that the ego is friendly to the instincts only so long as it is itself but little differentiated from the id. When it has evolved from the primary to the secondary process, from the pleasure principle to the reality principle, it has become, as I have already shown, alien territory to the instincts." Her expression, "the human ego by its very nature . . . ," deserves scrutiny. "By its very nature" could refer to a phylogenetic entity, a character determined by the gene composition of the germ plasm. It is improbable that Anna Freud entertained this thought since, by definition, the ego, as such, is not inherited except for the basic anatomy and physiology which the ego employs in expressing itself.

What then remains as regards the phrase, "the human ego by its very nature . . ."? Is it not the logical error of *petitio principii*, begging the question in which a definition which has not been proved is smuggled into the sequence of argument? "By its very nature" is an arbitrary postulation of what remains to be proved. Apparently Anna Freud assumed that something within the ego itself, independent of outside influences and parental attitudes (and presumably, independent of heredity), is operating. She admitted that the ego of a little child "regards instincts as dangerous because those who bring the child up have forbidden their gratification." Here she was on sound ground. Yet in her "instinctual anxiety" she seemed to think that the very young ego may reject certain id impulses apart from such parental attitudes which have been impressed upon the child. Was she here referring to Freud's (3) original theory of primal repression as "a first phase of repression which consists in a denial of entry into consciousness to the mental (ideational) presentation of the instinct"? How else can the ego differentiate from the id, and proceed from pleasure principle to reality principle except through impingement of the external and internal environment upon the id?

Let us postulate conditions in which the external necessity for repression is virtually eliminated. Let us imagine an ideal set of parents, utterly without personality distortions, possessed of perfect subtlety, imagination, and warmth. They note at once any mounting tension in the child and immediately provide adequate and generally acceptable forms of gratification. The surplus energy of erotism is channelized in such an understanding manner that there is "cathexis toward action that is acceptable as well as some object cathexis." There is no imposition of the necessity to repress from parental sources. The external figures resolve the emerging tensions in the child, so that they never reach the point of hostile aggression, renunciation or repression.

Granted this ideal external environment, would there not still remain the repressions necessarily resulting from internal drives and impulses of the child, which are beyond the capacity of the ego to integrate?

Repression is said to occur in the infantile ego because id impulses arise which the young ego cannot integrate into an acceptable pattern of behavior. This concept is based on the assumption that, even under ideal conditions of symbiosis between mother and child, the ego is unprepared at times to deal with mobilized id impulses. There is no doubt that in painful organic disease in the infant, the mother, no matter how subtle, can do little to relieve the child; hence there may be great rage and possibly the need for repression. But even if no such internal organic distress occurs, and even if external parental relationships were ideal, it has always been assumed that impulses would arise that are too powerful for the young ego to integrate acceptably.

Alexander (1) said, "the development of erotic drives does not run a course precisely parallel with the rest of either physical or mental growth; sexual impulses outstrip the rest. This discrepancy is clearly observable in the typical emotional constellation of this age, the œdipus complex." Alexander seemed to indicate that this discrepancy in development is a phylogenetically determined fact. On the other hand, Hartmann et al. (4), Benedek (5), and others no longer conceive of our being born with a reservoir of id impulses. They speak of the birth of an infant with an undifferentiated apparatus, out of which are crystallized or differentiated the ego and the id. With this latter view, many of us today are in agreement. Given no organic distressing disease and a theoretically ideal set of parents, are we still to believe that somehow the ego and id do develop from the original undifferentiated state at different tempos? If so, this would definitely constitute a negative adaptive reaction, which is indeed rare in biology.

Others have proposed the related concept that the child is driven by powerful impulses to attempt actions for which it lacks the necessary physiological and anatomical equipment. This dilemma mobilizes frustration, humiliation, and rage, and there emerges the need to repress. They refer to the little boy in the œdipal period who has genital impulses (it is maintained) but lacks the necessary physiological development for fulfilment. Hendrick (6) seriously questioned the concept of the growth and development of id impulses to act before the required physiological apparatus has appeared. In discussing the pleasure in mastery, he emphasized the fallacy of seeking to "define infantile life in terms of adult complexes" and he warned that we must be "on guard against ascribing to all childhood behavior the emotional intensity which is apparent in the neurotic episodes of the child, and in both the erotic and neurotic tensions of adults. This means that the goal of infantile erotism is not normally orgasm; it is not normally a compulsive need unless it is associated with anxiety and, therefore, differs dynamically from the adult's."

Hendrick suggested that when the impulse or need for a function arises, the physiology and structure are ordinarily ready. He cited multiple illustrations in growth. There is no compelling reason to think that the child has a strong impulse to walk or talk at three months. Yet, such an assumption is as defensible as the assumption that the child has a powerful impulse for intercourse at four years. Again, a child of four has no strong urge to drive a car as its father does, unless there is conflict and a compulsive need for competition. Five-year olds who are happy and have companions give no evidence of being frustrated and angry that they cannot play baseball with twelve-year olds. There is no intention to discard the œdipus, but to qualify its content and intensity, to call attention to Hendrick's redefinition of the goal of the heterosexually directed instinct of the four-year old, and to guard against our adult projections.

In other words, such a view would support the concept that the ego grows with and is integrated with the task which arises, which is not in keeping with the view of Freud, Anna Freud, and Waelder that somehow the ego's whole organization can be overwhelmed because of the strength of the instincts alone. This does not discount the possibility that the capacity of a phylogenetically developed disposition for repression may vary in children. My thesis is only that in the ontogenesis of the individual this adaptive capacity for repression is activated usually by external environmental factors.

It has been stated frequently that deprivation and repression are necessary for individualization and growth. Freud assumed that as long as all needs are gratified, under 'total' indulgence, the infant tends to experience the source of satisfaction as part of the self. Hartmann and his co-authors (4) said, "partial deprivation thus is probably an essential condition for the infant's ability to distinguish between the self and the object; to the extent to which indulgence prevails, comprehension of the breast as part of the self is dominant; to the extent to which deprivation is experienced, or indulgence delayed, the distinction becomes possible." (The qualification is added that "the distinction, however, seems to become impossible unless a certain amount of gratification is allowed for.") Granted that a degree of frustration is necessary for such basic developmental processes, it does not follow that the deprivation and frustration must be carried to a point necessitating repression. It would seem that a far more confident, colorful, adventurous child would evolve from a smoothly functioning symbiosis between mother and child in which frustration fails to reach the point where energy is dissipated in repression, and self-esteem and confidence are lost. As Alexander has emphasized often, severe deprivation may be a real stimulus to individualization of cultures and societies. However, such group deprivation does not necessarily involve repression in the individual, and does not make valid the concept that repression is a primary biological factor, or an adaptive mechanism to phylogenetic influences.

Anthropology can shed some light on our problem, even though it cannot provide ultimate answers, because it does not provide personal analyses of individuals in the societies it studies. Kardiner (7) was one of the first analysts in this country to explore more thoroughly the contributions of anthropologists in attempts to delineate more clearly what in behavior is primarily phylogenetic and biological in origin and what is contributed by external pressures.

Kardiner (7) and Linton emphasized that the long period of dependency of the human infant provides a potential advantage, if it is well managed. The loose integration and impressible plasticity of a long infancy afford maximal opportunity for the environment to mold and modify and to become channelized. They found that the influence of each culture studied varies with each type of behavior studied. "Not all impulses are equally susceptible of control. For example, the impulses generally denoted as sexual and aggressive are much more subject to control than eating impulses. . . . Some problems of adaptation in one culture create few difficulties, while in another they form the main façade." Anthropologists now describe how one culture may allow the widest sexual freedom between children, including even frottage against the mother; here sexual jealousies are minimal. But the nursing period is stormy. Food is scarce. Consequently, the major jealousies and conflicts in children and adults have to do with food rather than sex.

The only universal sexual taboo described by these investigators is mother-son incest. In general, different cultures display widely varied taboos, and, by the same token, widely differing human impulses subject to repression. There emerges compelling evidence for the importance of external rather than phylogenetic origins of repression. We have held the view that freedom in sexual play with themselves or each other in children would on the whole not decrease the inevitable phylogenetically determined sexual need for the parent. Anthropology so far lends little if any support to this view. Analyses of individuals in culturally different societies are sorely needed, and might provide crucial evidence on the point in question.

In our own culture, where individual analyses are plentiful, it is virtually impossible to determine whether freedom in autoerotism and sexual play between children diminishes the œdipal conflict because most parents, despite the best intellectual intentions to allow such childish gratifications, are so rooted in taboos as to frustrate the proclivity for such freedom by implied uneasiness. Hartmann and Kris (8), in criticizing Freud's concept of the phylogenetic source of castration fear, pointed out that implicit attitudes and anxiety in significant adults were sufficient to cause an intense fear in the child.

Probably no anthropologist commands greater respect from psychoanalysts than the late Ruth Benedict. Benedict (9) and Mead (10) and their group studied swaddling in certain European cultures. Greenacre and Buxbaum earlier touched on this subject, but without the detailed observations and the clear conclusions of Benedict and Mead. Benedict's and Mead's conclusion was that swaddling could not be relied upon to produce a single set of effects in different cultures: the parental motives for and attitudes toward swaddling were strikingly different in Russia, in Poland, and among Ukrainian Jews.

Benedict pointed out that any investigation of "comparative cultures must press the investigation to the point where the investigator can describe what is *communicated by* the particular variety of the widespread technique he is studying. Thus, in the case of swaddling, the object of investigation is the kind of communication which in different regions is set up between adults and the child by the procedures and sanctions used. . . . In Russia, swaddling is explicitly justified as necessary for the safety of an infant who is regarded as violent and being in danger of 'tearing its ears off or breaking its legs.' "

The Polish version of swaddling is that "the infant is regarded not as violent, but as exceedingly fragile. It will break in two without the support given by the bindings. . . . Swaddling is conceived as a first step in a long process of 'hardening' a child. Hardening is valued in Poland as suffering is valued. . . . In peasant villages it is good for a baby to cry without attention to strengthen the lungs; beating is likewise good since it is hardening."

The swaddling of the Jewish baby in the Ukraine is of still another complexion. "The baby is swaddled on a soft pillow with loose 'bindings,' the mother singing as she swaddles it. The stress is on warmth and comfort, and the confinement of the limbs is to be pitied. . . . Poor baby, he lies there nice and warm, but, poor baby, he can't move." This early warmth will later be contrasted with the hard benches and long hours at school. "The pillowed warmth of his swaddling period apparently becomes a prototype of what home represents." The mother "is starting the baby in a way of life where there is a lack of guilt and aggression in being the active partner." Of paramount importance, these parental attitudes are communicated to the infant. The Russian infant is imprisoned, the Polish infant is hardened, the Ukrainian Jewish infant is comforted.

In commenting on Benedict's conclusions in her report, Margaret Mead stated, "whenever any single practice was followed cross-culturally, a confusing number of contradictions were found, such as would have been the result if, to the material which Doctor Benedict presented today, we had applied a simple hypothesis that swaddling could be relied upon to produce a single set of effects. It has become increasingly clear over the last few years that it was necessary to include a variable, loosely described as *'tone of voice'* or the *quality of the interpersonal relationship* within which a given zone or stage of locomotion or mode of behavior was indulged and frustrated. I think that the research of the last six months makes it possible to proceed one step further and to advance the hypothesis that within the general framework of biological development the *significant specific character-forming elements will be those through which the adults attempt to communicate with the child*. This communication need not be an articulate type of 'character education' but it is *affect-laden and emphatic*. . . . By examining the system of communication between parent and child against a theoretical ground plan provided by the body itself, the pattern of family relationships in the society, and the tempo and rhythm of biological growth, we can distinguish those nuances of emphasis."

Hartmann, Kris and Loewenstein (4) have said, with others, that in restraining an active child the hostile response is greatly reduced when the child is handled by a friendly, imaginative adult; they stated, "cathexis toward action is transformed into object cathexis."

In certain long-standing communal groups (for example, one in Korea) aunts, cousins, and other relatives share in caring for the baby. In such children, with many mothers, sibling rivalry is far less a problem than in our society. Whether these children develop a sense of deprivation at the absence of a single mother could best be studied in several successive generations. However, the plausible suggestion is made that a girl with many mothers, later mature and herself a mother, is not required to give to her own baby as much as is demanded in our own society.

Similarly, we observe that demand feedings in infants result in calm, happy babies only if the attitudes communicated by the mothers are happy and calm. It is equally true that fairly early toilet training is compatible with serenity in the child depending upon the mother's attitudes. The view that early interruption of anal-erotic pleasures regardless of the mother's attitudes must lead to tragedy remains to be demonstrated.

Maternal attitudes and behavior may not constitute the infant's initial impact with the external environment. We may not correctly assume that the intense motor activity or immediate irritability of a baby at birth is due to only the two factors — inherited biology or the attitude of the mother in dealing with the baby. Evidence of nervous function other than such structural indications as myelinization is now available. Recent studies by neurophysiologists (11, 12) indicate electric activity of the cortex not only in newborn but even in utero as early as seven months. There is no switch thrown at birth which causes cortical cells suddenly to begin to function. Loud, repeated, disturbing noises or cramped positions causing uncomfortable proprioceptive discharges may stimulate cortical activity and adaptation in utero. We may doubt whether intrauterine life is the Nirvana we have assumed. This returns us again to the view of Rank and more recently of Greenacre (13) with regard to the factors of birth in anxiety. We may venture the hypothesis that perhaps some rudimentary distinctions between id and ego commence even before birth (14).

The point at issue may be formulated: repression is an adaptive mechanism of positive value to the organism, a response to and a defense against pathological change. Even with the most wisely educated parents, classical psychoanalysis views this mechanism as a necessity, since the strength of the id impulses is such that they cannot be integrated. I would suggest that the pathological changes might be essentially external in origin — changes in parental or cultural attitudes which interfere with the normal development of the capacity of the ego to perform its task.

In the classical view, part of the repression might be likened to the collateral circulation which develops in infants and children with coarctation of the aorta, an inborn defect. The view presented here would rather liken repression to antibody development in response to an infection of external origin.

The tendency or *Anlage* for repression develops ontogenetically and is activated essentially by the individual's experience with the external environment. In any case, it would appear that repression represents an adaptation of an ego whose integrative capacity has been burdened by pathological change usually having nothing to do with gene determined sources. It is making the best of what might be worse, at the cost of loss of free emotion and the binding of psychic energy.

IDENTIFICATION AND THE MEANING OF RESTITUTIVE BEHAVIOR IN THE CHILD

In a smoothly operating symbiosis between mother and child, the infant adapts itself to the maternal attitudes and demands in the most subtle detail, involving a striving for incorporation and identification. "The root of identification [according to Hartmann and his coworkers (15)] can be traced to those impulses of the id which strive toward incorporation; the psychological mechanism of identification is a correlate of and is built upon the model of this striving." Somehow, the child very early senses the slightest anxiety or finest shading of mood in the parent. All of the mother's reactions increase or decrease the child's security and, therefore, stir the reaction of the instinct for self preservation.

In discussing identification in early development as it relates to superego formation, Hartmann and his coworkers (4) stated that the little child, to escape conflicts between love, hate, and guilt, "does not identify with the parents as they are, but with the idealized parent; i.e., the child purifies their conduct in its mind and the identification proceeds as if they were consistently true to the principles they explicitly profess or aspire to observe."

I seriously question, as did Szurek (16) and Emch (17),

whether there is such a partial identification with the parents, a purification of parental conduct, or an incorporation of part of the parent and a discarding of the remainder. The child early incorporates all aspects of the parent, conscious and unconscious, including moral attitudes and the methods of dealing with everyday realities, with the multiple confusions involved in such incorporation.

In the symbiotic relationship the child must learn to integrate and adjust to all facets of the mother's personality, albeit in adjustment the child often represses quickly those aspects too disturbing for consciousness. Because such components are repressed, however, does not mean that identification is not operating, since identification operates unconsciously as well as consciously. For instance, the fact that the parents' sexuality has been repressed by the child does not indicate an identification with an asexual person. The child in our society quite generally desexualizes the parents and "purifies" them consciously only as it learns it must; the reality principle prevails. For our culture this is probably a fortunate and less painful adjustment. Nevertheless, just this necessarily repressed component of the parents makes for an unconscious hostile identification which must be resolved finally in "normal" adolescence if the child is to achieve such a healthy identification as to permit real independence. Collaborative therapy of the neurotic child and parent provides sound evidence that the child does not "purify" the parent except consciously; also, in the antisocial acting out of a psychopathic personality or a delinquent, it is common to portray the worst features of the parents' conscious or unconscious impulses.

In the process of total identification, in which the child normally learns to master all facets of the mother's personality, the parent is what may be appropriately called a "needed object."

The term "needed object," as contrasted with the common terms "love object" or "bad object," requires elaboration. These adult words, "love," sentimentalized and idealized, and "bad," judgmental in tone, lack scientific objectivity. The use of such terms as "love object" or "bad object," fraught with adult sentiment and emotion, has little justification in our thinking about dynamics. Rather, we must think in terms of multiple needs requiring satisfaction or frustration by someone. This someone, first the mother, becomes a "needed object." Rapaport (18) refers to the "need-satisfying" object, and Freud stated that "we do not say of those objects which serve the interests of self-preservation that we love them; rather we emphasize the fact that we need them. . . ." Such a "needed object" may provide widely varying degrees of satisfaction to the infant. Gitelson (19), discussing character synthesis in adolescents, especially those who hold one at arms' length, spoke not of loving an object or the therapist, but of the dependability of the object or therapist.

Collaborative therapy has revealed that we cannot understand the formation of the ego and restitutive behavior in many children in terms of guilt toward a loving object, with subsequent repression of forbidden impulses. We see many parents who satisfy such minimal custodial needs of the very little child as food, protection from injury, and provision for sleep, but who have no warmth or love, in the adult sense, to give to the child. Yet the child may comply completely with the parents' demands, develop anxiety, and make frantic efforts toward restitution. Is this a restitution born of guilt toward a "loving" object? Probably not. Rather, the child makes restitution because it fears the needed object will not fulfil its needs. The child responds to the mother's demands not primarily because of making restitution for guilt, but purely on the basis of the reality principle. This is the only way in which to deal with her. Parental love and warmth are not indispensable ingredients of this process of satisfying the child's primitive needs for food and protection which elicit responses to the mother's demands. This above concept is far removed from the concept of guilt in which "because she loves me, I must be good and make restitution." Rather, "because I need her, I must make restitution or lose the satisfaction of my needs." It goes without saying that, without consistent parental warmth, an emotionally healthy development of the child is impossible. Yet it must be emphasized that there is no need for love and warmth in the adult sense for the formation of an ego which will react restitutively or which will forbid antisocial behavior.

The word guilt, as used in the past, is meaningless if it is applied to all restitutive behavior. It appears more justifiable to view guilt as a need for punishment in an urge to make reparation to a "needed" object purely on the basis of the reality principle. To be sure guilt, in the accepted sense of making restitution, arises from parental love and the fear of losing that love. Such guilt is common. But there is less confusion genetically if we think not of a "love object" but of a "needed object," which covers the gamut of satisfactions or frustrations provided the child by the significant parent. Thus can we account for the restitutive behavior, fraught with anxiety, inhibition, and masochism, observed in many children with parents who are consistently unloving in the adult sense. To be sure, many such undependable, cold parents display every conscious and unconscious verbal expression of love for the child, and an immense concern for its welfare. In response, the child incorporates into its ego structure all the modalities of this pseudo love, exaggerated concern, and multiple, confusing inconsistencies in the parental attitudes.

In brief, Szurek's (16) and Johnson's (20) studies of little children and adolescents failed to support Hartmann's view that there is partial identification with the parents, an acceptance of the good elements and a rejection of the bad. Although children may and do repress those parts that may cause them the greater conscious conflict, nevertheless they probably early incorporate the whole parent en masse and then, as time goes on and the child sees confusing facets in the parent, it represses much of this which merely simulates idealization and purification. Children may be masochistic, with an intense need for punishment precisely because they learn that only by suffering may they make sufficient restitution to regain some lost sense of security in relation to the provider of basic minimal needs.

GENESIS OF HOSTILITY

This concept of total identification with the mother leads to a better understanding of the origin of hostility in the infant and child. If hostility is not essentially a primal sadism projected from masochism, how does this effect arise? It is said that frustration "causes aggression." It seems certain that aggressiveness is part of the biological apparatus of the newborn. But it is imperative to differentiate this from hostile aggressiveness, a distinction many fail to make. In the newborn baby, hunger gives rise to ineffectual skeletal, motor and autonomic discharges with crying, kicking, and flushing. The mother, if she is consciously or unconsciously ambivalent toward the baby, may see in this stormy display a hostile aggression. Unwittingly, she meets this hostility-by-interpretation with her own genuine hostility. The child's growing need for incorporation leads to introjection of the total attitude of the mother, including her hostility. There is no more compelling reason to assume that hostility is primary and phylogenetic than there is to assume that love originates thus. We should probably regard hostility as introjected, as we tend to do in the case of love. To be sure, such introjection probably does not begin until the infant has made the distinction between itself and the mother.

The incorporation of the ambivalent object leads to increased tension in the child and an augmentation of its demands, to be followed, in turn, by further estrangement and alienation of the mother as she observes the child's behavior. In the average family such alienation may be of moderate intensity, while in other families it may become a mounting, vicious spiral of mutual ambivalence. The prototype of hostility and love, then, is learned, but in one's growth becomes increasingly self-produced. The child and adolescent develop to hate just as they develop to love.

SUMMARY AND CONCLUSIONS

Repression is rather more in the nature of an adaptation to the impingement of external pathological change upon the developing ego than an adjustment to phylogenetically determined imbalances or changes in development. Although repression provides a useful means for coping with pathological change, the extent to which repression occurs is one index of the degree of departure from good health.

Restitutive behavior in the child seeks to preserve the source of gratification of primary needs by a "needed object," rather than seeking to appease a "loving object" with a view to preserving the love. Our concept of the meaning of guilt should be expanded to the more inclusive view that guilt is a need for punishment in an urge to make reparation to a "needed object," rather than limiting the meaning to the common situation in which restitutive behavior arises from parental love and the child's fear of losing it.

Hostile aggressiveness, as distinguished from biologically inherited aggressiveness, originates in the course of the infant's incorporation of the total maternal attitude, which includes the mother's own hostility.

REFERENCES

1. Alexander, Franz. *Fundamentals of psychoanalysis.* New York: W. W. Norton & Company, 1948.
2. Freud, Anna. *The ego and the mechanisms of defense.* New York: International Universities Press, Inc., 1946.
3. Freud, Sigmund. *Repression.* Coll. Papers, 4:86–97.
4. Hartmann, Heinz; Kris, Ernst; and Loewenstein, Rudolph M. Formation of psychic structure. In *The psychoanalytic study of the child* 2:11–37. New York: International Universities Press, Inc., 1946.
5. Benedek, Therese. The psychosomatic implications of the primary unit: mother-child. *Amer. J. of Orthopsychiatry* 19 (1949): 642–54.
6. Hendrick, Ives. Instinct and the ego during infancy. *Psychoanalytic Quarterly* 11 (1942): 33–53.
7. Kardiner, Abram. *The individual and his society.* New York: Columbia University Press, 1939.
8. Hartmann, Heinz, and Kris, Ernst. The genetic approach in psychoanalysis. In *The psychoanalytic study of the child*, vol. 1. New York: International Universities Press, Inc., 1945.
9. Benedict, Ruth. Child rearing in certain european countries. *Amer. J. of Orthopsychiatry* 19 (1949): 342–48.
10. Mead, Margaret. Discussion. *Amer. J. of Orthopsychiatry* 19 (1949): 349–50.
11. Smith, J. R. The electroencephalogram during normal infancy and childhood: I. rhythmic activities present in the neonate and their subsequent development. *J. of Genetic Psychology* 53 (1938): 431–53.
12. Lindsley, D. B. Heart and brain potentials of human fœtuses in utero. *Amer. J. of Psychology* 55 (1942): 412–16.
13. Greenacre, Phyllis. The biological economy of birth. In *The*

psychoanalytic study of the child, 1:31–49. New York: International Universities Press, Inc., 1945.
14. Hartmann, Heinz. Ego functions. Read before the meeting of the American Psychoanalytic Association, Montreal, May 1949.
15. Hartmann, Heinz; Kris, Ernst; and Loewenstein, Rudolph M. Formation of psychic structure. In *Psychoanalytic Study of the child*, 2:29, 33.
16. Szurek, S. A. Notes on genesis of psychopathic personality trends. *Psychiatry* 5 (1942): 1–6.
17. Emch, Minna. On "the need to know" as related to identification and acting out. *Int. J. Psa.*, 25 (1944): 13–19.
18. Rapaport, David. On the psychoanalytic theory of thinking. Read before the meeting of the American Psychoanalytic Association, Montreal, May 1949.
19. Gitelson, Maxwell. Character synthesis: the psychotherapeutic problem of adolescence. *Amer. J. Orthopsychiatry* 18 (1948): 422–31.
20. Johnson, Adelaide M. Sanctions for superego lacunae of adolescents. In *Searchlights on delinquency*, ed. K. R. Eissler, pp. 225–44. New York: International Universities Press, Inc., 1949. (Reprinted above, p. 113.)

22

FACTORS IN THE ETIOLOGY OF FIXATIONS AND SYMPTOM CHOICE

I. FUNDAMENTAL CONCEPTS

FREUD, in *Analysis Terminable and Interminable* (1), expressed scepticism about therapeutic achievements in many of his adult cases. Among the obstacles to success, he considered important the constitutional intensity of the instinct in some patients. Many writers following Freud's lead have accepted the constitutional strength of instincts as an explanation of therapeutic failure. But Freud, with his usual caution, stated explicitly that although "the constitutional factor is of crucial importance, . . . it is yet conceivable that the same effects might ensue from a re-enforcement of instinctual energy at some later period in life. If this were so, we should have to modify our formula and say 'the strength of the instincts at a given moment'. . . ."

As long understood, the term "fixation" refers to that level of emotional development corresponding with the last "successful adaptation." To that level the individual regresses when he fails, or is in danger of failing, at a higher level of growth. Fixation may be said then to refer to the level of emotional development beyond which further growth is arrested.

Fenichel (2) ably summarized the classical concepts of the origin of fixation in the following way.

1. The consequence of experiencing excessive satisfactions at a given level is that this level is renounced only with reluctance; if, later, misfortunes occur, there is always a yearning for the satisfaction formerly enjoyed.

2. A similar effort is wrought by *excessive frustrations* at a given level. One gets the impression that at developmental levels that do not afford enough satisfaction, the organism refuses to go further, demanding the withheld satisfactions. If the frustration has led to repression, the drives in question are thus cut off from the rest of the personality; they do not participate in further maturation and send up their disturbing derivatives from the unconscious into the conscious. The result is that these drives remain in the unconscious unchanged, constantly demanding the same sort of satisfaction; thus, they also constantly provoke the same defensive attitudes on the part of the defending ego. This is one source of neurotic "repetitions."

3. One frequently finds that excessive satisfactions as well as excessive frustrations underlie a given fixation; previous overindulgence had made the person unable to bear later frustrations; little frustrations, which a less spoiled individual could tolerate, then have the same effect that a severe frustration ordinarily has.

4. It is understandable, therefore, that abrupt changes from excessive satisfactions to excessive frustrations have an especially fixating effect.

5. Most frequently, however, fixations are rooted in experiences of instinctual satisfaction which simultaneously gave reassurance in the face of some anxiety or aided in repressing some other feared impulse. Such simultaneous satisfaction of drive and of security is the most common cause of fixations.

It will be well to examine what is meant by the concept "excessive indulgence or gratification," which Fenichel expressed as "excessive satisfactions." Long ago child analysts realized, as they observed ambivalence in the parent who spoiled the child, that "excessive love" or too much indulgence could not be regarded as healthy in the parent. Love which is not ambivalent has no strings attached; it permits growth and independence.

Ferenczi (3) wrote of parental seduction, the imposition of adult genital love on a child. (Similar brilliant reconstructions from analyses were described by Emch [4].) Although Ferenczi referred to parental indulgence of sexual instincts that patently were highly pathological and temporally inappropriate, his formulation is important to our present discussion of more subtle parental influences.

The most important change produced in the mind of the child by the anxiety-fear-ridden identification with the adult partner, is *the introjection of the guilt feelings of the adult* which makes hitherto harmless play appear as a punishable offense.

When the child recovers from such an attack, it feels enormously confused, in fact, split — innocent and culpable at the same time — and its confidence in the testimony of its own senses is broken. . . .

We have long held that not only superimposed love but also unbearable punishments lead to fixations. . . . The playful trespasses of the child are raised to serious reality only by the passionate, often infuriated, punitive sanctions and lead to depressive states in the child who, until then, felt blissfully guiltless.

Anyone can understand the disturbing forces that lead to fixations in an atmosphere such as Ferenczi described. And "excessive indulgence" on all other levels works dynamically in exactly the same way as Ferenczi elucidated. However, the mechanism is often far more subtle and unconscious than that described by Ferenczi.

In view of our recent work, we consider especially important Fenichel's statement: "Most frequently, . . . fixations are rooted in experiences of instinctual satisfaction which simultaneously gave reassurance in the face of some anxiety or aided in repressing some other feared impulse. Such simultaneous satisfaction of drive and of security is the most common cause of fixations." We agree with this statement as far as it goes. Fenichel does not explain how this reassurance comes about. We seriously question the concept of "security," which is only relative. The so-called reassurance stemming from some temporally inappropriate instinctual satisfaction, in the presence of anxiety, is an unhealthy reassurance and guilt-ridden satisfaction.

Since Fenichel's brilliant summary of the factors contributing to fixation, students of ego psychology, identification, and integration have emphasized that no process suddenly begins at birth. Hartmann and many others now conceive of our being born not with a reservoir of id impulses, but rather with an undifferentiated apparatus out of which are crystallized or differentiated the ego and the id. Investigators are more interested in observing the earliest mother-child relationship than in taking recourse to the old sharp divisions between phylogenetic anlage and environment. We may speculate about the most immature fantasy life of the preverbal infant, but for facts concerning communication between mother or parents and child we will start with the verbal child and its mother, although, to be sure, communication utilizes, in addition to verbalizations, other means such as tone, facial expression, and attitude. Our study, by its special technique, may help us better to understand the choice of neurosis as well as healthy development.

II. IMMEDIATE BACKGROUND FOR PRESENT STUDIES

Twelve years ago, in an attempt to understand and treat "school phobias" of children, a collaborative psychotherapy of child and significant adult was developed (5). The dynamic emotional interplay between the "significant" parent (usually the mother) and the child in these cases became clear. Children who previously had been under treatment without improvement were cured when the mothers agreed to be treated. Progress was accelerated when collaborative therapy was used from the beginning. With this technique, we were able for the first time to understand the etiology of acting out among antisocial delinquents (6).

Only such a technique, by which attention is focused equally on child and significant adult, could enable us to see clearly how the parent or parents, usually unconsciously, sanctioned and fostered the child's acting out of the parents' poorly integrated forbidden impulses. As the parent achieved vicarious gratification of these impulses, he often at the same time expressed the hostility inherent in his conflicts in a destructive fashion toward the child. Treatment often came to a standstill, or matters became worse, unless the significant parent were also under treatment. Simultaneous psychotherapy seemed a far more precise scientific therapy and method for research than reconstructive formulations from analysis of one or the other, which too often yield secondary and tertiary elaborations rather than primary etiology. In our method one therapist works with the child while another works with the parent or parents, and every therapeutic hour conducted by each therapist is reviewed fully in the research seminar. Thus the dynamic interplay of patient with patient, and of each patient with his therapist, is fully discussed. Such a method of therapy will not always be beneficial; in fact, in many cases only damage could result from the introduction of two therapists into the life of one patient or several members of the family. If there were no unresolved "blindspots" in either therapist, there would be no clinical need for the two members to get together to discuss their cases; but such discussion is always necessary for research.

III. PRESENT STUDIES

Our combined studies of parent and child have led us to reexamine rather closely some previously accepted views. In case after case, we have seen such tenacious fixation in the child at certain points that successful treatment, even at an early age, is nearly hopeless unless the parent's need of gratification through the child's operations within that fixation can be modified. The parent's healthy and neurotic needs, however, are only half the picture; for the child brings its own behavior to bear on the parent so that the earliest symbiosis gradually becomes closer and closer, like a spiral, as Grinker (7) has described it.

It appears from our research that a child is held at a certain level of fixation for at least two major reasons: (1) fear of something from which it regressed or which kept its development arrested, and (2) sanctions from one or both parents encourage the child to achieve instinctual gratification at the level where the child has become fixated. The parent unconsciously achieves gratification through the child; the young patient senses the ambivalent guilty demand from the parent that the child continue to afford him this gratification. Benedek (8) has recently called this process "regressive adaptation."

We do not contend that symptoms in the child are always determined by an unconscious compliance with the parent's unconscious wish for certain instinctual satisfactions. Piers (9) has pointed out that anal symptoms, for example, should not be confused with instinctual gratification. But we do believe the most rigidly fixed symptoms are correlated with parental wishes. For instance, long and intensive collaborative treatment of sexual aberrations in children and adolescents reveals that in every case a parent had serious problems at the genital level. We have found that this parent, (1) seduced the child; (2) then denied the final gratification; and (3) unconsciously gave specific stimulus for the outlet to the aroused instinctual drive. The hostile component in the parent plus other experiences in the life of the parent will determine the nature of the symptom choice. Such deep drives as frustrated oral and genital experiences of the parent, when they are present, only increase the complexities for the child. A simple case with obvious dynamics will illustrate this factor in choice of symptom.

Case 1

An intelligent mother brought her son, six years of age, because he stuttered and worst of all, as she said, still soiled and wetted, often with awareness and in particularly inappropriate places. To the mother this was a "public disgrace," so she sought help. A year before the boy had set several fires. His fantasy life, we found, was filled with rage but the only expressions of this permitted to him were soiling, wetting and, rarely, setting fires. No verbal expression of anger was countenanced by mother or father.

The father had been enuretic until adolescence and had no conscious concern about the boy's problem. The mother was in a panic about training him and his two-year-old brother. When asked gently in the early diagnostic interview how she imagined her son might react if she were more definite and firm with him about his soiling, she became agitated and said, "He would probably chisel the table legs, set fires, and burn the house down, and I would be sorry the rest of my life."

This was indeed a terrifying alternative she fantasied to the form of gratification she was permitting him; hence she dared not control the soiling. But how, in her own poorly integrated emotional life, did she arrive at such fantasies as were arresting the boy's development? In the first interviews the source of her fantasy life was revealed. When she was five years old, her only brother was born. Her father had been completely engrossed in her ten-year-old sister, whom this woman had always hated.

The mother now remembered with rage that her little brother "got away with murder with my mother for years; for instance, he just went outside and had his bowel movements wherever he wished." Her maternal uncle, as a boy of five years, had angrily set the house on fire, burning it down and killing himself. Our child patient's maternal grandmother, observing what her own brother had done in a rage, had permitted her son any liberty at the anal level, and our patient's mother, furious at her brother's license, was now permitting the same in her sons for fear firmness might lead to "burning the house down." The treatment of a mother like this is a colossal task.

The child, aware of the guilty, anxious, condoning and demanding attitude of the parent, may have a double burden of guilt to carry; its own (depending on age and other factors) and the parent's. It has a sense of obligation to the parent to continue in the symbiosis or spiral. The parent, however, denies his guilt and projects it onto the child, as Ferenczi described. The symbiotic instinctual gratification is disturbing to the child and is not well integrated into its emotional life. Although permitted by the parent, the gratification produces no healthy reaction, and a weak point results in the emotional development. This weak point offers a focus of fixation when pressures necessitate regression from a current level of adaptation.

From the mother's point of view, this temporary inappropriate satisfaction is preferable to the satisfaction she would derive if the child progressed to a higher level or at least to an alternative level. The child recognizes the mother's guilty sanction and must incorporate her unconscious sense of guilt if it is to maintain contact with the mother. The child's feeling of guilt is intense; it feels as guilty as — or even more guilty than — the well-trained child who steals or does some other act forbidden in its family.

Evidence in innumerable cases demonstrates that this fixation point or specificity of symptom is invariably related to the mother's own poorly integrated impulses; therefore these impulses in the mother may be roused and strengthened by the gratification she experiences from the child's questionable behavior. The complications of the spiraling relationship may so accumulate that the mother cannot free the child from experiencing gratification vicariously for her. A child under treatment will exhibit toward its therapist tremendous defensive anger and fear of giving up this relationship with the parent. It may feel that the therapist is wicked to question what the child feels is right and acceptable to the mother. The severity of the child's dilemma has to be observed to be believed.

As evidence we offer some representative cases. They do not show the blatant specificity seen in Case 1, which is unusual in that respect; often the fixation or symptom choice from generation to generation is more indirect. In our cases much of the usual analytic material is, for brevity, omitted; in general we include only such part of the child's material as relates to the parent's conflict.

Case 2

Eddie, four and a half years old, was brought to treatment because he wanted to be a girl and because, with the exception of a few months when a housekeeper was in the home, he continued to soil. For the year and a half previous to our seeing him, his soiling had become a ritual; he had to defecate into a diaper while lying on the bathroom floor. He abhorred odors and had to be cleaned immediately. As the bathroom ritual evolved, he became obsessive about numbers, where roads ended, how many times to chew a mouthful of food, and so on, with reaction-formations to all sorts of messing except defecation. He was the terror of the neighborhood and had no friends. The mother spontaneously admitted that his sister, Alice, two years old, was her favorite. Realizing that the mother was a very neurotic woman who would need long analysis, we decided to start intensive analytic treatment of the boy, leaving the mother untreated for the time being. The boy was permitted to regress to the infant level and he soon realized that he did not wish to be a girl but a baby. With indulgence and without pressure to grow up (since the therapist was without ambivalence toward him) he rapidly became satisfied; he no longer wished to be a baby or a girl and began to grow up to the level of a child five years of age, with a five-year-old's problems of ambivalence toward both parents. Within a year, Eddie was a happy child, possessed of friends, progressing well in kindergarten, competing normally for his age with his father, no longer victimizing his sister, and improving in other ways too.

One trouble, however, remained absolutely fixed — the soiling ritual in the bathroom. The mother reported that Eddie had asked, "What would you do if I used the toilet?" She replied, "I don't know." When he said, "When I'm six, I'll probably use the toilet," she could think of nothing to say.

This woman was paralyzed, so to speak, when she sought to make an appropriate response. Nevertheless, the fact that he now was asking such questions, and in play was insisting that Hopalong Cassidy and his other heroes go to the bathroom after breakfast, showed that Eddie was beginning to try to solve his problem. To his therapist he said, "My mamma doesn't want me to sit on the toilet."

About this time his sister, now three years old, was reported to be developing the same soiling difficulties. For the sake of research, and to avoid another long course of treatment, it was decided to try to engage the mother in treatment of as limited extent as possible. At first she was excessively sweet and ingratiating. After a time she talked regularly to her therapist about the children's bathroom habits, recurrently asking advice but discarding it before it was given. One day her therapist commented that the mother seemed troubled when she tried to be definite or firm about these functions in the bathroom. The mother replied that when her little daughter had seemed hesitant to urinate in the bushes with the neighborhood children, the mother had gone out and showed her how to do as the other little ones did. When the therapist asked the mother if she knew why she did this, the patient became defensive and very angry.

The mother then talked at length of many Pacific tribes "who can soil all their lives." She gave a considerable anthropological summary. When the therapist suggested that possibly the mother had some feeling not fully known to herself about the soiling impulses of people, the mother vehemently denied this. Immediately, she recounted, with many angry tears, that from her early childhood through late adolescence her own mother had permitted the family home to be unclean. The patient's father, a passive, inadequate man, and her mother had allowed the latter's alcoholic father and three alcoholic brothers to live with the family and the house was "constantly smeared with and smelled of vomitus and urine." The patient had been humiliated so often by this that finally she had ceased to bring friends home. She had not been conscious of her rage at her mother for permitting all this "mess" but had made an identification with her mother to the point where she was relieved of her feeling of hostility toward the mother. Now she was achieving ambivalent gratification through the soiling habits of her son and her daughter. She was of course crippling them as well.

The mother's fantasy frequently was that her son Eddie would be "an alcoholic, a dope fiend, or something worse." Her irritated, but guilty, anxious, and completely indefinite attitude toward the children about the whole matter of bathroom functions had been incorporated by them and had them greatly confused. The little daughter, in a diagnostic nursery group with a highly trained teacher, soiled herself and then, looking terrified of the teacher, asserted "My mamma doesn't care." The teacher, a very warm but definite person, said "But I do care." She then said that she would clean Alice, but that hereafter Alice should tell her when she wanted to have a bowel movement. This occurred during a period when the mother was very hostile toward her woman therapist and toward the teachers in the nursery school, defying them, declaring that they could not train the child. The terror and guilt which the three-year-old girl experienced with the teacher was the result not only of the child's incorporating her mother's anxiety and guilt, but was also derived from what she herself had observed of other children and from earlier training by her mother. This child was soon in the normal routine; the soiling never occurred again while she was under the instruction of this teacher.

The mother, having repressed her rage toward her own mother, was trying to solve the problem in this way: "I don't have to hate my mother for permitting that outrageous mess made by my uncles and grandfather, if I can be messy too — through my children."

Fostering this disturbance in the children also gave vent to much of her hostility. This hostility she imparted to the children; it was spoiling all their relationships with others.

When Alice began to use the toilet, Eddie was anxious and told his therapist, "You need to talk to me about something." Yet for a long time he was extremely angry with her for raising the question of soiling, declaring over and over, "My mamma doesn't want me to use the toilet yet."

The father, although not nearly so ill as the mother, also

gained much gratification from this soiling. Eddie was terrified at the thought of analyzing his confused identification with his mother in her guilty and angry wishes, and he was frightened by the suggestion that he go to the toilet, which he realized would anger his mother. Finally, when Eddie did begin to sit on the toilet to defecate, it was soon clear to his therapist that the heckling by his mother persisted, that he still was far from pleasing her. The mother awarded him a large candy bar for a big stool and a small piece for a small one. Arguments of course ensued over the size and the merited reward. His therapist found Eddie confused and angry. She first of all had to make clear to the child the reality that nobody can decide to have a large or small movement, which was counter to the mother's assumption. The anger against his mother, and the anger against the therapist in the transference and also as a person having a different view from his mother, had to be analyzed. The mother's therapist, apprised of this new form of unconscious attack and disapproval at home, could quickly identify it in the mother's vague and extremely distorted material. The mother finally volunteered the story of the rewards and bickering about the size of stools.

There were many indications of great confusion in Eddie's mind about realities, promises, and deceptions. It became increasingly clear to the mother's therapist that her patient might tell three different stories about one incident. She never could be sure when the mother was falsifying outright. Confronted with this fact, the patient told how her own mother used frequently to lie to spare her daughter from inevitable painful realities. Gradually Eddie's mother became better able to deal with realities and to avoid deceiving herself, her therapist, and her children. The effect on Eddie was immediate. The mother now began to work sincerely at her treatment. Her real personality emerged from the previous mist of vagueness, isolation and anxiety. Her treatment continued long, whereas Eddie's was now less difficult to complete.

The mother's hatred for men was tremendous and she early mistrusted her feelings toward her son. Her genital problem had never been solved. She had always used a weak man to protect herself against a masculine man; she would actually plan to include such an effeminate man on her dates with stronger men. The dates with the adequate man were consequently not repeated. She had married a man who proved stronger than she had judged and her son was her protector in a most peculiar arrangement. Her utter inability to train him stemmed from her drive to satisfy her need to soil which was, among other things, a defense against having to recognize her rage against her mother. Furthermore, her permission to soil, by crippling Eddie's personality, was an expression of the deep destructiveness the mother felt toward her drunken grandfather and uncles, father and husband. The child sensed her angry guilt at once if he thought of using the toilet, for she did not wish to be deprived of her vicarious gratification in his soiling or of this channel for discharge of her hostility to males. When finally she dealt with her own genital problem, the child was freed from her neurotic solution.

As stated above, a child, in the face of anxiety, may need to regress or achieve some instinctual satisfaction. If at the same time the parent, to satisfy his own neurotic needs, sanctions regressive satisfactions in the child, it is very ready to comply with the parent's wish and a fixation results as required by the symbiosis. The mother's ambivalence about Eddie's using the toilet favored his not using it and he subscribed to this wish of hers. His great guilt about using the toilet stemmed from denying her wish.

Possibly, the more overt the mother's wishes, the more direct is the relationship between them and the soiling. The more subtle the mother's ambivalence, the more doubting and obsessive-compulsive the child must become to deal with the instinct so subtly allowed, then denied, by the mother. During the subtle struggle with the mother over the size of stools. Eddie became very obsessive. The child could not believe his senses for any considerable length of time because of the mother's vacillation. This can occur at any level of emotional development, but since sphincter training constitutes the first serious training at the hands of the mother, we are not surprised when vacillating or obsessive (doing and undoing) behavior appears then.

If Eddie had been an adult and we had been analyzing his problem, we would have been clinically and therapeutically wrong to interpret his soiling ritual as expressing his wish to soil, and wrong to suppose that the guilt we observed was over his wish to soil. His guilt would be correctly interpreted rather as stemming from his wish not to soil in opposition to his mother's contrary wish.

Analysts have been conspicuously unsuccessful in treating obsessive-compulsive patients. Have we been imputing the wrong impulses to them? Possibly the parent, by simultaneously encouraging and discouraging instinctual gratification, causes in the child the unending confusion and vacillation that characterize obsessive-compulsive symptoms. Research on this point is now in progress.

Not always is the parent's unhealthy instinctual or neurotic gratification as directly related to the child's behavior as in the case of Eddie's soiling; yet a nucleus of specificity is found.

Case 3

A physician and his wife came to us complaining that their five-year-old daughter always had soiled. The consultant knew from outside sources that this child was so hirsute that playmates called her "monkey." The father's earnest account to the therapist included the fact that he resented the child greatly and pushed her away continually, saying, "You smell bad." About this his anxiety and guilt appeared only moderate. Finally the analyst told him she knew Marion was hirsute and asked him to say something about this. The father then appeared greatly disturbed and recounted that from birth the child had seemed a "monstrosity" to him — that he had examined her early in her life for possible hermaphroditism. He honestly stated that he loathed the child intensely, to his wife's distress. As time went on, it became obvious to the father that it was less painful to reject the child as a "soiling mess" than as one with a defective body. His own unresolved concern about enemas and bowel functions also became clear.

After the child had been under treatment for six months, she began to use the toilet. She soon resumed soiling, however, telling her mother: "Daddy says I don't have to have my movement in the toilet; he says I only have to try." The mother immediately took the father to task about this. The child again used the toilet for a week. Then one morning the mother heard Marion crying and, on entering the bathroom, found the father removing the child from the toilet before she was finished, ostensibly so that the older sister could use the toilet. The mother sent the sister to another bathroom and again reproached the father.

Obviously this father had an overwhelming need to foster and permit Marion's soiling. If her soiling is cured, there is danger that the father, deprived of one expression of his hatred and shame of the child, will be forced into some more subtle and destructive manifestation. Treatment of him may become a necessity for his sake as well as that of the child.

Case 4

A five-year-old girl had been masturbating openly and constantly since the age of two and one half years. The mother finally brought the child for treatment because her teacher was "so disturbed to see the child do this continuously in school." Treatment of the mother soon revealed that she had had exactly the same problem and the humiliation of harsh treatment in school because of it. Only with treatment of the mother could this child be successfully treated.

Case 5

This is a case in which transvestitism occurred early in life. The patient was a boy, six years of age. We have seen many cases of this sort. In this one, several striking etiologic factors came together. The mother was frigid, hated males, and completely favored the two-year-old sister. The little boy soon wanted to be a girl and insisted on wearing girls' clothes. The mother gave him many of her cast-off garments and was interested in, and amused by, his attiring himself in them. The boy was brought for treatment when the father finally became uneasy. The child soon realized he really wished to be the baby of the family rather than a girl. Strong remnants of his wish to be a girl remained, however, after the rivalry with his sister had been resolved by intensive therapy. The mother's hostility to males and her guilty fostering of his feminine identification augmented this fixation. Treatment of her revealed precisely how this operated unconsciously and from what it stemmed in her life. She was seductive with the boy; then by frustrating him she encouraged his retreat to femininity.

Case 6

Two brothers, nine and six years of age, created a serious problem at home and in restaurants by greatly prolonging meals and quarreling over vegetables and other foods with which they built dikes, tunnels, towers, and other structures at the dinner table. This sandbox behavior had been going on for years. The mother was thoroughly provoked by it and sought help. Her husband "seemed to take it very calmly." He came to analysis for problems apparently quite unrelated to the children's trouble. Only late in his analysis did the part he played in their unusual behavior become clear. He had feared to compete with his own father openly in a masculine way, but very early he and his brothers had learned that handling food at the table as has been described usually led their father to protest weakly and then to "leave the table for some peace." Only when this man, in analysis, became aware of this early neurotic expression of his genital hostility toward his father did he become firm with his own children. Almost immediately they gave up their distressing behavior at the table. To be sure, many facets of the boys' unresolved conflicts with their father were still obvious.

Case 7

Parents brought their ten-year-old son for consultation because he continually fingered his mother's dresses and recently had wanted to stroke her arms and legs. One could see the pleasure in the mother's face as she recounted that she loved clothes and that since her son could talk he had complimented her and her friends on their dresses. "He was a terrific hit with all of us, but now he is going too far — it looks queer." Her marriage had been in a precarious state for years. She said, "I love Jimmie's sweetness and compliments." As soon as the boy was with the therapist he stroked her dress and said, "I love that dress."

The etiology of this rudimentary fetishism is clear. The mother seduces, denies, and offers a solution.

Case 8

A minister, forty years of age, developed phobias at age four, began to practice compulsive bestiality at eleven, became ritualistic (counting and routine) at fifteen, and later developed obsessive intellectualization and indecision. His mother had used religion, about which she was ambivalent, in a hostile manner to control the boy. Finally she turned away from religion altogether. For years she kept her son's hair long. She dressed him in girls' clothes and throughout his adolescence allowed him to sleep with her.

When he was eleven his mother took him to a barnyard and told him a story about a boy who practiced bestiality, saying: "Now don't you ever let me catch you doing anything like that." The son was astounded, never having been aware that such a practice existed. In treatment he recalled with rage the look of gratification and the smile on his mother's face as she recounted the story. "It was almost as though she felt I would be capable of doing such a thing," he said, "and I went right out and did it." He had repeated his sexual relations with animals, feeling "horrible guilt" after each episode. He developed a ritual in which lengthy prayers of atonement alternated with the practice of bestiality. He had been consciously aware of the fact that the greater the atonement the more he enjoyed the next sexual act, and gradually the process had become exceedingly time consuming and burdensome to him.

We accomplished nothing for him in treatment until his obsessive prayers of atonement were interpreted as assuaging the guilt he felt for his murderous rage toward his mother for implicitly demanding this degrading bestiality from him and for playing into his need to seduce her. During the years he practiced bestiality his parents frequently, by ambiguous remarks, indicated that they knew he was doing some forbidden thing. They never had brought the matter directly into the open, however, and he had lived in fear that he would be discovered. What he really feared was that his death wishes toward his mother would be detected together with the guilt he felt for his rage toward his father and mother for the seduction.

The mother seduced, then withheld gratification. She stimulated the boy's bestiality. The son developed his obsessive reaction-formation as a way of coping with his mother's ambivalence about genitality, bestiality, and religion, and with his rage toward her. This man's ten-year-old son came to treatment because of sexual confusion and increasing anger with his parents.

Among our adult and child cases we found endless variations of infantile sexual gratification arising directly from a parent's need to fix the child at an immature level of instinctual gratification after seduction and denial (6).

With regard to the problem of enuresis, we have been able to supplement the fundamental studies of Gerard (10) by our finding that in a few cases enuretic children directly afford to a parent vicarious instinctual gratification. We still believe, however, that such direct parental gratification is more commonly achieved through a child's soiling, stuffing it with food, or sexual behavior, than through enuresis.

Children who long have had "intractable" constipation or malignant anorexia present a difficult problem. We feel from experience almost helpless in treating them while they are living with their parents unless the parents are accessible to treatment.

Overt hate can be unwittingly fostered in a child by a parent. The child does the acting and the parent, quite unconsciously, achieves vicarious gratification through the child's hostile behavior, in this way destroying the child. We have often seen this happen when, after a child has survived a serious accident or encephalitis, the parents have been told by a physician that the child's future state will be hopeless. The physician thus unwittingly gives permission to certain parents to let down their

Etiology of Fixations and Symptom Choice 373

own defenses and foster vicious forms of hostile behavior in the child (6).

We here cite one such case to support our belief that we cannot safely rob a parent of a deep gratification achieved through a child's pathological behavior without first resolving the parent's problem. Should we achieve health for the child but omit to help the parent to a healthy solution, we may destroy the parent or the sibling subsequently selected by the parent as a scapegoat. At times shortage of therapists may be used as an excuse for taking this risk, but the following case is a tragic illustration of what often happens when the therapist is unaware of the need for collaborative therapy, or when the facilities for it are lacking.

Case 9

Dick, one of identical twins, was severely hurt in an automobile accident when eighteen months old. A physician told the parents that, if he lived, he would be a "vegetable." At this, the mother wished he would die and felt relief at the prospect of his dying, for she realized she had always disliked him. The boy lived to become the terror of the neighborhood; he was utterly impulse ridden.

When he was brought for help, at the age of three, his intelligence and aptitudes were found to rate a trifle higher than those of the "well" twin. In a few play hours, his acting out was treated with friendly firmness, and he appeared to be a charming, active, fine little boy. The neighbors soon found him to be so, but with his mother he was his old self.

The boy's problems were not of organic origin, and the parents were told that in time he would be well. But a need for gratification through her son's acting out had been roused in the mother when the surgeon had given her permission to believe that her son was to be a psychotic "vegetable," and she should not have been deprived of this gratification without help from a collaborating therapist. Since the family was planning to move soon from the city, such therapy was not made available. To open up this woman's problems before the move seemed unwise.

Events proved that it was most unwise not to have offered therapy to the mother at once. For two weeks her vicious attacks on the boy were interspersed with long periods of dreamy withdrawal, in which she seemed to be out of contact with the world about her, even to the point of failure to feed the children. She was depressed and entertained suicidal thoughts. The development of these symptoms should have been foreseen, for experience should have suggested that this mother would be much disturbed to receive a hopeful prognosis for the boy. Such an event in general is clearly predictable.

In a few weeks the mother was so ill that she had to be hospitalized in a closed ward. Protected in the hospital, she relaxed, and study made clear that we were dealing with a highly sadistic woman. She had been successful in a career and had managed her family fairly well until the drastic diagnostic prediction about her son sanctioned in her a sadistic acting out in her relationship with him. Her own father had treated her ruthlessly; she hated and mistrusted men and had been seductive, in a hostile way, toward many. It became clear that hers was a malignant, hysterical personality, that she was not schizophrenic, and that she would be easily accessible to treatment, though it might be stormy. Before her illness, this woman had requested therapy, and undoubtedly her psychosis would have been averted had a therapist been working with her during her son's treatment.

Finally, we would emphasize that in estimating the severity of neurosis in a child, it is necessary to take into account, among others, the following factors: (1) the intensity of the child's sense of guilt in its neurosis; (2) the strength of the child's obligation to gratify a parent's unconscious wish; (3) the amount of fear and guilt the child will feel in giving up its inappropriate behavior.

IV. SUMMARY

Intensive collaborative treatment of parents and children (5, 6) has been used to study symptom choice and fixation. The child is found to be held to a particular point of fixation or type of symptomatology for at least two reasons: (1) fears of something from which it regressed or which arrested its development, and (2) the parental sanction granting to the child instinctual gratification at the level which becomes the point of fixation or symptom choice. By this sanction the parent achieves a vicarious, guilty satisfaction of his own instinctual needs. The child is guilty if it affords, or if it denies, this gratification to the parent. Successful therapy of the child often makes therapy imperative for the parent who is deprived of the vicarious gratification.

REFERENCES

1. Freud, Sigmund. *Analysis terminable and interminable* (1937). Coll. Papers, vol. 5.
2. Fenichel, Otto. *The psychoanalytic theory of neurosis*, pp. 65–66. New York: W. W. Norton & Co., 1945.
3. Ferenczi, Sandor. Confusion of tongues between the adult and the child (*the language of tenderness and passion*) (1932). *Int. J. Psa.*, 30 (1949): 225–30.
4. Emch, M. On "need to know" as related to identification and acting out. *Int. J. Psa.* 25 (1944) 13–19.
5. Johnson, Adelaide M.; Falstein, Eugene I.; Szurek, S. A.; and Svendsen, Margaret. School phobia. *Amer. J. Orthopsychiatry* 11 (1941): 702–11. (Reprinted above, p. 14.)
6. Johnson, Adelaide M., and Szurek, S. A. The genesis of anti-

social acting out in children and adults. *Psychoanalytic Quarterly* 21 (1952): 323–43.
7. Grinker, Roy R. Personal communication.
8. Benedek, Therese. Toward the biology of the depressive constellation. *J. Amer. Psychoanal. Assoc.* 4 (1956): 389–427.
9. Piers, Gerhart. Unpublished discussion of author's present paper at the meeting of the Chicago Psychoanalytic Society, Oct. 28, 1952.
10. Gerard, Margaret W.: Child analysis as a technique in investigation of mental mechanisms, illustrated by a study of enuresis. *Amer. J. Psychiatry* 17 (1937): 653–63.

23

OBSERVATIONS ON EGO FUNCTIONS IN SCHIZOPHRENIA

With Mary E. Giffin, E. Jane Watson, and Peter G. S. Beckett

The following is a theoretical elaboration evolved from an extended clinical study on schizophrenia. The clinical data on which this paper is based were presented in a companion paper that I had the privilege to read at the May 1955 meeting of the American Psychoanalytic Association in Atlantic City. The theoretical paper stands alone, but the interested reader is referred to the companion paper entitled "The Significance of Exogenous Traumata in the Genesis of Schizophrenia," in *Psychiatry: Journal for the Study of Interpersonal Processes*, 19 (1956): 137–42.

THE first of these papers has described a collaborative study of 27 schizophrenic patients which suggested that, first, a majority of persons who become schizophrenic have been subjected to overwhelming parentally instigated trauma; and, second, the intense hostility inherent in this trauma distorts the unfolding instinctual life and elicits the desperate survival response of psychosis. These observations have stimulated a re-evaluation of the ego functions in schizophrenia, in which it has become clear that many of these functions are directly related to the learned patterns of hypertrophied defense mechanisms fostered by the parents.

THE DEVELOPMENT OF DEFENSES – PROJECTION, DENIAL, AND CONSCIOUS LYING

Both in the study of 27 schizophrenic patients and their families, and in the earlier investigations which had prompted this study, we observed a high proportion of families in which there was inordinate use of projection both by the child and by at least one parent. We believe that this is significant.

All children project, but healthy parents define reality for them. Unhealthy parents not only fail to define reality, but, even worse, blame the child for parental actions, thus fostering in the child projection as a method for dealing with his own reality problems. In turn, the child's projections are accepted by the parents. In our cases, we found that frequently one parent used and fostered projection, and the other condoned its use, so that the child automatically learned the use of projection. In such families disowned hostility was constantly projected back and forth between family members.

But anger, hate, and unbearable reality must be denied before they can be projected, and the use of denial by the parents appeared frequently in our cases. Anna Freud has observed that a child's denial in play may be reinforced by a parent in a kindly effort to mitigate painful reality. (1) However, the parents of our patients utilize denial primarily to disguise their own hostile impulses. When these children perceived the anger and hostility of a parent, as they did on many occasions, immediately the parent would deny that he was angry and would insist that the child deny it too, so that the child was faced with the dilemma of whether to believe the parent or his own senses. If he believed his senses, he maintained a firm grip on reality; if he believed the parent, he maintained the needed relationship, but distorted his perception of reality. Repeated parental denial resulted in the child's failure to develop adequate reality testing.

Our experience with these patients was in accord with Waelder's concept that the denied is closer to consciousness than the repressed. (2) Yet denial and repression complement each other, in that the denial of threatening external reality reinforces the patient's repression of his own hostility toward the threatening object. We should mention, parenthetically at this point, that a paper on ego functions would not be complete without emphasis on repression. We have been profoundly impressed with the magnitude of the repression of traumatic episodes which occurred as late as midadolescence. We shall elaborate on this in our discussion of the theory of delusions.

We found the amount of conscious lying as a defense in these cases startling, even though we had expected discrepancies in the material given by various members of a family. Many parents consciously lied or withheld information about traumatic events reported by the patient or by other family members. They did this to preserve their own unassailable positions, even though in so doing they jeopardized the treatment of the patient, whom they consciously wished to help. As was noted in the preceding paper, some parents induced the patient to lie or to withhold information by means of dire threats as to what would happen to him if he disclosed the details of what had occurred at home.

IDENTIFICATION WITH THE HOSTILE AGGRESSOR

In our patients, identification with the hostile aggressor occurred in response to various experiences of intense hostility from adults, including incestuous attacks, repeated physical assaults, and the even more effective destructiveness of long-standing parental interference with ego development. The fact that such exogenous factors may have disrupted the instinctual balance has been emphasized by Ferenczi in discussing the severe neuroses. (3) He observed that patients with malignant hysteria actually had suffered sexual traumata in childhood, and accurately portrayed the process by which an adult may act out his own inappropriate sexual impulses toward a child and then blame the child for what has happened. Moreover, Ferenczi brilliantly recognized the child's introjection of the perpetrator of the sexual assault, emphasizing the child's taking over of the adult's guilt. In a paper given in 1932 he said:

Through the identification or let us say, the introjection of the aggressor, he [the aggressor] disappears as a part of the external reality and becomes intra- instead of extra-psychic. . . . In any case the attack as a rigid external reality, ceases to exist and in the traumatic trance the child succeeds in maintaining the previous situation of tenderness . . . almost always the perpetrator behaves as though nothing has happened and consoles himself with the thought, "Oh, it is only a child; he does not know anything; he will forget it all."

Our cases also provided ample evidence of continued parental interference with ego development. This occurred both through total isolation of the child and through total subjugation of the child. The enslavement was cemented when parents expressed fantasies that the child would eventually murder, become promiscuous, or become psychotic. The child's identification with, and acceptance of, such an image of himself is devastating to his ego development.

In all of our cases, the destructiveness instigated by one parent had been condoned by the other parent. Therefore, the helpless, unprotected child, if he were to survive within the family, had no alternative but to identify with the hostile aggressor. Here it must be emphasized that a child identifies to a greater or lesser degree with all facets of both parents. He cannot select only those aspects which appear safe.

Ferenczi has emphasized the introjection of the parental *guilt*, We have been more impressed with the child's introjection of (1) the fears felt by the destructive parent; (2) the parental projection of blame, used immediately and repeatedly with associated retaliatory threats; (3) the parental assertion that no one will believe the child; and (4) the parent's denial of his own acts and his own destructiveness.

Primarily through the child's introjection of parental denial, the assaulting aggressor becomes intrapsychic, and is no longer extrapsychic. This permits the child to maintain a relationship with the needed parent. The denial tends to obliterate reality testing, and reinforces the child's repression of his fear and rage.

THEORY OF DELUSIONS

These observations have led us to a reconsideration of earlier theories of delusions. Fenichel wrote, "In summary, delusions, like hallucinations, are condensed mixtures of perceptional elements, thoughts, and memories systematically distorted in accordance with definite tendencies; these tendencies will represent warded-off instinctual wishes as well as threats from the superego." (4) He went on to say that they can be interpreted like dreams, and mentioned that they contain an "historical kernel" of truth.

Waelder has pointed out that the usual theories concerning paranoid delusions have not explained their unique inaccessibility to influence. He referred to Freud's concept — which, like Fenichel's, held that there is a kernel of truth in delusions —

stating, "Something is denied — we leave it open whether it is a frustrating event or an instinctual drive . . . there may be a return of the disclaimed in distorted form. The knowledge of it as essential though distorted truth makes it inaccessible to influence."

We would freely grant that delusions contain powerful instinctual components. However, it appears that the initial schizophrenic delusion is largely an expression, albeit disguised, of the overwhelming exogenous trauma which the patient has experienced. The action described in the initial delusion with striking specificity represents a life experience of the patient. As repression fails, the fear and hatred felt toward the parental aggressor are rapidly displaced to other persons or objects. Thus, the delusion serves as a defense against reexperiencing consciously and affectively the original traumata. The content of the delusion closely reflects the details of an actual assault — an assault confirmed, in our cases, by interviews with other family members.

On the basis of our data, we conceive the steps in the development of a paranoid delusion to be as follows:

1. The patient has been the repeated target of marked intrafamilial hostility in the home in which he has been reared.

2. The patient has developed and learned the excessive use of projection, denial, or conscious lying through his years of adapting to parents who themselves excessively use these same mechanisms and foster their use by the child.

3. Discrete destructive actions toward the child, instigated by a parent, are superimposed upon the existing malevolent parent-child relationship.

4. The child, unprotected and helpless, must deny and repress these experiences if he is to preserve a relationship with the needed parent. He introjects the hostile aggressor, including the latter's denial and projection.

5. The parent and child continue the previous relationship, but now each increasingly needs to deny and repress the rage and fear engendered by the destructive experience. The parent reinforces the child's fear and guilt by utilizing subsequent incidents to convey to the child the latter's responsibility for the trauma. Parental denial and projection of responsibility distort the child's perception of reality.

6. As the traumata are repeated, the child's fear and rage crescendo, and his repression breaks down. Even after he has left the dominion of his parents, hostile actions of other persons toward him, similar to parental behavior, may increase the rage until repression cannot be maintained.

7. As the traumatic experiences emerge from repression, the child's fear of the previously introjected hostile aggressor and fear of his own counterrage force him to deny and to project, rapidly displacing the experience to other objects. This forms the content of the early delusion.

8. These distortions of reality defy resolution because they are invested with the emotional charge of the actual original experience. Until this central core is faced as true and as a part of reality, the patient cannot permit the desperately needed delusion or its derivatives to collapse.

In contrast to the concept that the core affect of the paranoid delusion is denied and projected homosexual love, reversed into hate and persecution, the delusions of our patients originally evolved from *hate*. Secondarily, erotization of the hostility occurred as a defense. The early delusion's inaccessibility to influence by initial interpretations of instinctual wishes becomes understandable with the recognition that the early delusion represents *not* a false belief, but a past reality.

The classicists have maintained that the patient, out of guilt over his instinctual wishes, develops an increasingly extensive delusional system in an effort to corroborate his innocence. They state that ideas of reference and hallucinations of derogation arise from a projected condemning superego. But the inference that a patient must be guilty because otherwise he would not continue to enlist outside forces to establish his guiltlessness commits the error in logic of the undistributed middle term.

We have observed *fear* rather than guilt as the motivating force determining the continuous displacement of the source of persecution with resultant extension of the delusional system. Fear of the internalized hostile aggressor and the counterhostility evoked by the threat to survival are denied, projected to outside objects, and continuously displaced. Thus the patient attempts to avoid reexperiencing the terror of the devastating hostility from and toward the person on whom he was entirely dependent.

TREATMENT IMPLICATIONS

The above observations have radically altered our treatment plan for patients in the earliest stage of schizophrenia. Most of our patients were seen within days of the initial appearance of symptoms of psychosis. Thus, their manifestations of psychosis lacked the confusing multiple displacements and regressive phenomena which commonly confront therapists whose patients arrive at an institution weeks after the onset of illness. Moreover, because of the high anxiety of the parents early in a patient's illness, the therapists found them more responsive to questioning than they would be at a later stage.

In therapy, we have first attempted to make it clear to the patient that we shall try to understand what he says, but that he must help. We ask the patient to present material slowly enough for each communication to be carefully considered. Highest priority is given to the possibility of truth inherent in the productions of the patient. The therapist tries, by words and actions, to clarify all reality distortions.

Later in therapy, it is, of course, necessary to use the transference relationship to understand reality distortions relative to parental influences and those related to instinctual drives. By deferring interpretations of the concomitant instinctual wishes to a later period in therapy, the therapist avoids reinforcing the patient's identification with the hostile aggressor who often told the patient that his impulses alone were at fault. As the patient experiences the therapist's protection against the introjected — and actual — hostile aggressor, the transference deepens, and the tendency toward regression comes into the scope of mutual therapeutic investigation and management. To be sure, sometimes the interpretation of the instinctual wishes cannot be deferred, and some reenforcement of the patient's identification with the hostile aggressor is unavoidable.

We agree completely with Fromm-Reichmann's emphasis on the need to analyze and to resolve the conflicts generated by the patient's hostility toward the object upon whom he is dependent — namely, the therapist or the parent. However, we explore very quickly with the patient the vastly important experiences by which he has developed the hostile, murderous wishes which he fearfully conveys to the therapist.

Early in treatment, using as clues the content of the schizophrenic delusion or the apparent meaning of the behavior, we push the patient and the parents for information concerning trauma which may be possibly related to the delusion or behavior. If the parents, thus directed, are able to recall and describe the traumatic events, with their consent we share our knowledge of these events with the patient. Once we can take this much initiative against the feared hostile aggressor, the patient is able to begin facing the introjected rage and his own counterrage. We are fully aware that later in treatment the patient must face the fear connected with his instinctual wishes.

With older patients, or when parental cooperation is not possible, we follow the same pattern, although without the catalytic effect of specific information. In only one case did the parents remove a patient from treatment, as the patient approached the disclosure of material about which the parents were very fearful.

As repression weakens in the patient and the therapist explores with the patient the possibility that the patient has experienced overwhelming trauma, the synergistic effect speeds the return of the repressed. When the early trauma begins breaking through repression to consciousness, the patient becomes horrified and full of shame; his next step is to deny the event, saying that it never really happened, that it is all in his imagination — just as his parents would have wished. He may beg the therapist to deny the trauma. But at this point we do not permit the patient to obstruct resolution of the traumatic reality through denial. We are not deceived by the denial. We encourage the patient to face the event which has occurred, and to reexperience fully and consciously the hostile, aggressive act directed toward him.

The strength of denial may be so great as to lure the therapist into making an interpretation on an instinctual level. However, such an interpretation would be inappropriate at this stage of treatment and might extend the delusional system. To be sure, the same emotional impact emerges later in the transference, with all the instinctual components, and every aspect of these must then be analyzed accordingly.

We believe that the profoundly repressed, overwhelming traumata which have occurred must be recovered and later analyzed in the transference for protection against recurrence of a psychotic episode. Unless this can be accomplished, many patients will continue to be vulnerable because the repressed material remains as a focus of further illness or will be channeled to the next generation. (5) By means of these techniques, applied in the early stages of schizophrenia, we believe that the episode of psychosis can be shortened and the future therapy structured, making it possible to diminish the suffering of the patient and his family.

A word should be added about the crossing of diagnostic lines. We have found that during the dynamic therapy of patients with severe neuroses, episodes of clinical schizophrenia have sometimes emerged. The delusion was ushered in by the return from repression of highly traumatic heterosexual or homosexual experiences. On the basis of our research observations, we have continued dynamic treatment in the face of such episodes, rather than regarding the schizophrenic episode as a signal for retreat.

Many investigators have observed that severe psychosomatic illness may alternate with acute schizophrenic psychosis. We have noted, in some of our patients, alternations between schizophrenia and psychopathic behavior or convulsive disorder. Collaborative studies of patients showing such alternation have revealed overwhelming exogenous traumata, similar to those we have observed in the other patients reported on here. Further research to clarify these observations is now in progress.

The distinction between the dynamics of the catatonic and the paranoid reactions remains obscure. Among the 27 patients included in this study, there was not one who was frankly catatonic. This absence of catatonia may be related to the short duration of psychosis in our patients, or the early initiation of treatment by the techniques we have described. Probably an equally intensive study of catatonic patients will clarify the relative importance of fear and guilt in these patients.

In summary, our research observations of 27 schizophrenic patients and their parents, studied by the collaborative method, have stimulated a reevaluation of ego functions in this disorder. It has become clear that many of these functions are directly related to the learned patterns of hypertrophied defense mechanisms fostered by the parents. The psychotic process is an adaptive technique developed in an effort to refute the experiences of parental assaultive behavior of an overwhelmingly destructive nature. The impact of the trauma leads to malignant distortion of the unfolding instinctual life. The theory of delusions can be seen as related to the introjection of the hostile aggressor, with repression and denial. We have found that the application of our concepts of therapy in the early stages of schizophrenia shortens the episode of psychosis and structures the future therapy.

REFERENCES

1. Freud, Anna. *The ego and the mechanisms of defence.* London: Hogarth Press, 1937.
2. Waelder, Robert. The structure of paranoid ideas: a critical survey of various theories. *Internat. J. Psycho-Anal.* 32 (1951): 167–77.
3. Ferenczi, Sándor. Confusion of tongues between the adult and the child. *Internat. J. Psycho-Anal.* 30 (1949): 225–30.
4. Fenichel, Otto. *The psychoanalytic theory of neurosis.* New York: Norton, 1945.
5. Johnson, Adelaide M. Factors in the etiology of fixations and symptom choice. *Psychoanalytic Quarterly* 22 (1953): 475–96. (Reprinted above, p. 353.)

24

THE INCEST BARRIER

With Maurice J. Barry, Jr., M.D.

There is some interesting history behind the last paper chosen for this section, "The Incest Barrier," written with M. J. Barry. The content of the last section of this paper pertains to the resolution of the oedipus conflict in the analysis of a male patient by a woman therapist. In a different form, this material was presented with some trepidation by Dr. Johnson at a seminar or staff meeting of a psychoanalytic group in Chicago in 1956 or 1957. There was considerable recoiling by the group since the paper forthrightly discussed strong positive feelings toward the patient by the analyst in place of the more traditional views of the time. Counter-transference had been fairly universally viewed as an undesirable contaminant of the analytic process. Since that time, Harold Searles and others have openly discussed the use of positive counter-transference. The topic seemed to fit rather naturally into considerations on the incest barrier, and the authors (Barry and Johnson) combined forces to write the paper that follows. It consists of an historical inquiry, clinical considerations of what happens after father-daughter incest, and a theoretical discussion leading into transference implications in analytic therapy.

INTRODUCTION

WHAT is the nature of the incest barrier in the family and in the psychoanalytic transference?

In an average analysis which proceeds in a reasonably predictable manner, the patient usually begins with residues of œdipal material expressed in his current living. Because of conflict at this level in the analysis, regression to preœdipal material is most common. Analysis of the pregenital strivings, with considerable resolution of ambivalence, then establishes a more stable foundation for what remains to be analyzed. With such a foundation of firmer emotional security and the patient's recognition of his basic capacity for loving and being loved, the œdipal conflict is again approached. In this final phase of analysis of the œdipal conflict, much castration anxiety and guilt are resolved. Upon resolution of these deterrents to the incestuous aim, the question arises as to what realistic barrier remains to prevent incestuous fulfilment in the analysis. If there is a barrier, what is its nature, origin, and advantage?

HISTORICAL INQUIRY

Freud (4) asked himself, "What is the ultimate source of the horror of incest which must be recognized as the root of exogamy?" He said, "To explain it by the existence of an instinctive dislike of sexual intercourse with blood relatives — that is to say, by an appeal to the fact that there is a horror of incest — is clearly unsatisfactory; for social experience shows that in spite of this supposed instinct, incest is no uncommon event even in our present-day society, and history tells us of cases in which incestuous marriage between privileged persons was actually the rule." After extensive consideration, in *Totem and Taboo*, Freud said, "At the end of our inquiry, we can only subscribe to Frazer's resigned conclusion. We are ignorant of the origin of the horror of incest and cannot even tell in what direction to look for it. None of the solutions of the enigma that have been proposed seems satisfactory."

Freud nevertheless felt impelled to mention another attempt at solving it: "This attempt is based upon a *hypothesis* of Charles Darwin about the social state of primitive men. Darwin deduced from the habits of higher apes that men, too, originally lived in comparatively small groups or hordes within which the jealousy of the oldest, strongest male prevented sexual promiscuity."

From Darwin's theory of the primal horde, Atkinson (1) hypothesized that in such a group the younger men inevitably would band together, revolt, and kill the paternal tyrant. Such a revolt would be followed by rivalry, fighting, and consequent disruption of the organization. To prevent the rivalry that would destroy the organization, it was necessary to erect the incest prohibition.

Freud recognized that it was difficult to explain the persistence of the incest barrier on the basis of this hypothesis. "I do not claim," he said, "that these problems have been sufficiently explained or that *direct communication* and tradition, of which one immediately thinks, are sufficient to the task." As an addendum he chose a phylogenetic answer: "A part of the task seems to be performed by the inheritance of psychic dispositions which, however, need certain incentives in the individual's life to become effective." He clarified this statement to some extent with the following: "We may safely assume that no generation is able to conceal any of its more important mental processes from its successor — everyone possesses in his unconscious mental activity an apparatus which enables him to interpret other people's reactions, that is, to undo the distortions which other people have imposed on the expression of their feelings." Freud does not explicitly state that this is a phylogenetic concept. One could just as well interpret this as unconscious behavior or concept of behavior learned by living together and understanding the unconscious attitudes of the older generation. The child senses the unconscious prohibition and disapproval of the parents whenever it makes sexual advances to either parent.

Freud certainly believed that castration anxiety was phylogenetic. In reviewing these concepts in 1945, Hartmann and Kris (5) disagreed, and wrote that implicit attitudes and anxiety among significant adults were sufficient in themselves to cause an intense fear in the child.

In 1939 Kardiner (7) published an analysis of several different cultural groups on the basis of descriptive data furnished by the anthropologist, Ralph Linton. In this work Kardiner delineated the relationships between personality and culture, elaborating "the common-sense observation that a Hindu is 'different' from an Eskimo." Without the aid of history, no satisfactory psychologic explanations of the origin of primary institutions could be achieved. Primary institutions varied greatly between cultures and included family organization and basic disciplines of feeding, weaning, and sexual taboos, including aim or object, or both. Kardiner demonstrated that the œdipus conflict was far from a basic universal phylogenetic structure, but was the resultant of a definite series of primary institutions. In the various cultures studied there were wide variations of rigidity, scope, and enforcement of the incest barrier. The one universally prohibited aim was found to be mother-son incest.

In 1945 Fenichel (3) wrote, "the œdipus complex signifies the combination of genital love for the parent of the opposite sex and jealous death wishes for the parent of the same sex. . . . In this sense the œdipus complex is undoubtedly a product of family influence. If the institution of the family were to change, the pattern of the œdipus complex would necessarily change also. It has been shown that . . . societies with family configurations different from our own . . . have different œdipus complexes. . . . The problem of the origin of the œdipus complex is thus reduced to the problem of the origin of the family, an interesting and still unsolved chapter." Fenichel appreciated Freud's postulate of the phylogenetic origin of the œdipus complex in the jealousy of the chieftain of the primal horde; however Fenichel concluded, "different environments provoke different reactions."

What are the sources of the child's castration fears in the œdipus situation? As Freud says, the child understands the conscious and unconscious attitudes and operations of its parents. In other words, in the œdipus situation the child appreciates the unconscious jealousy and prohibitive attitude of its elder rival. This is a factor in its guilt and castration anxiety. The child also has its own ambivalence to master. It is jealous and destructive in its motives toward the rival and also toward the frustrating object of its instinctual wishes. It realizes with anger the parents' special passionate love attachment for each other which excludes it. It is simple, then, for the child to project its hostile destructiveness toward the parents which, however, only intensifies its own fears. As Hartmann and Kris (5) put it, "the intensity of fear is not only linked to [the child's] present experience, but also to similar experiences in the past. The dreaded retaliation of the environment revives memories of similar anxieties when desires for other gratifications were predominant and when the supreme fear was not that of being castrated but that of not being loved. In other words, pregenital experience is one of the factors determining the reaction in the phallic phase. This simple formulation refers to a wealth of highly significant experiences which form the nucleus of early childhood; to the total attitude of the environment toward the child's anaclitic desires, when the need for protection is paramount, and toward the child's later erotic demands." These may be the total sources of castration fear in the little girl, and in both sexes the validity of such fear is apparently corroborated by the observation of the genital, anatomical differences between the sexes. We shall, however, consider whether an even deeper source of castration anxiety may not operate in the little boy within all cultures so far studied.

ABROGATION OF THE INCEST BARRIER

We have studied many cases of father-daughter incest, from little girls to young women. Some daughters have displayed little or no anxiety; other have manifested severe neuroses, perversions, promiscuity, and psychoses. We have seen many instances of the same symptoms among boys whose mothers have been highly "seductive." We have encountered no instance of literal mother-son incest. We are grateful to Dr. Irene Josselyn (6) for telling us of a case of mother-son incest in which there was no discernible anxiety. We have a number of cases of mother-daughter incest, and of mother-father-daughter incest, in some of which there were somatic and neurotic symptoms, some in which there was psychotic anxiety, and some in which there was no unusual anxiety. How can we understand the significance of these highly variable reactions?

If, as Fenichel and Kardiner observed, different environments provoke different œdipal reactions, we should find such evidence in our cases. We have had many cases which substantiate such views. The authors present two cases exemplifying father-daughter incest with little visible anxiety, fear, or guilt in the daughter where the mothers were passively collusive. Possibly, from such cases, we may achieve some further understanding of factors inherent in the incest barrier.

Case 1

Ten-year-old Marion was brought for consultation when the mother finally, after three months, became angry and disturbed, declaring that the father's sexual advances to the child must

The Incest Barrier

stop. From the time the child was four until she was ten, the mother had condoned the father's sleeping with Marion, his touching her genitals and placing his penis against her genitals. He had attempted intercourse, but had desisted when the child complained of pain. Marion was encouraged to fondle the father's genitals and the mother knew of this. The father became anxious and depressed when his wife finally prohibited this behavior. As a result, he sought a psychiatrist, who sent him to us. Recently, Marion had been making sexual approaches to boys in school and in the neighborhood.

Both parents were college trained. The frigid wife had always rejected the sexual advances of her handsome husband. Her father died when she was one year old and later, over a period of years, an uncle had been "seductive" with her. This woman preferred mutual masturbation to coitus. She had complained mildly for several years to her husband about his advances to the child, but had acceded limply when he replied that his behavior was the result of his wife's frigidity. The mother expressed no feeling that she was responsible on the basis of her complete vaginal anesthesia. The daughter was frequently allowed to watch the parents indulging in mutual masturbation. The wife suspected that her husband had some homosexual inclinations.

The father, a large, handsome man, was the son of a father who had been harsh to him and unloving to the mother. She had turned to her son for consolation with completely inappropriate expressions of affection. Her son, now the father of the child we were seeing, manifested intense hostility toward his seductive mother. When, as we have said, this man's wife finally interfered between him and Marion, he became depressed as his anger toward his mother and his wife was mobilized.

The child was pretty, neat, mannerly, and completely composed. She tried to please and attract attention from men with seductive mannerisms. She said that her mother and father had told her to tell "everything." She spoke calmly of her interests and friends. She often dreamed of snakes and falling off cliffs, she said. She talked in detail, without any anxiety, about her father's sexual play with her. She said she had not thought it wrong until recently; her father now always put the blame on her, or told her that her mother was the one who caused him to do such things. Lately she had been telling her mother about these episodes because her mother had told Marion to run to her if her father "bothered" her. The child said that she wanted to stay with her parents.

Case 2

A twenty-four-year-old nurse requested psychotherapy because of anxiety concerning her nursing career. Recently, she intensely disliked patients requiring considerable nursing care, especially elderly female patients. The genesis of this dislike stemmed from her hostile relationship with a paternal grandmother who had been rejecting and critical, but also physically seductive. Through the years, she had become aware of this hostility and expressed her anger toward the patients.

Purely as a matter of historical record and without anxiety, she spontaneously commented that she slept with her father until she left home at the age of eighteen to train to become a nurse. She literally took her mother's place in the parental bedroom when the mother deserted the father when the patient was twelve years old. Long before that, the mother had abandoned the child to the care of the father. For six years she had been her father's sexual partner, enjoying intercourse without any sense of guilt. The patient had never been aware that her father thought it was wrong, and the sexual relationship had never been questioned by her father's mother. When the grandmother was ill she would sometimes ask the patient to be her bed partner; when she did, mutual masturbation frequently ensued. In such instances the patient was aware that she and her grandmother were anxious. She became ashamed and then repelled by this, setting her own limits on it at the age of fifteen. She had never felt repelled or in need of abandoning the relationship with her father.

Case 3

In the case reported to us by Dr. Josselyn the patient was twenty-three years old. His father periodically deserted the family and was often in jail. They lived in an isolated Kentucky mountain community. The family physician told the boy that since he was the eldest, he should take his father's place in every way and help his sick mother become well. The young man was not mentally deficient, and recounted the details of his sexual relationship with his mother with no apparent feeling that it was of any particular significance. Dr. Josselyn found no evidence of psychopathology in the young man.

Among the cases presented, in which a sense of guilt was absent or only recently felt, the fact is that both parents condoned the incest. This is true in other similar cases. From our studies of father-daughter incest, collected from all economic classes, it is the rule that the daughter is compliant if the father manifests no sense of guilt and the mother is collusive or indifferent. When the mother is not permissive and the incest is consummated surreptitiously, both partners feel great anxiety and guilt.

We have histories of several ten and twelve-year-old boys from intellectual, "progressive" families who fondled their mothers' breasts in the presence of their fathers and others. At the time some were observed, the boys had no evident guilt or anxiety. The rage in these boys when they are made to understand that such actions must stop is tremendous: some boys with such a history have been apprehended for grabbing at women's breasts.

If mother-son incest occurs as often as father-daughter incest, we certainly do not hear about it; yet in our society there seems to be less prohibition against expression of partially seductive attitudes of mother toward son than against father toward daughter. This strict genital taboo may allow for greater expression of partial (polymorphous) sexual indulgence. The loosening to this extent of the incest barrier nevertheless produces its own pathologic processes in the genesis of sexual perversions (9).

Although we feel that powerful factors in conforming to or transgressing the incest barrier are dependent on conscious and unconscious communication between the parents and the child, we cannot but be impressed with the seeming universality of the mother-son incest barrier. Our investigations and research have failed to discover an account of a culture in which this barrier does not exist in a much more absolute form than the restrictions on father-daughter and brother-sister incest. Is this because there are no indifferent, permissive fathers, or should we look more closely into the whole process of growth for a possible answer? One is forced to consider the early personality developments of both male and female children as their object relations change. In this consideration, it is necessary to begin with the common and shared situation of early biologic infantile dependency. The most basic dependency in any child is on the mother, beginning with intrauterine existence, continuing through suckling, physical care, and the like. In most cultures the mother is at home with the child while the father is away. In general, the maturation process may be described as one in which an infant gradually acquires emotional and physical strength directly proportional to the satisfaction of its dependency needs by the mother and is thereby paradoxically enabled gradually to become free of dependence through a burgeoning self-sufficiency brought about by identification and introjection. The growing identification of the boy with his father is a powerful force in resolving his dependence on the mother. His maturation, however, carries with it the memory of earlier developmental stages, when all passive needs were satisfied simply and quickly and without effort, and when sustenance at the mother's breast was not gained by "the sweat of [his] face."

With growth, the task becomes more complex and difficult for the child. Passive longings tempt him to retreat from disappointments and difficulties to his retrospective memories of infantile omnipotence. Such an ultimate and permanent regression is physically and realistically impossible because the child's need for the mother is founded on dependency and is not reciprocated quantitatively or, in some ways, qualitatively. Even if it were, the protagonist would be faced with the difference in future life expectancy of mother and child, which necessitates a situation in which the offspring comes to assume that there will be many years in his life in which mother is no longer available. This is a *logical* reason for the relinquishment of the mother as an object.[1]

A mature heterosexual love relationship is one in which two adults share a mutual passion and a mutual reliance. The strength of the relationship is directly proportional to the equity and bal-

---

[1] Noting Freud's statement that the suckling experience, in its satiation, is the prototype of later adult orgiastic gratification, Dr. Lewis (8) suggests that the mother-son incest barrier is doubly strong because both have participated in consummated oral incest. In a sense he believes that this is the reason for the barrier which differs from the father-daughter and brother-sister relationships, as these were not influenced by the suckling contact of the former. A double barrier thus exists which must be guarded against not only because of the danger of a return of the repressed fantasy, but against the return of the repressed oral memory.

ance of the reciprocal interrelationship. An incestuous relationship is essentially one that has mutually exclusive aims.

Anthropologic studies reveal that Navajo Indian mothers frequently masturbate their male sucklings and kiss them passionately on the mouth while feeding them (8). Weaning is the relinquishment of sensuous satisfaction and pleasurable gratification for both mother and son. In this frustration there is a mutually transient vacillation between regression and development.

Regardless of the possible genital significances of this relationship at the oral level, its perpetuation into the genital phase is doomed to failure because of either unfulfilled infantile needs in the parent, or the perpetuation in the child of a dependency which would eventually leave him helpless and alone. In either eventuality, the fixation at an incestuous level carries with it the danger of an inherent degree of frustration and consequent hostility which is incompatible with the relative freedom from ambivalence that characterizes mature love. It is our feeling that an important source of castration anxiety, in the broadest sense, stems from the dependency-rooted urge toward incestuous fulfilment. In this situation, "castration" stands not merely for loss of the phallus, but for the loss of all the things for which the phallus is the symbol: independence, maturity, object relationships, potency in the broadest sense, and, most important, the ability to withstand separation and aloneness because of the recognition of one's potentialty for loving and being loved. Therese Benedek (2) has emphasized that growth means an oscillation between gratification and frustration and cannot be explained only as a repetition of the past. These factors constitute personal identity, and their acquisition comes about through the healthy resolution of the infantile state of helplessness. In other words, we cannot conceive of an incestuous relationship compatible with evolution from infantility for either child or mother.

TRANSFERENCE IMPLICATIONS

Let us examine the complications arising from the analysis of a male patient by a woman in the resolution of the œdipus conflict. Castration anxiety and guilt about the hostile components associated with frustration were analyzed. In the transference the rage at the frustrating analyst was recognized and resolved. As Benedek says, in such cases the analysis moves from the final œdipus to the late adolescent level where the patient is prepared to accept and to be accepted by an adult love object. If the patient is analyzable to the point of readiness for a genital object relationship, what then occurs in the transference and countertransference is not a simple repetition of the past relation to the mother. Toward the mother the multiple factors in the incestuous relationship are unconscious.

In our patient, at this level of analysis, powerful components of the incestuous striving and the taboo against it were made conscious. He was no longer an angry, frustrated, frightened little boy but felt himself to be a confident, lovable man. The ultimate resolution of this process was achieved with adult objects outside of the analysis.

When a male patient has achieved this stage of synthesis of tenderness and genitality, with minimal ambivalence, the analyst's feelings cannot be without content. It certainly was true during the analysis of the ambivalent œdipus in our patient, and there was no doubt as to why the analyst was frustrating to him. This is necessary while the patient is reliving his œdipal cravings; however, with a patient who has moved to the level of postœdipal maturity there is no reason for an analyst to continue to remain in the role of the frustrating parent. At this point the patient is aware that he is ready to abandon his œdipal fantasy and will sense this without its being stated. To the woman analyst the awareness of her reaction would be another item in the continuous analysis of her countertransference — positive and negative — throughout the therapy. This is not a black or white repetition of the unanalyzed mother-and-son relationship. If such intuitively empathic communications occur, is there no incest barrier operating? It appears that there is.

The patient has evolved beyond the stage in which the therapist was the omnipotent mother. The analysis of the transference does not, however, erase the positive transference memories. No relationship to another love object can ever be the same as the relationship to the mother for whom the analyst is a surrogate. To the patient it now seems, in part, a "normal" relationship being experienced with a mature woman not associated with his mother. But analysis cannot blot out forever the unconscious traces in the memory of such an important experience in his life. This can be a subtle and emotional experience for the patient who may be realizing for the first time a tenderness associated with sexual passion undistorted by hostility and at this time the patient, himself, recognizes the necessity for growth and control.

If at this point in an analysis there is such a qualitative empathic communication, the question of a seductive attitude on the part of the analyst arises. For example, a specific question or rumination was verbalized by our patient: "If time and circumstance were different, and I were as capable of loving and being loved as I now am, I am sure you could have fallen in love with me," or "I feel quite strongly at this stage that you find me an appealing adult man." Some analysts might say that if the œdipus were thoroughly analyzed such rumination would not arise. This may indicate that these analysts regard themselves first and last only as transference objects to their patients. This is to a varying degree undoubtedly true. As stated above, any sexual relationship that has incestuous implications is incompatible with maturity. Inherent in transference is the substitution of the analyst for various important relationships in the analysand's past. Whenever this transference is resolved by analysis, the analyst's task is completed, and the patient is ready to form attachments suitable to his needs. If his development had been relatively uncomplicated he would presumably have achieved this goal without analytic therapy.

We feel that these ruminations of the patient, although historically based on the transference, are directed more to the person of the analyst as a coequal human being. This is a transitional object relationship for the patient, and we must consider both its scope and its necessary limitations to avoid a seductive binding of the patient in this transitional phase. In our opinion, this transitional phase is the first step toward the recognition of the separate individualities of the analyst and the patient. At this stage an interpretation directing the patient back toward œdipal material in the transference may only bind and perpetuate the analyst as a transference figure, even if one's words says, "You must now go your own way."

We consider maturation as more than a simple repetition of the past. At this stage of the analysis, in addition, there should be extra-analytic maturation going on all the time with a mature heterosexual object such as the wife, or some other really loved and loving woman.

In the foregoing transitional phase the patient is really voicing the belief that he is ready for a more mature extra-analytic fulfilment and is commenting that he believes the analyst concurs in this belief on the basis of what he senses the analyst experiences in her own countertransference. The analyst knows that perpetuation of the relationship with the patient on a genital level would bring no real happiness or fulfilment to the patient or to the analyst. This is because of the historical roots of the relationship in the dependency and the temptation to a regression to this state. This could lead neither to growth for the patient nor to satisfaction for the analyst. By this time the well-analyzed patient should recognize this as clearly as does the analyst. At this stage the analyst *can* state that for the sake of the patient's own growth the patient must go his way. However, is this not redundant and would it not be stated in order to preserve the analyst's own feelings of superior maturation? If seductiveness on the part of the analyst means tying the patient to her by ambivalence, it seems to us that recognizing the patient's maturity to such degree as to allow the separation to be *mutually* agreed on is the best way to give the patient a real freedom, achieved partially on his own, rather than a spurious freedom which has within it the ambivalent results of being gratuitously rejected. If we are not trying to preserve the image of ourselves as a superior authority, we will recognize that the patient is not asking for a gratification that requires such rejection at this point.

The final stage of renunciation is coincident with a somber mood that is a state of mourning. The patient now poignantly experiences the sadness of separation from his childhood gratifications that he had not before — more diffusely — been capable of relinquishing bit by bit during his life. Analysis of a patient of the opposite sex may perhaps place a greater responsibility on the therapist. His or her countertransference in every instance requires careful scrutiny. Unless the therapist is quite secure, he or she may be threatened in final phases of the therapy by the patient's avowal of mature genital fantasies to the detriment of the patient's striving toward genitality. In the ultimate phase of analysis of a woman by a man, the patient's temptation toward regression to a dependence should not be so great; however, many women analysands under treatment by a subtle male analyst may necessarily have been carried through as profound a dependent mothering as any man treated by a woman analyst. As a matter of fact, if a woman has a deep-seated problem with her mother, the male analyst might be better equipped to resolve her mother-daughter dependence. When such a woman patient has resolved her ambivalent œdipus, the result will be equally successful if she is not discouraged from feeling that she has succeeded.

SUMMARY

To explore the origins of incest and the taboo against it, Freud was influenced by the Darwin-Atkinson hypothesis of the primal horde. Reexamination of incest from recent anthropologic data confirms that the taboo has its origin in the jealousy of the father. Such data indicate, however, that different ethnic groups have different œdipal conflicts according to variations in family habits and customs. Clinical instances of father-daughter incest demonstrate that such relationships have been fostered by both parents. This fact indicates that an important factor in the incest barrier rests on conscious and unconscious communication between the parents and the child.

A theoretical résumé of the terminal phase of analysis of a man by a woman analyst is presented. Thorough analysis of the castration complex, in the classic sense, may not be a deterrent to incestuous genital strivings toward the analyst. Examination of the last barrier in analysis indicates that in some instances it may be a mutual fantasy. In such instances it is believed that the analyst's countertransference can be a threat to her which she parries by attributing her patient's recently acquired genital attitude toward her as an infantile striving to his detriment.

REFERENCES

1. Atkinson, J. J. As quoted by Freud in *Totem and taboo*. In *The basic writings of Sigmund Freud*. New York: The Modern Library, 1938.
2. Benedek, Therese. Unpublished data.
3. Fenichel, Otto. *The psychoanalytic theory of neurosis*, pp. 97–98. New York: W. W. Norton & Co., Inc., 1945.
4. Freud, Sigmund. *Totem and Taboo*.
5. Hartmann, Heinz, and Kris, Ernst. The genetic approach in psychoanalysis. In *The psychoanalytic study of the child*, 1:21–23. New York: International Universities Press, Inc., 1945.
6. Josselyn, Irene. Personal communication to the authors.
7. Kardiner, Abram. *The individual and his society. The psychodynamics of primitive social organization*. New York: Columbia University Press, 1939.
8. Lewis, Harvey. Personal communication to the authors.
9. Litin, E. M.; Giffin, Mary E.; and Johnson, Adelaide M. Parental influence in unusual sexual behavior in children. *Psychoanalytic Quarterly* 25 (1956): 37–55.

SECTION

VII

Child Psychiatry

CHILD PSYCHIATRY

Probably one-third to one-half of Dr. Johnson's writing derived from her work with children and parent-child problems. Several of these papers have already been presented that might well have been included under the heading of this section. I have chosen three additional papers as representative of her general thinking in this field. They also serve as summary articles rather than as directed to specific or limited problems in the field. All three were written late in her career and reflect the distillation of her years of experience and thought.

25

SOME APPLICATIONS OF PSYCHOANALYTIC INSIGHTS TO THE SOCIALIZATION OF CHILDREN

With Mary E. Giffin, M.D.

THE socialization of a child is dependent upon the dynamic emotional interchanges occurring both consciously and unconsciously between the child and all other significant individuals. The personality attitudes and behavior of a child vary in intensity and expression dependent upon the interchange between intrapsychic, instinctual forces and familiocultural pressures. Insofar as psychoanalytic insights permit more accurate understanding of unconscious forces it behooves us to attempt to apply them to group interaction and socialization of the child. Typical is the following episode recently observed in a nursery school.

Teddy takes Jenny's hand and leads her into the doll corner room. After much giggling and many secretive glances, he announces to Jenny: "We're getting married, only the little kids don't know it."

Jenny stands in the center of the room looking very pleased,

Adelaide M. Johnson, M.D., and Mary E. Giffin, M.D., Some applications of psychoanalytic insights to the socialization of children. *American Journal of Orthopsychiatry* 27 (1957): 462–74. © American Orthopsychiatric Association, Inc. Reproduced by permission.

but makes no comment. Teddy crouches in front of Jenny and says in a pious and serious voice: "And before people get married they pray to God." He leaves her side, kneels in the cradle, shuts his eyes, and mumbles some unintelligible words. From there he goes to the closet of dress-up clothes, selects a man's vest, dons it, and announces to his bride reassuringly: "Daddies wear vests." He smooths his new costume, smiles and grabs Jenny around the waist, "And know what? For our honeymoon we'll have two babies — one for mommy and one for me."

She keeps smiling but pulls away — the tussle ends in their falling down, daddy on top of mommy. They get to their feet and Teddy says, "The mommy is loving the daddy so hard that sometimes they fall down." They both giggle — Teddy grabs her again and they fall once more. This time Jenny is more responsive. They roll and kick their feet in the air — much silliness and laughter. Teddy pauses to say, "We're having such fun on our wedding. Now let's dance." In a loud whisper — "They don't really let me go to dances, but I know how."

At no time did Jenny make one verbal comment but she certainly made no protest. The day following this episode, Teddy waited at the door for Jenny, took her hand, walked down the hall saying, "We're married." They have played together since but the wedding has not been repeated.

For years psychoanalysts were psychic archaeologists, uncovering memories and experiences of the distant past. Later, with the development of child analysis, therapists became as it were "war correspondents," immediate observers and participants in the living and in the recall of the unfolding instinctual life. Today, of course, all psychoanalysts are vitally concerned with the problems of immediate living, probing into the past only to detect and evaluate emotional and interpersonal distortions. With the refinement of collaborative therapy, a highly specific form of psychotherapy of the family unit, came the possibility of observing and influencing the intrapsychic and intrafamilial forces affecting each and all members of the primary group.

Review of psychoanalytic concepts. The focus of psychoanalysis has been that of studying human behavior, with particular emphasis on the less immediately observable phenomena, that is, on the unconscious roots from which man grows. Psychoanalysis emphasizes the developmental basis of object relationships and the impelling force of the sexual, aggressive, and acquisitive drives. Equally it emphasizes the potential for transition from narcissistic to mature love, and from deep dependency to pliable ego strength. Its therapy focuses on the analysis of defenses and conflicts, the resolution of which permits constructive direct or sublimated expression of the instinctual life. As conflicts are resolved in the transference the patient learns to love ever less ambivalently. As unconscious conflict material is faced on a conscious level, energy for constructive living is released from its bond with the no longer necessary defenses, resulting in the ability to make mature conscious choices of behavior. The goal of all psychoanalytic therapy is the resolution of unconscious conflicts, thus permitting freedom to love. In this respect psychoanalytic therapists and religious leaders share mutual goals — the technique of the former being that of analysis of unconscious conflicts, while the message of the latter is more conscious encouragement and embodiment of man's essential integrity.

Orthodox psychoanalysis has consistently protested against standardizing value judgments. Increasingly, however, psychoanalysts are dropping the more conventional role and setting firm limits on conduct which is unacceptable in our culture, that is, antisocial or delinquent behavior. Therapists have learned that happiness in our culture can only be attained by firm limitation on delinquent behavior, and that in dealing with delinquency problems the therapist must directly support and insist upon limits to antisocial behavior. Insofar as we have assumed such responsibility for the individual we must also extend our judgments to group activities.

There are many pitfalls inherent in an attempt to apply insights gained in one field to the practice of another. An awareness of such dangers must balance our attempts to serve social mental health. However, efforts to apply psychoanalytic insights may be important not alone for society's sake. They may be equally important as a means of validating our theoretical clinical insights. For instance, anthropologic observations have disproved the theory of the universality of the oedipal conflict. As Fenichel wrote in 1945, "The oedipal complex signifies the combination of genital love of the parent of the opposite sex with jealous death wishes for the parent of the same sex." He went on, "In this sense the oedipal complex is undoubtedly a product of family influence. If the institution of the family were to change, the pattern of the oedipal complex would necessarily change also. The problem of the origin of the oedipal complex is thus reduced to the problem of the origin of the family, an interesting and still unsolved chapter." (1)

Similarly, the multidisciplinary observations of collaborative therapists support the fact that not all behavior is in response to libidinal drives. Using the collaborative therapy approach investigators have clearly demonstrated that much in the behavior of a child is adaptive to external pressures compounded with the unfolding, ongoing libidinal life. Behavior is not an either-or proposition: it is the resultant of the libido operating mutually and interchangeably with the environmental forces, as Fromm-Reichman has emphasized.

Some Applications of Psychoanalytic Insights

The discoveries of psychoanalysis have clearly shown the enormous complexities of the child's mind. The discoveries of therapists working with patients are appropriate for practical application within the school, the home and all social institutions, that is, throughout the areas of influence in the socialization of children.

Psychoanalysis and education. Pertinent to the consideration of psychoanalysis and education, Freud wrote: (2)

> There is one subject, however, that I cannot pass by so easily, though this is not because I have any special understanding of it or have done much work on it myself. On the contrary, I have hardly ever occupied myself with it. But it is of immense importance, and rich in hopes for the future; perhaps, indeed, it is the most important of all the activities of analysis. I refer to the application of psychoanalysis to education, to the upbringing of the next generation. I am at least glad to be able to say that my daughter, Anna Freud, has made this her life-work, and is in this way making good my own neglect of the subject. One can easily see the path that has led to this application of analysis.

Concerning adult analysis Freud stated, "We were forced to acquaint ourselves with the psychological peculiarities of the years of infancy; and we learned a great many things which could not have been discovered except through analysis, and were in a position to set right a number of generally accepted beliefs about childhood." He emphasized the vital psychological significance of the first five years and specifically emphasized the importance of the first "expansion of sexuality" in the later adult sexual adjustment. Moreover, in this early paper he emphasized the struggle of the child to attain social adaptation and instinctual control. He conceived of education as an all-encompassing learning process and appealed specifically:

> *Let us get a clear idea of what the primary business of education is. The child has to learn to control its instincts.* To grant it com-

plete freedom, so that it obeys all its impulses without any restriction, is impossible. It would be a very instructive experiment for child-psychologists, but it would make life impossible for the parents and would do serious damage to the children themselves, as would be seen partly at the time, and partly during subsequent years.

For those neophytes who may have misunderstood Freud's concern for value judgments we would reemphasize that he specifically stated that complete freedom of impulsive actions would be harmful to the child as well as producing pandemonium for the parents. Today child psychiatrists emphasize even more firmly that for any specific culture certain impulsive acts must be *absolutely* forbidden. In our culture these include, among others, stealing, fire-setting, truancy, vandalism, incest and murder. Education in its broader sense must include the enforcement of necessary behavioral limits.

Freud's theoretical awareness of the need for proper limit-setting was tempered by his conviction that the suppression of instincts leads to neurosis. He was concerned about quantitating the forbidding, and tempering it to fit the constitutional susceptibility and disposition of the individual child. He did not clarify the fact that limits on certain behavior must be absolute and that it is the distorted, repressed, or dissociated anger over the frustration which leads to neurosis. Confusion about limit setting has befogged treatment to the present time. Recent experience of therapists specifically concerned with the treatment of delinquents has clearly shown that a little child can accept any necessary, culturally accepted limit on behavior *provided* that the limiting adult permits a healthy verbal channel for the expression of anger. Neurosis develops in relationship to parental attitudes about the expression of anger; the equivocal tempering of necessary limits merely confuses the child and enhances his anger.

Because of his position in the forefront of a beginning science Freud found it necessary to fall back on a "refractory instinctual constitution" to explain faulty educational results; he bemoaned the struggle of the educator in measuring for each child the proper amount of love and authority. Today we are in a vastly more fortunate position, for we know that limits on certain behavior must be absolute, that love to a child need never be titrated and that our major task lies in teaching the child properly and constructively to express his angry feelings verbally.

In the midst of his dilemma about education Freud beseeched educators to seek personal analyses. As he wisely pointed out, *"The analysis of teachers and educators seems to be a more practicable prophylactic* measure than the analysis of children themselves; and there are not such great obstacles against putting it into practice." He also noted the advantage attained by parents who had undergone analyses. He observed the benefit which could accrue to the child through such analyses and he saw this as a prophylactic educational measure. It was his hope that analyzed adults could treat children with better understanding, thus sparing the child unnecessary travail and trauma. Certainly subsequent observations have corroborated his belief and have offered a validation of his concepts. Collaborative therapy offers a type of secondary benefit similar to that Freud mentioned in that as parents and one child are treated all other children may also benefit.

Psychoanalytic insights into defenses. Freud's vision concerning *education* was carried into practical masterful expression by his daughter Anna. Her understanding ushered in a constructive elaboration of the whole psychoanalytic technique. The emphasis shifted from id analysis to the scrutiny of the defenses, with as we know it today the development of ego analysis. Anna Freud's classic text *The Ego and Its Defenses* (3) spread psychoanalytic insight into the classroom; this milestone became the educator's bible. Here was a systematic study of the ego's defensive measures for controlling threats from within as well as danger from the environment.

Out of this classic work came understanding and inspiration to all leaders working with children. Nursery school teachers, educators, social workers, psychologists, camp directors and recreational supervisors read and absorbed Anna Freud's lucid account of the integrative mechanisms of the ego. Insights thus gained permitted recognition of inhibition, altruistic surrender, denial or identification with the hostile aggressor, as they appeared in the classroom, the office or the sports field. No longer confused or discouraged by unexplained hostility or apparent deceit, children and parents could be more directly reached and helped.

Psychoanalysis in nursery school. Historically it was the nursery school teachers who first applied the insights of depth psychology to the socialization and education of the child. Susan Isaacs, among others, wrote graphically and lectured enthusiastically, appealing for a considered understanding of the "wider educational work of the nursery school." In 1937 she stated (4): "We can therefore look upon it as settled that the nursery school is a great help to the young child in his personal feelings and his intellectual life — it increases his happiness and helps him over the normal trials of early childhood." She and her sensitive colleagues put into practice the insights gained from psychoanalysis. They were themselves spontaneous enough emotionally to permit free play among their nursery school children. They recognized the constructive, integrating force and meaning of children's play activities. From their observations they gleaned the nonverbal, symbolic, emotional meaning of what had previously been accepted as emotional waste motion. These

Some Applications of Psychoanalytic Insights 417

teachers recognized the role of play in the expression of the child's libidinal fantasies, and its importance in the expression of aggressive feelings followed by restitutive processes. To them the play of children offered an insight to the conflicts of the child and incidentally also offered a concrete, workable proving ground for the validation of psychoanalytic theories and concepts. Sibling rivalry, regressive nursing, bisexuality, anal play and talk, oedipal drives, testing of limits all appeared on the scene with no prompting from any adult.

Freud encouraged personal analyses for parents and teachers: the early nursery school teachers verified the wisdom of such advice. In part at least because of their own greater knowledge gained through personal analyses, these pioneer nursery school leaders patiently but expectantly awaited the child's freedom to grow and by their observations permitted the weaving of present-day nursery school practices, a cloth formed by the interwoven threads of analytic insight and kindly undistorted observation.

We now take for granted many of the observations and formulations made by these educators twenty years ago, when their definition of a child's needs was startling, even dramatic. Until they put their formulations into practical application the details of the impact of the first five years were lacking to general knowledge. Their application of psychoanalytic formulations carried Freud's concepts into active life. It was these early nursery school teachers who first emphasized the fact that one cannot help a child with his major difficulties unless one is aware how real his feelings are — how to him his feelings are precious and intensely meaningful, just as are an adult's feelings to him. Theirs was a considered respect for the child.

Next they emphasized the need for active independent experience. They knew full well that it was the child's play, *his* experiences, *his* questions which increased his knowledge. Moreover, they recognized that only a generous environment could supply time and the tools for such learning.

These early, psychoanalytically experienced nursery school teachers never underestimated the importance of peer-play; they knew that parental security was necessary for basic orientation and that spontaneous togetherness of children of the same age enhanced the integration of the basic experiences.

Finally, these teachers clearly defined the parental responsibility of offering security of habit, activity and emotional expression upon which the child could pattern his own thoughts and behavior. Not only did they charge parents with the responsibility of offering proper identifications; they also emphasized the need at times for the child to regress from stress, thus restoring dependency resources. To the individual only recently indoctrinated in psychoanalysis these truths seem anything but startling; at the time of their initial description they represented an important concrete application of psychoanalytic insights. These teachers, psychoanalytically sensitized to neurotic conflicts, were, however, often unclear as to the sources of the behavior which they observed. They recognized many of the basic needs of the child but they did not prove whether child behavior was libidinal in origin, or patterned after and learned from the parents or both. Nursery school observations validated information from psychoanalytic patients about their own personality development. These observations, however, did not give the final clue as to the deepest sources of the behavior. These teachers did not presume to expand on the genesis of conflicts; they merely described what they saw. It was left to the analysts to probe further into the genetic sources of conflicts.

For instance, three-year-old Anne was constantly beaten down by her four-year-old sister, Marion. Marion had been in nursery school one year. The mother believed Anne should go to the same school to acquire her own friends. For three weeks little Anne would go only to Marion's room, calling it Marion's school. She pretended to the teachers and to her mother that she was four-year-old Christine. Quite correctly the adults recognized that Anne thought she would be more loved if she were the age of four-year-old sister Marion. Unknown to the teachers was the fact that the mother did love Marion more since she was more independent and spirited than Anne. Finally Marion was ill and out of school one week. Anne continued on her own, mastered the adjustment, won her mother's esteem and then left Marion's class at school to play happily with her own age group. During this week of mastery the teachers knowingly gave a great deal of support to Anne, who made the goal.

With nursery school corroboration there came renewed interest in determining the impact of environmental family forces on the phylogenetic biologic unfolding libidinal life. Today nursery school teachers are very aware of family attitudes that distort the developing personality.

Psychoanalysis and social work. Not only was Freud concerned with the application of psychoanalysis to education; he was deeply concerned about the effects of it on society. He was keenly aware of the possibility that his insights might be bent to destructive uses and he clearly warned analysts to avoid social partisanship in their treatment of patients.

Historically in America, along with the analysts it was the social workers, countless in numbers, who met his scientific challenge. Visionary leaders, such as Gordon Hamilton, Annette Garrett and Charlotte Towle, early taught and applied Freud's principles. In their supervision and in their handling of clients, children and adults, they antedated by decades the wider application of psychoanalytic concepts by general medical men.

Psychiatric social work in the United States has long been dynamic in understanding children's and adults' behavior. Schools and agencies have welcomed and sought the teaching and supervision of analysts. Their application of insights led directly to the home and its distortions of instinctual development.

Psychoanalysis and the home. As Erickson (5) has said, "Whatever reaction patterns are given biologically and whatever schedule is predetermined developmentally must be considered to be a series of potentialities for changing patterns of mutual regulation."

The application of psychoanalytic insights to the family milieu permits the parents to grow with the child. As Erickson again points out:

> We distort the situation if we abstract it in such a way that we consider the parent as "having" such and such a personality when the child is born and then, remaining static, impinging upon a poor little thing. For this weak and changing little being moves the whole family along. Babies control and bring up their families as much as they are controlled by them; in fact, we may say that the family brings up a baby by being brought up by him.

Once given knowledge of the oedipal conflict and the security of its normalcy a father may take some satisfaction in his daughter's verbal wish to marry him, but recognize the intensity and form of her feelings as a reflection of her developmental needs and wishes. Once aware of the normal jealousy feelings of this period a stable mother can accept her daughter's outburst, "I could kill you," without guilt or fear. Insight into child development and defenses gains constructive application within the home, and serves to the healthier living of all family members.

> One father said, "My daughter was an angel until three and a half years. Suddenly she had tantrums at bedtime, kept running into our bedroom for a drink or some triviality all night, acts so cross with her mother and me as soon as I come home at night. What is the meaning of this little tigress we now have at home?" When we explained the oedipal complex to this kindly intelligent father, he said, "I told my wife that I knew Freud would have an answer for this one."

Educating parents in understanding and anticipating the characteristic challenge and conflicts of each developmental period represents a culturally expansive application of psychoanalytic insights. As Susan Isaacs wrote 21 years ago, "It is thus of the greatest value to parents to gain a comparative knowledge of the record of achievement in all the ordinary personal skills and language, since this alone will bring a just perspective of the behavior of their own children." (6, p. 216) In her "Nursery as a Community" she emphasized the importance of a family-centered, not a child-centered nursery, a graphic reflection of her awareness that healthy self-sacrifice should include all family members. As she said, "It is in those families where the parents are able to respect and serve both their own personalities and those of the children that we find a happy and ordered community life, one which increasingly equips the child for the varied functions of his life in the larger community outside the nursery and outside the home itself." (6, p. 229)

It would seem almost unnecessary here to spell out the fact that the greatest factor in socialization of a child is his identification with the parent. His loving, his sharing, his growing independence, his conscience, his adaptation to hard rocks, his manners are largely dependent on the complexities of identification with parents.

We must be aware of the pitfalls of parental application of analytic insights. Parents, like ourselves, may be emotionally unable properly to apply the knowledge of psychoanalysis. True insight is built only upon the integration of psychodynamic understanding with emotional awareness of its meaning. Intellectual understanding alone may be grossly distorted in its application by the deep emotional problems and needs of the parent as well as the professional worker. To an unconsciously rejecting mother the injunction to be less insistent may lead to total rejection of the child.

Exemplary of this is the behavior of an emotionally cold, nonmotherly woman whose son was hospitalized for obstinate constipation. When her son was 2½ years of age she had been counseled to relax her habit training efforts; the result was that for an entire year she had completely ignored his toileting needs. Even when her child himself sought the stool and strained to the point of vomiting and fainting this mother showed not a glimmer of support. For this deeply rejecting mother a suggestion based on psychoanalytic insight boomeranged to the serious deprivation of her son.

Proper suggestions must be made only with an awareness of parental ability to discharge the understanding through constructive behavior.

Application of psychoanalytic insights to the socialization within the home must also include resolution of the parental need to be omnipotent or psychiatrically learned. Parents like therapists, to quote Frederick Allen, (7) must "not use the setting of a limit for the exercise of personal power." As he emphasizes, "To do that would be to destroy the meaning of the whole experience and make it the battle of wills the child may want." Parents must be encouraged to assume the role of benevolent protective authority, not that of the child's equal home companion. Some parents wear equality with the child as a badge of virtue; instead it is a reflection of the family's feet of clay.

Parents must also be protected against the misunderstanding that by applying psychoanalytic insights all anxieties and developmental conflicts will be eliminated. For example, a mother may quite correctly encourage in her elder child verbalization of jealous anger about a baby sibling, only to become angry herself when occasional sputtering by the child does not suffice. Parents must be educated not only in the knoweldge of psychoanalytic insights, but also in the assurance that successful resolution of conflicts, not the elimination of conflicts, provides the basis for the creative adult. Finally, parents as well as analysts and educators must strive for the combination of insight and discretion, an attitude exemplified admirably by Freud.

What then accrues to the parent and educator through knowing the developmental stages? Erikson wrote beautifully of the need of a wide understanding of the psychobiologic unfolding. He maintained that "we must try to chart the approximate sequence of stages when the nervous excitability as well as the coordination of the organs in question and the selective reactivity of significant people in the environment are apt to produce decisive encounters." He emphasized:

> We merely wish to gain an initial understanding of the timetable and the systematic relationship of the organ modes of pregenitality which establish the basic orientation that an organism or its parts can have to another organism and its parts and to the world of things. A being with organs can take things or another being into itself; it can retain them or let them out; or it can enter them. Beings with organs can also perform such modal acts with another being's parts. The human child during its long childhood learns these modes of physical approach and with them the modalities of social life. He learns to exist in space and time as he learns to be an organism in the space-time of his culture. Every part function thus learned is based on some integration of all the organ modes with one another and with the world image of their culture.

It is of interest that emphasis on the primary family unit followed Erikson's and others' emphasis on cultural forces. Actually adaptation to cultural forces is uniquely successful or unsuccessful depending upon the family adaptation; it is the parent-child symbiosis which largely determines personality variability and adjustment. The most significant applications of psychoanalytic insights, therefore, occur within the home. For purposes of further clarification let us consider a few examples of practical psychoanalytic applications within the family. We wish there were time to discuss many facets of the health and psychopathology of the dinner table. Here we see graphically portrayed the deepest analytic mechanisms operating comfortably or pathologically between parents and children. The dinner table is one of the dynamic centers for socialization of children and adults. We had in analysis the father of a four-year-old boy who swallowed his food infrequently and soon had an overflowing mouthful of food. In time it became clear that the father feared the child would choke to death, and constantly exhorted the boy to chew well before swallowing. If anyone consciously continuously concentrates on chewing and swallowing, one soon loses automatic smooth control. This father finally realized how his anxiety was disturbing the child, and when he analyzed the sources of his anxiety, the boy ate very well.

In the area of infant feeding, psychoanalytic insights support the belief that demand feeding based on the individual infant's desires can best serve the baby's needs. Breast feeding heightens the inclination for maternal body closeness, thus enhancing physical and emotional warmth. In general then, breast feeding is the method of choice. However, with a psychologically unmotherly woman as in the instance of a perfectionistic, highly scheduled mother, breast feeding or demand feeding would obviously only increase the anxiety of the mother and possibly create more problems than it solved. Corroboratively we find that, clinically, demand feeding is not the curative panacea for neurosis; its effectiveness varies directly with the relaxed maternal attitudes of the mother.

Similarly, insight concerning the natural history of the oedipal period can be of great assistance to parents. Parents grasp relatively easily the emotional attraction and jealousy typical of this period. If their own oedipal periods have been satisfactorily resolved they can gain a great deal from simple education and can successfully apply these insights to allay their own anxiety over the seemingly irrational outbursts of this period. However, if a mother has been ambivalently tied to her own mother and fixated on her father, she may be unable to accept her daughter's angry outbursts in spite of intellectual education.

Such a mother may well have slept with her own mother or in other ways may have been infantilized by her. Out of such knowledge has come the conviction that children should have their own rooms and be given the courtesy of modesty and respect. It is clear through insight into the unconscious that the oedipal conflict and its latency and adolescent exacerbations should not be augmented by excessive closeness to the primal scene. The quantity of anger over acceptance of oedipal frustrations is enough to resolve without adding extrapsychic stimuli. It is also clear that sleeping and bathroom privacy nurtures the independent strivings, quickening the growth away from dependency.

In contrast to the potential confusions which lie in the application of such knowledge is the relative clarity which can be conceived by parents in their understanding of regression and ambivalence. The concept of regression warrants universal understanding. Awareness of this response to stress allays much parental anxiety, as for instance in the regressive demand for a bottle by an older child in the face of the arrival of a new sibling. Parental understanding of the regressive need and value permits acceptance of the process and proper indulgence of the child, thus permitting quick recovery from the childish behavior. Conversely, parents can accept the fact that through misunderstanding parental rejection merely deepens and prolongs the regression. The child supported in his babyish behavior recovers quickly with parental acceptance. The regressed child chided for being a baby becomes increasingly anxious and demanding, adding temper outbursts, head banging or other destructive behavior to the original regression. Many parents with proper indoctrination gather the meaning of regression.

Somewhat more difficult for parents to grasp constructively is the fact of ambivalence. Parents enormously need the assurance from us that all individuals are born with the potential for both love and hate: their potentiation and object relations depend upon psychologic development. Psychologically illiterate parents may feel rejected or highly irritated by a child's angry outburst, moments after an obvious gesture of love. Knowledge that love and hate can be felt concomitantly toward the same individual permits healthier acceptance of both children and marital partners.

Thus could one continue with discussion of habit training, conscience development, bisexuality, curiosity, sibling rivalry and all the rest. Greater integrated knowledge leads to more secure application and integration by the child.

Validation of theoretical insight. Psychoanalysts must accept the responsibility for applying useful and validated insights. "Clinical knowledge, like any knowledge, is" as Erikson says, "but a tool in the hands of a faith or a weapon in the service of a superstition." (5) Properly to apply our insights to children we must interpret the word *faith* accurately. Scientific faith must be based on validation. Validation of psychoanalytic concepts by laboratory and clinical research is necessary but frequently misleading. For instance, David Levy's feeding experiments with puppies (8) are well known and interesting: this had the added advantage of confirming his earlier observation on human infants. As Hilgard points out, however, (9) "the final generalization need not be the original psychoanalytic one in order for psychoanalysis to have been of service. It is useful if it provides a first approximation to the generalization, and thus defines the field of inquiry."

Similarly, experiments on rats to test hoarding trends strongly suggest that early frustration about food may be of importance in later hoarding performances. Hilgard observed, "In the end, however, it will always be necessary to validate the principles through observations of man himself." We must also remember that just as animal experiments and the influences of frustration may not be analogous to their meaning in humans, so may they not be translatable from one individual to another. Poorly understood as yet is the entire subject of the good adaptation some people make in the face of what seems to be overwhelmingly frustrating.

Validation by means of anthropologic data has been suggestive, but again as Hilgard states, "Interesting as such parallel histories of development are, two important precautions need to be stated. First, there are many cultures in which the relationship between infant handling and adult behavior does not conform at all neatly to the hypothesis. (29) Second, children are influenced throughout life by the adults with whom they live, so that adult behavior cannot be attributed solely to training in infancy. Children who grow up in a friendly culture (or in a quarrelsome one) continue to learn what is expected of them as they grow up." Experiments testing the influences of the later years have not been carried out but certainly the stability and import of the early years could better be evaluated by subjection to stresses of an opposite culture in later childhood life.

Similarly analysts have maintained that early toilet training robbed the child of necessary erotic soiling gratifications. We have plenty of evidence that early training by some mothers is correlated with serious conflict and problems. No one, however, has done a study to see how early a very loving relaxed mother could train a child. It is possible that no evidence of conflict or deprivation would appear provided that such training was consistent with neurophysiologic readiness. In other words we have much information about the traumatic effect of neurotic maternal behavior and apparent developmental deviations but essentially none on the latitude of training practices available to the relaxed, comfortable mother.

From a practical clinical point of view a type of validation is possible in the predicting of conflicts expected but as yet not analyzed and in the clinical expectation of material which will be present in the background of parents, as judged by clinical symptoms and behavior in a child. For instance, if a child is sexually promiscuous it is predictable that one or both parents have also acted out sexually. Similarly, if a young girl chooses to marry a man 20 years older than herself it is predictable that her own father was too close to her. Validation of such predictions is possible through the gathering of further clinical data, and continued corroboration permits more active directed inquiry in subsequent cases.

Cultural validation has even greater potentialities. Observations must be made on the effects of widespread application of psychoanalytic insights. The change from rigid feeding to demand feeding offered an experimental protocol not statistically studied. Theoretically, of course, such a change was brought about by the philosophy that "infants are human beings" and that they could be expected to respond better if treated according to their status. In many instances children benefited; some did not. The specificities of success and failure warrant careful scrutiny with a view toward measurement of intrafamilial problems as they individually affect application of insight.

SUMMARY

We have reviewed some basic psychoanalytic insights and described their emergence in the socialization of the child.

Such insights are valuable in the awareness of the educator, the parents, the social worker, the psychologist and the physician.

Psychoanalytic concepts perceived in individual development need validation through every instrument at our command.

REFERENCES

1. Fenichel, Otto. *Psychoanalytic theory of neurosis*, p. 16. New York: Norton, 1945.
2. Freud, S. *New introductory lectures*, pp. 200–6. New York: Internat. Univ. Press, 1946.
3. Freud, A. *The ego and its defenses*. New York: Internat. Univ. Press, 1946.
4. Isaacs, S. *Childhood and after*. New York: Internat. Univ. Press, 1949.
5. Erikson, E. *Childhood and society*, p. 65. New York: Norton, 1950.
6. Isaacs, S. Nursery as a community. In *On the bringing up of children*, ed. John Rickman. New York: Robert Brunner, 1952.
7. Allen, F. H. *Psychotherapy with children*. New York: Norton, 1942.
8. Levy, David. From Hilgard (9).
9. Hilgard, Ernest R.; Kubie, Lawrence S.; and Pumpian-Mindlin, E. *Psychoanalysis as science*. Stanford, Calif.: Stanford Univ. Press, 1952.

26

THE DISTURBED CHILD

With Mary E. Giffin

GIVEN all the material, educational and medical benefits of our country, how can we account for the presence of so many unhappy, unpleasant and unproductive adults in our society? Given such basic assets as intelligence and physical well-being, how can we explain the misfits, the psychosomatics, the depressives, the school failures, the unmotivated, the psychotics, the maritally disabled, the individual delinquents and the sexually deviant? It is not sufficiently precise to view these disorders as the compounding of life's multiple pressures. We are in a position to speak with more exactness, and have no need to rely on generalities. The unhappy, the unproductive and the unpleasant adults of our society were the disturbed children of a generation ago — and what is more pertinent, they are the parents of our presently disturbed children.

The general practitioner is in a critical position; it is he who cares for 85 per cent of the children of this country. His detection, treatment and disposition of disturbed children can be a personal, medical, family and social contribution — or they can reflect inadequate understanding and the failure to assume responsibility for his patients in the largest sense. Practitioners for years have struggled with the fact that pediatric practice is a

Reprinted with permission from *Postgraduate Medicine* 22 (1957): 220–32.

combination of medicating the child and satisfying the family. Psychiatric understanding of the problems of the disturbed child has enlarged this concept to include the intervention and active treatment of many family members. Once again the general practitioner is called on not only to diagnose and to treat — he must also educate, as he has had to do with surgery, vaccination and infectious disease.

If a child contracts scarlet fever, is stricken with appendicitis or sustains a severe laceration, parents move quickly to enlist the physician's aid. Parents understand the need for medical care and quickly pay for the privilege of a healthy child. They would as gladly cooperate in the detection of the emotionally disturbed child if ignorance, superstition and poor advice could be overcome. Parents will not remain apathetic about seeking medical care for the emotionally crippled child if they can be educated to the need and potential for preventive and definitive treatment.

A concerned parent often voices recognition of unhappiness and maladjustment in a child, but is spuriously reassured by friends and uninformed relatives that the child is simply different congenitally or will outgrow this "phase." Since the symptoms do not constitute a life-or-death decision, the parents may be lulled into a mood of denial or of procrastination. Such parents often have an unconscious need to perpetuate such a personality distortion in the child, and thus readily concur with the well-intentioned friend.

Unfortunately, the offering of such poor advice is not limited to lay friends; it frequently comes from an equally well-intentioned physician. Because of unfortunate contacts with a few psychiatrists, or because psychiatric intervention may have temporarily inflamed a smoldering situation, or because of his own emotional problems, the practitioner may rationalize by depending on the elixir of time and the salve of sympathetic support. For years psychiatrists were in no position to expect a hearing: We had not yet defined the etiologic factors behind psychiatric entities. The situation is gradually changing. About certain conditions we can be very explicit with regard to etiology and treatment.

Insofar as the medical practitioner is dedicated to the principle of treating illness, he will be interested in acquainting himself with our ability to help parents and children achieve a healthier and more satisfying life. This paper is an attempt to outline some of the areas in which psychiatric understanding can help the general practitioner better treat his disturbed child-patients.

THE SOCIALLY DISTURBED: AN ILLUSTRATIVE CASE

As a prototype we will briefly discuss a case representing the socially disturbed.

Sam, eight years old, was referred for psychiatric attention because of incorrigible behavior at school, present since kindergarten but completely out of control in the prior three months. He was not only "sassy" and inattentive, but he had begun impulsively hitting things and children on the school grounds and in the classroom. He showed greater concern about breaking objects than about scratching, bruising and hitting his companions. Until the previous year he had had a small group of ruffian friends; at this time even they had deserted him in his defiant isolationism. The mothers in the neighborhood forbade their youngsters to play with him, and his siblings were ashamed to accept him as a brother. For three months he had not smiled, and any attempt to enforce regulations at home was met by severe outbursts of bad temper, including kicking the wall, hitting his mother, retaliatory fecal soiling and impulsive biting of his five year old brother. The younger brother, by contrast, was sweet, lovable and completely tractable.

Medically, Sam's condition was interesting because of encopresis and enuresis. During the taking of the history of the child from his mother, Sam was constantly in motion in the examining room. By the end of 10 minutes Sam had attempted to dismember every object in the room, and was demanding release.

Magically, with the dismissal of his mother, Sam became tractable and even cooperative. It took no psychiatric acumen to realize that Sam's mother represented the yeast in this child's ferment.

The physician who saw the child had confidence in psychiatry and quietly told the mother of the obvious need for specialized help. He was himself so calmly assured and so genuinely motivated in the child's behalf that no referral problem was presented. Psychiatric inquiry revealed a child who immediately began testing the limits in the playroom, throwing sand out of the box, crashing cars against the wall and turning on the water in full force.

The woman psychiatrist's initial comment, "There'll be none of that in here," was followed by a look of bewilderment; then the child's question, "You don't want me to mess things up?"

Slowly Sam shook his head and played quietly with the cars. A moment later he tried again; a car crashed against the opposite wall. The woman psychiatrist firmly but kindly said, "Sammy, I want you to have a good time and to talk about feelings — you're not to hurt the room, or me or yourself."

The boy angrily spat, "I hate you," to which the physician responded, "Of course you do, 'cause I won't let you do what you want."

A few moments later "disturbed" child and psychiatrist were

building a clay city — the reflection of a single constructive emotional experience. Sam had become convinced for a moment that one woman would limit his behavior but accept his angry words.

What of Sam's mother? As one would guess, she had never been able to limit her son's behavior, except when at long last she became completely torn asunder. Then *her* temper tantrum was even more startling than those of her son — she kicked, screamed, struck out and bit Sam — who could identify in only one direction: that of trying to release his anger as did his mother. During early childhood he had controlled the family, was rarely frustrated and seemed reasonably secure, except for enuresis and encopresis. With the competition of school, and especially since the birth of the younger brother, he had become more demanding and defiant.

The mother was completely overcome, withdrew in limit-setting even more, and began the ritual of saying, "Sammy, why can't you be as good as Brother Joe?" It was not surprising to find that a favored brother had never been restricted in her family. His name? Sam.

The physician-father sheepishly accepted responsibility for his passivity in the vacillating and irrational discipline which this child had received. He was quite aware of choosing attendance at medical meetings or retreat to the study rather than participation in the development and problems of the family.

Comment. — This kind of problem needs active and immediate intervention on the part of an interested and sensitized physician. We know many family physicians and pediatricians who have become subtle and expert at taking the kind of history that will reveal what is happening in a family to account for such a child's violent temper or his functional headaches, aching legs, enuresis, fears of going to school, insomnia, vomiting, night terrors — and even year-round asthma, behavioral problems and delinquency. The important thing is *active* and *learned* inquiry into the interpersonal factors behind such a child's family and social disturbance.

INTERVIEW TECHNICS

For those who might find it valuable, we briefly outline the salient aspects of collaborative interviewing. No psychiatric evaluation of a child is complete unless both parents are interviewed thoroughly with respect both to the child's problems and to the parents' own growth and development. The abundance with which psychodynamic material develops depends on the patience, subtlety, imagination and dexterity of the examiner as he detects and unravels the clues of the developing psychopathologic process. Experience permits insistence on the presence of interpersonal problems when symptoms are detected; and, as time proceeds, the examiner, to gain the facts necessary for accurate evaluation, feels no hesitancy in commenting on gross deceit or the withholding of information. It must, however, be remembered always that material is interpreted dynamically and in a manner constructive to each person as well as to the total family unit.

The following are the factors investigated with the parents. They constitute a brief outline of the orientation given to psychiatric and pediatric fellows rotating through the child psychiatry service.

1. Present illness: description and temporal correlation with family problems, separations, physical illness, school or social pressures. History of neurotic traits such as enuresis, nail biting, night terrors.

2. Developmental history: details of nursing, habit training and periods of jealousy, with particular emphasis on parental

emotional reactions to the conflicts common to these stages. Inquiry must always be made into the manner of handling biologic questions, particularly in the three to six year period.

3. Discipline patterns: specific examples of limit-setting, handling of frustrations and degree of consistency conveyed by each parent and both parents to the child. Inquiry into each parent's own pattern of discipline as a child.

4. Sleeping, modesty and affection patterns: These entail inquiry into actual arrangement of bedrooms and degree of privacy in sleeping, dressing and bathroom practices. Patterns of physical and verbal affection are obtained in detail.

5. School adjustment: Educational, disciplinary and social problems are elicited with particular evaluation of reading or learning difficulties.

6. Special interests and assets: particularly parents' awareness, participation and reaction to these. Patterns of sharing with friends and siblings.

7. Strength of conscience: evidences of dishonesty, delinquent trends, moral attitudes, religion.

8. Parental attitudes: which parent more kindred to child, expectations at conception and pregnancy, fantasies for child's future.

9. Parental marital adjustment: attitudes during courtship, sexual adjustment, interests, attitudes as spouses and parents.

10. Parental histories: taken in same orderly manner and detail as that of child.

   a. Specific symptoms suggest material to be sought: For instance, in case of school phobia, look for hostile-dependent relationship between child's mother and the mother's mother.

   b. Specific conflicts in parental development heighten awareness of present problems: For instance, if mother is overly affectionate to own father, marital adjustment undoubtedly is poor.

It should be pointed out that frequently parents withhold, deny or dissociate significant material, particularly in respect to discipline, seductive affection and sexual adjustment. It also happens that parents will attempt to keep the physician from interviewing the spouse "for fear the stories won't match." At times parents openly lie about serious emotional traumas. Such patterns are a reflection that the parents, too, are ill because of their unfortunate experiences. They cannot be condemned. They must be treated as sympathetically as a child. If parents become hostile toward the physician, a concerned comment regarding the source of this anger may further dynamic material. It is important that the interrogator not be deterred by the appearance of rage, disgust, tears or anxiety; these are the reflections of salient emotional factors. In spite of what at first may seem difficult hurdles, the facts must be gathered. Given time and experience, the interested practitioner can obtain a useful and dynamic history.

CONSIDERATION OF THEORY

We should at this point consider theory briefly. For two decades psychiatrists have been saying that the foundations of neurosis, psychosomatic states, certain psychoses and delinquencies are laid down in early childhood, and are in a large measure not constitutional. If detected early and if adequately treated, many of the disorders in question could be alleviated. Many primary emotional disturbances in children stem from the fact that these children are being reared by emotionally disturbed parents who themselves were reared by unstable parents. Neurosis leads to neurosis, and moderately concealed antisocial behavior in parents (delinquency) leads to more frank delinquency in the subsequent generation. This is due to interpersonal exchange and adaptation, not to heredity and the genes.

However, *all* emotional disturbances are *not* caused by disturbed parents; some are a result of disaster. If a mother dies when a child is three years old, for instance, this loss has a profound emotional effect on the developing personality, even in the most normal family. Insofar as parental attitudes and untoward disasters may be harbingers of emotional conflicts in children, they must be detected, and reparations made. Insofar as the emotional disturbances of children are reflections of parental conflict and unhappiness, the entire family deserves and has need of treatment.

Thus has arisen collaborative therapy of child and parents. (1) This technic has become a vital research tool as well, and has offered insights about specific etiologic factors not previously possible.

Basic to the understanding of all emotional illness is the understanding of anxiety, that ever-present feeling, common to the emotional disturbances of human beings. It may stand out so strikingly that no one could fail to see it. At other times it is covert, or acted on antisocially, or expressed by means of physical symptoms. What, then, is anxiety? It is akin to fear, but like a mathematical number raised to the fourth or the tenth power, it is beyond and above ordinary fear. It is overwhelming in its permeation, and more frightening because it is so nebulous, until its sources can be realized consciously. Anxiety is ill-defined fear, generated by unconscious conflicts, often not amenable to ordinary reassurance or will power, and usually pushed into greater chronicity by time and increasing environmental pressures.

Probably the greatest sources of anxiety in children today are their guilt, confusion and fear of retaliation related to their expression of anger. If children are to be healthfully reared, parents must expect outbursts of anger to follow frustrations, denials, limit-setting and disappointments. Wise parents do not make the child feel guilty about experiencing anger, but do afford guidance as to how the child may best express the anger; namely, verbally. The parents do not permit the child to destroy property, or to injure others or himself. The healthy parent instills a recognition of guilt about such acts, but at the same time guides the child in the moderate and constructive verbalization of his anger. If the parent is a comfortable person, he can set limits easily and accept the child's verbalized anger without alarm or hostility.

In contrast, the insecure parent responds in one of several ways: (1) He may brutally retaliate: spanking, depriving or rejecting inappropriately, so that the child is frightened about his physical well-being and is rejected emotionally; (2) he may himself be taken by panic, anticipating that the child of five years may indeed murder when he angrily says, "I could kill you"; the child in this instance senses the hostile fantasy of the parent and becomes more anxious as he is pushed in the direction of hostile behavior; (3) the parent may comment, "How can you say such things to your kind, dear mother? I love you more than anyone ever will. Some day, when I'm gone, you'll be sorry." Thus are generated in the child overwhelming guilt and the need to repress expressions of anger.

By these and other parent-child interchanges neurotic anxiety is instilled in the child to form the anlage for emotional illness. A large number of emotionally disturbed children and adults have so repressed their anger that they are not even conscious of it. They are aware only of anxiety or headache or a hundred other symptoms. It may take months in treatment to help the child or adult realize that anger underlies his neurosis. In his earlier investigative years, Freud believed that sexual conflicts underlay all neurosis. As Freud and other research workers looked more deeply into the unconscious, it became apparent that repressed anger was more the common denominator. To be sure, many sexual conflicts exist in emotional disorders, but this relates to the fact that anger is bound with sexual impulses.

This brings us to consideration of the theory of the presence and importance of the unconscious. In the latter years of the last century one of the greatest discoveries in biologic science was made. Freud perceived and tested the existence of the unconscious; he developed technics for observing and exploring its operations. He proved beyond all doubt that vast reservoirs of the emotional and mental operations that drive us reside in the unconscious, an understanding of which has permitted psychiatry to become a truly scientific specialty. It is now accepted that unconscious mechanisms push and pull us in directions we frequently would prefer to believe consciously maneuvered. This does not mean that nothing can be decided on consciously without interference from the unconscious. It does mean, however, that if painful and conflictual facts have been repressed in the unconscious, rational behavior becomes very difficult.

Of vital importance also in behavioral patterns is the developing conscience. Reflecting and caricaturing the strengths and weaknesses of parental conscience is the mosaic of the child's conscience. A child's conscience is not inherited but is developed, especially during the first six years of life, by means of imitation in great detail of the total behavior of parents. This imitation embraces the conscious and unconscious operations of the parents. To an equal extent, conscience develops from the parents' conscious and unconscious image of the child and from their concepts and hopes for their child. The amalgam of these detailed and specific identifications in the realms of honesty, social behavior, sexual concepts and moral principles forms the child's conscience, basic to the constructive social control of the individual.

Finally, a word about love. In the earlier days in child psychiatry, great emphasis was placed on the need to give the child sufficient love. No one seemed to recognize in those days that the parents were giving as much love to the child as they were capable of mustering. To suggest to such parents that their disturbed children needed more love and affection was redundant. Until such parents could understand their inability to give what should be natural — that is, parental love — they could not act differently. Today we recognize that the parents had parents, too, and that we must help parents if we are to help the child. We have learned that the handling of the child's sexual questionings, his testing of social behavior, his response to discipline, all reflect parental security or uncertainty. With these concepts and technics as a background, let us consider specific disorders.

ACUTE EMOTIONAL DISTURBANCES

Neurotic, psychotic, delinquent or psychosomatic problems may show signs of acute decompensation with the eruption of an acute emergency. The acutely disturbed child needs quick and dynamic evaluation of family psychopathology, with active intervention by a sensitized and confident physician.

Problems to be considered in this discussion of acute disturbances will be limited to: (1) sudden development of severe and incapacitating anxiety and phobic symptoms in reaction to a traumatic event; (2) riotous temper tantrums and allied symptoms so severe as to be dangerous to the patient and people around him; (3) reactions to death and other disturbing incidents; (4) the appearance of massive emotional regression in response to surgical operation. In all these cases the previous personality development decides the "stress-tolerance level" of the child and thus determines how he will react to a serious psychologic trauma, such as death of a parent, divorce, vicious hostile attack by a parent, terrifying cataclysms, birth of siblings or failure at school.

Sudden, Overwhelming Panic

Let us consider the children in whom overwhelming anxiety abruptly develops to the point of panic. Such children may be screaming, trembling and clinging to the mother, from whom they refuse to be separated. As the attacks progress these children may voice fears of dying, may show extreme motor excitement and the various symptoms of either hyperventilation or hallucinations.

Example 1. A boy of five years was brought for consultation by his father because of the boy's acute hallucination of predatory spiders about to overtake him. Our knowledge that his paranoidally psychotic mother, three days before, had almost choked him to death permitted rapid interpretation of his need to hallucinate symbolically the maternal assault — until such a time as a believing therapist could share with him the actual life-threatening attack which had occurred. Sudden sexual assaults or destructive threats of all kinds may precipitate panic in a child. Such insults are, of course, highly hostile, and the child is terrified by the destructive intent. The child is overwhelmed not only in a physical sense but also by the knowledge that parental "love" in the instance at hand is destructive. The child's fear and shame at accepting such knowledge precipitate overwhelming anxiety and may necessitate hallucinatory dissociation. Active, interpretive psychotherapy is obviously imperative in such instances, and referral to a competent child psychiatrist is the treatment of choice.

Example 2. In contrast, one might consider a child suffering from a school phobia, another form of an acute anxiety state reflecting morbid fear of separation. Children thus affected may be brought to the practitioner with the complaint of acute attacks of abdominal pain, vomiting, headache, pallor and sweating — and in such states they obviously represent diagnostic problems. In our practice it has become customary to urge that a high index of suspicion be entertained that these symptoms are reflections of anxiety if they: (1) occur before school, only to subside by noon; (2) rarely occur in summer; (3) are seen in families in which parent and child show difficulty functioning away from one another. The factors behind such conditions will be discussed under "separation anxiety," later in this paper. If the symptoms are of recent onset and the truancy marked, immediate psychiatric referral is indicated. In the past, in many of these cases, the condition has been mistaken for rheumatic fever. Rest in bed only made the entire situation worse.

Riotous Temper Tantrums and Allied Symptoms

Another type of acutely disturbed child who presents a difficult problem dangerous to both himself and those around him is the one with riotous temper tantrums and allied symptoms. Such children are best handled in the hospital, away from the situation at home. This type of management in itself may eliminate the outbursts and allow the physician to make therapeutic contact with the child. All catastrophic temper tantrums are initiated and fostered unconsciously by the parents, who need treatment if the child is to return home.

We all know today that the setting of reasonable limits is absolutely necessary in the rearing of children, and in many instances in therapy at the onset. The calm, unhostile, consistent adult rapidly has less and less trouble with this, for the patient, removed from the parents, is intensely relieved to have a firm, friendly adult take a guiding hand in control of the riot.

Allen (2) puts it this way: "A skillful therapist has no interest in proving he can *make* a child put away his playthings or clear up the mess he has made during the hour. He will not use the setting of a limit for the exercise of personal power. To do that would be to destroy the meaning of the whole experience, and make it the battle of wills the child may want. Valid limits grow from the situation and belong to it. They do not spring from the personal whims or control of the therapist. Around the natural limits that emerge, a therapist, by clearly defining them, helps the child to face them or to express his feeling about them."

Example 3. Typical of the catastrophic reactions is the condition of an acutely disturbed 17 year old farm boy in whom convulsivelike seizures suddenly developed. They were associated with violent hyperactivity, including attempts to throw himself through a window. His condition at first was thought to be epileptic, and anticonvulsants were prescribed and he was restricted from driving the tractor, his pride and joy. This restriction contributed to deterioration of the situation to the point where commitment of the boy was being demanded by the neighbors. The boy was then hospitalized three weeks. During psychotherapy he came to recognize consciously his feeling of helplessness in the face of his enormous rage toward his semi-invalided and hemiplegic father, who blatantly favored the patient's lazy older brother. The patient was doing practically all the farm work, but his father, possibly partly because of organic deterioration, derogated requests the patient made for machinery and supplies, while lavishing money on the spendthrift elder brother. Before his father's illness the patient had worked closely with his father on the farm, but since that time he could not bring himself to express his real feelings of rage. Long treatment after the brief hospitalization helped this patient to face and to deal with his anger more consciously, and no seizures supervened, in spite of the withdrawal of drugs. The boy finally was able, without a temper tantrum, to tell his father that he would leave the household unless matters were radically changed. By that time the patient could speak with such firm conviction that his father knew the situation was serious and that the boy meant what he said. The parent then complied.

Acute Reactions to Death and Catastrophe

We cannot omit from the subject of the more acute reactions a discussion of the effect of the death of a parent. By the age of two years the child is devoted to his parents. Little children regard death as abandonment, and are terrified and enraged.

Example 4. John, a boy of four years, said, "Mommy is in heaven. She went to Milwaukee last year and came home. Why don't she come home now?" Members of this child's family thought they were supportive when they said, "Mommy was sick, but now she's happy in heaven." This infuriated the child, who immediately assumed she had not been happy at home. In addition, he was driven by the belief that his angry thoughts might have caused her death. This boy needed a chance to grieve openly with the other mourners and to talk of his hate and terror and love. If feelings are smoothed over, all emotion is repressed — the love along with the panic and hate. When the love is repressed along with the hate, the child grows up to be a cold person, unable to realize his potential for loving. If the relatives hesitate to talk about such a catastrophe with the little child, then the physician should do this recurrently and often for some weeks. The practitioner can serve a very useful purpose in these cases by insisting on the child's right and his need to speak of his feelings, to cry and to be angry.

Massive Emotional Regression

Symptoms of acute neurosis or psychosis, as we have said, may be the results of long hostility and cruelty on the part of adults, exposure to accidents, death or long absence of a loved one, or disturbing experiences, such as introduction to perversion or adult genital exposure. The intensity of the reaction depends on the level of security previously felt with the parents. The inexperienced therapist may, in these catastrophic cases, confuse schizophrenia with massive emotional regression. Typical is the following case.

Example 5.[1] A 12 year old boy underwent craniotomy for removal of a medulloblastoma. The mother had refused the neurosurgeon permission to orient the boy preoperatively. The boy first learned he was to have his head operated on from the barber, who appeared to shave his head at five o'clock in the morning. After the operation, this 12 year old boy regressed to an infantile level, soiling and wetting his clothing, sucking, taking only fluids, whimpering and speaking only a few words of baby talk. This regression was not to be explained by any neurologic or radiologic interference, according to the specialists in these fields. It was immediately obvious that the patient now feared greater physical injury, and especially something castrative. When this fear was discussed in simple terms with him, he manifested his first confidence in the physician. The hostile, destructive mother was forbidden access to the boy, since she had always terrified him. The passive father for once stood his ground and supported us. The psychotherapist encouraged the boy to face his rage and terror at the sudden surgical insult, and correlated these feelings with significant ones from his past. In many such cases intensive work also is done with the parents.

1. [This case is presented in an expanded version in paper 17, p. 267. *Editor.*]

Mention should here be made of an area in which psychologic preparation seems to be preventing acute anxiety and postoperative pain; namely, in instances of amputation.[2] We encounter almost no phantom limbs with pain if four simple matters are discussed with the child (or adult) before the operation. The physician need not be a psychiatrist to manage this well. Often the physician must work very rapidly, since for sound reasons surgical treatment cannot be delayed. The parents give the history, which alerts the physician to the presence or absence of insecurity, physical fears and anxiety, and undue guilt about hostility chronic in the child. We now handle several points in the treatment of all children.

First, we support the surgeon's decision that amputation is necessary, and we encourage the child to face his anger at us about this amputation before and after the operation.

Second, we discuss with the patient his sadness and mourning about losing his old friend — his limb.

Third, we tell him there will be a phantom phenomenon and explain what he will feel.

Fourth, and especially with the older child or adult, we help him verbalize his concern about disposition of the limb. This is a grave concern, particularly in the chronically disturbed patient, and must be discussed freely.

Above all, we do everything we can to help the patients face their anger and sadness. Often much work must be done with parents, surgeons and nurses toward their understanding of and acceptance of the angry, mourning child who has undergone amputation. At first the surgeons felt we only made troublesome patients for them. This attitude has now largely subsided. It is time for these procedures to become part of the medical regimen for patients who must undergo amputation.

2. [For more on this topic see paper 9, p. 108. *Editor*.]

THE SCHIZOPHRENIC CHILD

Some of the most disturbed children are those struggling with schizophrenic thoughts, fears and physical drives or inhibitions. They may show their disturbance either in the form of acute excitement or pitiful withdrawal, colored by hallucinations or delusions, or muted by apathetic desensitization. As soon as the diagnosis is suspected, psychiatric consultation is necessary. The condition of these children, and especially the more autistic ones, often is confused with mental retardation or damage to the brain. Hospitalization may be the only course open, for both proper control and accurate diagnostic observation. Children presumed to be schizophrenic ought to have careful and detailed psychiatric observation, so that those exposed to violent intrafamilial threats may be evaluated for possibilities of treatment.

Some very competent physicians today still maintain that schizophrenia is constitutional and organic, whereas others see it as developing in relation to disturbed and very destructive parents. Certainly, some, at least, of those patients previously considered hopeless now can be treated satisfactorily. This particular field is still open for research, but our observations on the procedure in which we collaboratively and concomitantly treat parents and child incline us more toward the environmental than toward the constitutional view. The most open mind is that which does not, at this stage of research, stoutly maintain an either/or attitude but considers every avenue for exploring the environmental and constitutional factors. For the practitioner this means the referring of such patients *early* to the interested child psychiatrist.

CHRONIC EMOTIONAL DISTURBANCES

Children with chronic emotional disturbances are more usually seen in outpatient clinics, to which they are brought for treatment by the parents or by means of urging from teachers.

Inhibition of Learning

One of the most common evidences of emotional disturbance that teachers observe is the inhibition of learning, of greater or lesser degree. Children formerly doing brilliant work may suddenly fail and lose interest. Emotional conflicts with anxiety, inhibitions and depression may account for this. Children thus afflicted are best handled by psychiatrists, but the family physician can clarify emotional problems.

If the learning problem centers largely around reading, a psychiatrist should decide if this is an educational matter or an emotional, conflictual problem. If it is the former, excellent *individual* tutoring five days a week (not after school hours) by a very pleasant, encouraging tutor is the best approach; most parents are unsuitable tutors. If the problem is emotional, the psychiatrist must help the child face his emotional inhibitions. Fear about questioning in biologic and sexual matters often is at the basis of general inhibitions of learning. In these instances, parents have harshly squelched the little child's early guileless questions about sexual matters; subsequently the child is afraid to ask questions about anything for fear of a harsh, rejecting and shaming answer.

Separation Anxiety

One of the commonest chronic emotional disorders is separation anxiety,[3] frequently a cause of absence from school and erroneously considered a phobic reaction to school. A year ago, within three days of each other, two 14 year old girls arrived at the hospital on stretchers. They appeared to be critically ill; the possibility that Addison's disease and other systemic conditions might be present was investigated. The girls were thin, without

---

3. [For exposition of this topic and for a therapeutic example see paper 19, p. 298. *Editor.*]

appetite, very weak, and had been in bed for three months. Investigation showed that the mothers, unhappy in their marriages, had been overly concerned about any aches or colds in the children, and had fostered regression and hostilely frustrated growth in many ways. They were attempting to hold these girls close, to buttress their own insecurity. The results were very sick children, on whose continuing invalidism the mothers were parasitically dependent. In a few days of collaborative treatment, each mother and daughter were coming to our offices. Active, intensive early treatment broke up the destructive physiologic and school problems, and permitted a return to school with a foregoing of the immature gratification of their neurotic tie to the mother.

Boys become involved in separation anxiety exactly as do girls, and many times the fathers may be important etiologic factors in the hostile-dependent tie. Whoever is of greater importance must be treated with the child. Twelve years ago such problems were not understood; these children became invalids or at best inadequate and neurasthenic. Separation anxiety, with all its ramifications, is the core-conflict of many adult neuroses. Papers published elsewhere describe the details of actual psychotherapy. (3, 4) Any interested practitioner can apply the technics as described in these papers.

Psychosomatic Illness

Although not so obviously disturbed emotionally as are members of the preceding groups, the psychosomatically ill are afflicted with a degree of disturbance which must not be overlooked. A case may illustrate.

Example 6. Rickie was seen at the age of two years, because of chronic constipation. Toilet training had been begun when he was 18 months old and success had been obtained for a month.

Then the child began to refuse to cooperate with the routine, and constipation started. The pediatrician suggested that the mother quiet her fears and allow the child to decide about toilet habits. One and a half years later the child was admitted to the hospital with obstipation and fecal impaction. Megacolon was demonstrated by roentgenograms, and there was a stricture at the rectosigmoid. Surgical intervention was deferred because of the *surgeon's* belief that psychiatric intervention would be more appropriate.

It became quickly apparent that this child's mother expected and admired automation, that the pleasure of maturing and of play of any kind was foreign to her psyche and that the child's independence had indeed met a testing ground in the matter of bowel performance. This child was disturbed in all testing situations; on the part of the mother there were constant nagging, whining and demands. On the other hand, with the play therapist, once limits had been set, this child was lovable, imaginative and spontaneous, without undue demands. The mother had indeed relaxed her concern about toilet habits but she had almost totally rejected the child, in play, by vacillating limits and by absolutely no support in the child's attempts to overcome obstipation. Even when she learned of the child's successful evacuations of the bowel in the play situation she "neglected" to provide ready accommodations for such an action for the child at home. Wise was the surgeon who saw this anxious child whose physiology also was disturbed.

It is impossible to discuss the mechanisms present in all, but patients with the following symptoms should be studied with a view to defining the etiologic importance of emotional factors: enuresis, tics, vomiting, constipation, soiling, nail biting, year-round asthma, refusal to eat, phobias, unexplained paralysis of an arm or leg, blindness, episodes of fainting, obsessive fears and thoughts, the need to do things by rituals, inhibition in activities, negligible interest span, inability to make and hold friends, continuous crying, sensitivity and sadness, terror of leaving the mother, violent bursts of hatred, bizarre pains and disorders of the skin.

THE DELINQUENT CHILD

Still another category of disturbed children compels our attention; namely, the delinquent child who becomes the psychopath at a later age. In contrast to the overly guilty neurotic person, in these cases we see too little guilt. Two large categories of antisocial behavior can be defined: the individual delinquent and the gang delinquent.

The Individual Delinquent

First, let us consider the lone delinquent. Mystery enveloped causation here until 15 years ago, when several of us began to treat these children collaboratively. (5, 6) Startling facts emerged, and we never fail to find similar facts in every case of delinquency. The facts are that the parents are unconsciously fostering and condoning the delinquent behavior. The parents of delinquent children unconsciously gain satisfaction from the specific antisocial behavior of the children. Interns and residents, early in training, are shocked and skeptical about such an assertion. When, however, they interview parents in the manner we outline, they too emerge in possession of such disturbing facts.

Always we find that impulses toward behavior similar to that in the child are present in these parents: These impulses are unconscious, poorly inhibited and close to breaking through into consciousness. These impulses do break out, sadly enough, by means of fostering such behavior in a child.

Consciously, most of these parents are deeply concerned at

the child's misguided behavior, and have no idea that they are actually promoting it. These parents foster conscience defects in their children. There is rarely generalized weakness of the conscience, but rather, a lack of conscience in certain of the circumscribed areas of behavior. The child's antisocial behavior is correlated with the specific area of weakness in the parents' conscience.

The reader will immediately ask two questions: "How do you explain the fact that only one child in a family of three or five children may be delinquent?" and "If the parents do initiate and foster such a defect in conscience, just how do they do it?"

Suffice it to say that each child in a family has a particular emotional meaning to the parents and therefore is subject to highly specific identification and fantasies. For example, a mother with a lying father sooner or later chooses one son to identify with her disliked father, and unwittingly assumes she will never be able to train that boy to tell the truth. She is paralyzed in patiently training him as she trains the other children about truth. Conscience defects are molded in a child in scores of ways of which the following are examples.

1. The parent is vacillating, and may say one thing, only to undo it in the next breath. A mother says it is wrong to steal, but when her child is caught, she covers up for the child. A 14 year old boy brought to us because of extortion said that when his father accused him, quite correctly, of stealing from his wallet, the mother intervened with the statement that she had spent the money. She was deriving unconscious gratification from her son's stealing.

2. Parents will say, "You may not play with fires," but undo the prohibition by adding, "But if you must get it out of your system, we can set fire to papers in the sink." It should be clear that no one has to get fire-setting out of his system.

3. Issues are so befogged by parents that the child can only be confused. Told on the one hand to be honest, the child detects dishonesties in the parents. The parent, with a sly smile, may remark that the grocer shortchanged himself, yet overlook a healthy challenge from the child to tell the grocer. Instead of making clear that dishonesty under all conditions is wrong, parents act as if there can be exceptions.

The same double standard recently was clearly shown in newspaper accounts of the father of an adolescent who, with a group, killed an old man. The father of one of these adolescents said, "I can see murder for money; but just to murder, I can't understand that in my boy."

4. Interested, smiling responses are seen on the parents' faces as a child recounts forbidden behavior at school. Such glances portray parental vicarious gratification obtained by the child's misbehavior. These parents later may spank the child; however, punishment after ardent listening serves as no prohibition. The child will repeat what he feels gives the parent gratification.

5. Once the child notes parental deception, he begins to blackmail the parent. For instance, a mother may write an illicit excuse to the school to cover an absence. It is not surprising that the child will demand another excuse whenever it seems opportune. The problem of delinquency becomes compounded by temper tantrums which the child soon learns are effective in overwhelming a vacillating, corrupt parent.

In a normal home, consistent, never-faltering training goes on daily with regard to truth, possessions and person. The normal parent knows emphatically that with training her children will develop consciences like her own, in which there is no alternative about antisocial impulses. The training is consistent, so that little thefts and untruths are immediately curtailed. The mother or father who permits minor thefts with the idea that the child "will outgrow it" is only fostering further trouble. The normal parent knows that constant training is necessary, but it never occurs to her that her child will ever reach a delinquency court or a reform school. Such fantasies are expressions of what the parents think of the child; they are common among parents of delinquent children.

Among the sexual delinquents, too, parents unconsciously foster the particular form of misbehavior. (7, 8) Children behave sexually in accordance with the parents' conscious and unconscious image for the child. Reflective of problems which may develop is the following.

Example 7. A depressed 42 year old woman came to consultation complaining of the sadistic promiscuity of her 20 year old son. Since his adolescence, the mother had intently listened to the minutest details of his intimacies with girls. She was most unhappy with her passive and submissive husband. The sources of her ambivalent seductiveness with her son were easily adduced. Her own father had been a Don Juan. From her early adolescence he had come to her bedroom nightly to fondle her, and he had even made attempts to enter her bed. At the first such instance, this patient sought protection from her mother. The mother did not dare to reproach the father "lest he kill her." From the father, to the patient, to her son, sanctions of the forbidden are evident in three generations. The son, refusing treatment, will provide still another generation of pathologic involvement.

The Gang Delinquent

What distinguishes the individual delinquency just discussed from that great mass of sociologic or gang delinquency? In the individual delinquent from "acceptable" families there develops a conscience defect *unconsciously* fostered by the parents. There is a conscience defect in sociologic delinquencies by our standards, but it is *conscious*; the parents are quite consciously in accord with the child; there is nothing unconscious about it. It is their world against our world. Their culture avows it is all right to steal or to betray the other world. Trickery, vandalism or extortion against the other group is consciously condoned. In the instance of sexual misconduct the parents' own sexual aberrations are overtly revealed to the children without guilt, and later the grown children behave accordingly. These children are not being driven by the parents' unconscious wishes, but rather, by a gregarious need for acceptance.

It is of interest that in areas of delinquency one may find many well-behaved and stable children because they are being reared in families in which the parents are truly normal, setting limits effectively, guiding their children consistently and affectionately, uninfluenced by the culture of the area. One of our foremost educators was reared in a slum area in which delinquency was rampant. Six of his early friends had been sent to the gas chamber. The educator, however, had been reared by poor but affectionate, consistent parents who emphatically set limits about all behavior that tended to deviate. His family did not accept the mores and standards of the underprivileged of the area in which they lived; thus the child did not become delinquent.

Identification of the type of delinquent must rest with the psychiatrist, the sociologist, social worker and psychologist. A thorough study must involve the parents as deeply as the delinquent. Treatment of either kind is a monumental challenge. The individual delinquent cannot be treated, if the child remains in the home, unless the parents also are treated intensively. Such treatment must be done by specialists, and it is as difficult as any treatment that ever confronts the psychiatrist. If the parents are not motivated or cannot be treated, then treatment of the child must be carried out in a hospital over a very long period. Treatment of the sociologic delinquent is best conducted through sociologists, community leaders and those working in the antisocial areas. Psychiatric treatment is illogical and ineffective for members of these sociologic antisocial groups. This is a formidable task requiring improved living facilities and new leadership.

SUMMARY

We have briefly reviewed some of the problems presented by disturbed children. Their presence is everywhere, and our plea to the general practitioner is that of sensitization to their ubiquity. The socially disturbed, the acutely anxious and the delinquent need immediate psychiatric referral. The schizophrenically disturbed need careful psychiatric observation, preferably in a hospital.

With regard to the chronically emotionally disturbed, much depends on the time available to the practitioner for inquiry into intrafamilial and intrapsychic conflicts. As practitioners gain confidence in the importance of emotional factors, they will feel more assured about their own inquiry, and psychiatric referrals will be made without apology. Children rarely show embarrassment at seeing a psychiatrist, but the physician's apologetic referral may heighten the parents' shame to the point of great and unnecessary distress. With our present emphasis on total medical care, inquiry into emotional problems must become an integral part of a medical evaluation.

REFERENCES

1. Johnson, A. M.; Falstein, E. I.; Szurek, S. A.; and Svendsen, M. School phobia. *Am. J. Orthopsychiat.* 11 (1941): 702–11. (Reprinted above, p. 14.)

2. Allen, F. H. Psychotherapy with children, 1st ed. New York: W. W. Norton and Company, 1942, 311 pp.
3. Robinson, D. B.; Duncan, G. M.; and Johnson, A. M. Psychotherapy of a mother and daughter with a problem of separation anxiety. *Proc. Staff Meet., Mayo Clin.* 30 (1955): 141–48. (Reprinted above, p. 298.)
4. Estes, H. R.; Haylett, C. H.; and Johnson, A. M. Separation anxiety. *Am. J. Psychotherapy* 10 (1956): 682–95.
5. Johnson, A. M. and Szurek, S. A. Etiology of antisocial behavior in delinquents and psychopaths. JAMA 154 (1954): 814–17.
6. ———. The genesis of antisocial acting out in children and adults. *Psychoanalyt. Quart.* 21 (1952): 323–43. (Reprinted above, p. 145.)
7. Giffin, M. E.; Johnson, A. M.; and Litin, E. M. Specific factors determining antisocial acting out. *Am. J. Orthopsychiat.* 24 (1954): 668–84.
8. Litin, E. M.; Giffin, M. E.; and Johnson, A. M. Parental influence in unusual sexual behavior in children. *Psychoanalyt. Quart.* 25 (1956): 37–55.

27

THE ADOLESCENT AND HIS PROBLEMS

I HAVE been asked to discuss the adolescent's problems as they may be encountered by the occupational therapist. The latter must communicate with adolescents who are neurotic, psychotic or delinquent. No one can hope to understand the multiplicity of unusual reactions in these emotionally ill children if one does not have a basic familiarity with the complexities of behavior in the normal adolescent.

THE NORMAL ADOLESCENT

Adolescence is a physical phenomenon associated with profound psychologic changes. The emotional problems and the emotional growth have their biologic origin in the glandular-hormonal changes that occur at pubescence and in the physical changes that result from the hormonal readjustment. Physiologically, the childhood bodily structure fairly rapidly matures. Synchronous with this physical growth is an intensification of the psychologic impulse to grow up.

The two major psychologic changes are: (1) An awakening of sexual interest, (2) A more independent adult status.

How these two major changes evolve is drastically determined by the experiences of the child with his family in the years gone by. All of this needs considerable elaboration.

Reprinted with permission from *American Journal of Occupational Therapy* 11 (1957): 255–61.

The composite picture of the behavior of adolescence often is apparently contradictory and confused. It is no simple step to cross the terrain between childhood and adulthood as it stands in our world today. In our culture marriage must be delayed until a greater degree of independence can be achieved through education and greater economic growth. Obviously in our western culture, then, many complex external checks of a social nature are imposed upon the spontaneity of the physical process of maturation. Many paradoxes result.

Josselyn (1) describes this particular paradox clearly.

> On one hand, the adolescent is accepted as a maturing preadult. Permission is given to modify the character of his social life . . . Supervision of leisure time activity by the parent is either markedly reduced or not existent at all. The school takes cognizance of this change by introducing the departmentalized type of education in which more responsibility is placed upon the student and in which the intensity of the relationship with a teacher is diluted by the presence of several teachers. The child is now expected to solve his problems himself, or to seek help upon his own initiative.
>
> On the other hand, parents and teachers, frightened by the apparent instability of the adolescent, tend to inhibit where freedom formerly was implied. Some parents who, during the latency period of the child, gradually gained confidence in his judgment, now, as the child enters adolescence, become, and not without some justification, unsure of this unpredictable person's capacity to evaluate situations. This unsureness in the parents is particularly true in parents rather unstable themselves. This contradictory attitude is nicely illustrated in a common struggle — the struggle between the parent and the child concerning the hour of coming in at night. The adolescent is not only allowed but is usually encouraged by the modern parent to date. Any of these dates are acceptable — if the child returns at a stated hour . . . Many parents are surprisingly inflexible about the hour . . . Parents often rationalize this stand by saying that the child needs rest; late hours result in fatigue. This rationalization may be justified, but too often the same parent recounts with pride how parent and child talked for an hour after his

The Adolescent and His Problems

return from a date about "all that happened." Where then is the needed rest?

But to forget the paradoxes for a time, let us not believe that all is confusion. In a family background of respect and love for the child, the transition to adulthood is a rather solid, tangible and understandable phenomenon. If there has been easy and frank discussion with the mother from earliest childhood, the young girl listens without anxiety to her mother's explanation of menstruation — its relationship to the egg or ovum produced by the ovaries each month as the girl matures. To grown-ups whom they trust, girls normally are able to express their pleasure at the onset of the menses.

The boy needs education about his growing up at this time, too. He has questions about nocturnal emissions about which he is too anxious and too shy to ask. He needs to know that this is normal for the maturing sexual organs. He has questions also about menstruation in girls. Undoubtedly, if he were wisely informed, he would become protective and kindly, aware of the young girl's shyness and right to privacy in these matters.

Toward the end of pre-adolescence we observe in boys and girls increasing uneasiness over any display of affection from the parents. Although this is a source of pain to some possessive parents, it is an indication of the normal onset of puberty and the child's need to defend himself against his earlier emotional attachments to the parents. It can become very confusing for the child if the parents resent this withdrawal, and thus increase the child's feeling that he has failed his parents. The occupational therapist will do well to respect this typical adolescent withdrawal from physical evidence of affection.

By the age of 12 and 13 years the girls begin again, as at 4 and 5 years, to enjoy adorning and displaying their bodies. To be comfortable, they must conform to the prevailing style. Boys of the same age are thinking not so much of making themselves handsome as of becoming important through some achievement in the world. Normally, there is no sudden ushering in of puberty, but the observer sees emotional and bodily changes gradually taking place.

In the case of sick adolescents, occupational therapists see many children who are not going through adolescence as I have described the normal process. One of the common features you see is the regressed adolescent: the child whose insecurity and conflict are so great that he judges it to be safer to remain more childish and less grown up. Shyness and obesity are common defenses: Emotional immaturity is a necessary defense; such a child cannot be pushed or superficially talked out of it.

CONSERVATISM OR REVOLT

What is happening specifically in the adolescent? The body is now flooded with the hormones from the sexual glands which become increasingly active with puberty . . . Since all this feeling associated with the body makes for new adjustments, they may become insecure. A common mode of handling insecurity at any age is to try, consciously or unconsciously, to deny it through expressions of defiance and daring. The wise adult does not suppress rebellion rigidly nor does he play into the revolt permissively. (2)

Instead, he does what he can to reassure the child of his attractiveness and worth-whileness and indicates his confidence in the basic good sense of the son or daughter.

Because the responsibilities and changes are so great at this age, the adolescent has to develop a deep conservatism as a protection against failure and unhappiness. Characteristic of the basic biology of all organisms is the tendency toward self-preservation. Adults can rely on the normal adolescent's sense of good taste, his eagerness to conform. The responsibility of the adults is to guide them into activities that are appropriate to their age and emotional growth. Their tendency to conform does the rest.

The insecurity of adolescence makes boys and girls highly sensitive to criticism. What they wish more than anything else is to be loved. They do not want this love expressed in emotional demonstrativeness, but in confidence and respect from adults. Every child responds unconsciously to what the parents wish him to be, even though these inner wishes are not put into words. If the unconscious wishes of the parents are for illicit or questionable behavior, the adolescent responds accordingly. He identifies you and all adults as having the same wishes for him as the parents, and at first responds according to that view.

The adolescent must be able to assure himself that he is lovable and that he knows how to love. The child who unconsciously and consciously knows he has been truly loved by his parents finds his task infinitely easier than the child who has suffered uncertainty. To reassure himself that he is not childishly dependent solely on the parents for love, the normal adolescent resorts for a time to the age-old defense of his denial of his need for the parents, withdrawing from the parents or turning a borderline incident into a full-fledged battle to prove he has no need for the parent.

Adolescents strive to reassure themselves that they are not "different." Girls turn to girls and boys to boys at first, simply talking things over and speculating about things. When they are alone, face to face, they get down to their more troublesome worries. Sometimes, when their insecurity is great and their self-esteem is at a low ebb, they build themselves up to each other; often some are taken in by accounts of seductive charm or "masculine" prowess. Many normal girls, who are lovable and able to love and therefore hesitate to invest their fine, deep feelings brashly, may be envious of the shallow girls who have less to lose by flirting. The same could be said of the boys.

A close relationship with teachers is of basic importance in the total growth of these young students. Here, too, the recreational and occupational therapists may have great appeal to members of this age group and can make capital of such adolescent yearning. The normal adolescent has a large fund of energy, and with the thought of years ahead, given reassurance, he feels he can achieve much.

BOY MEETS GIRL

The normal adolescent emancipates himself only gradually from his parents. To find his way to the opposite sex he often seeks, first, friendliness, confidence and closeness to members of his own sex. This bond, this realization of loving and being loved by a dear friend of one's own sex, is a boon to the adolescent. It is only a passing stage in the growth of the child's confidence in himself which helps him later to make a comfortable relationship with members of the opposite sex. A secure, normal adolescent moves ahead. If, however, a boy or girl finds it impossible to have more than one friend at a time and has no capacity to share his or her interests with others, then parents and educators should recognize this as an indication of insecurity, and they should encourage the child toward greater self-confidence, or, if need be, they should get some professional help.

In your work in the hospitals you will encounter adolescents who have become fixated in some overt homosexual adaptation. You will need close co-operation with the psychiatrist to be sure that your relationship to the child cannot be maneuvered by her into compounding the complexities of the established fixation. All workers and therapists should be suspicious of themselves and their motives if they tend in any way to feel possessive with a patient.

There are facts about relationships between the sexes that should be available to the concerned and wondering child. Should boys and girls kiss or neck, and how far should they go? If they were certain that they really were lovable and loving, there would be little question. No adolescent child, however, can be completely sure of his acceptability, since this comes about only with the gradual process of growth. Short cuts to the assurance of being loved never work. By "short cuts" we mean sexual experimentation without experiencing at the same time the heightened self-esteem and security that come with enjoying friendliness, warmth and admiration from the partner. Sexual play alone leaves both partners dissatisfied with themselves, empty or perhaps depressed. Only the growing, maturing boy and girl can become fine friends, loyal, admiring, protective, fair and generous.

The sexual relationship should in no way jeopardize the health or happiness of another individual. Therefore, genital sexuality is confined to the security of marriage. This statement carries with it nothing prudish or mid-Victorian, but implies the essence of the highest morality among human beings. With this attitude, any intimate sexual relationship between two people would be based on a mature sense of responsibility toward each other. Only when the young man has grown sufficiently that his own happiness is concerned with the total welfare and security of his partner and child can he be considered mature and ready for love and the sexuality that goes with it. When a young girl is still so insecure about her feminine loveliness and capacity to love that to hold a boy she feels she must enter into promiscuous sexual intimacy, she needs to grow up more or, if necessary, to have some professional help.

What is the adolescent to do about the physiologic tension

created by the sexual hormones which now flood the body? To some extent this is drained off quite acceptably through dancing and moderate "petting." About masturbation, an age-old normal means of discharging sexual tension, there is much dubious folklore which is terrifying to insecure young people. According to scientific knowledge, the only unsatisfactory and emotionally disturbing aspect of masturbation is that relief of physiologic tension alone is not enough to make one happy. If a child is unhappy, if he finds it difficult to be friendly and feel loved, then masturbation may leave him more lonely, depressed and self-critical. If the depression and unhappiness become marked, then the child is obviously insecure in his total emotional adjustment and is projecting all his anxiety onto the problem of masturbation.

If, by the end of adolescence, inner security, with warmth and friendliness for both sexes, has developed, there need be little concern for the future healthy emotional adjustment of the boy or girl. Such young people can accept a generous, responsible attitude in marriage and grow steadily toward maturity together.

FAULTY ADJUSTMENTS

Since, in the lives of most people, relationships from birth to marriage are never completely free of misunderstandings, we turn to a consideration of some of the clinical evidences of faulty emotional adjustment in adolescence.

Neurosis

From descriptions of the earliest phases of emotional development, with which you are familiar, it is not difficult to see what makes for distorted personalities. When the distortion is not severe, we call it "neurosis." When the personality is so extensively involved that the individual becomes incapable of seeing the basic realities about him, we speak of his suffering from a "psychosis."

It has become clear through research that if fear or anxiety or hate or sexual impulse creates greater discomfort than the individual can bear, such impulses are pushed out of consciousness by a psychologic mechanism called "repression." The impulses continue to exist in the unconscious, however, and are always in danger of returning to consciousness should the repressive mechanism fail to work. If some frustration or fright of considerable magnitude were added to the individual already carrying a burden of repressed hostility, the repressive mechanism at this point might not be able to block all this from consciousness. If the person has a strong conscience, he cannot bear to let himself express so much hate or antisocial feeling directly. Another line of defense must therefore be brought into play. The repression partially gives way and a complicated psychologic twist occurs which lets the hate or the sexual impulse come out, not directly, but in some disguised form in which it remains acceptably hidden from the individual and others about him. These disguised expressions of his forbidden hostility or sexuality are symptoms of neurosis. The patient may suffer because of such symptoms, but not to the same degree that he would suffer from the fear and guilt which would result from giving way directly to the impulse which was unacceptable to his conscience.

What are some of these neurotic symptoms? Let us take a simple example. A young girl may be too embarrassed to face her sexual feelings. Every time a boy speaks to her she may blush violently. She is not aware that unconsciously she has fantasies of guilt about her sexual feelings, but the tell-tale somatic expression of her embarrassment appears. Most adolescent girls blush some, but gradually their anxiety about sexuality normally subsides and with it the blushing. If the young woman continues to find herself so uneasy that she cannot converse freely with men, she may need help.

In the psychiatric hospital population the occupational therapist will certainly encounter the hysterical adolescent girl or her counterpart in the boy. This is the girl often dressed and tinted for an older age or dressed in paradoxes. For instance, she may wear bobby sox with long earrings and much make up. She is seductive and exhibitionistic with men immediately — this is far less apparent when she meets women. On the other hand, the hysterical boys are seductive and winning with the women. Why are such girls so seductive with much hostility just below the surface? We always find in their background that the father has been seductive with his daughter, the mother usually condoning it. The mother may even foster this seductive air about the girl through all manner of suggestive remarks to the girl about men. The same kind and variable degrees of seductiveness go on between mothers and sons which account for the adolescent boy's seductive, veiled, hostile approach to women. Great hostility is close to the surface in all hysterical seductive patients because when the parent stimulated them, this generated anger, since the parental stimulation led only to frustration sexually. When the occupational therapist does not respond to the seduction the resentment at the thwarting may emerge at once, and this is natural. The therapist should not compound the damage done by the parents by adapting, as have the parents. The hysterical girl inappropriately stimulated to a hostile competition with the mother will always be easily angered by women. These patients with such seductive backgrounds require a very close understanding between psychiatrist and occupational therapist.

Most people at some time have experienced such terror that for a second they could not catch their breath. When this is carried further and becomes interlinked with some deep and frightening unconscious conflict, we call it "asthma." If buried terror or rage is constantly plaguing us, the blood pressure may gradually go up and stay at a high level. There have been many discussions of the relationship of stomach ulcers to unconscious longing for love (food), and such investigators have shown how the organs can react to emotional conflicts. These organ reactions to emotional conflicts are the concern of the entire medical profession today.

Chronic ulcerative colitis, with its gross emotional innerlay, is well known to all of you. What you are called upon to do with a neurotic adolescent with this disease, of course, depends first of all upon the psychiatrist's evaluation of the patient with his disease. Illustratively, let us consider a case of ulcerative colitis. The patient is very sick when a stage of remission is not present. I believe with Margolin that such patients, when an active phase of the disease is present, should not be burdened in any way. They all want to regress emotionally to a less burdensome, more childlike existence. This regression should be permitted and encouraged, but the patient concomitantly should be afforded unstinting emotional support. In a permissive setting such regression may proceed to an infantile stage. Occupational therapy with a disease in such an active phase is too burdensome, and requires too much productiveness from the patient. No effort should be made to push him in any way. When he begins to improve physiologically and the depression subsides, associated with evidences of his wishing to be more mature, then opportunities for occupational therapy may be offered with safety.

Another symptom of neurosis is withdrawal from people. For instance, a young girl, anxious since childhood because she thinks she is not loved, avoids awareness of this burdensome humiliation by withdrawing from social contracts. She dares not risk a further rebuff, for this might unleash to consciousness the early painful feelings. Certain personality traits may develop as neurotic symptoms. Coldness, withdrawal, extreme sensitiveness or shyness, rigidity of behavior, intolerance, submissiveness, meticulousness and many other character traits are known to be neurotic defenses which have developed as protection from awareness of early hurt, fear and hate, long since buried in the unconscious.

When the occupational therapist sees these shy, withdrawn adolescents, it becomes obvious that they are most uncomfortable in group situations. They prefer to work alone. Often the parents have been crowding them for years to be more outgoing, in spite of their insecurity. To crowd them to participate in group activities is to compound their burden. The withdrawal is a defense against insecurity and anxiety, and until the psychotherapist has resolved the sources of such tension the patient should go at his own pace. At times the psychiatrist will advise you to press the patient into the group. This may be because the psychiatrist wishes to mobilize more conscious anxiety in the patient. With such a procedure you may well encounter evidences of irritability and resentment in the patient which are therapeutically in order. A comment to the patient that you can observe this and yet not retaliate can constitute a therapeutic step for the patient.

One of the most common defensive adaptations in adolescents is that of the blasé behavior. Probably this is one of the most exasperating symptoms occupational therapists encounter. When you suggest work in which adolescents might achieve some gratification, you are met with indifference, boredom and patronizing glances or remarks. A child emotionally healthy and happy from early childhood has been working at jobs with the mother and father. The blasé, bored, unenthusiastic adolescents have had no such happy, productive experiences in their backgrounds and underneath there is little security or joy in working with you. It does no good to scold and resent them, because this is what they have experienced and have adapted to, with deaf ears. The occupational therapist would make more basic strides if she only chatted with such a child for a long time. These adolescents will never move until they begin to like you.

When the adolescent assumes the sullen, silent approach, then the worker really feels blocked. I have had sullen, blasé adolescents spend nine months to a year, hour after hour, in my office, saying little. If we realize the basic mistrust and accept the fact that this child will take infinite patience about the time necessary to build up confidence, we can settle down without irritation and with no sense of failure.

Many neurotic behavior reactions develop in people secondary to minor or major organic disease. The emotional problems of the child and adolescent poliomyelitic patient can assume major proportions, including loss of self-esteem, rage at the disability and the defective appearance, regression to a more dependent childlike leaning on others, with or without overt hostility, withdrawal from peers, depression with no urge or drive to sublimate or substitute new areas for achievement. The attitude may be "what's the use — I am finished." All these neurotic or depressive attitudes, if prolonged in the patient, are greatly augmented by the neurotic reactions of the parents. The disfigurements and handicaps caused by severe burns comprise a formidable psychotherapeutic task on any hospital service.

Absolute honesty and frankness are necessary if we are to enlist the confidence of these handicapped, disfigured adolescents. For instance, if they say, "I look awful," or "I look ugly," and they really do, the occupational therapist should admit the truth. If you admit that you recognize the true state of affairs, and yet can like the patient in spite of the defect, then he can begin to trust you. If you like a patient he feels it — you do not have to verbalize your positive feelings. Any patient will be able to detect whether or not you feel resentment toward him. If he irritates you by his behavior, admit it openly. Of course, if you have inner sources of resentment of your own, unrelated to the specific patient, then tell him, "You irritate me, but it is not simply you; it is partly my problem which I must work on." We psychotherapists must recurrently face such personal problems with our patients.

Psychosis

When a person is so overwhelmed by his fears and feelings that he loses insight into what is real, we call his illness a "psychosis." The psychotic person does not believe his fears or thoughts are irrational, and consequently he makes misinterpretations of everything; these are called "delusions" and "hallucinations." For example, he may be convinced that his physician or his brother is planning to kill him, and no argument will dissuade him from such a conviction. He may twist a harmless remark into what, to him alone, is absolute evidence of evil intention. Often these patients are so frightened that they trust no one.

The therapist would understand far more about how to respond to and deal with the schizophrenic adolescent if he knew more of the causation and evolution of the disorder. The group at the Mayo Clinic has no inclination to be dogmatic about the nature of such etiologic factors, but a large research group there recently has formulated some fairly definite impressions as to how this disease develops. We intensively studied 27 schizophrenic patients by means of collaborative psychotherapy — that is, concomitant treatment of the two parents as well as the patient. Our studies showed, first, that a majority of the patients had been subjected to overwhelming, parentally instigated trauma, and, second, that the intense hostility inherent in this trauma distorted the whole developing instinctual life of the child. In these families the common defenses were exaggerated projections, denial and conscious lying. The destructiveness toward the child consisted of assaults of a physical or psychologic nature. First were those cases in which parents interfered with normal ego differentiation. Second were discrete parental physical and psychologic assaults classified as murderous (choking), castrative (brutality and threats) and incestuous. Other trauma were parental intentions to drive the patient insane by many means and threats to the patient that he would go insane. Other threats that terrified children were that parents believed the child would become murderous. In all our cases, the destructiveness instigated by one parent had been condoned by the other parent. Therefore, the helpless, unprotected child had no alternative but to identify with the destructive parent, and take on all of these parental attitudes and fantasies about himself. Children identify to a greater or lesser extent with all facets of both parents. They cannot select only those aspects of the parents which appear healthy and safe. Therefore, all therapists dealing with these patients are also dealing with the destructive parents within the patients. These patients are terrified that the destructiveness in them will come out toward the therapists on whom they are dependent for help. It is to be hoped that therapists in all departments do not have such destructive wishes toward the patient. In spite of his delusional projections in which the patient at first sees the therapist as destructive, like the parent, the patient finally, after long treatment, comes to realize that the therapist is not behaving and feeling like the assaultive parent. When occupational therapists begin to realize that the patient is behaving like an exaggerated caricature of the parents' behavior, the therapists come to feel that the patient does not seem so strange and senseless. The sensitive schizophrenic patient senses immediately this altered feeling in all therapists, and reacts to this new reality of feeling that he is understood. Since our research led to greater understanding of the patients, it has been strikingly evident that young psychiatrists feel less strange with, and puzzled by, the patients, and in turn the patients respond to this. If you find the patient's delusions incomprehensible, you will still find that much of him makes sense to you as soon as you have heard his background. Before occupational therapists make their first contact with a schizophrenic patient, they should know his history, not simply his symptoms, so as to have a basic feeling of knowing the meaning of his present predicament.

In the case of depressed adolescents the occupational therapist should know that the patient is always too guilty about repressed intense hostility. Depending upon the depth of the hostility from consciousness, one's management of the patient varies. If the patient is deeply depressed, support and reassurance and the offering of simple tasks work best. In the case of hostility close to the surface, the psychiatrist may suggest that the occupational therapist should push more firmly, and if the patient appears angry, to tell the patient you realize he is irritated, that that is all right, but that, nevertheless, he should get on with his work.

Delinquency and Acting-Out

In addition to neurosis and psychosis, there is another great category of adolescent problems: the problem of the delinquent. By "delinquent behavior" we mean antisocial behavior such as stealing, fire-setting, vandalism, sexual promiscuity and truancy.

Such patients have conscience defects, so that they act-out when any inner tension begins to arise. They never have had the proper training and restrictions for the development of guilt in the area in which they act-out.

Mystery enveloped causation here until 15 years ago, when several of us began to study and treat the parents as intensively as the child, or even more so. Startling facts emerged in that research, and we never fail to find similar facts in every such instance that now comes into our hands. The facts are that one parent, or sometimes both, is unconsciously fostering and permitting continuation of the delinquent behavior. You are all familiar with the fact that parents achieve gratification from children's good behavior and successes. There are also parents who unconsciously enjoy satisfaction from children's delinquent behavior. In the case of the individual delinquent, I must emphasize that what is operating in the parents is unconscious, until by certain technics we bring it into the parents' conscious awareness.

Although we find that antisocial impulses are unconscious in these parents, nevertheless such trends are poorly inhibited and are close to breaking through into consciousness. These parental impulses emerge and are deflected by fostering the antisocial behavior in the child. Consciously, most parents are deeply concerned at the child's misguided behavior, but neither has any idea that he or she — the parent — actually is promoting it.

This brings us to the problem of one's individual conscience: that part of us which knows what society regards as right and wrong. How do we get our conscience? A child's conscience is not inherited but is developed, especially during the first six years of life, through imitation of the total behavior of parents. This imitation embraces the conscious and unconscious operations of the parents. To an equal extent, conscience develops from the parents' conscious and unconscious image of the child, and from their concepts and hope and fears for the child.

The individual learns to lie, steal, set fires, destroy and misbehave sexually by unconsciously copying the pace set by the parents.

There is not time here to discuss the details of how the destructive parents unconsciously foster such behavior, why only one child of five in a family is chosen to do the stealing. I have written extensively in many papers of these matters. Psychiatrists vary in how they handle such acting-out. I feel that the occupational therapist should take a stand with society on the matter and let no behavior of stealing or other antisocial acting-out go by without setting limits with the patient and telling him that such behavior will be discussed with his psychiatrist. It is then the responsibility of the psychiatrist to handle this in terms of the conscience defect. For instance, a child may have been made to feel very guilty about sibling rivalry, but nonetheless have been permitted to steal. Thus, until the stealing has come under control, whatever mounting anxiety there may be about unconscious sibling rivalry, is immediately drained off by resort to stealing. This is something with which the psychiatrist must deal.

SUMMARY

The need for an understanding of the problems of the normal adolescent is basic if we are to interpret the behavior of the neurotic, psychotic and delinquent child. I have delineated the prominent features in normal adolescence and have illustrated problems the occupational therapist may encounter in dealing with adolescents in the three major pathologic emotional disorders: neurosis, psychosis and delinquency.

REFERENCES

1. Joselyn, Irene M. *Psychosexual development of children.* New York: Family Service Association of America, 1953.
2. Johnson, Adelaide M., and Ross, Helen. Psychiatric interpretation of the growth process, part ii. Latency and adolescence. *J. Social Casework*, 30 (1949): 148–54.

28

SOME SUGGESTIONS FOR PRACTICE IN INFANT ADOPTIONS

With Barbara Kohlsaat

A fourth paper, written with Barbara Kohlsaat, addresses itself to the problems inherent in infant adoption. Dr. Johnson observed that a disproportionately large number of children brought to her for help were adopted children. She came to believe that adoptive parents were less restrained from projecting onto these children their own unresolved conflicts and antisocial impulses (conscious or unconscious). If the child acted out antisocially, the fault could readily be attributed to "bad genetic endowment." She also observed that behavioral problems in these children often followed closely on the revelation to the child of his illegitimate origins — i.e., he had "bad" parents or wasn't wanted. Either way, the child's sense of identity was threatened with "badness." With Miss Kohlsaat as senior author, the following article was published for social workers, hopefully to help prevent unnecessary failures and tragedies for adopted children and their foster parents.

Two fundamental conditions are necessary for the healthy emotional life of any child or adult who is influenced predominantly by our western culture. First, each person wants above all else to be sure that he is loved by his parents, natural

Reprinted with permission from *Journal of Social Casework* 35(1954): 91–99.

or adoptive. Second, since conscience is developed by identification with and incorporation of the moral parents, it is necessary that everyone be certain that his parents were good people of excellent character. Any degree of poverty or simplicity can be accepted, but children must believe their parents were decent, honest citizens. Antisocial acting out in children comes about through identification with antisocial sanctions in parental figures. Particularly pertinent here is sexual acting out by parents. Illegitimacy is of concern, not only because of sociologic prejudices, but because of a much deeper implication that is involved — that a child cannot make a normal solution of the oedipal conflict unless he is certain his mother is wholly the father's in fact. Thus, education of the public to a more tolerant attitude about illegitimacy is all to the good but this does not touch the oedipal implications for the child, which are primitively profound in our culture. In other words, the child or the adolescent cannot integrate healthily illegitimacy in his family. Personality traits and structure, including the conscience, are not inherited but evolve as environmental influences interact with the child's potentials.

This discussion is confined to children adopted in infancy. Older children frequently have had experience, in fact or by hearsay, with natural parents under circumstances in which the unhealthy image is already relatively well established. These older children constitute problems in psychiatric management not relevant to this paper; about such children a great deal of understanding is developing.

If the opening remarks are accepted, we now ask the question: How can infant adoptive practices be so facilitated as to ensure the child's having a satisfying image about his natural parents, an image of lovableness and decency, by our standards? To find the answers will involve scrutiny not only of what the prospective parents seem to be and will mean to a child, but also of what the social agency should or should not reveal to them about the baby's background. How can the social worker help the adoptive parents in dealing with the child's adoption, to ensure his basic image of security about his natural parents? Would it not be well, too, to reconsider the most appropriate age at which to tell a child of his adoption?

The last point will be considered first. For a number of years, progressive agencies have suggested that a child be told of his adoption early, some advocating that the word "adopted" be used with him as soon as he can talk. This has been suggested to avoid the child's hearing of his adoption outside the home. Acknowledging the possibility of such outside pressure, we always have questioned that much of anything can be understood by the child until he is old enough to be curious, to learn and to integrate the simple biology of birth. When the 3- to 4-year-old sees and hears of new babies, he asks where they come from. Given the answer that they grow inside their mothers, usually one's child then asks, "Did I grow inside you?" The answer from the adoptive parent is, "No, we had no baby and we saw you at a little baby nursery, loved you, and were so happy to get you."

Anyone with sensitivity can see now what the next question will be and this may frighten adoptive parents. It is the point at which they need careful help early in their relationship with the worker, and possibly later. That next question is, "If I grew inside my mother, why didn't she keep me?"

IMPORTANCE OF PARENTAL IMAGE

At this point it might be well to reemphasize certain facts that come to mind in evolving the basic thinking of good adoption practices. In general, the child develops outlines of character structure, especially in the area of conscience, like the parents' image of the child and like the child's image of the parents, interwoven. So children are not told that Great-grandfather embezzled money, that Aunt Ethel had an illegitimate baby, that Great-uncle Ned was a psychopath and deserted from the army. Indeed not, but, rather, the attempt is made to hold up the best of the family ideals to a child, and never is the child's personality likened to that of any of his faltering relatives. Because of the possibility of neurotic character traits in the adoptive parents, they and the child must be protected by keeping from them any knowledge about the child's background which they can use as a cudgel.

It is hardly necessary to discuss here the simple dynamic implications of what has just been said; but it is better to err through repetition than through obscurity. It is a clinical fact, confirmed over and over, that adults unconsciously use each other and their children to live out both their healthy and their poorly integrated impulses. Such transactions exist in every family; no one is self-acting.

A few examples will show what is meant. As we know, some people who cannot produce children, whether or not demonstrable organic disease is present, have deep neurotic feelings of inferiority about femininity and masculinity. Such people, therefore, may be hostilely envious of those who can bear children. Is it surprising, then, that an adoptive mother may be hostilely envious of the baby's natural mother, whether the natural mother was married or not? This conclusion seems elementary to anyone who spends a moment thinking about it. It is not difficult to anticipate that the adoptive mother's hostile envy would come easily to the surface on provocation by the child and, with it, a wish to depreciate the woman who could bear a child. Ten-year-old Anne, say, becomes angry over some issue and says to her adoptive mother, "You are mean to me. My own mother would have loved me more. I wish I had my own mother."

Here is a tailor-made opportunity for the envious woman, in word or in tone, to depreciate the child's natural mother, which would be devastating. Also, adoptive parents are heading for disaster if they have a self-righteous need to feel that they gave the child a "wonderful break," and that the child should know how much more they are doing for him than his natural parents ever would have done. Any such hostile attack on the child who is being naughty at the moment will be a frightful boomerang, only driving the child further away. The normal adoptive mother, who really feels sorry for the unmarried young mother, is the mother who will regard herself as the fortunate woman and will not depreciate the child's own past.

Most children, when angry momentarily, wish they had a different set of parents, but in a normal family they do not remain fixed in such fantasies. Adopted children, likewise, remain bound to fantasies of how wonderful their own parents might have been only when the adoptive parents neurotically drive them to such a pitch.

Any unfavorable criticism, in tone or word, of the child's parents, especially if it has to do with social opprobrium, is devastating. The child immediately feels shame and humiliation and, of course, hates both his natural mother and his adoptive mother who precipitated the humiliation. An adolescent boy or girl has a need to believe that his natural mother or father never acted out antisocially. Adolescent boys and girls are more likely to hold themselves in line sexually when they sense in their parents mutual esteem and protective respect toward each other. Through identification with such parents, adolescents come to treat persons of the opposite sex with similar generosity and kindliness. If they hear of serious disrespect or antisocial acting out on the part of parents, their own sense of security is shaken; they hostilely identify with such parents and may act out similarly, their sexuality fused with sadomasochism. In other words, the girl feels, "I am so ashamed of my mother's affairs, and therefore so angry, that I don't care what I do." The boy feels, "Women are not to be trusted, I hate them all and will use them as I wish." This applies to children with adoptive parents as well as to those who remain with their real parents. What they will hostilely do sexually if they hear of antisocial sexual behavior in their parents is highly predictable.

When a prospective adoptive mother tells us of her fantasy that her child may get into sexual trouble because of "heredity," we have to conclude that she is not yet ready to adopt a child. Children tend to become what parents consciously and unconsciously fantasy they will become as far as general character structure goes. This declaration is based on clinical experiences and not on supposition. We interviewed a woman recently who came to us because she hated her 5-year-old daughter. This patient said, "The child is a lovely child and it is all my problem."

It seems that this woman had been adopted at the age of four years and, from innuendo on the part of her adoptive mother, had gathered the impression that her own parents were "no good." After a number of years, a well-intentioned priest had assisted the patient to find her family, and when she had seen them, she came to realize that her mother and older sister were, in fact, "promiscuous sluts" and her father "a bum." It is interesting that the patient never had dared to go to see what her parents were like until she had been safely married to a warm, stable man. Her repressed rage, which she felt toward her natural and her adoptive mother, returned and was displaced onto her little daughter. This patient is to be treated.

Some agencies have a questionable practice of making it possible for an adopted child to come to them at the age of 16 or 18 years to learn the facts of his background. For the protection of the child *and* of the adoptive parents, legislation should forbid the giving of such information to the child. Knowledge of unfortunate or illicit matters may jolt an 18-year-old greatly; a previously adequate self-esteem may be seriously jeopardized.

REVISING AGENCY PRACTICES

If the child adopted in infancy is to be given an unequivocally reassuring concept of his natural parents' love for him, if he is to gain the impression that they were fine citizens — and by this time we have sufficiently indicated that we believe both to be fundamental — how are social agencies to handle the problem with integrity? Assuming that the current and potential health of the baby has been thoroughly evaluated by responsible medical consultants, the agency should take the responsibility of withholding, both from the child and the adoptive parents, all facts that experience has shown it to be dangerous to reveal. Secure in the knowledge that personality traits and conscience are *not* inherited, an agency can and should take the firm position that no personal information is pertinent to the baby's future development. An agency then can withhold the fact that emotional instability had been evident in the baby's forebears and assure the adoptive parents that the baby will develop well emotionally if conditions remain fairly comfortable in the home.

The agency that investigates prospective parents, of course, will encounter very anxious, narcissistic, and unconsciously sadistic parents who demand knowledge of the child's past. Social workers know already the meaning of such concern, and we do not need to re-emphasize that such conditions constitute psychiatric problems. It does, however, seem necessary for us to offer some avenue out of the dilemma of outright rejection of such parents. Even greater care must be taken with overly compliant parents who operate submissively and masochistically, for they may accept all too willingly the withholding of information by the worker. Masochism is always fused with equal quantities of unconscious sadism; in time, the latter recurrently emerges, and, in circumstances here under consideration, would be directed toward the adopted child.

Now, to return to the question that the child addressed to his adoptive mother: "Why didn't my mother keep me?" If the adoptive mother answers, "She could not take care of you," the child says or thinks, "Why? Didn't she like me?" That is, he will say it unless he is intimidated by the anxiety he senses in the adoptive mother. At the age of 3½ years, he may not know of death, but a year later he may ask if his own mother died. What can the adoptive parent say about the reasons for the natural parents not keeping the baby? Here we shall merely state that adoptive parents who are presumed to be normal can be helped to think (and feel) through, ahead of time, what they will answer when the child asks his questions. That is, if the adoptive parents are comfortable, they may realize that they would say to the child: "We know you must have had good parents who loved you because you were a dear baby. We have no idea what happened but it must have been some very sad thing and there must have been no relatives who could help out; so the ladies and doctors at the nursery were only too happy to have you. It must have been something like that because one could not help loving you. That will never happen to you again though, because we have lots of aunts and uncles and grandparents who are well and love you as well as Daddy and I do." Interviews with very neurotic adoptive parents and with more normal parents will be presented later, in which the outcome of such a course will be evident.

Before we present this material, however, we should like to consider the feelings of the social worker. In any relatively large adoptive agency, the worker who must deal directly with the adoptive parents should be placed on firm ground. This could be accomplished if all confidential background material were cleared through a few selected administrative supervisors and consultants who certified to the good health of a baby. There would be no reason then for the background material to be passed on to the worker. The worker's attitude could be, "I know this to be a fine baby because my investigating chief and consultants have so agreed; that is enough for me." In a small adoptive agency it would, of course, be more difficult to work out and maintain such levels of confidential investigative work, but this should be the aim nevertheless.

Healthy adoptive parents certainly would tend to identify with the social worker's conviction that everything had been done to make sure that the baby was potentially ready for growth in a stable environment. Undoubtedly, as workers gain experience they are freer to deal with adoptive parents regardless of their own knowledge of a child's past. Like physicians, who are schooled in withholding material that cannot be integrated by patients and families, social workers should be able to handle such situations.

AN AID IN EVALUATING PROSPECTIVE PARENTS

Some readers, knowing the difficulties inherent in casework with adoptive applicants, will doubtless speculate about the ways these ideas can be translated into practice. How will the caseworker know when a couple is sufficiently mature to function well as adoptive parents? One thing is clear: The caseworker cannot tell adoptive parents only that a child is healthy and then assume a "take it or leave it" attitude, in the hope that those who would be uncomfortable under such an arrangement will withdraw their applications. Only hostilely aggressive applicants are likely to do this, and if they did, still the healthy would not be separated from the submissive but resentful applicants. The effect of their masochism, on the child, has been explained.

The necessary sorting out will depend on three things: (1) acceptance by the adoption worker, without undue anxiety and conflict, of the agency's position that background data concerning the baby should be withheld from adoptive parents; (2) the securing of a really critical history of each prospective parent; (3) a type of interviewing that draws out from the applicant attitudes and fantasies that leave no doubt that what is expressed are his real feelings and intentions and not statements designed, consciously or unconsciously, to win the caseworker's approval and to result, therefore, in placement of the child.

A word about the content of these personal histories: Information should be secured concerning, and particular attention should be paid to, both past and current interpersonal relationships. This is needed not only to assist in predicting the individual's capacity for parenthood, but also in order that the relationship to the worker can be observed in the light of other significant relationships. Thus, it can be determined that one is not getting a false picture because of the urgent wish of the adoptive parent to secure a child. Let it be assumed, on the one hand, that an applicant appears completely to agree with the agency's thought and method; that the applicant makes no demands counter to the agency's position. Let it be assumed, on the other hand, that the personal history reveals that the applicant is constantly imposed upon by others, and when asked what he does about it, says, "I don't say anything; it wouldn't do any good."

Immediately the suspicion would arise that the applicant's attitude toward the worker is the same. The worker, then, must try to find out how the applicant really feels.

Interviewing, then, must be designed to draw out as purely

as possible the individual's feelings, fantasies, and associations. The opinions and attitudes of the caseworker must remain largely undisclosed, so that what is elicited in no way reflects these attitudes. This calls for patience, lack of anxiety, the capacity for conscious, silent listening, and the ability to ask unloaded questions which will, nevertheless, stimulate association. Such an approach undoubtedly will cause the development of transference attitudes, for which the worker must watch and with which the worker must deal.

The process is perhaps more easily illustrated than described. We shall present two illustrative interviews. In one, the B family has difficulty in accepting the agency's position. In the other, the S family shows healthy responses to the application situation.

THE B FAMILY

Mr. B was the oldest of four children and he had been given a great deal of responsibility for the care of his siblings because his mother had been ill frequently. His father's work had taken him away from home much of the time. This father had been a rather severe person, who had discouraged dependency, fear, or display of feeling. Mrs. B was the only child of a domineering mother who continued, even after her daughter's marriage, to interfere with her life. In this, the mother encountered little opposition from Mrs. B. The worker had several interviews with the B's and believed that, since they had not initiated any discussion about what they would tell a child, the worker would need to initiate it. The worker's report follows:

Mr. and Mrs. B were seen together at the office. I had not stated any definite reason for asking them to come in and I noted that they were tense. After a few minutes in which inconsequential subjects were introduced by them, I said that I was interested that they had not yet said anything about the problem presented by questions that a child would ask about himself. Mrs. B quickly and rather defensively answered that she knew the agency would not give them any background information about a child, and she thought she would just do the best she could when the time came. She followed this with a remark that was designed to change the subject. Mr. B was sitting quietly, playing with his watch chain. No feeling was revealed by his facial expression.

I returned to my question, saying that it can be pretty tough to meet such situations without thinking them through ahead of time, and I suggested that we imagine it now. Tears came to Mrs. B's eyes as she picked nervously at her handkerchief. Suddenly, and with strong feeling, Mr. B said that he had been trying to go along with us because his wife wanted a baby so badly, but he couldn't see, "for the life of him," why we thought children shouldn't know the truth about themselves. When I asked him why he thought they should, he answered in a very rigid way that he knew full well that most adopted children are illegitimate and so did everybody else and he figured a child might as well know it first as last. "If there's one thing my father beat into my head, it's that you'll never get along in this world if you can't face up to the facts of life!"

By this time, Mrs. B was crying openly, and Mr. B looked uncomfortable after his outburst. I picked up Mr. B's remark about having kept quiet because his wife wanted a baby so badly and said I wondered how he felt about it. He said that he wanted one too, but that it was even more important to her because he had to be away from home a lot. I then asked Mr. B if he could ever remember a time when he had been told a "fact of life" that had been hard to take. He answered that he didn't think so, that, for instance, it had helped him to have his father tell him as a child that his mother was very delicate and had to be protected so she wouldn't get too upset and get sick. That way he could keep the other children quiet. I said: "Some children would be frightened to be told that and they'd wish their mothers were stronger, so that they didn't have to do so much of the mothering themselves."

Mr. B looked rather stunned by this remark and said, quite defensively, but without so much belligerence, that that's the way things were and it was no use wishing they were different. I agreed that that was the way things had been and nobody could help it, but I said that it must have been hard for him. He softened considerably at this and said that he loved children a lot but that sometimes he had not minded too much that he and his wife hadn't had any because he had got "such a snootful" of looking after them from the time he was a child until his marriage.

Mrs. B became very anxious when her husband said this and tried to smooth things over. When I suggested that perhaps they needed to talk things over between themselves a little more before going on with their application, Mrs. B began again to cry. She said that she just couldn't face her mother's questions if that were to happen; that it had been bad enough when Mrs. B had had to admit to her mother her inability to have a baby of her own. I said that I wondered if she couldn't tell her mother that she and Mr. B were not being refused as parents but that they themselves had decided to give the matter some more thought. Mrs. B looked rather helpless at this idea but her husband took over and assured her that he wouldn't mind saying it. He then turned back to me and said that the only thing that worried him was what to do if they couldn't come to some agreement about it. I told him that sometimes, in the process of applying for a child, people came to feel that they had had experiences as children which made it hard to decide, and that they got some help with these feelings before going on with their applications. The B's seemed interested in discussing this idea more fully and finally they left, planning to call and let me know what they decided. I told them I would want them to, and that I would be glad to see them again when they felt they might wish an opportunity for further discussion.

A week later Mr. B said by telephone that Mrs. B and he had talked to their minister about their problem since they had seen me and, as a result, they had decided to see Dr. M [a psychiatrist] to get some help in working things out. Mr. B said that both he and his wife felt much better; they wanted to be assured that we would hold their application until they knew definitely what they wished to do. I told him that we would.

THE S FAMILY

The S's are a couple in their twenties, who cannot have children of their own because of proved organic disease in Mrs. S.

Both have been able to express their disappointment, frustration, and sorrow over this disability. Full personal histories have been taken and Mr. and Mrs. S have been evaluated as being essentially free of any pathological emotional condition. The worker's account of an interview with the S's follows:

Mr. and Mrs. S were seen in the office. They had come to sign permission for me to get a report from their physician. I wanted to determine what they were thinking, so I asked what they would like to discuss this time. Mr. S said that they had been thinking about the questions a child would ask concerning where babies come from.

Mrs. S then commented that it seemed to her that the child would surely ask at this time if he grew in *her* tummy. I nodded to indicate that I thought so too, but otherwise remained silent, to see what they would do with this thought. Mrs. S went on to say that she would explain that she wasn't able to grow babies in her tummy and that they had asked me to help them get a baby. I still remained silent.

Mr. S then broke in to say he would think the next question might easily be concerning why the mother didn't keep him. I asked, "What would you say?" Both Mr. and Mrs. S sat without talking for several minutes; both looked worried and as though they were thinking hard. I felt I could let their silence continue because they were not waiting for me but were aware only of their own struggle. Mr. S finally said that this was "sure some hump to get over" because he knew that most adopted children are illegitimate. A somewhat more relaxed expression now came into Mrs. S's face. She said she was remembering a time when she was about 15 and talking with her mother about a child they knew who was illegitimate. She could remember that her mother had said that it was sad but that this in no way altered her feelings toward the child. Mr. S broke in to ask his wife if she remembered Mary J whom they had both known in high school. They both recalled very sympathetically what a "tough break" she had had and wondered what had happened to her and her baby. Mrs. S then brought herself back to the present with a comment about needing to think about *their* baby. She knew what she wanted to do for her child but, also, that it wasn't going to be easy. They both settled down in their chairs as though they had hard work ahead of them and slowly began to spell out their thoughts.

Mr. S said that in the first place he and his wife didn't know, but he thought that he would want first to say that he was sure the child's mother and father were nice people who loved him very much; maybe he would go on to say that the child had been a lovely, special baby and that they were lucky he could come to be their baby because there were lots of people who would have liked to have had him.

Feeling that they were on the right track, I put in a remark here about sometime getting over the idea that babies are special and cannot be bought like dolls at a store. The S's noted this, and then Mrs. S said she wondered how many questions would be asked at one time, whether to go ahead and tell a lot at once or wait for further questions from the child. I felt that the S's recent experience with children was so limited that they could not be expected to know this, so I told them that if questions are answered without anxiety or evasion, and if no more are asked, it is safe to assume that the child has asked all he wants to know at that time. The whole story could come out in a considerable number of instalments and might also need to be repeated several times.

I suggested that for the purpose of discussion we pretend it *was* the next time. What did they suppose might be the next question? Mrs. S said she thought the child again would want to know why his mother and daddy didn't keep him. She thought that the best thing would be first to say they didn't know. She supposed that this wouldn't be enough but they would wait for further indications of his wanting to know more, then or later. If the child again asked why they couldn't keep him, she would repeat that all she knew was that he was a lovely baby and ask if he would like to imagine about what could have happened that prevented his mother and daddy from keeping him. I asked what she would imagine. She thought she would picture with him that maybe his mother and daddy died or were sick or some other sad thing and maybe there weren't any uncles or aunts or grandparents who could help out, so the worker had found a new mother and daddy for him. I wondered how they would feel about imagining things this way. Mr. S answered that he had been brought up not to lie and he would not want to; so he would be glad not to be loaded down with information that would put him in a spot.

We spent the rest of the interview talking about this in a little more detail. I did not bring up the questions that might come again in adolescence or early adulthood, when the child might learn about illegitimacy. Since these questions seemed not yet to have occurred to the S's, I would rather wait to see how and when such questions might come.

COMMENT

The technique of deferring some of the discussion with adoptive parents carries with it, of necessity, the responsibility on the part of the agency to encourage the return of these parents to the agency in the child pre-adolescent period. Undoubtedly, further questions about the coming adolescent phase will have occurred to the parents. These matters could be better worked through before adolescence. The worker could merely indicate to the parents that, since adolescence brings its own particular problems, it would be well for them to return when the child reached the age of 9 or 10 years. Many of the parents would handle the adolescent period well and without help, but we believe it is the agency's responsibility to leave every avenue open for discussion. The adopted child who has had a healthy, satisfying relationship with his adoptive parents and who always has been allowed to respect his natural parents will be only momentarily concerned by the possibility of his being illegitimate when he first becomes aware of such a thing in society. Should the child raise the question, adoptive parents who have generously reared a child would, with complete ease, respond that the subject was something with which they had not concerned themselves in the slightest.

Comment so far has not been made with respect to the intensity and length of an adoption study conducted in the manner we have suggested. The essence of the method is that we wait for, and help, the applicant to verbalize his own feelings. At the same time that we are uncovering conflict material, we threaten the defenses as little as possible. If we work in this way, the problems of the adoptive parent will be clarified between him and the worker. The conflicts will be identified as the parents', and can be used by the worker in assisting parents to a helpful decision. It will not be necessary to subject the parents to the blow of an unexplained and unexplainable rejection. This technique of interviewing cannot be applied under pressure or by formula. It will in all probability take more time and require more interviews than an approach in which the worker is more active and directive and of which the result is more likely to be filled with artifacts.

In interviewing prospective parents there is no sidestepping the fact that the social worker is engaged in psychotherapy. Any psychotherapy that is valid must be genetic and dynamic. In other words, if a therapist is always alert to handling responses dynamically, neither the worker nor the patient ever will get into a corner from which there is no escape. This constitutes some of the most complicated and hazardous psychotherapy undertaken by any social worker. To carry it on without the continuous, dynamic supervision of a psychiatrist would be equivalent to undertaking psychotherapy of any patient without the safeguards demanded by law and by medical ethics in this country. This matter is discussed fully in a recent publication. (1)

It may be well, for a moment, to focus attention on Mr. B's assertion that children should face all the facts of life. This parent's unconscious resentment at having been so burdened as a child drove him to a revenge that he rationalized as a realistic philosophy for living — as "honesty and frankness." Every physician repeatedly faces a parallel problem. He has cases whose outcome worries him greatly. If he thinks out loud, in the presence of relatives, about all the possible dire complications, he may be immature, anxious, perhaps sadistic, and in dread of the consequences of whatever decision he makes. A physician can imagine all kinds of hazardous complications but if he is mature he does not burden the relatives with *all* this knowledge. If there is grave danger, of course he prepares the family for it, but if he were to let the family in on all the worries, the members of the family would need care themselves. Maturity carries with it the obligation to withhold certain knowledge that might be devastating if revealed.

SUGGESTIONS FOR PRACTICE

We believe two things are essential to a child's healthy solution of his oedipal and pre-oedipal emotional life: (1) He should have a sense of being loved, with all the security implicit in such love. (2) He should believe in the simple decency (good citizenship) of his natural parents. If he is illegitimate, he is much more deeply affected by such a sociological problem as illegitimacy than he would be otherwise.

We believe that, to ensure achievement of the considerations just mentioned in relation to an adopted infant, two further conditions should be met: (1) Any history not pertinent to the baby's future development should be withheld from the adoptive parents. (2) The thinking implied in taking such a position with prospective adoptive parents must be worked through dynamically so that one can be assured that the stand taken is thoroughly integrated.

We suggest that the foregoing fundamental considerations can be put into effect by mature caseworkers who are carrying out infant adoption practices, if: (1) The agencies re-examine issues relevant to the physical and emotional health of a baby. (2) The responsibility for evaluation of the child is delegated to persons on administrative and consultative levels who do not work directly with the adoptive parents. (3) The worker dealing immediately with the adoptive parents is given only the knowledge of the baby's potential for good health.

REFERENCE

1. Johnson, Adelaide M. Collaborative psychotherapy: team setting. In *Psychoanalysis and social work*, ed. Marcel Heiman, pp. 79–108. New York: International Universities Press, 1953. (Reprinted above, p. 245.)

BIBLIOGRAPHY OF WRITINGS BY ADELAIDE JOHNSON

Auto-transplantation of the adrenal cortex. *American Journal of Physiology* 97 (1931): 392–95. (With Victor Johnson.)

Secondary rise in blood pressure following peripheral splanchnic nerve stimulation. *American Journal of Physiology* 99 (1931): 160–66. (With Victor Johnson.)

Studies in the physiological action of glycerol on the animal organism. *American Journal of Physiology*. 103 (1933): 517–34. (With A. J. Carlson and Victor Johnson.)

Application of personality study to patients. In *Contributions dedicated to Dr. Aldolph Meyer*, pp. 61–64. Baltimore: Johns Hopkins Press, 1938. (With Henry M. Fox and Paul Lemkau.)

Vertigo as the primary manifestation in anxiety neurosis. *Illinois Medical Journal* 77 (1940): 86–89.

School phobia. *American Journal of Orthopsychiatry* 11 (1941): 702–11. (With E. Falstein, S. Szurek, and M. Svendsen.)

Collaborative psychiatric therapy of parent-child problems. *American Journal of Orthopsychiatry* 12 (1942): 511–16. (With S. Szurek and E. Falstein.)

Evaluation of therapeutic results in psychotherapy. *Proceedings, second brief psychotherapy council discussion*, p. 15. Chicago Institute for Psychoanalysis, January 1944.

Analysis of a disturbed adolescent girl and collaborative psychiatric treatment of the mother. *American Journal of Orthopsychiatry* 14 (1944): 195–203. (With Dora Fishback.)

Emergency psychotherapy of pathologically severe feeding disturbances in children. *Proceedings, second brief psychotherapy council discussion*, p. 15. Chicago Institute for Psychoanalysis, January 1944.

Brief psychotherapy in bronchial asthma. *Proceedings, second brief psychotherapy council*, pp. 14–21. Chicago Institute for Psychoanalysis, January 1944. (With Thomas French.)

The growing science of casework. *Journal of Social Casework* 27 (1946): 273–78. (With Helen Ross.)

A case of migraine. *Proceedings, third brief psychotherapy council*, pp. 69–120, including discussion. Chicago Institute for Psychoanalysis, October 1946.

Psychoanalytic Psychiatry. *Proceedings, conference on science*, pp. 109–16. Rockford College, Rockford, Illinois, February 21–23, 1947.

Preliminary report on a psychosomatic study of rheumatoid arthritis. *Psychosomatic Medicine* 9 (1947): 295–300. (With Franz Alexander and Louis B. Shapiro.)

Psychiatric interpretation of the growth process, part I. The earliest years. *Journal of Social Casework* 30 (1949): 87–92. (With Helen Ross.)

Psychiatric interpretation of the growth process, part II. Latency and adolescence. *Journal of Social Casework* 30 (1949): 148–54. (With Helen Ross.)

Variations in goal and technique. In *Psychoanalytic therapy*, ed. Franz Alexander and Thomas French, pp. 291–324. New York: Ronald Press, 1946.

Psychotherapy in bronchial asthma. In *Studies in psychosomatic medicine*, ed. Franz Alexander and Thomas French, pp. 249–58. New York: Ronald Press, 1948.

Psychosomatic study of rheumatoid arthritis. In *Studies in psychosomatic medicine*, ed. Franz Alexander and Thomas French, pp. 489–98. New York: Ronald Press, 1948. (With Franz Alexander and Louis B. Shapiro.)

Migraine. In *Studies in psychosomatic medicine*, ed. Franz Alexander and Thomas French, pp. 522–43. New York: Ronald Press, 1948.

Sanctions for superego lacunae of adolescents. *Searchlights on delinquency*, ed. K. R. Eissler, pp. 225–45. New York: International Universities Press, 1949.

A contribution to the treatment of super-ego defects. *Journal of Social Casework* 21 (1950): 135–38.

Some etiological aspects of represssion, guilt and hostility. Chicago

Psychoanalytic Society, September 27, 1949. *Psychoanalytic Quarterly* 20 (1951): 511–27.

Treatment of acute painful phantom limb. *Proceedings of the staff meetings of the Mayo Clinic* 27 (1952): 110–18. Discussion by Adelaide Johnson of paper by L. C. Kolb, L. M. Frank, and E. Jane Watson.

The genesis of antisocial acting out in children and adults. *Psychoanalytic Quarterly* 21 (1952): 323–43. (With S. A. Szurek.)

Collaborative psychotherapy: team setting. In *Psychoanalysis and social work*, ed. Marcel Heiman, pp. 79–108. New York: International Universities Press, 1953.

Psychoanalytic therapy. In *Twenty years of psychoanalysis*, ed. Franz Alexander and Helen Ross, pp. 242–57. New York: W. W. Norton and Company, 1953.

The essentials of psychotherapy as viewed by the psychoanalyst. Scientific proceedings, American Psychoanalytic Association. New York Meetings, December, 1952. *Journal of the American Psychoanalytic Association* 1 (1953): 550–61.

Factors in the etiology of fixations and symptom choice. Chicago Psychoanalytic Society, October 28, 1952. *Psychoanalytic Quarterly* 22 (1953): 475–96.

Some suggestions for practice in infant adoptions. *Journal of Social Casework* 35 (1954): 91–99. (With Barbara Kohlsaat.)

Etiology of antisocial behavior in delinquents and psychopaths. *Journal of the American Medical Association* 154 (1954): 814–17. (With S. A. Szurek.)

Psychoanalysis and psychotherapy: dynamic criteria for treatment choice. Scientific proceedings, American Psychoanalytic Association, New York Meetings, December, 1953. *Journal of the American Psychoanalytic Association* 2 (1954): 346–50.

Specific factors determining antisocial acting out. Symposium: Antisocial Acting Out. American Orthopsychiatric Association, New York, March, 1954. *American Journal of Orthopsychiatry* 24 (1954): 668–84. (With M. E. Giffin and E. M. Litin.)

The emotionally disturbed child — signs, symptoms and causative factors — psychiatrist's point of view. *Proceedings, fourth annual conference on crippled children, Roanoke, Virginia*, pp. 7–18, March 1955.

Parental sanction of delinquency. *Focus* 34 (1955): 44–49. (Journal of the National Probation and Parole Association). (With S. A. Szurek.)

Individual antisocial behavior. Joint meeting, Sections of Pediatrics and of Nervous and Mental Diseases, American Medical Association, San Francisco, June 25, 1954. *American Medical Association Journal of Diseases of Children* 89 (1955): 472–75.

Psychotherapy of a mother and daughter with a problem of separation anxiety. *Proceedings of the Staff Meetings of the Mayo Clinic* 30 (1955): 141–48. (With D. B. Robinson and G. M. Duncan.)

A specific factor in symptom choice. *Proceedings of the Staff Meetings of the Mayo Clinic* 30 (1955): 227–43. (With S. H. Frazier, Jr., Mary H. Faubion, and Mary E. Giffin.)

Etiology and therapy of overt homosexuality. American Psychoanalytic Association, New York, December 3, 1953. *Psychoanalytic Quarterly* 24 (1955): 506–15. (With L. C. Kolb.)

Book review of *Psychoanalysis: practical and research aspects*, by Willi Hoffer (Baltimore: Williams & Wilkins Company, 1955). *Psychoanalytic Quarterly* 24 (1955): 573–74.

Parental permissiveness and fostering in child rearing and their relationship to juvenile delinquency. *Proceedings of the Staff Meetings of the Mayo Clinic* 30 (1955): 557–65. (With Edmund C. Burke.)

Parental influence in unusual sexual behavior in children. American Psychoanalytic Association, New York, December 4, 1953. *Psychoanalytic Quarterly* 25 (1956): 37–55. (With E. M. Litin and M. E. Giffin.)

Book review of *Maternal dependency and schizophrenia*, by Joseph Abrahams and Edith Varon (New York: International Universities Press, 1953). *Psychoanalytic Quarterly* 24 (1955): 300–2.

Book review of *Psychosomatic case book*, by Roy R. Grinker and Fred Robbins (New York: The Blakiston Company, 1954). *Psychoanalytic Quarterly* 24 (1955): 304–6.

Recurrent urinary retention due to emotional factors. *Psychosomatic Medicine* 18 (1956): 77–80. (With George E. Williams.)

Factors in the growth and development of the psychotherapist. Panel discussion, Adelaide Johnson, Chairman, Scientific Proceedings, American Psychoanalytic Association, Atlantic City Meetings, May, 1955. *Journal of the American Psychoanalytic Association* 4 (1956): 170–75.

Role of the dynamic psychiatrist in a clinic setting. I. Recognition of dynamic factors in the patient-doctor relationship. *Proceedings of the Staff Meetings of the Mayo Clinic* 31 (1956): 145–50. (With S. H. Frazier and M. E. Giffin.)

The emotionally disturbed child. Dedication, Children's Psychiatric Unit, Ann Arbor, Michigan, February 11, 1956. *University of Michigan Medical Bulletin* 22 (1956): 98–109.

Studies in schizophrenia at the Mayo Clinic. I. Significance of exogenous traumata in the genesis of schizophrenia. *Psychiatry* 19 (1956): 137–42. (With P. G. S. Beckett, D. B. Robinson, S. H. Frazier, Jr., R. M. Steinhilber, G. M. Duncan, H. R. Estes, E. M. Litin, R. T. Grattan, W. L. Lorton, and George E. Williams.)

Studies in schizophrenia at the Mayo Clinic. II. Observations on ego functions in schizophrenia. *Psychiatry* 19 (1956): 143–48. (With M. E. Giffin, E. Jane Watson, and P. G. S. Beckett.)

Causation of juvenile delinquency. American Academy of Pediatrics, Chicago, 1955. *Pediatrics* 17 (1956): 934–39.

Role of the dynamic psychiatrist in a clinic setting. II. Criteria for the selection of patients for referral to the section of psychiatry. *Proceedings of the Staff Meetings of the Mayo Clinic* 31 (1956): 400–6. (With M. E. Giffin and S. H. Frazier, Jr.)

Book review of *The yearbook of psychoanalysis*, vol. 10, ed. Sandor Lorand, M.D. (New York: International Universities Press, 1955). *Psychoanalytic Quarterly* 25 (1956): 263 65.

Prevention and treatment of juvenile delinquency. Governor's Conference on Juvenile Deliquency, University of Maryland, College Park, Maryland, September 10, 11, 12, 1956. *Proceedings of Governor's Conference*, p. 30.

Separation Anxiety. *American Journal of Psychotherapy* 10 (1956): 682–95. (With H. R. Estes and C. H. Haylett.)

Psychotherapy in facial disfigurement. *Proceedings of the Staff Meetings of the Mayo Clinic* 31 (1956): 537–44. (With E. J. Watson.)

Portrait of a nurse. *Nursing World* 130 (1956): 12–14.

Internist's role in treatment of anorexia nervosa. *Proceedings of the*

Staff Meetings of the Mayo Clinic 32 (1957): 171–82. (With M. E. Giffin, S. H. Frazier, D. B. Robinson.)

Some applications of psychoanalytic insights to the socialization of children. *American Journal of Orthopsychiatry* 27 (1957): 462–74. (With M. E. Giffin.)

The adolescent and his problems. *American Journal of Occupational Therapy* 11 (1957): 255–61.

The sexual deviant (sexual psychopath): causes, treatment, and prevention. *Journal of the American Medical Association* 164 (1957): 1559–65. (With D. B. Robinson.)

The disturbed child. *Postgraduate Medicine* 22 (1957): 220–32. (With M. E. Giffin.)

Depth electrographic recording of a seizure during a structured interview. *Psychosomatic Medicine* 19 (1957): 353–62. (With U. C. Groethuysen, D. B. Robinson, C. H. Haylett, and H. E. Estes.)

Emotional significance of acquired physical disfigurement in children. *American Journal of Orthopsychiatry* 28 (1958): 85–97. (With E. J. Watson.)

Self-destructive factor in the medical patient. *Journal of Michigan State Medical Society* 57 (1958): 400–3. (With S. H. Frazier.)

The incest barrier. *Psychoanalytic Quarterly* 27 (1958): 485–500. (With M. J. Barry, Jr.)

Etiological factors in first-degree murder. *Journal of the American Medical Association* 168 (1958): 1755–58. (With G. M. Duncan, S. H. Frazier, E. M. Litin, and A. J. Barron.)

Ego distortions: some modifications in therapeutic technic. *American Journal of Psychotherapy* 13 (1959): 809–25. (With M. J. Barry, Jr., and D. B. Robinson.)

Juvenile delinquency. In *American Handbook of Psychiatry*, ed. Silvano Arieti, pp. 840–56. New York: Basic Books, 1959.

Transmission of superego defects in the family. In *A Modern Introduction to the Family*, ed. Norman W. Bell and Ezra F. Vogel, pp. 623–35. Glencoe, Ill.: Free Press, 1960.

INDEX

Abdominal pain: in urinary retention, 102

Acting out, 145–54; adolescent, in treatment, 296; child as scapegoat, 146–47; defined, 215; of patient against patient, 288; offsetting of, 125; parental response to, 117; sexual, in adolescent, 173–79; of therapist, 320–21, 322

Adolescence: conservatism of, 156; defined, 459; parental accusation, 118; parental superego defects, 126; in sex relationship, 481; treatment of, 282

Adoption: discussions with child in, 479, 484; and exhibitionism, 195; procedures in, 477–95; scapegoat child, 146, 147, 219; unconscious parental needs, 116

Agorophobia: mentioned, 41

Allergies: in asthma, 47

Ambivalence: effect on infant, 349; hostile-dependent bond, 299; parental fostering of, 187–88; parental insight, 426; parents, in delinquency, 453; in soiling, 366

Amputated body parts: disposition of, 108–10; psychological preparation, 447

Anaclitic therapy. *See* Supportive therapy

Animals: concern of child for, 8

Antisocial behavior: in adolescence, 10; collaborative psychiatric treatment, 34, 35; limitations, on, 412; parental prohibitions, 158. *See also* Acting out; Delinquency; Sexual deviations

Anxiety: in adoptive parent, 486; amputated body parts, 109; apprehension in analysis, 261; birth during, 344; in breast feeding, 424; at child's behavior, 123; child's use of mother's, 21; defined, 438; in homicide, 274; in incest, 396–97; in masturbation, 466; in migraine, 71, 74; as panic, 442–43; in repression, 334–35; in school phobia, 14–21 *passim*; self-preservation instinct, 345; in sex development, 461; sex impulses, 48; in vertigo, 41–44

Arthritis: in women, 55–66; mentioned, 6

Asthma: in adolescent, 469; psychotherapy in, 45–54; mentioned, 6

Bathing: and exhibitionism, 195; parental seduction in, 185
Bestiality, 370–72
Bisexuality: in child, 193, 417. *See also* Masculine protest reaction
Black sheep, 158–63
Blasé adolescent, 470–71
Breast: infant feeding, 424; oral

attack on, 62; in sexual deviation, 189, 191; of stepmother, 74
Brutality: and masochism, 257; parental, in murder, 205

Castration anxiety: in arthritis, 61; in blindness, 268–70; phallic symbol, 400; phylogenetic origin, 341, 392–93; in surgery preparation, 446
Catatonia: mentioned, 387
Childbirth: in arthritis, 57; fear of death at, 91
Choice of symptom. *See* Symptom choice
Classical analysis: defined, 322
Collaborative treatment: antisocial adolescent, 356–57; defined, 252; interviewing technique, 435; libido and environment, 412; mother and daughter, 282–97; neurotic children, 26–36, 115; parent and child, 228–29; as research tool, 438; of schizophrenic adolescent, 472; secondary benefit, 415; in separation anxiety, 282–97; team setting, 245–81
Competition: and arthritis, 56; compulsion for, 338; in hysterical adolescent girl, 468; intellectual, 75; in masculine identification, 58, 59; mother and daughter, 289, 302; in migraine, 72, 74; of therapists, 28, 248, 296, 308–9
Concomitant treatment: parent-child, 35, 308; in school phobia, 12, 18, 23–25; in symbiosis, 255. *See also* Collaborative treatment
Confession: in asthma, 45, 46, 50, 54
Conflicts: cause of emotional distress, 7; conscious level, 411; independence of child, 20, 21; and mature ego, 321; prediction of, 428; in superego lacunae, 113; and ulcers, 469; in urinary retention, 99
Conscience: in adopted child, 483; defect in, 115; in delinquency, 158, 474; development of, 157, 440; molding of defects, 453; in normal parent, 454; origins of, 475; parental acting out, 126; parental identification, 217–18; in sexual deviation, 182, 200; treatment of adolescent, 128, 129, 131
Corrective emotional experience, 321
Corruption: adolescent superego lacunae, 122–38 *passim*; in mother, 12; in stealing, 222
Countertransference: fears of, 320; resistance in therapist, 260; in superego lacunae, 140; in woman analyst, 402
Conversion hysteria: in arthritis, 61, 62
Cremation: of amputated body parts, 110
Culture studies, 392; and infant handling, 427; sociologic delinquency, 231–37; and swaddling, 340–42; validation of insight, 428

Deafness: in vertigo, 39
Death: and arthritis, 57, 63, 64; conflicts at childbirth, 93; as desertion, 302, 445; and fixation, 169; from malignancy, 270; in migraine, 68, 73, 77, 80; of mother, 258, 438, 484; of parents, 8
Defensiveness: and acting out, 152; in adolescent regression, 462; in adoption applicant, 493; aggressive impulses, 62, 65; awareness of conflicts, 251; hostility toward

men, 78; insights into, 415; intensification by therapist, 135; neurotic adolescent, 470; normal adolescent, 463; by repression, 334; in schizophrenia, 378–79
Delinquency, 155–67, 207–40; defined, 207, 474; limitations, 412; parental satisfaction, 475; psychopathy in, 452; in sexual deviation, 183; in successive generations, 437–38. *See also* Antisocial behavior
Delusions: defined, 381, 383; in psychosis, 472, 474; in schizophrenia, 382, 448
Denial: in normal adolescent, 463; in schizophrenia, 379, 381–82, 386
Dependency: in arthritis, 60; in asthma, 49, 51, 54; and confession, 46; in exhibitionism, 197–98; on husband, 83; in incest, 398–99; in migraine, 78; mother-daughter, 288; in school phobia, 16–20 *passim*, 25; in soiling, 264; in superego lacunae, 141
Depreciation: of father, 94; of husband, 71, 94
Depression: in migraine, 76; obstruction by mother, 288; in vertigo, 40
Deprivation: necessity for growth, 339
Diagnostic formulation, 314–15
Dinner table: as socialization center, 424
Disinheritance: effect of, 196, 198
Domination, female: in arthritis, 56, 61, 65; school phobia, 19
Dreams: in arthritis, 61; in disturbed adolescent girl, 287–91 *passim*; incestuous, 102; in migraine, 70–85 *passim*; in separation anxiety, 305, 306, 307
Dynamic interplay: in team setting, 246

Education: function of, 211–12; in delinquency, 239–40; need for treatment, 431; of parents, in sexual deviation, 202; and personal analysis, 415; and psychoanalysis, 413; for strengthening superego, 130
Ego: analysis of defenses, 415–16; at birth, 356; in repression, 335–38 *passim*; in schizophrenia, 379, 380, 388; in utero, 344
Emotional assimilation: in therapy, 72
Ephedrin: mentioned, 52, 53
Epilepsy: mentioned, 279, 280
Equivocation. *See* Ambivalence
Excessive satisfactions, 354–55
Exhibitionism, 117; in sexual deviation, 191–97 *passim*

Failure: and parental gratification, 160
Fainting: in migraine, 83
Fantasies: in adopted child, 481; of amputated body parts, 109; of beating, 289; in migraine, 72, 84, 86, 90; parental, 11, 123, 150, 188, 359, 360, 361, 432, 453, 455; of parent and physician, 276; between patients, 288; in sexual acting out, 173
Father: in adoption interview, 488–92 *passim*; in antisocial behavior, 217; in arthritis, 57; in asthma, 49, 50, 51; in castration anxiety, 268, 269; conflict with sons, 370; depreciation of, 61; at dinner table, 421; in homosexuality, 148, 149, 150; in incest, 174, 175, 394–95; in migraine, 69–94 *passim*; paranoia in, 284; in school phobia, 24, 25; seduction by, 189–90; in soiling, 364–68 *passim*; in vertigo, 42, 43

Fear: in arthritis, 60; of castration, 393; child's, 8, 45, 46, 152; in fixation, 358; of homosexuality, 74; in delusions, 384; of dependence on therapist, 81; in migraine, 9, 72, 82, 88; in school phobia, 14; in urinary retention, 101, 103

Fetishism, 178, 182; and seductive mother, 370

Fire setting: prohibition ambivalence, 453; in superego lacunae, 133; wish for deaths, 30, 31, 128

Firmness: defined, 144

Fixation, 353–75; causes of, 169, 354–55, 358; and collaborative treatment, 254, 263; defined, 353; dynamics of, 279; homosexuality, 464

Foster parents: in sexual deviation, 196; in superego lacunae, 136

Frigidity: and incest, 395

Frustration: and aggression, 349; of child, 8; in delinquency, 226; in fixation, 354; genital, 192, 196; in incest, 189; individual adaptation, 427; and motor discharge, 63; and repression, 337, 339; result of fear, 92; violence as solution for, 206

Gang delinquent. *See* Sociologic delinquent

Genitals: in exhibitionism, 177, 194; protective clutching, 274–75; in transvestitism, 172; in urinary retention, 101–2

Guilt: and antisocial acting out, 151–52; in arthritis, 57, 63, 64, 65; absence in incest, 397; and anger verbalization, 439; child's, 8, 21; in fixation, 360; in frequent interviews, 324; of individual delinquent, 211–12; parental, 34, 116, 118, 147, 185, 190; in regression, 255; in restitutive behavior, 347–50 *passim*; in school phobia, 17; in sexual deviation, 200; toward stepmother, 79; of therapist, 142, 262, 309

Hallucination: in panic, 442. *See also* Delusions

Homicidal impulse, 271, 283

Homosexuality: in adolescent, 464; fear of, 74, 80; fostered aberrations, 148–50; in girls, 179; maternity as defense for, 291; mother-daughter, 289–90

Hostile-dependent bond, 299, 307. *See also* Dependency; Hostility

Hostility: in adoptive mother, 480; in arthritis, 57, 62–65 *passim*; in asthma, 53; in delusions, 383; in disturbed adolescent, 286, 468, 474; expression of, 439; male exhibitionism, 198; in migraine, 67–94; origins of, 349–51; parental, 8, 34, 147; school phobia, 18; sexual, 165, 182

Husband: in arthritis, 61, 63, 64; in migraine, 70–94 *passim*; of therapist, 53, 290; in vertigo, 42, 43

Hypochrondriasis: in separation anxiety, 307

Id: at birth, 356; in repression, 335, 337; in utero, 344

Identification: child socialization, 421; and conscience, 217–18; of delinquent type, 456; with hostile aggressor, 379–85 *passim*; and normal superego, 130–31; with parent, 11, 114, 118, 473; purification of parental conduct,

346; root of, 345; with therapist, 95
Illegitimacy: in adoption, 478, 492; and oedipal period, 494
Incest: barrier, 389–405; effect on child, 174, 175, 189; as universal taboo, 341; in urinary retention, 103–4
Individual delinquent, 209–12, 218–29; fostering from parents, 452–55
Infant feeding: insights on, 424
Infidelity: and arthritis, 58, 59, 62
Inheritance, biological: behavioral patterns, 333
Insight, 412, 416, 421, 422; application in home, 423; in child's play, 417; in collaborative therapy, 295, 296; in ego mechanisms, 416; parental, 258, 418, 420
Integrated parents: in conscience, 217–18; defined, 145–46, 163; and superego, 117–18; and stealing, 221
Intellectuality: in migraine, 67, 69, 70, 72, 75
Intrafamilial interpersonal relations, 27; in collaborative treatment, 411

Jealousy: for father's attention, 71; over food, 340; homo-heterosexual, 291; and incest taboo, 391, 405; mother-daughter, 30; of patient, in treatment, 259; toward stepmother, 74. *See also* Sibling rivalry

Limitations: in adolescent psychosis, 476; craving for, 138; for individual child, 414
Latent tendencies, 169
Learning: inhibition of, 449

Loneliness: in migraine, 85, 86, 89
Love and warmth: defined, 145; lack of, in superego lacunae, 114; need for, 441
Lying: in "black sheep," 159, 161, 162; parental, 365; in schizophrenia, 379

Marriage: impotence in, 196; incestuous, 390; relationship significance, 465; sex hostility in, 165; treatment of both partners, 295
Masculine protest reaction: in arthritis, 56–65 *passim*; in migraine, 75
Masochism: in adopted child, 482, 484; in arthritis, 56–64 *passim*; and brutality, 257; as overwhelming influence, 333; mother-daughter, 289; mother-son, 30; punitive superego, 214; and restitution, 349
Masturbation: anxiety in, 466; in incest, 395; mother-daughter, 368–69
Meniere's syndrome, 40, 44; pseudo-, 41
Menstruation: in adolescent, 292, 461
Migraine, 57–95; and fear, 9
Miscarriage: and arthritis, 57, 60
Mother: in acting out, 150–51; and adolescent daughter, 283–97; in adoption, 479–82, 488–92 *passim*; ambivalence in, 299, 349–50; in asthma, 45, 46, 61; in breast feeding, 424; corruptibility in, 12; corruption of therapist, 137; and delinquent son, 453; and dying child, 270; in genital problems, 274–75, 366; homicidal impulse toward, 271–73; in homosexuality, 148–50; hostility in, 29; identification

with, 142; and infant feeding, 343; and insight applications, 422; and lying, 159–60; in massive regression, 446; in masturbation, 369; in migraine, 77, 87; in pregenital period, 172; resistance to treatment, 261; in school phobia, 16–25; seduction by, 186, 372; and separation anxiety, 299–309; in soiling, 264–67, 359; in transvestitism, 172–77 *passim*, 193, 369; in stealing, 122; vicarious gratification in, 276–77

Mourning: of amputated body parts, 109; for childhood gratifications, 404; in migraine, 76, 91; necessity for, 445

Murder: etiology of, 205–6

Muscular tonus: in arthritis, 64, 65

Narcissism, 133, 291

Needed object: defined, 347

Neurasthenia: mentioned, 39

Neurosis: in adolescent, 466–72

Nocturnal emissions: in adolescent, 461

Normal superego, 114–15; in conscience, 217, 218; with mature parents, 130

Nursery school: psychoanalysis in, 416

Nurture and release: in separation anxiety, 299

Nystagmus: mentioned, 39

Obesity: in adolescent regression, 462; and asthma, 47, 48, 49

Occupational therapy: with disturbed adolescent, 468–74 *passim*

Oedipal conflict, 91; in adolescent's mother, 291; culture studies and incest, 390, 392, 405; defined, 412; double, in soiling, 254; in illegitimacy, 478; insight into, 424–25; in male patient, 401; movement toward, 325; and parental understanding, 420; in school phobia, 32; in stealing, 141; and superego, 117; and taboos, 341

Oedipal period: in arthritis, 60, 61; death of mother, 73, 80, 81, 93; father in, 172; genital impulses, 337; need of child, 494; in sexual aberration, 148

Optimism: mentioned, 65

Oral incorporation, 58, 59

Orgasm: in arthritis, 59; in exhibitionism, 194; in infantile eroticism, 338; in migraine, 73

Orphanage: and exhibitionism, 194–95

Paranoia: and ego problems, 133; in father, 284

Parent-child problems, 27–35

Parents. *See* Father; Mother

Parent substitute, 225

Permission: in therapy, 124–25

Permissiveness, parental, 155–67; in conscience defects, 129; in stealing, 122; in superego lacunae, 113

Personal analysis: for parents and teachers, 415, 417; for therapists, 5, 142

Personality: adolescent superego lacunae, 140–41; in adoption, 480, 483; in child behavior, 409; in choice of treatment, 317; and cripple psychology, 65; in disturbed child, 431; and mother's death, 438; in illegitimacy, 478; in neurosis, 466, 470; nursery school observation, 418; parental destruction of, 190; predelin-

Index

quent, 226–27; psychopathic, defined, 208; sexual crime, 165; sexual deviation, 182–83, 200; in sociologic delinquent, 235

Perversions: development of, 175–79; male hostility in, 194; parental role in, 164–65, 188, 191–92; warning of patient, 125

Phallic symbols: use of body as, 58, 62

Phobias: treatment of, 327

Physician: in adoption, 494; in diagnostic formulation, 315; in delinquency referral, 457; and disturbed child, 430–31; and psychosomatic symptoms, 251; in sexual deviation, 182–83, 201–3; in surgery, 447; therapist's role as, 261

Play, role of: child's expression, 417

Poliomyelitis: and emotional problems, 471

Pregenital conflict: exposure in analysis, 324

Pregnancy: fear of death, 96; fear of mother, 151; and male exhibitionism, 197, 198

Privacy: child's need for, 172–73; and dependency, 425; in parental seduction, 185–86; in sexual deviation, 192

Prohibitions: and conscience, 157–58; in healthy home, 163; and incest, 391; and juvenile delinquency, 165–66, 211; and unconscious permission, 161

Projection: in schizophrenia, 378–82 *passim*

Promises: and superego development, 134

Psychoanalysis: defined, 411

Psychoanalytic psychiatry, 3–13; defined, 322; therapy in, 313–29

Psychosis: in adolescent, 472–76

Psychosomatic problems: in child illness, 450–52; and schizophrenia, 387. *See also* Arthritis, Asthma, etc.

Puberty, onset of, 461–62

Punishment: and arthritis, 63; child's wish to give, 29; and delinquency, 156, 208; need for self-, 114; parental inconsistency, 133; and restitution, 349; in school phobia, 21; in stealing, 138; in urinary retention, 101; in vicarious gratification, 220

Racial prejudice, 10

Rape: by uncle, 103

Regression: in adolescent, 462, 469; in castration anxiety, 268–70; control of, 320; indulged, 326; limiting of, 257: parental gratification, 254; parental insight, 425; in poliomyelitis, 471; and schizophrenia, 446; in soiling, 255

Regressive adaptation: defined, 358

Rejection: in subcultures, 232

Relapses: in treatment, 308

Repression: dangers in, 467; defined, 344, 350; in identification, 346; in infantile ego, 334, 336, 338; necessity for growth, 339

Resident treatment: in homicidal impulse, 272

Running away: causes of, 119–22 *passim*

Sanctions, 113–43; cause for deception, 124; in delinquency, 157, 166–67; in fixation, 358; of homosexuality, 149–50; in individual delinquency, 218–19; in noncollaborative treatment, 253; in parental seduction, 169, 455; in sexual deviation, 188; in steal-

ing, 147; and transvestitism, 171–72; treatment of parent, 127
Scapegoat: adopted child, 146–47, 219; in daughter, 303; antisocial behavior in, 153; individual delinquent, 236; neurotic parent, 309; selection of, 253
Schizophrenia: in adolescent, 472–74; in child, 448; ego functions in, 377–88
School phobia, 14–25; dynamics of, 293; and separation anxiety, 299, 305, 443; treatment of mother, 123
Seduction: by analyst, 402–4; defined, 170, 184–86; and fixation, 355; hysterical adolescent, 468; by parent, 149, 169, 173, 179, 189, 201
Self-flagellation: and incest, 175
Separation anxiety, 298–309; and collaborative treatment, 449–50; defined, 298
Sex: in arthritis, 56, 57, 62; in asthma, 48–50, 52; child's questions, 164; in delinquency, 455; discussion in family, 185; education in, 465; feelings for father, 93; force of impulses, 333, 337, 440; in migraine, 67, 72, 73, 93; to punish parent, 29; of therapist, 296; in treatment, 405; and urinary functions, 104; and vertigo, 42–43; unusual behavior, 168–79; wish for therapist, 53, 54
Sexual aberrations. *See* Perversions; Sexual deviations
Sexual deviations, 148–50, 181–203; defined, 182; in delinquency, 456; pathogenesis of, 188–89, 203
Sibling rivalry: in arthritis, 57, 60, 61; in child's play, 417; in communal groups, 343; in migraine, 73; of parents, 147; in school phobia, 18; in soiling, 254; and superego defect, 152–53
Socialization: and disturbed child, 432–34; factors in, 409
Social worker: in adoption, 483–85, 493; in extra-office relationship, 256; and insights, 416; in parent-child problems, 27; psychoanalytic application, 419; school phobia, 23; and stealing, 139; team setting, 245–52 *passim*, 280
Sociologic delinquent, 225–26, 229–40; conscience defect in, 455; in culture studies, 230–39
Sociologist: in delinquency, 238–39
Soiling, 254, 263–76; erotic gratification in, 427; in fixation, 359–66 *passim*
Stealing: causes of, 121–22; in child, 34; individual and gang delinquent, 237; parental duplicity, 147–48; parental sanction, 124, 152, 161, 220–21; in superego lacunae, 129, 130, 135–41 *passim*; in subcultures, 232–33; tendencies in mother, 31
Stepmother: in asthma, 48, 49; in migraine, 68–93 *passim*
Stoicism: in cripple psychology, 65
Superego: and parental sanctions, 124; of parents, 113–15; relapse in treatment, 132
Superego lacunae, 113–43, 212, 214, 218; defined, 113
Supportive therapy: and ego, 319; in team setting, 247, 256
Surgery: amputation of body parts, 108; on brain, 267; and constipation, 451
Swaddling: cultural differences in, 341–42
Symbiosis, 255, 258–59; family adaptation, 423; in fixation, 360; ideal conditions, 336, 339, 345,

346; prevention of destruction in, 260; unusual sexual behavior, 170
Symptom choice, 30, 35; determinant factors, 359. *See also* Fixation

Teacher: and adolescent, 460, 464; defining parental responsibility, 418; as disciplinarian, 22; and insights, 416; and personal analysis, 415, 417; and soiling, 364
Temper tantrum, 443–45; in delinquent, 454; in mother, 434
Threats: parental, 128; of therapeutic success, 227
Time: in analysis, 7; in collaborative treatment, 229; in psychoanalytic treatment, 323–26 *passim*; in residency treatment, 227; school phobia treatment, 24
Transference: in acting out, 214–15; in conscience lacunae, 129; control of, 319; degree necessary, 95; diagnostic formulation, 315; frequency of interview, 325; incest barrier, 401–3; in migraine, 67–85 *passim*; in mother, 273; negative, 275; psychoanalytic concept, 411; reality test, 326; in resistance, 261; and running away, 120–21; in schizophrenia, 385; in school phobia, 17, 23, 24; and social worker, 247, 248; in soiling, 365; and superego, 140–43 *passim*
Transurethral resection, 98, 99
Transvestitism, 171, 175–77, 187, 191; and mother, 193, 369

Trauma: in parental assault, 473; in schizophrenia, 377–84 *passim*
Truancy. *See* Running away; School phobia
Twins: in parental gratification, 32; one as scapegoat, 276–77

Ulcerative colitis: in neurotic adolescent, 469
Unconscious, theory of, 440
Uncovering therapy: and ego, 319; and frequency of interview, 325; team setting, 247, 256
Urinary retention, 98–107; infections in, 101

Vertigo: in anxiety neurosis, 39–44
Vicarious gratification: in antisocial behavior, 113, 116–17, 154, 157, 168; in fixation, 357, 361, 375; in juvenile delinquency, 216, 220, 223; and punishment, 454; robbing of, 276; in soiling, 366; wish at childbirth, 288
Voyeurism, 177–78, 192; and exhibitionism, 195

Weaning: mentioned, 400
Weeping: in adolescent girl, 283; for amputated body parts, 110; in migraine, 74–89 *passim*
Well-adjusted parents. *See* Integrated parents
Whirling sensations, 39, 40, 44
Withdrawal: in adolescent neurosis, 469

RC454
J64

DISCARDED
URI LIBRARY